This is a collection of fourteen original essays from a t‹ ‹ ‹ ‹ ‹ ‹ ‹RARY in the field. In this wide-ranging volume, the contrib ‹ ‹ ‹ ‹ a healthy sampling of Williams's works, from the early apprenticeship years in the 1930s through to his last play before his death in 1983, *Something Cloudy, Something Clear.* In addition to essays on such major plays as *The Glass Menagerie, A Streetcar Named Desire,* and *Cat on a Hot Tin Roof,* among others, the contributors also consider selected minor plays, short stories, poems, and biographical concerns. *The Cambridge Companion to Tennessee Williams* also features a chapter on selected key productions as well as a bibliographic essay surveying the major critical statements on the dramatist.

THE CAMBRIDGE
COMPANION TO
TENNESSEE WILLIAMS

CAMBRIDGE COMPANIONS TO LITERATURE

THE CAMBRIDGE
COMPANION TO
TENNESSEE WILLIAMS

EDITED BY
MATTHEW C. ROUDANÉ
Georgia State University

CAMBRIDGE
UNIVERSITY PRESS

PUBLISHED BY THE PRESS SYNDICATE OF THE UNIVERSITY OF CAMBRIDGE
The Pitt Building, Trumpington Street, Cambridge CB2 1RP, United Kingdom

CAMBRIDGE UNIVERSITY PRESS
The Edinburgh Building, Cambridge CB2 2RU, United Kingdom
40 West 20th Street, New York, NY 10011–4211, USA
10 Stamford Road, Oakleigh, Melbourne 3166, Australia

First published 1997

Printed in the United Kingdom at the University Press, Cambridge

Typeset in Sabon 10/13 pt. [CE]

A catalogue record for this book is available from the British Library

Library of Congress cataloging in publication data

The Cambridge companion to Tennessee Williams / edited by Matthew C. Roudané.
p. cm. – (Cambridge companions to literature)
Includes bibliographical references and index.
ISBN 0 521 49533 4 (hardback). – ISBN 0 521 49883 X (paperback)
1. Williams, Tennessee, 1911–1983– Criticism and interpretation.
2. Southern States – In literature. I. Roudané, Matthew Charles, 1953– . II. Series.
PS3545.I5365Z614   1997
812'.54–dc21   97–40036
CIP

ISBN 0 521 49533 4 hardback
ISBN 0 521 49883 X paperback

For Susan and Nickolas

CONTENTS

ILLUSTRATIONS

NOTES ON CONTRIBUTORS

THOMAS P. ADLER is Professor of English and Interim Dean of Liberal Arts at Purdue University, where he has taught dramatic literature and film since receiving his PhD from the University of Illinois at Urbana-Champaign in 1970. He has written widely on both modern and contemporary British and American playwrights, including especially O'Neill, Albee, and Pinter. His extensive work on Williams includes a monograph, *"A Streetcar Named Desire": The Moth and the Lantern* (1990), and two lengthy chapters in his most recent book, *American Drama, 1940–1960: A Critical History* (1994).

JAN BALAKIAN is an Assistant Professor of English at Kean College of New Jersey. Her essays on Arthur Miller and Wendy Wasserstein are forthcoming in the Cambridge Companions to those writers. She is currently writing a book about Wendy Wasserstein's plays.

CHRISTOPHER BIGSBY is Professor of American Studies at the University of East Anglia. He has published more than twenty books on British and American culture, including *Confrontation and Commitment: A Study of Contemporary American Drama 1959–1966* (1967), *Albee* (1969), *The Black American Writer* (1969), *The Second Black Renaissance* (1980), *A Critical Introduction to Twentieth-Century American Drama* (1982–85), *David Mamet* (1985), *Modern American Drama 1940–1990* (1992), and, as editor, *Contemporary English Drama* (1981), *Arthur Miller and Company* (1990), and *The Portable Arthur Miller* (1995). He is also the author of three novels: *Hester* (1994), *Pearl* (1995), and *Still Lives* (1996).

JOHN M. CLUM is Professor of English and Professor of the Practice of Drama at Duke University. He is the author of *Acting Gay: Male Homosexuality in Modern Drama* (1992; revised edn. 1994) and other books and numerous essays on twentieth-century British and American drama, gay drama, and musical theatre. He is the editor of *Staging Gay Lives* (1996) and co-editor of *Displacing Homophobia: Essays on Gay Literature and Culture* (1989). Professor Clum has also directed over sixty dramatic and operatic productions and five of his produced plays have been published by Dialogus Play Service and Publishing. He is currently at work on studies of twentieth-century musical theatre and bodily mutilation in American drama.

RUBY COHN, Professor Emerita at the University of California (Davis), has written and edited several books on modern drama and on the work of Samuel Beckett.

GILBERT DEBUSSCHER is Professor of English and American Literature at the University of Brussels in Belgium. He is the author or editor of books and articles on Edward Albee, Tennessee Williams, Jack Richardson, Edward Bond, Willy Russell, and avant garde drama.

ALBERT J. DEVLIN is a Professor of English at the University of Missouri, Columbia, who specializes in modern and Southern American literature. He has authored and edited books on Eudora Welty (*Eudora Welty's Chronicle: A Story of Mississippi Life* [1983], *Welty: A Life in Literature* [1987]) and Tennessee Williams (*Conversations with Tennessee Williams* [1986]). He served as consultant for the Tennessee Williams film project, "Lion of the American Stage" (PBS, 1995), and is at work (with Nancy Tischler) on an estate-authorized edition of "The Selected Letters of Tennessee Williams," to be published by New Directions.

ALLEAN HALE, Adjunct Professor of Theatre at the University of Illinois, is a specialist in Tennessee Williams studies. Her many publications in literary and theatre journals include "Tennessee Williams" in Gale's *Contemporary Literary Criticism*, volume 45. She was an opening lecturer at the Twentieth-Century American Playwrights Exhibit at the University of Texas in 1994 and has participated in scholarly panels nationwide. A consultant for two PBS television documentaries, *Tennessee Williams – Orpheus of the American Stage*, and *Tennessee Williams' Dragon Country*, she is also a contributing editor of the *Tennessee Williams Literary Journal*. In progress is a book with Nancy Tischler on Williams's late plays.

FELICIA HARDISON LONDRÉ is Curators' Professor of Theatre at the University of Missouri, Kansas City, and dramaturg for Missouri Repertory Theatre, Nebraska Shakespeare Festival, and the Heart of America Shakespeare Festival. In 1993 she was a Visiting Foreign Professor at Hosei University in Tokyo, and in 1995 she held the Women's Chair in Humanistic Studies at Marquette University. Her first book was *Tennessee Williams* (1979). Her books since then include *Tom Stoppard, Federico García Lorca*, and *The History of World Theater: From the English Restoration to the Present*. *The History of North American Theater: The United States, Canada, and Mexico from Pre-Columbian Times to the Present* is a book in progress, with Daniel J. Watermeier. She currently serves on nine editorial boards and is Vice-President of the American Theatre and Drama Society.

BRENDA MURPHY is Professor of English at the University of Connecticut and the author of *Miller: Death of a Salesman* (1995), *Tennessee Williams and Elia Kazan: A Collaboration in the Theatre* (1992), *A Realist in the American Theatre: Selected Drama Criticism of William Dean Howells* (1992), *American Realism and American Drama, 1880–1940*, Cambridge Studies in American literature and culture (1987), and with George Monteiro, *John Hay-Howells's Letters* (1980). Work in progress includes *The Cambridge Companion to American Women Playwrights* and a study of dramatic representations of the House of Committee on Un-American Activities in American theatre, film, and television.

JACQUELINE O'CONNOR is Assistant Professor of English at the Stephen F. Austin State University in Texas, where she directs the graduate program and teaches courses in American and modern drama, women's literature, and advanced writing. She has published essays on David Rabe and Anna Cora Mowatt, and her book, *Tennessee Williams Dramatizes Dementia*, is forthcoming from Bowling Green University Popular Press.

R. BARTON PALMER is Calhoun Lemon Professor of Literature at Clemson University in South Carolina and also serves as Executive Director of the South Atlantic Modern Language Association. As a medievalist, he has edited and translated six volumes of the narrative poetry of Guillaume de Machaut, Chaucer's most famous French contemporary. Two of these have been selected by *Choice* magazine as "outstanding academic books." As a film scholar, he has published two books on the American *film noir*, *Hollywood's Dark Cinema: The American Film Noir* and *Perspectives on Film Noir*, and edited a collection on film theory, *The Cinematic Text: Methods and Approaches*. Current film projects include *Screening Modern Literature: W. Somerset Maugham and the Cinema* (with Robert Calder) and *Joseph L. Mankiewicz: A Critical Guide* (with Cheryl Lower).

MATTHEW C. ROUDANÉ is Professor of English at Georgia State University in Atlanta, where he specializes in modern drama. He has published *Understanding Edward Albee* (1987), *Conversations with Arthur Miller* (1987), *American Dramatists* (1989), *"Who's Afraid of Virginia Woolf?": Necessary Fictions, Terrifying Realities* (1990), *Public Issues, Private Tensions: Contemporary American Drama* (1993), *Approaches to Teaching Miller's "Death of a Salesman"* (1995), and *American Drama since 1960: A Critical History* (1996). Roudané is editor of the *South Atlantic Review*.

NANCY M. TISCHLER is a Professor of English and Humanities at the Pennsylvania State University and Director of Summer Sessions. She has also taught at the University of Arkansas, the George Washington University, and Susquehanna University. She wrote the first dissertation on Tennessee Williams under her maiden name, Nancy Patterson, and also wrote the first full-length critical study, which was reviewed favorably by Brooks Atkinson in the *New York*

Times Book Review. She has written books and articles on various other subjects – Southern literature, modern drama, religion, and women, but has continued to work on Tennessee Williams. She has been a member of the editorial board for the *Tennessee Williams Newsletter* and *Journal*, and has contributed to a number of collections and studies of Williams. Currently, with Albert Devlin, Professor of the University of Missouri, she is editing the "Collected Letters of Tennessee Williams" for publication by New Directions in 1999.

1911   26 *March*   Born Thomas Lanier Williams in Columbus, Mississippi to Cornelius Coffin and Edwina Dakin Williams. Sister Rose Isabel born on 17 November 1909.

1911–18 Tom and Rose live with their mother and her parents, the Rev. and Mrs. Walter Dakin, in the Episcopal rectory of various Southern towns, as Tom's father is often absent as a traveling salesman. At five, in Clarksdale, Tom has diphtheria with complications that leave him an invalid for two years.

1918   *July*   Family moves to St. Louis, Missouri to live with father who has been made branch manager of International Shoe Company. Tom fears father, who taunts him, calling him "Miss Nancy."

1919   21 *February*   Brother Walter Dakin born.

1924–26 Writes first story, "Isolated," for junior high-school newspaper, and later, travel articles for the high school-paper, finds his first girlfriend in Hazel Kramer.

1927   Wins third prize ($5) from the magazine *Smart Set* for his answer to the question "Can a Good Wife Be a Good Sport?" and published there. Also wins a prize for a movie review of *Stella Dallas*.

1928   *July*   Short story "The Vengeance of Nitocris" is published in magazine *Weird Tales*. Tours Europe with his maternal grandfather.

1929   Enters the University of Missouri in September and joins a fraternity. Becomes the first freshman ever to receive honorable mention in a contest, for his play *Beauty Is the Word*.

1930   Earns money during summer vacation by selling *Pictorial Review*.

1932   Father withdraws him from the university after the winter semester, presumably for failing ROTC. Begins working at International Shoe Company and spends his nights writing.

1934   Story "Stella for Star" wins first place in amateur contest.

1935   *Spring*   Claims he has a heart attack, and recuperates at his grandparents' home in Memphis.
12 July   First production of his one-act play *Cairo! Shanghai! Bombay!* by Memphis Garden Players.

1936   *Autumn*   Sees Alla Nazimova perform in Henrik Ibsen's *Ghosts* and is inspired to be a playwright. Enrolls in Washington University, St. Louis, where he published poetry in the college magazine, *Manuscript*, and wins top prize in a poetry contest. "27 Wagons Full of Cotton" is later adapted into two plays and a film.
Begins his literary association with Clark Mills. Receives an acceptance letter from Harriet Monroe of *Poetry: A Magazine of Verse* for "My Love Was Light," a poem. This is the first hint of a national career in the making.

1937   First full-length plays are produced, *Candles to the Sun* and *Fugitive Kind*, by the amateur group the Mummers in St. Louis, whose director, Willard Holland, became another early influence of Williams. Transfers to the University of Iowa, where he studies playwriting and production. Has several short plays produced.

1938   *August*   Graduates with BA degree in English from the University of Iowa.

1939   Lives briefly in several places in the Midwest, South, and West, including New Orleans in the French Quarter, and it may have been here that he has his first extended homosexual experience. First uses the name "Tennessee" as the author of "The Field of Blue Children," published in *Story* magazine.

Four plays under the title *American Blues* win $100 in a contest organized by the Group Theatre. His plays are sent to literary agent Audrey Wood. Travels to Taos, New Mexico, where he visits Frieda Lawrence, and returns to St. Louis, where he works on *Battle of Angels*.

September   First meeting with Audrey Wood, who becomes his agent.

December   Awarded a Rockefeller Foundation grant of $1,000.

1940   *January*   Moves to New York to enroll in an advanced playwriting seminar taught by John Gassner at The New School for Social Research. In February, students stage his one-act play *The Long Goodbye*, the first of his plays to be seen in New York. Leaves New York for travels to Memphis and Provincetown, on Cape Cod, where he has his first sustained homosexual affair.

30 December   *Battle of Angels* opens in Boston but quickly closes after a censorship controversy; is revised as *Orpheus Descending* in 1957.

1941–42 Lives in a variety of locations, including Key West, Florida, and New Orleans, and works at a variety of jobs. Starts the story "Portrait of a Girl in Glass," which will be developed into *The Glass Menagerie*.

1943   *Spring*   Returns to St. Louis. His sister Rose is institutionalized for schizophrenia and undergoes prefrontal lobotomy.

April   Audrey Wood gets him a job as a scriptwriter for MGM and he moves to California.

May   While writing a film script for Lana Turner, develops "Portrait of a Girl in Glass" into a screenplay, "The Gentleman Caller."

October   Loses his Hollywood job. *You Touched Me!* opens in Cleveland.

1944   *6 January*   Grandmother dies.

April   Awarded $1,000 by the National Institute of Arts and Letters for *Battle of Angels*.

July *The Purification* is produced in Pasadena, California, under the direction of Margo Jones.
26 December *The Glass Menagerie* premieres in Chicago.

1945 *January or February* Starts working on *A Streetcar Named Desire*.
31 March *The Glass Menagerie* opens on Broadway and wins the New York Drama Critics' Circle, Donaldson, and Sidney Howard Memorial awards.
25 September *You Touched Me!* opens in New York.

1946 *27 Wagons Full of Cotton and Other Plays* published.
January or February Starts living with Pancho Rodrigues y Gonzalez.
Summer Beginning of friendship with Southern novelist Carson McCullers. May begins work on *Summer and Smoke*.
October May begins drafting *Camino Real*.

1947 *8 July* *Summer and Smoke* opens in Dallas.
3 December *A Streetcar Named Desire* opens in New York starring Jessica Tandy, Marlon Brando, Karl Malden, and Kim Stanley. It wins the Pulitzer Prize for drama and the Donaldson and New York Drama Critics' Circle awards, the first work ever to win all three.
Meets Frank Merlo.

1948 Visits Europe, including London, where John Gielgud is preparing a production of *The Glass Menagerie*. A first collection of fiction, *One Arm and Other Stories* and *American Blues: Five Short Plays*, published.
6 October *Summer and Smoke* opens in New York. This same month, Frank Merlo moves in with him, the beginning of a fourteen-year relationship. He moves Rose to a private clinic. Meets Maria Britneva, the Lady St. Just.

1949 *April* Goes to London, where *A Streetcar Named Desire* is about to open.
Winter Works on *The Rose Tattoo*.

1950 A novel, *The Roman Spring of Mrs. Stone* is published, and the film of *The Glass Menagerie* is released.
29 December *The Rose Tattoo* opens in Chicago.

1951   *3 February*   *The Rose Tattoo* opens in New York, and wins a Tony award. Film version of *A Streetcar Named Desire* released.

1952   *A Streetcar Named Desire* film version wins the New York Film Critics' Circle Award. Elected to the National Institute of Arts and Letters.

1953   *19 March*   *Camino Real* opens in New York.
Works on *Cat on a Hot Tin Roof*.

1954   Publishes *Hard Candy: A Book of Stories* and continues working on *Cat on a Hot Tin Roof*.
October   Starts filming *The Rose Tattoo*.

1955   *14 February*   Maternal grandfather dies.
24 March   *Cat on a Hot Tin Roof* opens in New York, where it runs for 694 performances, winning the Pulitzer Prize, and the New York Drama Critics' Circle and Donaldson awards.
Film version of *The Rose Tattoo* is released.

1956   Film *Baby Doll* opens in New York. A first collection of poems, *In the Winter of Cities*, published.
Spring   Relationship with Frank Merlo deteriorating.
Summer   In Rome, verging on a nervous breakdown.

1957   *21 March*   *Orpheus Descending* opens in New York.
May   Father dies.
June   Starts psychoanalysis with Dr. Lawrence Kubie.

1958   *7 January*   *Garden District* (*Suddenly Last Summer* and *Something Unspoken*) opens off-Broadway and (16 September) in London.
30 January   *Cat on a Hot Tin Roof* opens in London. The film version starring Elizabeth Taylor and Paul Newman is released.
June   Breaks off analysis with Dr. Kubie and leaves for Europe.
29 December   *Period of Adjustment* opens in Miami.

1959   *15 January*   *The Rose Tattoo* opens in London.
10 March   *Sweet Bird of Youth* opens in New York.
April Goes to Cuba, where he meets Ernest Hemingway and Fidel Castro.

Screen version of *Suddenly Last Summer* starring Elizabeth Taylor, Katherine Hepburn, and Montgomery Clift, is released.

1960   *10 November*   *Period of Adjustment* opens in New York. *The Fugitive Kind* (the movie of *Orpheus Descending*) is released.

1961   *28 December*   *The Night of the Iguana* premieres, and he later wins his fourth New York Drama Critics' Circle Award.

1962   *11 July*   *The Milk Train Doesn't Stop Here Anymore* opens at the Spoleto Festival in Italy. Film versions of *Sweet Bird of Youth* and *Period of Adjustment* released.

1963   *16 January*   *The Milk Train Doesn't Stop Here Anymore* opens in New York. *September*   Frank Merlo dies of cancer. Williams enters period of depression.

1964   Film version of *The Night of the Iguana* released.

1965   Receives Brandeis University Creative Arts Award.

1966   *22 February*   *Slapstick Tragedy* (*The Mutilated* and *The Gnädiges Fräulein*) opens in New York. *The Knightly Quest: A Novella and Four Short Stories* published.

1967   First version of *The Two-Character Play* produced in London.

1968   *27 March*   *Kingdom of Earth* (*The Seven Descents of Myrtle*) opens in New York. *Boom!*, the film version of *The Milk Train Doesn't Stop Here Anymore* opens.

1969   *January*   Baptized as a Roman Catholic in Key West. *11 May*   *In the Bar of a Tokyo Hotel* opens in New York. *September–December*   Enters Barnes Hospital, St. Louis, for psychiatric care.

1970   *Dragon Country: A Book of Plays* published. Interviewed on "The David Frost Show."

1971   First volume of *The Theatre of Tennessee Williams* published by New Directions. Second version of *The Two-Character Play* (titled *Out Cry*) revived in Chicago. Audrey Wood, Williams's literary agent for thirty-two years, is replaced by Bill Barnes.
March   *Summer and Smoke* (opera by Lanford Wilson and Lee Hoiby).
November   *The Eccentricities of a Nightingale* produced in New York.

1972   *April*   *Small Craft Warnings* opens for a successful run off-Broadway. Williams makes his acting debut as Doc.

1973   *1 March*   Third version of *The Two-Character Play, Out Cry,* has its New York premiere.
Awarded the first Centennial Medal of the Cathedral of St. John the Divine. Notorious *Playboy* interview appears in April.

1974   *Eight Mortal Ladies Possessed: A Book of Stories* published.
May   *The Latter Days of a Celebrated Soubrette,* a reworking of *The Gnädiges Fräulein* opens and closes after one off-Broadway performance.
July   Revival of *Cat on a Hot Tin Roof* in Connecticut, and in September, on Broadway.

1975   Receives Medal of Honor for Literature, National Arts Club. A second novel, *Moise and the World of Reason,* and his autobiographical *Memoirs,* which deals openly with his homosexuality, are both published.
June   *The Red Devil Battery Sign* plays briefly in Boston and New York opening postponed; revised versions later produced in Vienna (1976) and London (1977).
August   *Out Cry* opens in New York.
September   Revival of *Summer and Smoke* in New York.
October   Revival of *Sweet Bird of Youth* in New York.
December   Revival of *The Glass Menagerie* in New York.

1976   *16 January*   *This Is (An Entertainment)* opens in San Francisco.
Letters to Donald Windham 1940–1965 published.
A second volume of poems, *Androgyne, Mon Amour,* is published.

1977   *11 May*   *Vieux Carré* opens in New York.
June   *The Red Devil Battery Sign* opens in London.

1978   *June*   *A Lovely Sunday for Creve Coeur* opens in Charleston, South Carolina and at Spoleto Festival.
Tiger Tale, stage version of the film *Baby Doll*, opens in Atlanta.
Where I Live: Selected Essays published. Mitch Douglas becomes Williams's third literary agent.

1979   *10 January*   *A Lovely Sunday for Creve Coeur* opens in New York.
September   *Kitche, Kutchen, und Kinder* opens in New York.
December   Honored at Kennedy Center by President Carter.

1980   *24 January*   *Will Mr. Merriweather Return from Memphis?* inaugurates the Tennessee Williams Performing Arts Center, Key West.
26 March   *Clothes for a Summer Hotel* opens in New York.
1 June   Mother dies.
Appointed Distinguished Writer-in-Residence at the University of British Columbia, Vancouver.

1981   *Spring 1981/Spring 1982*   *A House Not Meant to Stand* produced, Chicago. *The Notebook of Trigorin*, Williams's adaptation of Chekhov's *The Seagull*, produced at Vancouver Playhouse.
24 August   *Something Cloudy, Something Clear*, his last play to be produced in New York during his lifetime, opens. He, along with Harold Pinter, wins the prestigious Commonwealth Award, which carries an $11,000 prize.

1982   Receives honorary doctorate from Harvard University.

1983   *24 or 25 February*   Dies at the Hotel Elysee, New York City, from choking on a cap from a medicine bottle.
5 March   Funeral at St. Louis Cathedral.

1984   Publication of *Stopped Rocking and Other Screenplays*.

1986   New Directions publishes *Tennessee Williams: The Collected Stories*, with an introduction by Gore Vidal.

1987   *Ten by Tennessee*, two evenings of one-act plays, produced in May in New York. *Conversations with Tennessee Williams*, a collection of interviews, is published.

1990   *Five O'Clock Angel, Letters of Tennessee Williams to Maria St. Just, 1948–1982* published.

1995   New Directions publishes *Something Cloudy, Something Clear.* Lyle Leverich's *Tom: The Unknown Tennessee Williams, volume 1,* which Williams authorized, is published.
George Crandell's *Tennessee Williams, A Descriptive Bibliography*, which documents every work by Williams, is published.

1996   *5 September*   *The Notebooks of Trigorin* opens at Cincinnati Playhouse in the Park.

MATTHEW C. ROUDANÉ

Introduction

If such playwrights as Eugene O'Neill, Susan Glaspell, Thornton Wilder, and Clifford Odets dominate American theatre in the first half of the twentieth century, and Arthur Miller, Edward Albee, Lorraine Hansberry, Sam Shepard, and, among many others, David Mamet the second half, Tennessee Williams animates the middle years of the century. In a very real sense, then, Tennessee Williams inhabits a central place within the American theatre. The centrality of Williams's theatre, however, has less connection with chronology and more with the original nature of his theatrical imagination. While O'Neill was the tragic dramatist and Miller remains the theatrician of the ethical, Williams emerged as the poet of the heart. He took quite seriously Yeats's epigraph: "Be secret and exult."

Ultimately Williams would become less secret about his life and art, and his exultations less clear of purpose, but he worked assiduously in creating poetic stage moments, moments in which social fact, psychological collapse, and eroticized encounter form a still point in which the imagination, itself, becomes the last refuge for his fated characters. In Williams's cosmology, of course, the imagination is the source of both great strength and weakness. Strength because the imagination creates, for Amanda Wingfield in *The Glass Menagerie*, Blanche DuBois in *A Streetcar Named Desire*, or Hannah Jelkes in *The Night of the Iguana*, a heroic resistance against a contingent and bewildering universe. Weakness because, for Val Xavier in *Orpheus Descending*, Sebastian Venable in *Suddenly Last Summer*, or Chance Wayne in *Sweet Bird of Youth*, the human imagination finds itself consumed (by blowtorch, cannibalism, and castration) by those whose sensibilities annihilate the heroic, the romantic, the creative. Within such a paradoxical world Williams succeeded in expanding the boundaries of theatricality itself, combining a lyricism and experimentalism that revolutionized American drama after World War II.

Williams was hardly the first to reconfigure through dramatic experimentation the American stage. Before Williams became a teenager O'Neill entranced the nation with such Strindbergian expressionist works as *The Hairy Ape* and *The Emperor Jones*. As a young man Williams would have been aware of the contributions of Susan Glaspell and Elmer Rice, who stand as but two representative examples of other notable American dramatists who, like Williams, were engaged with psychologizing as well as mythicizing the Real. Williams was a child of both World War I and the Great Depression and, like Clifford Odets and Thornton Wilder, was aware of the social dimensions of his theatre, an awareness that allowed Laurette Taylor as Amanda, Eddie Dowling as Tom, and Julie Haydon as Laura to move – physically and symbolically – beyond the scripted text of *The Glass Menagerie* and into a broader collective social context. Thus, for all his acclaim as a dramatic innovator, Williams is plainly indebted to some literary forebears. From Hart Crane and D. H. Lawrence he took the imagery of the repressed desires, of an inscribed sexuality that is at once visible and thinly veiled. From O'Neill he inherited the imagery of the tragic, of a sense of personal betrayal born out of characters who seem increasingly unable to communicate with self or the other. From Strindberg he inherited the imagery of the expressionist, which helped him to restructure the modern stage. From Karl Huysman, and Villiers de l'Isle-Adam, Williams drew upon the technical and imagistic possibilities implicit in the Symbolist movement. He often commented that he was influenced by Brecht, Sartre, Rimbaud, and van Gogh. From Chekhov, especially, he learned the importance of setting and emblem, replicating the particular milieu of Belle Reve, New Orleans, or St. Louis while simultaneously transforming those localized settings to the level of symbol.

Yet even as Williams borrowed from his literary and theatrical past, he also, when he was at his best, reinvented the American stage. This certainly was the case on December 26, 1944 when *The Glass Menagerie* premiered at the Civic Theater in Chicago and when *A Streetcar Named Desire* opened on December 3, 1947 at the Barrymore Theater in New York City. A connoisseur of the visual and a celebrant of the magical textures of the human body live on a stage, Williams nonetheless was foremost attracted to the word itself. Indeed, of all the creative forms which Williams indulged in – poetry, short fiction, memoirs, letters, his production notes, and stage directions – it is his use of language that most animates his stage.

Williams celebrates language. His is a poetic language that makes the word flesh, creates an alluring stage ambience, that becomes the visible means to performance grace. His attention to language liberated the American stage from the constraints of Ibsenesque realism as it suggested other metaphoric possibilities to Williams and his contemporaries. Arthur Miller, for one, reports that after seeing *A Streetcar Named Desire*, he was inspired to work even more precisely with his language in a play he was struggling with at the time. It was then called *The Inside of His Head*, the working title, of course, of what would become *Death of a Salesman*. Seeing *Streetcar* "strengthened" Miller. It was a play, Miller reveals in his autobiography *Timebends: A Life*, that opened "one specific door," one that didn't deal so much with "the story or characters or direction, but [with] words and their liberation, [with] the joy of the writer in writing them, the radiant eloquence of its composition, [that] moved me more than all its pathos. It formed a bridge . . . to the whole tradition of unashamed word-joy that . . . we had . . . turned our backs on."

Indeed, Williams "formed a bridge," whose foundation is the word, and he, Miller, and other dramatists suddenly were able to cross a creative bridge more freely and enter into a new theatrical world. What Miller suggests has everything to do with the animating principle of Williams's theatre. He sought to find the verbal equivalents for his characters' tortured inner selves, a search that led him away from the realism of Ibsen, O'Casey (the later) O'Neill, Clifford Odets, and Lillian Hellman and toward a new dramatic form. Williams reinforced his language, moreover, by refining what he termed his "plastic theatre": the use of lights, music, sets, and any other forms of nonverbal expression that would complement the textual version of the play. This willingness to open up his theatre to more than the traditional forms of realism, then the dominant mode of theatrical expression in America, allowed Williams to create a lyric drama, a poetic theatre. Stage symbol, scenic image, body language were to assume important roles, roles accentuating the conflicts that the characters themselves were articulating to audiences through their language.

Allean Hale begins the *Companion* by interweaving Williams's life and career prior to *The Glass Menagerie*. She chronicles the conflicting influences that father, mother, and sister exerted on Williams, and other such key events as the devastating family move to St. Louis, Williams's formative creative years at three universities, and the impact of laboring in a factory during the Great Depression. Hale also writes about other early experiences, the outcomes of which inspired the playwright to write short stories, poems, and his first plays. His early career, we learn, is of astonishing if amateurish productivity: before *The Glass Menagerie* opened, Hale writes, "he had written more than thirty-five plays, twenty-five stories, the forty pages of verse published in New Directions' *Five Young American Poets*," and other items Williams could not remember.

Perhaps Williams's apprenticeship, which lasted at least a decade, partially explains, to borrow John Barth's words, the "passionate virtuosity," of his "first" breakthrough work and the subject of C. W. E. Bigsby's essay, *The Glass Menagerie*. Bigsby suggests that Williams, like Chekhov, explores "a world of private need beneath the routines of social performance," a private need poignantly revealed through Tom Wingfield's poetic reconstructions of past familial experiences. Working carefully with the pretexts of Williams's published text – "The Catastrophe of Success" essay, character and production notes, the richly textured opening stage directions – Bigsby pinpoints the multivalency of *The Glass Menagerie* and the ways in which these pretexts influence audience reception. Bigsby also discusses the multiple origins of the play, the ideographic backdrop of the Great Depression in the United States, and how these and other factors make the Wingfields victims of fate, of time, and of "a prosaic and destructive reality." Reflecting on the play's ending, Bigsby writes, "Art can never really be a protection against the real. Chamberlain's betrayals, Franco's victories, Hitler's barbarity were not defeated by wishing they might be so, and, as Auden lamented, poetry did not save a single Jew. Williams was acutely aware of this." Then acknowledging the political and personal dimension of Williams's play, Bigsby concludes, "At the same time [Williams] was wedded to art, whose power does indeed lie in its ability to outlive even the traumas of history. He was wedded to theatre whose form and whose substance exposed the nature of the paradox, as it offers truth through lies and reveals a tensile strength in the most fragile of creations."

As Felicia Hardison Londré argues, *A Streetcar Named Desire* fulfilled the promise and aesthetic brilliance of *The Glass Menagerie*, catapulting its author "to the front rank of American dramatists." Londré analyzes the play in its historical context, situating its theatrical and cultural impact during the time of original performance, demonstrating, as does R. Barton Palmer in his contribution on Williams and Hollywood, just how startling *A Streetcar Named Desire* was for 1947 audiences. She also provides a fresh reading of the ending of the play, bringing to bear current critical debates regarding Williams's portrait of Blanche. Through a careful discussion of each of the play's eleven scenes, Londré analyzes what many regard as Williams's greatest achievement.

Jan Balakian addresses one of Williams's most innovative, and misunderstood, plays, *Camino Real*. Tracing the elements of melodrama, farce, pagan ritual, romance, satire, tragedy, and comedy, Balakian suggests that "never before had the American theatre seen a play that exploded realism" in quite the way the surreal *Camino Real* did. In this mythicized poetic allegory, Balakian argues, Williams reveals just how indebted he was to the Romantic sensibility, a sensibility energized by the enabling imagination of the self. More than merely a fanciful indulgence celebrating the wondrous if baffling powers of the imagination, though, *Camino Real*, like Miller's

The Crucible, problematizes the ideological realities of a Cold War conservatism within the United States. Balakian also covers the notorious critical reception of the original production and surveys key landmark productions over the years. Despite the carnivalized world in which Kilroy finds himself, Balakian concludes, "*Camino* is ultimately an affirmative play because the violets break the rocks, and imagination and love triumph over cruelty and tyranny. Indeed, Williams's most crucial metaphor is Kilroy's retrieval of his heart from the state because this is a play about reclaiming one's heart." Perhaps as we enter the twenty-first century, audiences will be better prepared to appreciate the wonderful theatricality of this 1953 work.

After the alleged failure of *Camino Real*, Williams's next major play two years later, *Cat on a Hot Tin Roof*, emerged as "a great critical and financial success," as Albert J. Devlin writes. In addition to his reading of plot, character, and theme, Devlin provides background information regarding the original composition of the play, the various third-act versions, and why such revisions were made. Devlin also demonstrates the ways in which Williams culturally inscribed the drama by exploiting "the plantation setting and ideology" of *Cat on a Hot Tin Roof*. Relying on the theories of Georg Lukács and Julia Kristeva, as well as a number of unpublished Tennessee Williams letters, Devlin contextualizes our understanding of Big Daddy, Big Mama, Maggie, and Brick in this fresh reconsideration of a drama whose figures try, with uneven results, to come to terms with the "mendacity" and the "clicks" infiltrating their very existences.

Thomas P. Adler takes as his subject two important plays within the Williams *oeuvre*, *Summer and Smoke* and what Adler calls "the dramatist's last Broadway success," *The Night of the Iguana*. Analyzing the intertextuality of Williams's scripts, particularly the interfolding of his own and others' poetry into the plays, Adler explores central patterns long associated with the playwright's verse and drama: "Dissolution and decline – purity giving way to corruption, a sanctuary or safe harbor invaded by harsh judgment and condemnation – these are, indeed, recurring motifs in the verses from his own pen that Williams includes in his plays." Adler charts the competing narratives of Alma and John, the rich symbolism of *Summer and Smoke*, and discusses the relationship between two who should or could have been close, but whose fates are, like those of Laura and Blanche, defined by separation and loss. Still, Adler locates, especially in *The Night of the Iguana*, the classic Williamsesque theme concerning the importance of "tenacity and endurance," a sense of acceptance that tempers, however ambiguously, Hannah's life. If all the figures in the play are at the end of their ropes, to allude to a key metaphor of the play,

Williams also outlines a redemptive force. Shannon, Maxine, and Hannah, Adler concludes, are able to carry on. Hannah, especially, "in a kind of Beckettian endurance beyond endurance, serves Williams well as a potent image of humankind's condition after the Fall." This is why both *Summer and Smoke* and *The Night of the Iguana* invite theatregoers to "consider our torturous growth from innocence to experience and the need for finding a way to live in the ruined Eden of the present."

No American playwright before Williams eroticized the stage the way Williams did. Ever since the audience gazed at Marlon Brando – and his body – in 1947, Williams presented what John M. Clum calls a "sex/gender system" that only recently has been more fully appreciated by both homosexual and heterosexual audiences. Clum focuses on three plays of the late 1950s, when homophobia was rising to its high point during the McCarthy era: *Orpheus Descending, Suddenly Last Summer,* and *Sweet Bird of Youth.* Sebastian Venable, Val Xavier, and Chance Wayne, Clum suggests, are "sacrificed for violating their proscribed roles in the patriarchal sex/gender system. The possibility of a new sex/gender system is seen through the two central female characters in each play, one mutilated, the other healed." With reference to such scholars as David Savran, Gayle Rubin, and, among others, Eve Kosofsky Sedgwick, Clum begins with a theoretical discussion of the many ways in which the relationship of homosexuality and heterosexuality influences both American culture and our ways of rethinking Williams's stage. Clum concentrates "on the beautiful male as sexual martyr in these three plays, on the dynamics and erotics of the martyrdoms, and on the ways in which his relationship to the fugitive woman suggests a liberating possibility."

As Bigsby, Adler, and Balakian locate an essentially Romantic sensibility in Williams, so Nancy M. Tischler explores even more explicitly what she calls the Romantic textures in selected short stories and plays. Like Hale, Tischler gives careful consideration to biographical issues, showing that the playwright had a profound "inclination to observe the world and its people through the eyes of the romantic," a vision that "came as naturally to Williams as writing did." Citing personal letters (many of which will be published for the first time by Tischler and Devlin), early rough drafts, selected pieces of short fiction, and, of course, numerous plays, Tischler concludes, and rightly so, that the "life on stage was for Tennessee Williams an image of the human condition, not simply a chronicle of individual experience." For Williams, the personal insight and private doubts, as Christopher Bigsby reminds us, outline the political concerns and moral anxieties of a nation whose faith in the future, though ever present, seems as indeterminate as the troubled heroes of Williams's theatre.

In his carefully documented essay, Gilbert Debusscher spotlights the extent to which Williams borrowed from the past, refurbished the present through his own original plays, and left his unmistakable imprint on a future generation of playgoers and playwrights. Although the European and American models and influences, from Oscar Wilde, Hart Crane, and Bertolt Brecht through Federico García Lorca and Jean Cocteau, remain vital forces inscribed in a Williams text and performance, Debusscher insists on the playwright's originality. "Williams is not a derivative artist," concludes Debusscher, "and his plays are nothing if not recognizably his own: he was in life as in the best of his art a devourer, a predator who seized upon his own experience and that of his literary predecessors to feed his imagination and trigger his creativity."

Moving from page to stage was, for Williams, tricky business. Like any self-respecting Romantic, Williams poured out his soul in solitude, typing out scripts for that ideal Beckettian audience, an audience of one, himself. Whether in text or performance, though, Williams's words have since become part of the collective vocabulary of a nation. Amanda Wingfield's reminiscence about entertaining "*seventeen*! – gentlemen callers!"[1] or Blanche DuBois's "I don't want realism. I want magic!"[2] or, in some of the most famous lines in American theatre, her last utterance in *Streetcar* – "Whoever you are – I have always depended on the kindness of strangers"[3] – remain familiar to audiences a half a century after they were first voiced. But Williams knew that the transference to live performance, the most public of arts, required help.

More so than any other literary form, playwriting quickly becomes a collaborative effort, involving a whole range of players who never take the stage on opening night: set and costume designers, lighting and sound technicians, stage managers and stage hands, producers, and, of course, directors. Indeed, in the case of Williams, the role of the director has been enormously influential – and at times controversial. In her careful examination concerning the relationship of Williams and directors, Brenda Murphy raises such issues as the nature of artistic integrity, authorial control, commercial viability, and, above all, the way in which the playwright and the director's relationship became, for Williams, a contentious one. As Murphy puts it, "from his first protector in the theatre, Margo Jones, to his last, José Quintero," Williams ". . . had worked with some of the best directors of the twentieth-century theatre . . ." Like so many of his antiheroes, however, Williams himself was filled with ambivalence and contradiction. "He desired both protection and control," Murphy concludes. "He sought collaboration and resented it. He needed an emotional connection, and he sabotaged it. He could be the most amiable of collaborators and the most difficult. He was fortunate in finding so many talented collaborators who saw the genius in the plays and were willing to take on the playwright in order to participate in their full realization on the stage."

The collaborative issues Murphy articulates seem equally evident in Williams's major contributions to Hollywood film, the subject of R. Barton Palmer's essay. Palmer pursues the various issues that relate to the adaptation of Williams's plays for the screen. These issues relate largely to the different requirements of the commercial cinema, which was itself in a process of transition during the 1950s and 1960s for institutional and economic reasons. In particular, Palmer addresses the notion that the more radical, disruptive thrust of the Williams play is generally blunted by Hollywood treatment (though not entirely, because it is Williams's somewhat scandalous reputation that provides the motive in part for the screen adaptation of his work). Palmer opens his essay with a survey of the Williams film adaptations, seen within the context of American filmmaking as an institution in the process of self-transformation in the 1950s and 1960s. Williams's dramatic materials, Palmer demonstrates, provided Hollywood with important sources for a new kind of film – adult, naughty, pessimistic, filled with intense and complex characters – that proved popular because of changing conditions of production and, especially, reception. Palmer then shifts to a close examination of the most important adaptations: *Cat on Hot Tin Roof*, *A Streetcar Named Desire*, *Rose Tattoo*, *Sweet Bird of Youth*, *Suddenly Last Summer*, and *Baby Doll*. Here Palmer's analysis centers on the ways in which Williams's materials were adapted to key elements of "the classical Hollywood text," particularly the Production Code, and the genre system, especially the melodrama or woman's picture. Palmer rightly concludes, "If the American cinema of the late fifties, sixties, and early seventies is densely populated by attractive yet emotionally sensitive men who lack decisiveness and are prone to failure, then Tennessee Williams must be credited for inaugurating what is, in part, a revolution in taste, but also, and more important, a transformation of the national character. And this would never have happened without the wholesale transference of his artistic vision from the stage to the commercial screen."

The author of some seventy plays (if one counts the combinations of earlier plays expanded into new and newly retitled works as well as the unpublished works) Williams established his reputation, of course, with *The Glass Menagerie* and *A Streetcar Named Desire*, but also extended his artistic excellence, most agree, with at least *Summer and Smoke*, *The Rose Tattoo*, *Camino Real*, *Cat on a Hot Tin Roof*, *Orpheus Descending*, *Sweet*

Bird of Youth, and *The Night of the Iguana*. If the plays of the last twenty years of Williams's life are "failures," Ruby Cohn may cause scholars, or at least actors, to reconsider the merits of such lesser-known works as *The Chalky White Substance, Small Craft Warnings, Vieux Carré, A House Not Meant to Stand*, and, among others, *Something Cloudy, Something Clear*.

The specifics of Williams's originality remain varied and complex, but his use of set and setting, of lights, music, screen projections and so on all coalesce in the plays in ways that remain as fresh as they are original. The music and lighting in *The Glass Menagerie* and *A Streetcar Named Desire* seem almost too notorious to require much comment here, but within many of his last twenty plays before his death in 1983, Williams, as Cohn writes, "expanded both his visual and sonic repertory: soap bubbles, iron gates, spotlights, dancing, and manipulation of props; the noise of knocks, rattles, sea, wind, and giant wings." Cohn, too, spotlights the playwright's verbal accomplishments. In her reading of selected plays after *The Night of the Iguana*, Cohn suggests that "almost always, these devices [Williams's stage effects and expressive dialogue] function dramatically, even when the plays are slim. Without exception, these late plays, like the earlier ones, provide opportunities for passionate acting."

Jacqueline O'Connor surveys the major critical statements in her bibliographic essay. She evaluates the biographical studies, from Edwina Dakin Williams's *Remember Me to Tom* (1963), the first biography of the dramatist, written by his mother, through Lyle Leverich's *Tom: The Unknown Tennessee Williams* (1995). O'Connor also reviews the extant bibliographies, such as George Crandell's *Tennessee Williams: A Descriptive Bibliography* (1995), and she notes the *Tennessee Williams Literary Journal*, edited by W. Kenneth Holditch; this journal remains an invaluable source for information about The Tennessee Williams Literary Festival, an annual gathering of critics and performers each spring in New Orleans. She also reports on the many book-length studies on Williams, including, for instance, Nancy M. Tischler's *Tennessee Williams: Rebellious Puritan* and Signi L. Falk's *Tennessee Williams* (both 1961) through several studies published in the 1990s – Thomas P. Adler's *"A Streetcar Named Desire": The Moth and the Lantern* (1990), Brenda Murphy's *Tennessee Williams and Elia Kazan: A Collaboration in the Theatre* (1992) and, among others, Alice Griffin's *Understanding Tennessee Williams* (1995).

O'Connor also highlights the various collections of critical essays, including Jac Tharpe's *Tennessee Williams: A Tribute* (1977) and Philip C. Kolin's *Confronting Tennessee Williams's "A Streetcar Named Desire": Essays in Critical Pluralism* (1993). O'Connor mentions several key books whose chapters include provocative and enlightening considerations of Williams. C. W. E. Bigsby has written particularly engaging commentaries in his well-known *A Critical Introduction to Twentieth-Century American Drama, volume 2* (1984) and in *Modern American Drama, 1945–1990* (1992). So, too, have David Savran in *Communists, Cowboys, and Queers: The Politics of Masculinity in the Work of Arthur Miller and Tennessee Williams* (1992) and Thomas P. Adler in *American Drama, 1940–1960* (1994). Finally, O'Connor's second contribution brings the *Companion* to a close by surveying selected key premieres through the years and the sometimes laudatory but often hostile receptions the plays received from theatre reviewers and critics.

If Williams began to lose control of his mimetic powers in the later years, he nonetheless produced an *œuvre* that forever altered, and enhanced, the American stage. The following essays, which address not only the plays, but also the poetry and short stories in roughly chronological order, chart the enormity of such alterations and enhancements.

I would like to thank the contributors, whose intelligent efforts and advice to me over the months made the editing process a pleasurable one. Albert Devlin, Allean Hale, and Nancy Tischler provided valuable information for the chronology, and I thank them for their suggestions. Jan Rieman also helped with proofreading, for which I am very grateful, and I appreciate the work of Ralph Norris, who assisted with the index. Finally, a special thanks to Sarah Stanton of Cambridge University Press for her encouragement and excellent help.

NOTES

1 Tennessee Williams, *The Glass Menagerie*, in *The Theatre of Tennessee Williams*, vol. 1 (New York: New Directions, 1971), p. 148.
2 Tennessee Williams, *A Streetcar Named Desire*, in *The Theatre of Tennessee Williams*, vol. 1 (New York: New Directions, 1971), p. 385.
3 *Ibid.*, p. 418.

I

ALLEAN HALE

Early Williams: the making of a playwright

How did Thomas Lanier Williams III become Tennessee Williams the playwright? What in his apprentice years predicts the masterworks which became classics of the American stage? While we cannot explain his genius, we can trace elements in his nature, nurture, and circumstance which fostered its expression. Even as a small child Tom showed a gift for drama, entertaining the grown-ups in the family with stories which grew increasingly exciting as he told them. He would also act out the cartoons from the newspaper. Reared in the rectory of his grandfather, the Reverend Walter Dakin, he felt both the prestige and burden of being called "the preacher's boy." His parents were virtually separated, his traveling-salesman father appearing only often enough to upset the tranquil household and frighten his children. His mother, Edwina, had the beauty and social inclinations of a Southern belle and, if not the wealth, the status that the Episcopalian ministry held in the small cotton center of Clarksdale, Mississippi. She often performed as a singer and, since Tom's grandmother was a music teacher, music early became a component of his life. Tom and his sister Rose, only sixteen months apart, were as inseparable as twins and were called "The Couple." They were so attuned that when one was ill, the other developed symptoms. Where Tom was sensitive and quietly observant, Rose was vivacious in a way he adored. She sufficed as his only companion. Growing up in this female-dominated environment doubtless gave Tom the empathy shown in the woman characters created by the playwright Tennessee. He later remembered his childhood as idyllic, although he spent two years as an invalid with some mysterious aftermath of diphtheria, and a fit of strangulation left him with a fear of choking to death – a prophetic fear, as it turned out.

The Southern idyll was shattered with a forced move to St. Louis, when his father got a managerial job with the International Shoe Company, the largest in the world, and sent for his family. At seven, Tom was transported overnight from his agrarian Eden to an immense, smoky city. Here Edwina

Figure 1 Maureen Stapleton, Cliff Robertson, and Gramham Denton in *Orpheus Descending* at the Martin Beck Theatre, New York, 1957, directed by Harold Clurman

felt herself a nobody and, with a sort of reverse snobbery, impressed on her children that in St. Louis only money and status mattered. Thus Tom first got the sense of being an outsider, which would become a pervasive theme in his writing. To his father Cornelius Williams, St. Louis was the city of opportunity, in 1918 fifth largest in the United States, with a fine school system, universities, libraries, a famed symphony orchestra, a splendid art museum. "C.C." made a good salary, but as the frustrated Edwina held back affection, he held back money. Their life together became a battle of opposites. Edwina, aggressively prudish, became a scold as Cornelius, lusty and ebullient, took his disappointment out in drink and occasional "light ladies." Edwina used Tom as confidant; C.C. retaliated by calling his delicate son "Miss Nancy." Caught in-between, Tom felt trapped. It was perhaps on his escape to the nearby Forest Park Zoo that he found his metaphor of home-as-menagerie. St. Louis would turn out to be *his* city of opportunity, though he called it "The City of St. Pollution." Whereas much of his work has St. Louis origins, he would transpose it into the South. And, just as he would convert a respectable middle-class apartment on Enright Avenue into the tenement of *The Glass Menagerie,* he would adopt his mother's nostalgia for an aristocratic idealized South, more *belle rêve* than reality.

Lost in the huge city, Tom was miserable through grade school. Rose was growing away from him as she approached puberty. Unable to attract her father's affection, she had lost confidence, was becoming quietly strange. Perhaps to compensate for Tom's loneliness, his mother bought him a second-hand typewriter at twelve whereupon, he recalled, he never stopped typing. It was through this he found his place at Ben Blewett Junior High, which had a newspaper. At thirteen his first published story, "Isolated," appeared in *The Junior Life,* poems followed, and a full page of the June 1925 yearbook featured "Demon Smoke," an ecological protest by Thomas Williams, 9th grade. On the class rolls he was "our literary boy." At fourteen, he had found his vocation.

At sixteen, entering a contest in *Smart Set* magazine for the best answer to the question "Can a Good Wife Be a Good Sport?" his reply as the wronged husband, citing "my own unhappy marital experiences," won a five-dollar prize. At seventeen he sold a horror story to *Weird Tales* for thirty-five dollars. "The Vengeance of Nitocris" describes how an Egyptian princess revenges her brother's death by inviting his enemies to a banquet at which she opens sluice gates to the Nile and drowns them all. This violent tale portrays the first of the author's strong women and is, incidentally, the first of his brother–sister situations. Now Tom was convinced that he could make writing pay and thus earn his father's respect. To "show" the old man became one of his strong motivations and he decided on a career in journalism.

In 1929 the University of Missouri had the outstanding School of Journalism in the country, but Tom found the classes boring. His first "beat" was to report the market prices of chickens and eggs. When finally assigned a news story, the death of a dean's wife, he carelessly buried the dean – and his journalistic career was over. He had at least learned to read the newspapers, which would later furnish ideas for other works. The university then had a series of contests in Poetry, Essay, Story, and Play-writing, each with the magnificent prize of fifty dollars. Tom, whose campus jobs paid thirty cents an hour, entered all of them. The drama contest included the incentive of seeing one's play produced by the Missouri Workshop. Modeled after George Pierce Baker's '47 Workshop at Harvard, it was outstanding for its time and place and was the most popular student activity outside of football. Weeks ahead, the newspaper listed the 100 best one-act plays for study and now in preparation Tom read O'Neill and Strindberg. He also audited playwriting under Dr. Robert Ramsay, who used the *ouroboros* symbol – the snake with tail in mouth – to describe the perfect plot. The end must be implicit in the beginning. The scenario for tragedy was "opening situation," "complicating circumstances," "apparent success" until "the flaw discovered," then "thickening clouds," "sudden catastrophe," and "aftermath." Whether or not Tom was impressed by this formula, it describes accurately the plot line of *A Streetcar Named Desire*. That play may have been more directly inspired by the Workshop's expressionistic performance of *The Hairy Ape*. Both deal with an upper-class female's scorn for the sweaty proletarian she compares to an ape.

So, in the hope of making money, Tom wrote his first play, *Beauty is the Word*. He did not make a financial gain, but became the first freshman ever to receive honorable mention in a contest. Traditionally, a writer's first play will be about leaving home. *Beauty* is a rebellion against his religious upbringing; *Hot Milk at Three in the Morning,* the following year, a goodbye to the bonds of family. These two plays, the one lyrical, the other grittily realistic, illustrate an opposition which would mark his future work. As an apprentice playwright, Tom would experiment, choosing a different master as model each time. He had just read of Jeanne Eagle's tremendous success in *Rain* so, like Somerset Maugham, he set his play in the tropics, as a contest between a sensual woman and a puritanical missionary. He was also reading Shelley; his title reflects that romantic's gospel of beauty. *Hot Milk at Three in the Morning* is "kitchen sink" drama of the type John Osborne would popularize thirty-five years later. The play's triad, Moony, the nagging wife, and the baby, parallels the situation of Tom, his mother, and the increasingly helpless Rose, anticipating *The Glass Menagerie. Hot Milk* may have been influenced by O'Neill's *Before*

Breakfast just as its character "Moony" resembles *The Dreamy Kid*. Its later version called *Moony's Kid Don't Cry* shows the influence of D. H. Lawrence's story "The Rocking Horse Winner."

Tom's father thought that joining a fraternity would help make Tom a man, but he was as much a misfit among the ATOs as he had been in grade school. The brothers found him shy and socially backward, a loner who spent most of his time at the typewriter. When he failed military training in his junior year, his father pulled him out of the university, considering it a lost investment. But Tom took away from Missouri the college background he would use in *Cat on a Hot Tin Roof*, and from his fraternity experience two key characters for future plays: Mitch, of *Streetcar*, and Jim O'Connor of *The Glass Menagerie*.

The Great Depression hit St. Louis in 1932, and Cornelius Williams felt he was doing well to get his son work in the shoe factory. Though Tom considered it a disaster, the job proved a leavening influence. It forced him out of the pretentious gentility of a home where his mother's social ambitions focused on becoming Regent of the DAR and into a nine-to-five blue-collar world. Without this he might have become the elitist poet he would picture later as Sebastian in *Suddenly Last Summer*, for his close attachment to Edwina tinged him with her snobbery and detachment from reality.

Instead he learned what it was like to be a wage-earner at sixty-five dollars a month, in a tedious job – dusting hundreds of shoes, or typing columns of figures all day to be fed into the mimeograph machine. He also learned to appreciate his co-workers and would dedicate the one play based on his factory experience, *Stairs to the Roof,* to Eddie, Doretta, Nora, Jimmie, and Dell. The factory was, in fact, a thorn-in-flesh which pricked him to work even more furiously at writing. He set a schedule of one story a week, writing on Saturday, polishing on Sunday, working into the night, stoked by coffee and cigarettes. Significantly, on the eve of his twenty-fourth birthday, a physical and nervous breakdown released him from his job. He took with him the memory of a co-worker, Stanley Kowalski, who would become perhaps the best-known male character in any American play.

Recovering at his Dakin grandparents' in Memphis, Tom read Chekhov, the writer who above all others would affect his work. Drawn into an amateur theatre group, he wrote his third play, *Cairo! Shanghai! Bombay!,* a comedy-fantasy about two sailors on shore leave. His audience was non-paying, but their applause was another spur to becoming a playwright. On returning home Tom entered Washington University, his grandmother supplying the funds. Here he met Clark Mills (McBurney), a French scholar and recognized poet, who would have a primary influence on him for many years, introducing him to Rilke, Rimbaud, and Hart Crane, who became his idol. Mills was editor of the university literary paper *The Eliot,* which published twenty of Tom's poems in 1936–37. Rhymed ballads and sonnets, reminiscent of Edna St. Vincent Millay, these showed above-average skill. Their subjects of frustrated desire and loss – several describing his sister – revealed themes he would develop in his plays. Mills also introduced Tom to the Union of St. Louis Artists and Writers, a bohemian mix of literati, radical activists, and pseudo-Marxists. Their organizer was Jack Conroy, ex-miner, labor leader and writer, who published *The Anvil: The Magazine of Proletarian Literature.* Although it portrayed the oppression of the capitalist system, Conroy's real crusade was to make *The Anvil* the mouthpiece for a Midwestern cultural revolution of worker-writers. Among those he published early were Richard Wright, Langston Hughes, Nelson Algren, and James T. Farrell. Tom submitted two stories, which were accepted but never published. He was never more than a peripheral member of Conroy's group but the contact made him see his surroundings in a new light. During the Depression St. Louis had a "Hooverville" stretching a mile along the Mississippi riverfront where people lived in shacks built from crates and foraged food from the refuse on boats. This was an atmosphere for revolution and as a strike organizer, Conroy was their local hero. His book, *The Disinherited,* called the most representative work of the Depression era, gained him the label "the American Gorki." Williams would also choose society's outcasts as a subject, and Conroy's influence would be visible in his next three proletarian plays.

At Washington University Tom came under two other important influences: Professor William G. B. Carson's Playwriting Class and an amateur theatre group, the Mummers, with a dynamic director, Willard Holland. Producing Irwin Shaw's anti-war play, *Bury the Dead,* on Armistice Day, Holland needed a curtain-raiser and heard that Tom had written plays. Having flunked ROTC, Tom was happy to deliver a twelve-minute satire against militarism, *Headlines.* It was typical of him to convert real-life failure into dramatic success. Holland became Tom's mentor and his experience with the Mummers, more than any other factor, sealed his future as a playwright. The Mummers never put on a show that didn't "deliver a punch," Williams wrote later.[1] That emotional impact became his dramatic aim and was realized in *Candles to the Sun.* A play of social significance about coal miners – of whom Tom had no direct knowledge – it was described in the *St. Louis Post Dispatch* of March 19, 1937, as incorporating "poverty, degeneracy, accidents on the fifth level below ground, a strike and brutal murder, ending with beans for everybody, hope and the singing of 'Solidarity Forever.'" This Marxist hymn had been the actual finale to a St. Louis hunger march and the mining details may have come from Conroy's books, along with Tom's portrait of "Birmingham Red," who resembled Conroy himself. Tom's next play for the Mummers, *Fugitive Kind*, was laid in a men's flophouse, peopled by the skid-row characters he had met on the levee. The set called for the skyline of the city, as "a great implacable force . . . crowding its fugitives against their last wall." The plot, along with an uneven mix of poetic passages and colloquial dialogue, owes something to Maxwell Anderson's *Winterset*, which Tom had recently seen and to Mielziner's striking backdrop of Brooklyn Bridge. *Fugitive Kind* was a failure, but Tom reserved the title for future use, little dreaming that one day the great Mielziner would design the sets for his plays.

Professor Carson's class at Washington University centered on a year's-end contest in which each student had to write a one-act play. Williams, probably the only class member who had had a work produced, now considered himself a playwright. During the year he had written several sketches about a homebound girl and her mother which Carson found touching, but for the contest he submitted the wildest of melodramas. *Me, Vashya!* concerns a ruthless munitions maker who supplies both his country and its enemies with ammunition and so prolongs the war. This scandal discovered, he threatens to blow up the world but is killed by the Princess, his young wife. Tom was doubtless thinking of Sir Basil Zaharoff, "the butcher of Europe," who was in the news in the mid-thirties. When Tom's play lost the contest to a light comedy, he was furious. He quit Washington University. Reading the play, one who knows his history can understand why he found its failure so destructive. The Princess, who had had a mental breakdown and was suffering delusions, was a revealing portrait of his sister at the time. It was characteristic of Tom, who never forgot a detail or abandoned an idea, to use the arms villain and the crisis situation in *The Red Devil Battery Sign*, four decades later. In these early plays he was trying out pieces of a puzzle which would find their place in a finished picture later on.

In the fall of 1937 Tom was well aware that, as he went off to the University of Iowa and freedom, Rose was going into confinement at Farmington State Hospital. Whereas before writing had been an escape from the reality of home, from now on it would be his escape from the fear of insanity. There was insanity on both sides of the family, and Tom's psychological balance was always precarious. His journals of these years show his struggles with depression, his "blue devils." As Harry Rasky put it beautifully in *Tennessee Williams: A Portrait in Laughter and Lamentation*, Tom and Rose were like Siamese twins joined at the heart.[2] Tom would always bear the guilt of the one who survived. The Williams household itself seemed to have the craziness of a cartoon script. The previous December, Cornelius, in a poker party brawl, had his ear bitten off. Tom, reminded of van Gogh cutting off his ear, saw parallels with his own life: the religious background, the unsympathetic father who opposed his career, the fear of madness, the passion for art. Enrolled at Iowa to study playwriting, he began a script about the painter called *The Holy Family*. Van Gogh would be his model for one of his portraits of the artist-against-society, *The Two-Character Play*.

The University of Iowa in the thirties was an exciting place to be. It had just constructed a splendid Dramatic Arts building with the latest staging facilities – "the theatre is the most completely equipped in the world," Tom wrote his mother.[3] One of the first college radio stations, WSUI, was at Iowa, the future-famous Writers' Workshop was forming, there was a literary magazine, *American Prefaces*. On the faculty, painter Grant Wood and playwright E. P. Conkle stressed the "regionalism" which was currently part of the "Iowa Renaissance." Professor E. C. Mabie, who headed the Department of Dramatic Art, was forging new concepts in theatre education. Although he taught and emphasized playwriting, he required all students to have practical experience in stagecraft and acting as well. Tom's Modern Drama reading course was equally comprehensive: a dozen plays a month, covering notable drama from *Camille* to *Of Mice and Men*. Playwriting students were to turn in a short play every two weeks; the three best were produced. Mabie was influential nationally as Midwestern Director of the Works Progress Administration's Federal Theatre whose emphasis on social drama encouraged the "Living Newspaper" agit-prop productions. Tom also studied under Conkle, whose current Broadway success, *Prologue to Glory,* inspired his students with dreams of the New York stage. Most of Tom's short plays written as class assignments have a political thrust, especially one on socialized medicine. His experience with the many doctors unable to cure his sister fueled him to take the medical profession apart. (Mabie, who had physician friends, tore up his script.) Among Tom's Living Newspaper plays produced at Iowa were *The Big Scene,* a satire on a Hollywood producer, and *Quit Eating,* a prison play. He also wrote a radio script which ran into censorship problems, causing the director to resign in protest. He was not trying to be difficult. The few classmates who remember him described him as quiet, shy, unobtrusive. He simply marched to a different drummer.

At year's end, assigned to write a long autobiographical play, he wrote *Spring Storm,* with a byline from T.S. Eliot's *The Waste Land,* "April is the cruelest month." His foreword called it a tragedy about the sexual struggles in youth, "a psychological treatment of problems I have felt deeply." (A significant statement, in that he would become known as a psychological dramatist.) Identified as a Southerner at Iowa, and steeped in the current regionalism, Tom set his play in the South, although it refers to actual sites in Columbia, Missouri. Whereas his previous plays had used only Mid-western speech, here his character Helen's is deeply Southern. In Helen he apparently combined his high-school sweetheart, Hazel Kramer, with Anna Jean O'Donnell, to whom he wrote ardent verses in college. The situation deals with four young people entangled in a frustrating relationship where each is in love with the wrong person. Arthur (the Williams character), in love with Helen, unwittingly causes Hertha, who loves him, to commit suicide. Helen, abandoned by her lover Dick, must settle for Arthur. Overcome with guilt, he comes to her for comfort. Coldly, the siren Helen lures him into the moonlight where she drops her gown to stand naked. This, Williams's first portrait of the castrating female and the subjected man, suggests his models as Strindberg and Ibsen. When Tom read it to the class there was a stunned silence. Finally Professor Mabie, kindly for once, said "Well, we all have to paint our nudes."[4] Mabie did not grant Tom the scholarship he sought to continue for a Master's degree after he graduated that summer. Failing to get on the Federal Theatre project in Chicago, Tom, jobless, had to return to St. Louis, "that dreaded city."

Iowa was a milestone in Williams's professional career: it focused him as a playwright. It gave him his first systematic exposure to dramatic theory and theatre literature, his first obligation to meet deadlines, practice in writing the dialogue and monologues which would become his trademarks, enough stagecraft to suggest the practical aspects of putting on a play, even two minor acting parts which helped him to understand the actor's view-point. He left Iowa with two other "firsts" – his first and last sexual affair with a girl, and a new name, "Tennessee," dubbed him by some of his schoolmates who couldn't place his Southern accent. Strangely enough, Iowa helped him to find himself as "the Southern playwright."

Back home, he wrote his last long social drama, *Not About Nightingales*. Based on a news story of a prison disaster, it is remarkable for its cinematic technique, each episode fading into the next, marked only by lighting changes. Thematic titles are flashed on the screen: "Miss Crane Applies for a Job!" Theme music is specified throughout, "Tchaikhowsky's 1812 Over-ture" written in one margin. Most innovative for the day is the device of showing two sets on the same stage, alternately lit. There is effective use of offstage noise and action. This play was his most powerful indictment of an uncaring society. Prisoners who staged a hunger strike are placed in a steam cell until they will concede. Here, either accidentally or on purpose, they are scalded to death. This was perhaps the most "proletarian" of Tom's early plays, with characters like Butch, Schultz, Black Ollie, and the Queen speaking very real dialogue. The Queen was also his first treatment of a homosexual character. Like virtually all of his plays so far, *Not About Nightingales* centered on the theme of escape.

By December Tom could stand home no longer and decided to make a final try for a Works Progress Administration job in New Orleans. En route he mailed a packet of plays to a Group Theatre contest for writers under twenty-five. Tom was twenty-seven but, always oblivious of rules, he dropped the three years he had worked in the factory as "lost time" and became twenty-four. Under the title *American Blues* he sent four one-acts, with two of his long plays, for the first time signing himself "Tennessee Williams." Meanwhile, he settled in to the raffish life of the French Quarter, working as a waiter when his last hope of getting on the Writers' Project failed. With war coming on, the Project would soon end. By February he was on the road West, with a friend who had a saxophone and a Ford V-8. They visited Hollywood, where Jim failed to find a band gig and Tom had a brief stint as a shoe salesman. In March, six days before his twenty-eighth birthday, came the wire saying he had won a special one-hundred-dollar award for *American Blues*. This was followed by a letter from Audrey Wood, literary agent, offering to represent him. Though he did not realize it at the time, these two messages would change his life. He was only dimly aware of the importance of the Group Theatre, which was headed by Harold Clurman, Cheryl Crawford, and Lee Strasberg. Their acting company included John Garfield, Lee J. Cobb, Karl Malden, and Elia Kazan, with Tom's admired playwrights Clifford Odets, Paul Green, and Irwin Shaw. A less naive person would have headed for New York immediately, but Tom spent the hundred dollars on a lazy summer at Laguna Beach reading D. H. Lawrence. He had decided to write about Lawrence so he went home by way of Taos where brash enthusiasm got him accepted into the Laurentian inner circle.

Back in his St. Louis attic, he began a play about his experiences to date and by November sent Audrey *Battle of Angels*. Christmas at home brought a crisis. Visiting Rose at the sanitarium he found her delusional, uttering obscenities he hadn't imagined she knew. "Horrible, horrible!" he wrote in his journal.[5] Rose, with the same strong sexual drives as her father and brother, had had no outlet. That night he felt he, too, would go mad unless he could get away. The next morning, miraculously, came the news that he had won a thousand-dollar Rockefeller scholarship. Audrey, who had urged him to apply for the award, now enrolled him in the playwriting seminar of John Gassner and Theresa Helburn at The New School for Social Research which had opened that spring of 1940. This brought him to the attention of those two most important persons in the New York theatre. The school's Dramatic Workshop was headed by Erwin Piscator, who had been noted in Germany for such theatrical innovations as the moving stage, the use of projections, and a narrator involving the audience. His influence had reached the American left-wing theatre of the 1930s, in the Federal Theatre's Living Newspaper and documentaries. Like his associate Brecht he advocated political theatre, the stage as a forum for discussion. Williams would use this technique briefly in two late plays, *A House Not Meant to Stand,* where Cornelius steps forward to address the audience about the decay of America and at the ending of *The Red Devil Battery Sign.* His use of projected captions and the narrator in *The Glass Menagerie* are often attributed to Piscator's influence, although he had already suggested these in *Fugitive Kind.* Piscator, regarding Williams as his most impressive pupil, helped get *The Long Goodbye* produced at the Dramatic Workshop. This memory play about a brother and sister leaving the apartment later pictured in *The Glass Menagerie,* was Tom's first New York production. Although he stayed at the New School only from January to April, contacts there would result in *Battle of Angels* being optioned by the Theatre Guild.

He saw *Battle* as the record of his youth and wrote in his journal: "My next play will be simple, direct and terrible – a picture of my own heart . . . It will be myself without concealment or evasion . . . a passionate denial of sham and a cry for beauty" (Leverich, *Tom,* 301).

It is important that by now he was admittedly a homosexual. In 1939 a homosexual was outside the law, outside the Church, branded a pervert by conventional society. This laid a particular onus on Williams, with his religious upbringing, and might account for his deterministic point of view. *Battle of Angels* continues his theme of the marginal character. In this, his first long Southern play, he also establishes his territory: the Clarksdale of his childhood, between the Sunflower River and the Mississippi. His "Two Rivers County" with its "Glorious Hill," "Blue Mountain," and its Cutrer family would become as endemic to Tennessee Williams's works as was Yoknapatawpha County to the novels of Faulkner. The two mythical kingdoms were only fifty miles apart.

Battle of Angels, as the first long work in which Williams finds his own voice, makes a useful study in how he composed. Each play usually evolved from an image spelled out in an early title. Trial titles for *Battle* were *The Memory of an Orchard, The Snakeskin Jacket,* and *Something Wild in the Country,* all of which are motifs in the drama. The orchard memory was of a sad lady his grandfather would take him to visit in a house surrounded by blooming trees. She had a set of hanging glass prisms which the child delighted to touch. So the visual image for *Battle* was of a woman in an orchard, and the magic of delicate glass. In the play, the confectionery decorated as an orchard represents the sweetness in life that Myra seeks, contrasted with the "dry goods" of the mercantile store to which she is condemned. When she discovers that she is no longer barren and decorates herself with glass ornaments, she reinforces the visual magic of the prisms Tom remembered. Myra is important in the Williams canon, and in American theatre, as his first of many women characters who are allowed their eroticism. His plays would shatter the stereotypic chaste heroine/whore dichotomy to show women in their complexity, just as his subject matter would bring maturity to the American stage.

The Snakeskin Jacket names the primary metaphor of the play, the emblem of Val, the vagabond musician with guitar who suggests the Orpheus legend on which the drama is based. It would be characteristic of Williams to construct his plays on a frame of Greek mythology. As an invalid child, reading voraciously in his grandfather's classical library, Tom learned of Orpheus and his bride, Eurydice, who was bitten by a snake and died; how he pursued her to the underworld and played music so enchanting that Pluto released her on condition that Orpheus would not look back as she followed him to earth. About to reach the upper world, Orpheus glanced backward, and Eurydice vanished. When the grieving Orpheus repulsed the Thracian women who tried to comfort him, they tore him to pieces in their fury. This tragedy forms the legendary background of Williams's play. Its contemporary plot relates to D. H. Lawrence's *Lady Chatterley's Lover* in which a barren woman, tied to an invalid husband, meets a virile man who unlocks her passion and gets her with child. *Something Wild in the Country* describes the protagonist, Val – the uninhibited stranger whose arrival threatens the complacency of the narrow-minded Southern community. These literary overtones caught by the play reader are not necessarily apparent to the viewing audience, which was one problem of the play. The title Williams finally chose, *Battle of Angels,* points to Revelations 12:7: "Now war arose in heaven, Michael and his angels fighting against the dragon [Satan]." It is ironical that, although Williams would come to be considered a sensational purveyor of sex and this particular play would be condemned as filthy, he was almost as much a preacher as his priest-grandfather. Many of his plays would enact symbolic crucifixions or resurrections; in *Battle*, names of the two protagonists disclose the framework of a Passion Play. Val, as "Valentine Xavier," connotes both Saint and Savior. He is thirty, the age of Christ's Passion. "Myra" suggests "Mary," both Virgin and Madonna. Myra's tyrannical husband, Jabe, is the Pluto/Jehovah figure. The play takes place at Easter and Val's fate is to be hanged on the lynching tree, a Crucifixion.

As a playwright, Williams would become known for his unforgettable characters. Much of his characterization is accomplished through dialogue. Once his people speak, it is impossible to confuse them. The Southernisms, the speech patterns and rhythms of his small-town gossips, the Sheriff and his redneck pals are absolutely on target. Val's speech is consistently dreamy, other-worldly, poetic. His monologue about the bird which, having no feet, must fly forever, is a forecast of the *aria* Williams will assign his central character in each play. Myra is most real when tough. The job interview scene where Myra asks Val for his credentials is richly funny; another Williams skill is his ability to commingle comedy and tragedy, as in life. Here he does it by juxtaposition, pitting Val's flowery description of his implausible "credentials" against Myra's sardonic commentary on them. This scene illustrates another trait that would mark all of Williams's plays, his mixture of realism and fantasy. Although critics, unable to find an exact label, would at first call him a realist, he was never just that; one mark of his genius was his refusal to fit into any slot; his plays would mingle naturalism, as in *Streetcar,* with the romantic (*Summer and Smoke*) or the allegorical, as in *Suddenly Last Summer.*

In *Battle of Angels* Williams first uses his hallmark technique of splitting the authorial self into several characters. Sandra, the passionate sensualist, embodies Val's wildness carried to the extreme. Vee, the primitive painter, represents Val the artist, while the black Conjure Man is Val the mystic. He uses characters to forward his theme; these three are Williams's angels who do battle against the Satanic figure of Jabe, Myra's husband, the cancer-ridden invalid who represents Death. Hades is not below but is the upstairs of the store, where he summons Myra by pounding on the bedroom floor. Minor devils are the Sheriff, his pals and their women, who act as a chorus furnishing the play's exposition. Like the Furies, they are as ready as the chain-gang dogs to tear Val apart. In this battle, the angels are defeated – a typical Tennessee Williams twist. His characters seldom win; in his existential world it is the struggle that counts.

Williams would be criticized for his one-to-one symbols, but would point out that a symbol, even a character's name, is a shortcut to the play's meaning, replacing many lines of exposition. It is the allusive content of Williams's plays that makes them so rich. Exploring a Williams play has the fascination of archaeology, as one uncovers a layer of mythology, a layer of religion, stray nuggets from other writers, on a bedrock of personal history. Examining this last is always a matter of speculation; Val is obviously an idealized Tom Williams, his memory of himself on his first trip to Mexico in 1939, an early "hippie," his only luggage not a guitar, but a typewriter. *Battle* also expresses his childhood fear of his father who, like

Jabe, was the unseen but frightening presence in his childhood. Val's fatal attraction for women follows the Orpheus myth rather than life. The women in Tennessee's life at the time were his mother and sister. The ambiguity of the Myra character suggests his ambivalent feelings towards both: mother, the older woman who clings to the young man as a substitute for a loveless marriage; sister, the unfulfilled virgin, like Eurydice condemned to eternal hell. Tom's attachment to Rose is the apparent subject of two other works which help to explain *Battle of Angels*. Recreating the atmosphere of Taos from that same Western trip was a 1940 verse play, *The Purification*. It is a dark Lorca-like drama of a brother and sister caught in an incestuous passion, brought to trial in their New Mexican village and condemned to death. Related to this is a 1940 poem "The Legend," picturing a young boy and a girl who is forbidden to him, coming together sexually almost against their wills:[6]

> they knew only
> the hot, quick arrow of love
> while metals clashed,
> a battle of angels above them,
> and thunder – and storm!

That the name Myra might also refer to Myrrha of Ovid's legend who committed incest and courted death for her sin is another possible reference. Finally, Williams seems to have had in mind Rilke's *Sonnets to Orpheus*, written to a dead maiden.[7] Williams's own poem, "Orpheus Descending," became the title for his revised *Battle of Angels*.

These allusions are all imbedded in the play, like various threads combined to form a rich texture. Although in production only one or two threads can be extended to the end, the multiple facets leave it open to many interpretations. In *A Streetcar Named Desire*, Stanley can be played either as insensitive destroyer or as a primitive husband defending his home; Blanche as fragile and idealistic or as a ruthless manipulator. The varied components which form a Williams play illustrate what he called his "organic" method of writing, where visual image becomes a poem, poem develops into scene, a series of scenes becomes a one-act and finally a full-length play. By age twenty-eight, Tennessee Williams was already a master of scenes, characterization, dialogue, monologue, and had introduced music, sound effects, movement, and lighting to express abstract themes and to create theatrical excitement. These expressionistic techniques, common today, were an early embodiment of Williams's manifesto for a "plastic" theatre and, according to Esther Jackson, may be one of his most lasting contributions to American dramaturgy.[8]

There was too much theatrical excitement when the play opened in Boston. Its swift transfer from paper to stage overwhelmed the novice playwright. Before Tom knew it, the play was in rehearsal. Dazed at the speed at which he was being propelled towards Broadway, in his inexperience he left the realization of his precious work to others. When asked for daily rewrites which seemed to change the intent of his play, he could only say, "I put it down this-a way, and that's the only way I know to put it down" (Leverich, *Tom*, 392). Thereupon director, producer, actors all made their own changes. Gassner later said that Williams was so poorly guided in revising that the play as produced was inferior to the script as accepted. The technical effects were a special problem, as the crew tried to translate into reality the author's imaginings: off-stage trains, hound-dogs, thunder, lightning, calliope music, and the final holocaust.

Why the play was opened in puritanical Boston was a question Williams would ponder later. The audience was unresponsive until the ending, which burst into violent melodrama. Lady tells Val she is pregnant; Jabe shoots Lady; Val is seized by the mob who blowtorch the confectionery and drag him off to be hanged. As red lights glared and clouds of smoke blew into the audience, they fled, coughing and choking. Most of the reviews were equally disastrous, calling the play "Delta dirt" written by a hillbilly author and stating that it gave the audience the sensation of being dunked in mire. Tennessee was completely taken by surprise. How could his honest portrayal of human needs be declared immoral? Faced with closure by the police, the Theatre Guild closed the show and the "hillbilly" author retreated in despair, convinced that his career was ended. Instead, it had established him with the public as a Southern writer and he had learned that to be successful a playwright must consider audience reaction.

This first big failure would drive Williams into rewriting the play for the next nineteen years. As *Orpheus Descending* in 1957 it kept the Greek legend but downplayed the religious references. The most important change was to rewrite Myra, now Lady, with the fiery Italian actress, Anna Magnani, in mind. Still not popular on Broadway, its 1960 film version, *The Fugitive Kind*, was perhaps better realized. It was not until 1989, after Williams's death, that his faith in *Orpheus* was justified. Revived with Vanessa Redgrave in a brilliant performance as Lady, and a production which emphasized the surreal aspects of the play, it received almost unanimous praise both in London and New York. It was now seen as a tragedy and, according to Frank Rich, in the January 15 *New York Times*, "a landmark production full of implications for the American theater."

Penniless after his Boston failure, expecting to be drafted, Tennessee returned to wandering. These were the years when the cities swept around him "like dead leaves."[9] In Acapulco he lived in the setting he would use in *The Night of the Iguana,* encountered the Nazis of that drama, and met Paul Bowles, who would compose the music for his future Broadway plays. In New Orleans, he had to sell his only suit, pawn his typewriter, and sleep in a cubicle crawling with roaches. He used the scene for a play he wrote in pencil in one day: *The Lady of Larkspur Lotion,* a sketch for his future Blanche. So he converted life into theatre, desperation into art. New Orleans was the city to which he would most often return, the city which represented freedom against the encagement of St. Louis. If St. Louis was his goad, New Orleans was his inspiration. The contrast between the two symbolized Williams's eternal struggle between opposites – the tension with which he lived and on which his plays are built. In less than three months in 1941 in New Orleans, he produced an astonishing amount of work: two long plays, at least eight one-acts, and nine stories for a proposed book. His vagabondage was not wasted. In Macon he found his model for Big Daddy in *Cat on a Hot Tin Roof.* Back in New York for a cataract operation, he worked as a singing poet in a Village bar, wearing an eye-patch. (His poor eyesight kept him from the draft.) He was briefly an elevator operator until he forgot to close the door to the shaft. As an usher at the Strand he saw *Casablanca* night after night and from Sidney Greenstreet got his model for Gutman in *Camino Real.* Along the way, he made those friends who would figure throughout his life: Jay Laughlin, head of New Directions, who became his publisher, Hume Cronyn, who took an option on his short plays, while confessing he didn't know how they could be used. Audrey Wood deplored them as non-commercial, but was busy getting them published: *Moony's Kid Don't Cry, At Liberty, This Property is Condemned, The Last of My Solid Gold Watches* were all in print by 1943, most included in Mayorga's *Best One-Act Plays* of the year. These poignant sketches would become classics, in some ways Williams at his best. Gems of characterization, compassionate, observant, funny and sad; Chekhovian glimpses portraying gallant losers, caught at a moment from which we realize all will be downhill, these one-acts would never go out of repertory.

But at thirty-two his financial future depended on a long play. Hopeful when summoned by Piscator to discuss producing *Battle of Angels* at The New School, he found the latter had taken his play apart, reassigned his speeches, and converted his lyric drama into a Brechtian treatise on social injustice with the South as a fascist state. Williams withdrew. *You Touched Me!,* the D. H. Lawrence adaptation he had written with his friend Donald Windham, and his fantasy, *Stairs to the Roof,* still had no takers, although each would eventually be produced. Discouraged, he returned to St. Louis, to find his grandmother dying of cancer, his sister lobotomized. (In 1943 the lobotomy, which involved drilling a hole into each side of the skull, was a new operation thought to be the solution for schizophrenia; that it was mutilating, returning the patient to an infantile passivity was not yet understood.) Although Tom was not told of the operation until after it was done, he would always feel guilt at not having prevented it. If he had avoided seeing Rose for years, her presence had never left his subconscious or his writing. "Portrait of a Girl in Glass," "Oriflamme," and *Portrait of a Madonna* were portraits of Rose. Now he worked on *The Gentleman Caller*, a crystallization of all those painful family memories. On April 30, 1943, came a telegram telling him to report to Hollywood at once. Audrey had secured a contract at MGM for $250 a week! Anxious to copyright all his work before MGM might make claims, she asked her client for a list of his unpublished writing to date. His "List of Properties" in bumpy type-script surprised even her. Since the Mummers days in 1936 he had written more than thirty-five plays, twenty-five stories, the forty pages of verse published in New Directions' *Five Young American Poets*, and other items "I can't recall."[10] What he could not know at the time was that he was also listing the initial drafts for at least five of those later groundbreaking dramas which would transform the American stage. When the Hollywood venture did not work out, he offered MGM *The Gentleman Caller,* saying it would last longer than *Gone With the Wind*. They turned it down, but his prophecy, uttered in bravado, proved true. As *The Glass Menagerie* it would become "the great American play," one of the most performed and most anthologized in modern theatre history, translated into more than thirty languages, universal in its appeal.

NOTES

Information on St. Louis, Ben Blewett, the University of Missouri, and the University of Iowa is based on the author's own experience in each place, along with her research at the State Historical Society of Missouri, Columbia, the University Archives, Iowa City, and numerous personal interviews.

1 Tennessee Williams, *Where I Live* (New York: New Directions, 1978), 11.

2 Harry Rasky, *Tennessee Williams: A Portrait in Laughter and Lamentation* (New York: Dodd, Mead 1986), 51.

3 Tom Williams to Edwina Williams, quoted in *Remember Me to Tom*, by Edwina Williams as told to Lucy Freeman (New York: G. P. Putnam, 1963), 90.

4 Nancy M. Tischler, *Tennessee Williams: Rebellious Puritan* (New York: Citadel Press, 1965), 56. In 1996 a version of *Spring Storm* with a more ambiguous ending was discovered by Dan Isaac, a Williams historian. Written around 1940 this script contains the seeds of many later plays. Produced as a staged reading

in New York at the Ensemble Studio Theatre, it was revealed as a mature study in human relationships, whose vivid characterization, humor, and poignancy rival *The Glass Menagerie*. A professional premiere is planned for 1997–8 with publication by New Directions.

5 Lyle Leverich, *Tom: The Unknown Tennessee Williams* (New York: Crown, 1995), 335.

6 Tennessee Williams, *In the Winter of Cities* (New York: New Directions, 1964), 83.

7 Rainer Maria Rilke, *Sonnets to Orpheus*, ed. J. B. Leishman (London: Hogarth Press, 1946). Williams was reading Rilke shortly before he wrote *Battle of Angels*. The young girl is referred to in Part 1, sonnet 2, and Part II, sonnet 28. Sonnets specifically mentioning Orpheus are 1, 5 and 26. In II, 4, the linking of unicorn/virgin/mirror may have been one source for Williams's unicorn symbol in *The Glass Menagerie*.

8 Esther Merle Jackson, *The Broken World of Tennessee Williams* (Madison: University of Wisconsin Press, 1965), 89.

9 Compare Tom's final speech in *The Glass Menagerie*, Scene 7. *The Theatre of Tennessee Williams*, vol. I (New York: New Directions, 1971), 237.

10 Tennessee Williams, "List of Properties" (unpublished typed manuscript, 1943), 3. Courtesy of Lyle Leverich.

BIBLIOGRAPHY

Crandell, George W. *Tennessee Williams, A Descriptive Bibliography*. University of Pittsburgh Press, 1995.

Ley-Piscator, Maria. *The Piscator Experiment*. Carbondale: Southern Illinois University Press, 1967.

Van Antwerp, Margaret and Sally Johns (eds.). *Tennessee Williams. Dictionary of Literary Biography, Documentary Series*, vol. IV. Detroit: Gale, 1984.

Wixson, Douglas. *Worker-Writer in America: Jack Conroy and the Tradition of Midwestern Literary Radicalism*. Urbana: University of Illinois Press, 1994.

Williams, Tennessee. *American Blues*. New York: Dramatists Play Service, 1948.

Battle of Angels, in *The Theatre of Tennessee Williams*, vol. I. New York: New Directions, 1971.

Beauty is the Word. Published in *The Missouri Review*, vol. VII, no. 3, 1984.

Candles to the Sun, Me, Vashya!, Fugitive Kind, Spring Storm, Not About Nightingales, Stairs to the Roof, are unpublished manuscripts in the Tennessee Williams Collection, Harry Ransom Humanities Research Center, University of Texas, Austin.

27 Wagons Full of Cotton and Other Short Plays. The Theatre of Tennessee Williams, vol. VI. New York: New Directions, 1981.

Orpheus Descending. The Theatre of Tennessee Williams, vol. III. New York: New Directions, 1971.

2

C. W. E. BIGSBY

Entering *The Glass Menagerie*

In *The Seagull* Chekhov's Trepliov insists that "We need new art forms . . . and if they aren't available, we might just as well have nothing at all."[1] The statement is not without its irony given Trepliov's own incapacity, but it carried the force of a playwright who was himself dedicated to such innovation. Fifty-five years later, and in a world as much in transition as Chekhov's, Tennessee Williams was conscious of trying to create just such a new form, a "plastic" theatre which owed something, indeed, to the Russian writer for whom a detailed realism was never really a primary objective. As Stanislavsky had remarked of Chekhov's work, "At times he is an impressionist, at times a symbolist; he is a 'realist' where it is necessary."[2] A tracery of the real was an essential scaffold for his exploration of character and subtle recreation of mood, but his characters inhabit more than a tangible world and reach for something more than the merely material. Much the same was true of Williams, so that what Stanislavsky said of Chekhov could equally well be said of him:

> A purblind eye would see only that Chekhov lightly traces the outward lines of the plot, that he is engaged in representing everyday life, the minute details of ordinary living. He certainly does these things, but he needs all this only as a contrast to set off the high ideal which is ever present in his mind and for which he longs and hopes all the time. In his dramatic works Chekhov has achieved an equal mastery over the internal as well as external truth . . . he knows how to destroy both the inner and outer falsity of the stage presentation by giving us beautiful, artistic, genuine truth.[3]

Williams was concerned with exploring precisely this internal truth, a world of private need beneath the routines of social performance. For Stanislavsky "These subtle moods and emotions which Chekhov conveys through his art are suffused with the undying poetry of Russian life."[4] Williams's work is also suffused with poetry. His, though, derives from a region of America which has self-consciously invested itself with a romantic mythology, as it does from characters whose struggle with the real leaves a

29

Figure 2 *The Glass Menagerie*, Zoe Wanamaker and Claire Skinner. Donmar Warehouse Theatre, 1995

residue of poetry in their broken lives. His dramatic strategy, however, is close to that pioneered by his Russian master whose plays, as Stanislavsky explained, "are full of action, not in their external but in their inner development. In the very inactivity of his characters," he insisted, "a complex inner activity is concealed."[5]

This was precisely the quality singled out by Arthur Miller in his memorial tribute to Williams, following his death in 1983. For Arthur Miller, though, what was most striking was his celebration of a lyrical quality in characters whose lives were, indeed, in one sense inactive but which constituted the action of plays which set out to stage the drama of the self's encounter with the ineluctable fact of mortality. As he remarked, Tennessee Williams

> broke new ground by opening up the stage to sheer sensibility, and not by abandoning dramatic structure but transforming it. What was new in Tennessee Williams was his rhapsodic insistence on making form serve his utterance. He did not turn his back on dramatic rules but created new ones. . . . With *The Glass Menagerie*, the long-lost lyrical line was found again, and supporting it, driving it on, an emotional heroism, that outflanked even values themselves; what he was celebrating was not approval or disapproval but humanity, the pure germ of enduring life.[6]

You could say of Williams's work what Jean Cocteau said of his own, that "the action of my play is in images, while the text is not: I attempt to substitute a 'poetry of the theater' for 'poetry in the theater.'"[7] Nowhere, perhaps, were the above observations more relevant to Williams's work than in his first Broadway success, *The Glass Menagerie* (1945).

When New Directions published *The Glass Menagerie* as part of the first volume of the collected plays of Tennessee Williams, they included an essay entitled "The Catastrophe of Success."[8] Indeed the reader entering the play text passes through a series of other texts, including this essay, character notes, production notes, and elaborate stage directions. Each one modifies our response to the play and in some sense throws light on Williams's own reading of it.

In the essay, which he published in the *New York Times* to mark the third anniversary of the Chicago opening of *The Glass Menagerie*, Williams described the life which he had led prior to the success of that play as 'one that required endurance, a life of clawing and scratching along a sheer surface and holding on tight with raw fingers to every inch of rock higher than the one caught hold of before" (136). It was a description which could have applied to virtually any of his principal characters, from Blanche, in *A Streetcar Named Desire*, and Val, in *Orpheus Descending*, through to

Maggie, in *Cat on a Hot Tin Roof*, and Shannon, in *The Night of the Iguana*. It could certainly apply to the characters in *The Glass Menagerie*. In the essay he speaks of his paranoid response to finding himself suddenly in the limelight, in a world in which the ordinary seems imbued with threat, and explains the pressures which had led him to write. He had turned to writing, he explained, because it is "only in his work that an artist can find reality and satisfaction, for the actual world is less intense than the world of his invention and consequently his life . . . does not seem very substantial" (138). Again the observations which he makes about himself could apply with equal force to his characters for whom the imagination is a principal resource, while "the actual world" is the origin of threat and a destructive banality.

It is ironic, therefore, that in that same essay Williams speaks disparagingly of the Cinderella story, with its account of moving from rags to riches, as a primary and destructive American myth, for it is the fate of his characters, and particularly those in his first Broadway success, to miss life's party, to be left with no more than the ashes of a once-burning fire. However, where Cinderella succeeds and inherits a suspect world of tainted wealth, his characters transform their lives with nothing more than a fantasy born out of need. The irony is, however, that the imagination which sustains them also isolates them, insulates them from those others pressed to the margins of a society whose priorities have little to do with the artist, the dispossessed, or the abandoned.

The essay is a curious document. Much of it is taken up with Williams's confession of guilt at moving so easily into the role of successful playwright, living in expensive hotels and treating the staff as social inferiors. In particular he denounces a service economy which requires social inequity. He announces that American ideals can no longer even be stated, let alone enacted, and insists on the importance of struggle. "Security," he announces, "is a kind of death." The essence of that struggle, however, does not so much lie with challenging the class system as resisting the deprivations of time because, as he reminds us, "time is short and it doesn't return again. It is slipping away while I write this and while you read it, and the monosyllable of the clock is Loss, loss, loss, unless you devote your heart to its opposition" (140–41). The need for social justice thus becomes entwined with a more fundamental struggle to discover meaning and identity in the face of absurdity.

On the face of it his insistence that security can be equated with death would seem a curious observation when applied to *The Glass Menagerie*, a play set during the Depression. What Amanda needs more than anything else, both for herself and her daughter, is, arguably, precisely security. It was what the Depression had destroyed. His own sense of self-disgust, however, leads him to celebrate the insecurity which had characterized his own earlier life. Yet in a sense if Tom, his alter ego in the play, had settled for what he had got, if he had offered his mother and sister the security they needed, he would have destroyed himself as a poet. *The Glass Menagerie*, then, is concerned with the insecurity which on the one hand drives some to a lonely desperation, redeemed only by hermetic fantasies and myths, and on the other creates poets scarred by guilt but elevated by their avocation.

As Williams himself insisted, in the production notes which precede the printed text, this is a "memory play" which, "because of its considerably delicate or tenuous material," justifies "atmospheric touches and subtleties of direction." He chooses the occasion to reject the "straight realistic play with its genuine Frigidaire and authentic ice-cubes, its characters who speak exactly as its audience speaks." Everyone, he insists, "should know nowadays the unimportance of the photographic in art" because "truth, life, or reality is an organic thing which the poetic imagination can represent or suggest, in essence, only through transformation, through changing into other forms than those which merely present in appearance" (131). This is something more than a manifesto, though, at the beginning of his career, it is certainly that. For the fact is that this is not only a description of the play's dramatic tactics, it is an accurate account of the strategy of characters who themselves distrust the real until it is transformed by the imagination.

All the key words of Williams's work are to be found in these introductory notes: paranoia, tenderness, illusions, illness, fragile, delicate, poetic, transformation, emotion, nostalgia, desperation, trap. These defining elements are to be projected not merely through character and dialogue. He envisages a production in which all elements will serve his central concern with those who are the victims of social circumstance, of imperious national myths, of fate and of time as the agent of that fate. He envisages the projection of magic-lantern slides which will amplify elements of a scene. He calls for music to give "emotional emphasis," music which is to be "the lightest, most delicate music in the world" emphasizing "emotion, nostalgia, which is the first condition of the play." He identifies the need for non-realistic lighting, "in keeping with the atmosphere of memory," a lighting which, when it falls upon the figure of Laura should have "a pristine clarity such as light used in early religious portraits of female saints or madonnas." Indeed, he suggests that "a free, imaginative use of light can be of enormous value in giving a mobile, plastic quality to plays of a more or less static nature" (133–34). As Jo Mielziner, the play's designer and lighting director, remarked of Williams: "If he had written plays in the days before the technical development of translucent and transparent scenery, I believe he would have invented it." Explaining his own use of translucent interior walls, he insisted that, "it was a true reflection of the contemporary playwright's interest in – and at times obsession with – the exploration of the inner man." As he remarked, "Williams was writing not only a memory play but a play of influences that were not confined within the walls of a room."[9] Those influences were in part artistic and in part social for the pressure which threatens to break not only Laura but all the characters in this St. Louis apartment derive, at least in part, from the brutal urgencies of 1930s America, from the imperatives of a society dedicated, in the words of Jim, the "gentleman caller," to *Knowledge – Zzzzzp! Money – Zzzzzp! – Power! . . . the cycle democracy is built on!* (222).

The opening stage direction seems somewhat curious, a hangover from the radical plays he had written in the 1930s. The Wingfield apartment, we are told, is

> one of those vast hive-like conglomerates of cellular living-units that flower as warty growths in overcrowded urban centers of lower middle-class population and are symptomatic of the impulse of this largest and fundamentally enslaved section of American society to avoid fluidity and differentiation and to exist and function as one interfused mass of automatism. (143)

It is true that the apartment is both literally and metaphorically a trap which Tom and his mother, at least, wish to escape, but the determinism is not primarily presented as politically or socially rooted. The alienation and despair go deeper than this. His characters are, beyond anything, the victims of fate (Laura), of time (Amanda), and of a prosaic and destructive reality. However, the social and political backdrop is not as irrelevant as it may appear.

The Wingfields live on credit. The electricity is cut off following Tom's failure to pay the bill. Amanda scrapes together money by demonstrating brassieres at a local store, itself a humiliation for a woman of her sensibility. Otherwise she has to suffer the embarrassment of selling subscriptions to women's magazines over the telephone, enduring the abrupt response of those she calls. The daughter's failure to complete a typewriting course is more than a blow to her self-esteem. Amanda has invested what little money she has to free both herself and Laura.

In this context her son's decision to leave has financial as well as personal implications. He earns a wretched sixty-five dollars a month but in Depression America any job is valuable and, though Tom feels suffocated by work which leaves him little time or space for his poetic ambitions, it has at least served to sustain the family. By leaving he condemns mother and sister to something more than spiritual isolation. The gentleman caller, Jim, meanwhile, recalls visiting the Century of Progress Exposition in Chicago, an exhibition not without its irony in Depression America (an irony frequently invoked by David Mamet thirty years later). To Jim it reveals that the future of America will be "even more wonderful than the present time is!" (212). But we have seen the present, a present in which the Wingfields have been reduced to something approaching a subsistence existence. Indeed Jim's confidence is paper thin for within a few moments he confesses that "I hoped when I was going to high school that I would be further along at this time, six years later, than I am now" (216), his high-school yearbook having predicted inevitable success. If knowledge, money, and power do, indeed, constitute democracy then democracy is itself under threat. And, indeed, Tom is seen, at one stage, reading a newspaper which announces Franco's triumph, a curious stage direction but one which goes to the heart of Williams's sense of the imperious and implacable power which threatens all his characters.

Tom's first speech reiterates that sense of social oppression which Williams had sought to imply through the stage set. "In Spain," he tells us, "there was revolution. Here there was only shouting and confusion. In Spain there was Guernica. Here there were disturbances of labor, some-times pretty violent, in otherwise peaceful cities such as Chicago, Cleve-land, Saint Louis." This, he asserts, "is the social background of the play." The middle class of America, he tells us, had "their fingers pressed forcibly down on the fiery Braille alphabet of a dissolving economy" (145). And there is a powerful sense not merely that the animating myths of America have failed those who look for some structure to their lives, but that those myths are themselves the root of a destructive materialism or deceptive illusion.

The play is set at a moment of change, change in the private world of the characters but also in the public world, as though it resonated this private pain. As Tom tells us, "Adventure and change were imminent in this year. They were waiting around the corner for all these kids. Suspended in the mist over Berchtesgarden, caught in the folds of Chamberlain's umbrella. In Spain there was Guernica! . . . All the world was waiting for bombard-ments!" (179). It is a speech which does more than situate the play, provide a context for what, by contrast, must seem a minor drama. It is an invitation to read the events ironically, and to see in the desire to live with comforting fictions, rather than confront brutal truths, a doomed and ultimately deadly strategy. For, as Tom indicates in the same speech, whatever consolations or distractions existed – hot swing music, liquor, movies, sex, glass menageries (the last hinted at by his reference to a chandelier) – flooded the world with rainbows which he characterizes as "brief" and "deceptive."

The Glass Menagerie is more than a lament for a tortured sister (Laura is based on Williams's mentally damaged sister, Rose); it is an elegy for a lost innocence. The Depression had already destroyed one American dream; the war destroyed another, and Tom looks back on the events which he stages in his memory and imagination from the perspective of an immediately postwar world. Neville Chamberlain's piece of paper promising "peace in our time" was no less a product of desperation, no less a symbol of the triumph of hope over despair, than Laura's glass menagerie. Chamberlain's piece of theatre, as he emerged from an aircraft and waved the flag of surrender, believing it to be evidence of his triumph, was no less ironic than Amanda's stage-managed drama of the gentleman caller. In the end brute reality trampled on both.

The Glass Menagerie is no more a play of purely private emotions and concerns than Chekhov's *The Cherry Orchard*. In both cases society, no less than the characters who are its expression and in some senses its victims, is caught at a moment of change. Something has broken. We even hear its sound. In Chekhov "A distant sound is heard, coming as if out of the sky, like the sound of a string snapping, slowly and sadly dying away."[10] In *The Glass Menagerie* "There is an ominous cracking sound in the sky . . . The sky falls" (233). The snapping of the horn from a glass unicorn thus stands for something more than the end of a private romantic myth. It marks the end of a phase of history, of a particular view of human possibility.

The origins of *The Glass Menagerie* lie in a short story which Williams wrote around 1941. "Portrait of a Girl in Glass" differs in certain respects from the final play version, not least in the absence of that detailed social and political context which broadened the metaphoric significance of *The Glass Menagerie*. The character of Laura is much closer to being a portrait of his sister, Rose. In the play she suffers from a deformed foot; in the story the flaw is more cruel. She is mentally rather than physically fragile. At the age of twenty she believes that stars are five-pointed because they are represented as such on the Star of Bethlehem which she fixes to the top of her Christmas tree. She treats the characters in her favorite book as real and responds to her gentleman caller not because they had shared the same high school but because, in her mind, he resembles a character from that book, though there is an echo of that in the play when Laura suddenly addresses Jim as Freckles, the protagonist of the novel which is no longer alluded to.

The setting is similar, though with certain crucial differences. There is no dance hall across the street, with its overtones of a smoldering sexuality. Instead the alleyway is a scene of death as a dog regularly attacks and kills stray cats in a cul-de-sac which mirrors that confronting the characters in the story. That sense of entrapment, social and metaphysical, survives into the play version, though without this reminder of mortality.

Other elements fed into *The Glass Menagerie*. A projected series of plays, to be called "Mississippi Sketches," included a comedy entitled "The Front Porch Girl," in which a shy girl ultimately finds companionship with one of the lodgers in her mother's boarding house. Expanded into a play called *If You Breathe, it Breaks! or Portrait of a Girl in Glass*, it featured a girl who sat on the front porch of her house awaiting gentlemen callers while finding consolation in a menagerie of glass animals, which becomes an expression of the fragility she believes characterizes those so easily broken by the world. Finally, under contract to Metro-Goldwyn-Mayer in Hollywood, Williams worked on a script, then titled *The Gentleman Caller*, about a woman awaiting a gentleman caller. This, revised, became *The Glass Menagerie*.

Story and play are rooted firmly in Williams's own life. As he explained, speaking in the year of the play's first production, his family had lived in an apartment not essentially different from that featured in his drama. He recalled his sister's room which was "painted white" with shelves which he had helped her fill "with the little glass animals" which constituted her menagerie. "She was the member of the family with whom I was most in sympathy and, looking back, her glass menagerie had a meaning for me . . . and as I thought about it the glass animals came to represent the fragile, delicate ties that must be broken, that you inevitably break, when you try to fulfill yourself."[11]

This, indeed, is a clue to why Tom, the narrator who shares Tennessee Williams's first name, chooses to "write" the play, in the sense of recalling what seem to him to have been key moments in his past life. For the fact is that the play does have a narrator and his values and perceptions shape the way we see the action, indeed determine what we see. The story is told for a purpose and serves a need outside that story. Tom Wingfield recalls the past for much the same reason that Willy Loman does in *Death of a Salesman*: guilt. He revisits the past because he knows that his own freedom, such as it is, has been purchased at the price of abandoning others, as Williams had abandoned his mother and, more poignantly, his sister. He "writes" the play, more significantly, perhaps, because he has not effected that escape from the past which had been his primary motive for leaving. The past continues to exert a pull on him, as it does on his mother and sister, as it does on the South which they inhabit.

For his mother, Amanda, the past represents her youth, before time worked its dark alchemy. Memory has become myth, a story to be endlessly repeated as a protection against present decline. She wants nothing more than to freeze time; and in this she mirrors a region whose myths of past grace and romantic fiction mask a sense of present decay. In Williams's words, she clings "frantically to another time and place" (129). The South does no less and Williams (here and in *A Streetcar Named Desire*), like William Faulkner, acknowledges the seductive yet destructive power of a past reconstituted as myth. At the same time she knows that compromise is necessary. Survival has its price and Amanda is one of Williams's survivors. She survives, ironically, by selling romantic myths, in the form of romance magazines, to other women.

For her daughter, the glass animals of her menagerie transport her into a mythical world, timeless, immune from the onward rush of the twentieth century. It is an immunity, however, which she buys at too high a price for, in stepping into the fictive world of her glass animals, she steps out of any meaningful relationship with others in the present. She becomes one more beautiful but fragile piece in the collection, no longer vulnerable to the depredations of social process or time but no longer redeemed by love.

Tom, meanwhile, prefers the movies, or, more importantly, his poetry. A poet in an unpoetic world, he retreats into his writing because there he can abstract himself from the harsh truths of his existence in a down-at-heel St. Louis apartment. It is not, however, a strategy which has brought him success or peace of mind. He narrates the play in the uniform of the Merchant Marine. He has traded a job in the warehouse for one at sea. There is no suggestion that his desertion of mother and sister has been sanctified by the liberation, or public acknowledgment, of his talent. Like his father before him he has fallen in love with long distance, mistaking movement for progress. Williams himself may have seen Laura's glass animals as representing the fragile, delicate ties that must be broken "when you try to fulfill yourself,"[12] but it is clear that in *The Glass Menagerie* Tom has not fulfilled himself. Tennessee Williams may have felt guilty that his success with the play was built on the exploitation of others; Tom lacks even the consolation of success. Fired from his job in the shoe warehouse, he wanders from city to city, looking for the companionship he had failed to offer his sister. In the story version he tells us that he has grown "firm and sufficient." In the play there is no such assurance as, in that Merchant Marine uniform which is the very symbol of his homelessness, he returns, in his memory, to the home he deserted for the fulfillment he failed to find. When his mother asks him to "look out for your sister . . . because she's young and dependent" (175), she identifies an obligation which Tom refuses. In his own life Williams never quite absolved himself of a feeling of guilt with respect to his sister.

For Tom, memories of the past are a distraction from present failure for though situated in time they exist outside of time. In summoning those memories into existence, he transposes experience into a series of images, transforms life into art, and in so doing mimics the process which his namesake Tom Williams adopts in creating plays, for, as Williams has remarked, the virtue of a play lies in the fact that it occurs "*outside* of time," indeed that it is "*a world without time*."[13] It is, to his mind, time which renders experience and, indeed, people, inconsequential. Art ascribes meaning to the moment, neutralizes a fear of "*not meaning*." It is a world in which "emotion and action have a dimension and a dignity that they would . . . have in real existence, if only the shattering intrusion of time could be locked out" (52). The theatrical metaphor, indeed, is central, with Tom as author of a metadrama in which he self-consciously stages his memories as a play in which he performs as narrator. But if he is the primary author, he acknowledges the centrality of Amanda as director, designer, and lighting technician of the drama which has been his life and the life of his tortured sister.

Early in the play Amanda is presented as an actress, self-dramatizing, self-conscious. Her first part is that of martyred mother. When she removes her hat and gloves she does so with a theatrical gesture ("a bit of acting" [151]). She dabs at her lips and nostrils to indicate her distress before melodramatically tearing the diagram of a typewriter keyboard to pieces. When the gentleman caller arrives for her daughter she changes roles, dressing herself in the clothes of a young woman and becoming a Southern belle, rendered grotesque by the distance between performer and role. But at the end of the play all such pretences are abandoned. As we see but do not hear her words of comfort to her daughter, so her various roles – shrewish mother, coquettish belle, ingratiating saleswoman – are set aside. The tableau which we see as Tom delivers his final speech is one in which mother and daughter are reunited in their abandonment. "Her silliness is gone," Williams tells us. Amanda "withdraws through the portieres," retreating from the stage which Tom has summoned into being but also from the arena in which she has chosen to play out her own drama. Just as Stanislavsky had rejected those who try to "act" or "pretend" in a Chekhov play, praising only those who "live them . . . and follow the deeply buried arteries through which their emotions flow,"[14] so Williams presents Amanda as most completely human when she lays aside her performance and allows simple humanity to determine her actions.

Laura, too, is an actress, though of a different kind. If she has learned "to live vitally in her illusions" (129), she is forced to deceive when her enrollment in a typewriting course ends in fiasco. Each day she leaves home supposedly to go to the business college but in fact to watch movies, visit museums, the zoo, or the botanical gardens. At home she pretends to study a keyboard chart. When this performance proves futile she is cast in a part of her mother's making for the visit of Tom's friend, Jim, the gentleman caller. Laura is costumed by Amanda ("The dress is colored and designed by memory," her breasts enhanced by powder puffs). She is made up ("The arrangement of Laura's hair is changed; it is softer and more becoming") and placed center stage ("Laura stands in the middle of the room"). The stage has been set and the lighting adjusted by Amanda as stage manager ("The new floor lamp with its rose silk shade is in place, a colored paper lantern conceals the broken light fixture in the ceiling, new billowing white curtains are at the windows, chintz covers are on the chairs and sofa . . ." [191]). She even directs the action ("Laura Wingfield, you march right to that door!" [197]). The failure of this performance, however, leaves Laura with only one theatre in which to live out her life, that of her glass menagerie.

Even Jim, the gentleman caller, is an actor. Once the baritone lead in *The Pirates of Penzance*, he is studying public speaking, the better to enter the public stage. He, too, has his fantasies. In his own mind he is something of a psychoanalyst. He is interested in "electro-dynamics" and taking a course in radio engineering at night school. Each new enthusiasm implies a scenario which will transform him, including his engagement: "The power of love is really pretty tremendous! Love is something that – changes the whole world" (230). Once again, however, this is a performance which fails quite to convince as his prosaic description falls some way short of the life-transforming experience which he claims: "She's a home girl . . . and in a great many ways we – get along fine" (229). The dash indicates a momentary hesitation as he reaches for a language adequate to the self-confident role he wishes to project. Recognizing the inadequacy of "get along fine" he moves quickly to a confession of love, born on a moonlit boat trip and leading to the construction of "a new man" (280). It carries no real conviction. Jim is a huckster for success, no longer confident of the substantiality or inevitability of his dream, an actor increasingly uncertain of his lines or his role.

One of the ironies of the play lies in the fact that performance, the imagination's abstraction of the self from its social environment itself, leads into a cul-de-sac not dissimilar to that which lies just beyond the windows of the St. Louis apartment. Tom is fated to restage his drama of the glass menagerie as surely as Ishmael is to recount the story of a white whale, as surely as is his sister to dramatize the lives of animals who are touching at least in part because they, like Amanda and Laura in Tom's memory, are unchanging. No matter how many times Tom steps forward to introduce the memories which haunt him, Laura will never escape on the arms of her gentleman caller, nor Amanda redeem her own failed life by finding romance for the daughter she loves but who must always stand as a reproach. The theatre offers a certain grace, as does all art, but beyond the obvious irony always implicit in an unyielding beauty, uncorrupted by time and hence uncontaminated by an imperfect humanity, is the hermetic atmosphere conjured by a world constructed by the imagination out of memory and desire.

The theatrical metaphor was to remain central to his work. *A Streetcar Named Desire* ends with Blanche DuBois, always a performer but now a pure actress, walking out of a New Orleans apartment towards the sad theatre of the madhouse, no longer able to distinguish fantasy from the real, no longer able, therefore, to reach out to those who might have been able to rescue her from despair. *Camino Real*, whose title is doubly ironic, stages the lives of the dispossessed and the marginal wholly through fictional characters who are never allowed access to the tangible world of tortured humanity, acting out their romantic scenarios entirely in the fictive world which is their protection against time but which also defines the limits of their possibility. Fiction as consolation: fiction as imprisonment. Decades later he was to write a play, *Out Cry*, in which the theatre is presented as the central metaphor, as two characters perform their lives in an empty theatre in a country whose coldness is itself an image of their lives, drained of human warmth because abstracted from time, from mortality, and hence from humanity.

Why this theatrical metaphor? In part, perhaps, because his plays are set in a South which is self-dramatizing, which performs its history as myth refusing the dynamic of time because this contains an account of failure and defeat. In part because the self he wishes to present is one sustained essentially by the imagination. The real proves so relentless and unforgiving that it has to be transformed, restaged, so that it becomes tolerable to those who lack the qualities required for survival. The national drama of progress, albeit denied by a national reality of Depression, is one which has no place for the fragile, the poet, the betrayed, the deserted. For progress, beyond its insistence on the material, invokes time and time, as we have seen, for Williams and his characters, was always the enemy. In his personal life he, like Tom, like Blanche, and like so many of his characters, sought some ultimate meaning in an art which granted him the only real refuge from the deprivations of natural process while at the same time leaving him to rely on the comfort offered by "the nearest stranger."

When Amanda says that "in these trying times we live in, all that we have to cling to is – each other" (171), she voices a conviction which was equally Williams's own, as she does when she observes that "Life's not easy, it calls for – Spartan endurance!" Indeed, though in interviews he often derided his mother, on whom Amanda was modeled, it is clear that it is Amanda who bears the greatest burden, twice abandoned and left to watch over her daughter. Though querulous and puritanical, she is allowed moments of touching vulnerability when she exposes the nature of her own pain ("I've never told you but I – loved your father. . ." [172]). And though she sustains herself with memories and fantasies of a reassuring future, she is forced to an acknowledgment of her situation, as Tom is not. Indeed, Williams himself confessed as much, remarking that, "the mother's valor is the core of *The Glass Menagerie* . . . She's confused, pathetic, even stupid, but everything has got to be all right. She fights to make it that way in the only way she knows how."[15] By necessity she has a practicality which none of the other characters show. At the beginning of the play she proscribes the word "cripple"; at the end she uses the word herself. It is her first step towards accepting the truth of her daughter's situation and hence of the need which she must acknowledge and address.

Williams comments on her cruelty and tenderness, on her derisory yet admirable character, her confused vitality, confused because it appears to lack real purpose. As he remarks in the character notes which precede the play, "she is not paranoiac, but her life is paranoia" (129). The conspiracy of which she is a victim is a fact of existence: youth gives way to age, beauty decays, optimism is subverted by experience, fantasies ground on the rock of the real. She has, he insists, "endurance," but as William Faulkner was to say in his Nobel Prize acceptance speech, endurance is not enough. It is simply the ability to live with irony. He looked, at least in the rhetoric of his speech if not in the action of his novels, for a degree of triumph. There is no real triumph in Williams's plays and precious little in Faulkner's novels. What there is is "a kind of heroism," and that is precisely the quality which he has ascribed to Amanda. Deserted and betrayed, she stays and continues her losing battle with time in the company of her doomed daughter and, in what is virtually the play's final stage direction, Williams finds a "dignity and tragic beauty" in that sad alliance. It is no longer the absurdity of this abandoned woman he chooses to stress. At the beginning of the play he had described her expression as "grim and hopeless" (151). She shakes her head in despair, having just learned of her daughter's deception in abandoning her typing course. At the end we are told that her "gestures are slow and graceful, almost dancelike" (236), as she comforts that same daughter.

Early in the play we are told that her face has "aged but childish features," that it is "cruelly sharp, satirical as a Daumier print" (169). At the end, with her words inaudible to us, she is once more presented to us in visual terms in a kind of *tableau vivant*. This time, though, it is an image drained of irony. What communicates is less cruelty than charity, less sharpness than a soft maternal attentiveness. At least in memory Tom embraces the woman he has otherwise blamed for his own problems, for the suffocating years in the shoe warehouse and for the guilt which has made him return, in memory, to St. Louis where he had abandoned her and failed to redeem his sister from her isolation.

In a world "lit by lightning," Laura's candles cast a softer glow. In the end the lightning will prevail, at least in the short term. Art can never really be a protection against the real. Chamberlain's betrayals, Franco's victories, Hitler's barbarity were not defeated by wishing they might be so, and, as Auden lamented, poetry did not save a single Jew. Williams was acutely aware of this. Why else have Tom open the play with a reminder of what lay in wait for those caught in the Depression and consoling themselves with movies, glamor magazines and dance music entitled, "The World is Waiting for the Sunrise"? At the same time he was wedded to art, whose power does indeed lie in its ability to outlive even the traumas of history. He was wedded to theatre whose form and whose substance exposed the nature of the paradox, as it offers truth through lies and reveals a tensile strength in the most fragile of creations.

NOTES

1 Anton Chekhov, *Plays*, translated Elisaveta Fen (Harmondsworth: Penguin, 1959), 123.
2 *Ibid.*, 7.
3 *Ibid.*, pp. 7–8.
4 *Ibid.*, p. 8.
5 *Ibid.*, p. 7.
6 Arthur Miller, "A Memorial Tribute to Tennessee Williams," a speech to the American Academy, 1984. Unpublished typescript.
7 Manuel Duran, *Lorca* (Englewood Cliffs, 1962), 172.
8 Tennessee Williams, *The Theatre of Tennessee Williams*, vol. 1 (New York 1971). Further references to this essay, and *The Glass Menagerie*, which also appears in this volume, appear in parentheses in the text.
9 Jo Mielziner, *Designing for the Theater* (New York, 1965), 124.
10 Chekhov, *Plays*, 398.
11 Tennessee Williams, *Conversations with Tennessee Williams*, ed. Albert Devlin (Jackson: University Press of Mississippi, 1986), p. 10.

12 *Ibid.*, 10.
13 Tennessee Williams, *Where I Live* (New York: New Directions, 1978), 50.
14 Anton Chekhov, *Plays*, 8.
15 Williams, *Conversations*, 14.

3

FELICIA HARDISON LONDRÉ

A streetcar running fifty years

The thirty-two-cent United States postage stamp commemorating Tennessee Williams, issued in 1996, features a portrait of Williams in a white linen suit against a twilight sky and, in the background, a streetcar. The choice of the streetcar as the only element in the design that can be specifically tied to one of Williams's plays testifies to the centrality of *A Streetcar Named Desire* in his dramatic canon as well as in the American cultural consciousness. Whether or not *A Streetcar Named Desire* is Tennessee Williams's "best" play, or even his most performed play, it is probably the one most closely identified with the dramatist, and it is certainly the one that has elicited the most critical commentary.

When *A Streetcar Named Desire* premiered at the Ethel Barrymore Theater in New York on December 3, 1947, Tennessee Williams was essentially known to the public for one other play, *The Glass Menagerie*, which had ended a 561-performance run at New York's Playhouse Theater just sixteen months earlier. The elegiac tone and coming-of-age crises of *The Glass Menagerie* did not prepare theatregoers for the searing adult drama of *A Streetcar Named Desire*, with its references to unspeakable aspects of sexuality. Indeed, one reviewer called it the product of an "almost desperately morbid turn of mind,"[1] and another found it "not a play for the squeamish."[2] And yet, it was recognized as "an enormous advance over that minor-key and too wet-eyed work, *The Glass Menagerie*."[3] It fulfilled the promise of the earlier work and catapulted Williams to the front rank of American dramatists. *A Streetcar Named Desire* ran for 855 performances and became the first play ever to win all three major awards, the Pulitzer Prize, the New York Drama Critics' Circle Award, and the Donaldson Award.

Despite the obvious differences between those two early Broadway successes, they also have much in common, as do most of Tennessee Williams's plays. In fact, *A Streetcar Named Desire* might be read as a compendium of his characteristic dramaturgy, verbal and visual language,

Figure 3 Karl Malden as Mitch and Jessica Tandy as Blanche in Scene 6 of *A Streetcar Named Desire*, directed by Elia Kazan

and thematic preoccupations. Such elements include the episodic structure; the lyricism of dialogue and atmosphere interspersed by comedy; the psychological realism of the characterizations set against striking departures from realism in the staging; the evocatively charged use of scenic elements, props, sound effects, gestures, and linguistic motifs; and the focus on characters who are psychically wounded or otherwise marginalized by mainstream society: characters seeking lost purity, or escape from the ravages of time, or refuge from the harshness of an uncomprehending world, or simple human contact. Their specific application in *A Streetcar Named Desire* will be incorporated in the scene-by-scene analysis below.

It is interesting to note some striking resemblances between *A Streetcar Named Desire* and *Cat on a Hot Tin Roof*, which premiered seven years later, on March 24, 1955. Blanche is like Brick in wishing to deny the passage of time, which robs both characters of a golden age of innocence. Both loved someone who was probably homosexual and who committed suicide after his implicit pleas for help met rejection. Just as Blanche carries a sense of guilt for what she said to Allan Grey on the dance floor, Brick knows that he was at fault for hanging up the phone on his friend Skipper. Both turn to drink, Brick drinking until he hears the click in his head that makes him peaceful, just as Blanche in Scene 9 remains gripped by the polka tune in her head until she hears "the shot! It always stops after that." Blanche and Maggie the Cat regard themselves as once-soft people who have become hardened in the process of survival. Stanley Kowalski and Big Daddy share traits – notably their ebullience and vulgarity – that make them compelling figures. The bed is a central feature in the settings of both plays, and the bathroom functions as a place of refuge for both Blanche and Brick. Both plays include interrupted birthday festivities, and both move metaphorically from desire to death, balanced by the birth of the Kowalski baby and the promise of new life in the body of Maggie. Certainly, these kinds of parallels could be found in almost any selection of plays by Williams, but it is instructive to note them in *A Streetcar Named Desire*, the play he regarded as his best, and *Cat on a Hot Tin Roof*, his most perfectly crafted work.

In the fifty years since *A Streetcar Named Desire* made its initial impact on the American stage, new modes of literary criticism as well as changing styles of theatrical production have affected our understanding of the play, without diminishing our appreciation of its beauty and power. Some of those evolving or altered viewpoints will be discussed below. First, however, it is important to place the play in its original context, to assess its importance in its own time. Broadway in the post-World War II years was dominated by musical comedies and revivals of works by Aristophanes, Shakespeare, Chekhov, Shaw, Wilde, Synge, and others, while the supply of new plays fell far short of their prewar abundance. Few playwrights of the 1920s and 1930s made the transition into the anxiety-ridden 1940s. Theatregoers, though buoyed by the Allied powers' victory and a rising tide of postwar prosperity, did not easily shake off lingering apprehensions that were born of the 1930s Depression and nurtured by the 1945 unleashing of nuclear weapons. Their entertainment expectations could no longer be satisfied by the standard packaging and tidy ending of the "well-made play." In this climate, the loose structure and moral ambiguities of *A Streetcar Named Desire* struck a chord of truth. Harold Clurman wrote in February 1948 that "its impact at this moment is especially strong, because it is virtually unique as a stage piece that is both personal and social and wholly a product of our life today."[4] The poker games of Scenes 3 and 11 bring together men who fought in the war, and Blanche carries memories of her encounters with off-duty soldiers at Belle Reve. All the characters are trying to build lives for themselves in the changing postwar world.

While it was certainly a product of its time, *A Streetcar Named Desire* also shocked audiences in that "outside of O'Neill's work, this was the first American play in which sexuality was patently at the core of the lives of all its principal characters, a sexuality with the power to redeem or destroy."[5] The play might be further credited with reinvigorating theatrical convention by its symbolic use of stage space, which juxtaposed the small flat (two rooms and a bathroom, with varying degrees of privacy) and the public arena of the street. Thomas Postlewait has insightfully analyzed the dynamics of this use of space in an article treating a number of Williams's plays.[6] The physical interior and exterior of the simultaneous setting also reinforce the mingling of objective reality and the subjective reality that is seen through the eyes of Blanche DuBois. The skillful incorporation of different levels of reality in an essentially "realistic" drama is another of the play's accomplishments.

Ultimately, it is sheer artistry that has made *A Streetcar Named Desire* seem so immediate and yet so transcendent: the verisimilitude and poetic power of the dialogue, the compelling characters squared off in a finely balanced struggle on which are brought to bear all the resources of theatre. In 1989, Philip Kolin asked a number of American dramatists to write a paragraph or two on the importance of *A Streetcar Named Desire*.[7] The thirty-six responses include three (those of William Hauptman, Terrence McNally, and Paul Zindel) that refer to the "mystery" of the play; they evoke both the mystery of creativity that produces art of this magnitude and the mystery of this particular work of art that always holds more secrets and more riches no matter how many times it is described, analyzed, or interpreted. This essay then is but one attempt, much indebted to five decades of scholarly study and theatrical production, to mine some of the play's incalculable wealth.

The first indication of the play's brilliance lies in its title, *A Streetcar Named Desire*, which signals the importance of theatrical metaphor in the work. In addition, the mundane concreteness of "streetcar" and the abstract quality of aspiration evoked in "desire" point to the many antinomies – thematic, symbolic, and imagistic oppositions – imbedded throughout the play.[8] The title also ties the action to a specific locale (the French Quarter in New Orleans was actually served by streetcars named "Desire" and "Cemeteries"), and it plants the notion of movement from one place to another (the action might be summed up as Blanche's emotional journey from desire to madness). Williams settled on the title only after submitting the completed manuscript to his agent Audrey Wood in 1947. For at least two years he had been working through revisions, the various drafts titled *The Passion of a Moth, Go, Said the Bird!, Blanche's Chair in the Moon, The Moth, The Primary Colors, Electric Avenue*, and *The Poker Night*.[9] Audrey Wood objected to the title on the manuscript she received, because to her *The Poker Night* sounded like "a Western action novel." Williams had apparently been holding the *Streetcar* title in reserve all along.[10]

In her study of the manuscripts, Vivienne Dickson found that Williams had also considered various epigraphs, each of which pinpoints a theme or image that has survived in the final version: blind hope, delicate moths in a world of mammoth figures, flight from reality.[11] The epigraph he finally chose for *A Streetcar Named Desire*, the fifth verse of Hart Crane's 1932 poem "The Broken Tower," epitomizes the play in a less obvious way:

> And so it was I entered the broken world
> To trace the visionary company of love, its voice
> An instant in the wind (I know not whither hurled)
> But not for long to hold each desperate choice.

Blanche might be said to have entered "the broken world" when her young husband Allan Grey died many years before the action of the play begins. His was the brief "visionary company of love," the loss of which – and the desire to "trace" or recapture it – leads her to make so many desperate choices.

The action of *A Streetcar Named Desire* is divided into eleven scenes. There are no act divisions, but the original production placed the customary two intermissions after Scenes 4 and 6. Those breaks also mark the seasonal divisions of the play, as Scenes 1 through 4 take place on two consecutive days in early May; Scenes 5 and 6 on a hot August evening; Scenes 7 through 10 on the afternoon and night of Blanche's birthday, September 15; and Scene 11 "some weeks later," a kind of October coda. The same three groupings of scenes may be defined in terms of their dominant genre. According to Roxana Stuart, who played Blanche in two different productions, "the first four scenes are comedy; then come two scenes of elegy, mood, romance; then five scenes of tragedy."[12] In his rehearsal notebook,[13] director Elia Kazan summarized each of the eleven scenes in terms of what Blanche wants, makes happen, or has happen to her.

Kazan's articulation of Blanche's through-line of action shows that, like most readers of the play, he considered her to be the protagonist. The protagonist is traditionally the character who faces obstacles in pursuit of a goal, one who makes things happen while holding the interest and sympathy of the reader or audience member, and the one whose crucial choice (crisis) determines the outcome of the action. According to Kazan's scheme, Blanche's crisis comes in Scene 9, when she makes a "last desperate effort to save herself by telling the whole truth. *The truth dooms her.*"[14] It is generally considered dramaturgically most effective if the crisis is closely followed by the climax (the emotional high point for the audience) and if the story is wrapped up fairly quickly after the climax. The climax of *A Streetcar Named Desire* is undoubtedly Stanley's rape of Blanche, which occurs at the end of Scene 10. Thus some critics pinpoint Stanley's decision to violate his antagonist as the play's crisis, and this would identify Stanley as the play's protagonist. Indeed, it very often occurs in productions of the play that Stanley is the one who garners the audience's sympathies. This was the case even in Kazan's production, in which Marlon Brando's exuberant portrayal of Stanley Kowalski not only had the audience rooting for his victory over Blanche, but skyrocketed Brando to overnight fame as an actor.

Tennessee Williams intended a balance of power between Blanche and Stanley, to show that both are complex figures whose wants and behaviors must be understood in the context of what is at stake for them. The action proceeds through clashes of these two opposites to the inevitable show-down by which one wins and the other loses. And yet, Scene 11 hints that the nominal winner, Stanley, has also lost, in that the relationships he values most – those with his wife Stella and his best friend Mitch – will never again be quite the same. Williams's characters, though often wrong-headed, are not agents of evil intent, but victims of their own limited perceptions.

Williams resembled his favorite dramatist, Anton Pavlovich Chekhov, in the depiction of characters whose superficial miscommunications mask a subterranean tumult that sends their lives spinning out of control. In fact, *A Streetcar Named Desire* is often compared to the Russian writer's *The Cherry Orchard* (1903), for both plays concern a genteel way of life obliterated by the brash energy of a lower social order on the rise. Both plays begin with an arrival and end with a departure. Blanche's fall, precipitated in part by her desperate flight from reality toward an illusory refuge, has much in common with that of Nina Zarechnaya in Chekhov's *The Seagull* (1896). The endings of Chekhov's *Uncle Vanya* (1899) and *Three Sisters* (1901) are echoed in Eunice's line in Scene 11 of *A Streetcar Named Desire*: "Life has got to go on. No matter what happens, you've got to keep going" (406). An important Chekhovian feature of Tennessee Williams's drama, including *A Streetcar Named Desire*, is the use of music (often from an offstage source) and sound effects to heighten or comment upon a dramatic moment. When Blanche panics, for example, we hear a cat screech in the alley or a locomotive thundering past.

From the opening moment of Scene 1, the atmosphere is evoked by a tinny "blue piano" being played in a bar-room around the corner. Colors and scents also described in the opening stage directions underscore the poverty, decay, and quaint charm of this New Orleans street named Elysian Fields. Its lively multi-ethnicity is established by the two women, "one white and one colored," chatting and joking on the steps of the building where Stanley and Stella Kowalski occupy the street-level flat.

An exchange of ten short lines introduces Stanley and Stella, hinting at her good breeding in contrast to his coarseness. His initial action, tossing her a package of meat, sets up his association with food and drink that will become apparent throughout the play (along with other physical needs). They have scarcely left for the bowling alley when Blanche appears, an incongruously delicate figure in white. Eunice, the landlady who lives upstairs, asks if she is "lost," a question that becomes prescient in retrospect. Blanche's first line, a reference to the streetcars that brought her here, suggests a movement beyond physical needs to ineffable matters of the spirit: "They told me to take a street-car named Desire, and then transfer to one called Cemeteries and ride six blocks and get off at – Elysian Fields!" (246). We will see her progress from the sexual "desire" that caused her to lose her job as a schoolteacher, to a mere desire for "rest!," to the burial of her hope for redemption, to her going mad, which might be seen as a crossing over to a "paradise" beyond personal responsibility (thus the allusion to the classical Greek concept of the Elysian Fields).

Left alone in the downstairs flat to await her sister Stella, Blanche reveals in her actions both the nervous strain she is struggling to keep under control and her duplicity. Helping herself to the whiskey she finds establishes a precedent for what will become a summer-long pattern of secret drinking. Stella's arrival unleashes in Blanche a torrent of manipulative and defensive remarks. The scene serves not only as exposition, but it also sets up the contrasting characterizations of the sisters. When Blanche criticizes the flat and the neighborhood in literary terms ("Only Mr. Edgar Allan Poe! – could do it justice!"), Stella responds with a matter-of-fact reference to gritty reality: "No, honey, those are the L & N tracks" (252). Blanche explains her departure from school before the end of spring term as a leave of absence occasioned by nervous exhaustion; this will later be revealed as a lie. Her vanity comes to the fore when she points out Stella's weight gain, and that she hasn't put on an ounce in the ten years since Stella left home. Thus the first scene deftly sketches some of Blanche's character flaws. There are more to come.

Blanche is dubious about the arrangements for her visit: the bed is (like Blanche herself) "one of those collapsible things" (256), and the absence of any door between the two rooms of the flat raises a question of decency – and perhaps metaphorically heralds the ill-defined boundaries in her coming struggles with Stanley over territorial space. At the same time, the urgency of her insistence on staying here ("I want to be *near* you, got to be *with* somebody, I *can't* be *alone!*" [257]) announces her basic motive: need for refuge and desire for human contact. Elia Kazan found the spine of Blanche's character in similar terms: to "find protection," which in the tradition of the old South "must be through another person."[15]

The opposition of Blanche and Stanley is foreshadowed even before they meet. Stella refers to Stanley as "a different species" (258), but she cannot describe the difference and resorts to showing her his photograph. This kind of literalism will emerge as common to both Stella's and Stanley's outlook in contrast to Blanche's facility with allusion and metaphor. At this point we learn from Stella only that Stanley was a Master Sergeant in the Engineers' Corps, that his civilian job takes him "on the road a good deal," and that his essential trait is the powerful physical attraction he exerts on Stella. The latter factor somehow triggers Blanche's resentment; she begins reproaching Stella for having left her with the responsibility for holding things together at home, a tirade that culminates in the accusation, "Where were *you*! In bed with your – Polack!" (262).

The kernel of Blanche's outburst is the news that Belle Reve is lost. Belle Reve had earlier been mentioned by Eunice as "your home-place, the plantation . . . a great big place with white columns" (249). As any student of elementary French recognizes, the plantation's name is incorrect; the French noun *rêve* (dream) takes the masculine form of the adjective "beautiful"; thus it should be *Beau* Reve. The logical assumption is that the plantation was originally named Belle *Rive* (beautiful shore), and that over the generations the name has been corrupted as the family's fortune dwindled. What had been a solid *shore* is now but an evanescent *dream* of lost splendor. Blanche becomes hysterical as she blames the loss of the plantation on the expense of "all that sickness and dying," the long series of family deaths she was forced to witness: "the struggle for breath and bleeding. You didn't dream, but I saw! *Saw! Saw!*" (262). Her stress on *seeing* something that shatters an ideal or an illusion will be echoed ("I saw! I know!") in her story in Scene 6, the play's central scene. The thought will be reiterated as a theatrical metaphor at the beginning of Scene 10 when Blanche's romantic fantasy is cut short by a glimpse of herself in a hand mirror, which she then smashes. But the brutal realities of death and desire inflicted on her by those she loves have left their mark on her even before she meets her match in Stanley.

Reduced to tears by Blanche's diatribe, Stella runs into the bathroom to wash her face. This leaves Blanche alone for her initial meeting with Stanley. Faced with a surprise house guest, he takes the situation in his stride. His words add up to nothing more than cheerful vulgarity. But to the high-strung Blanche, his comments and gestures (holding up the liquor bottle, taking off his shirt) must seem calculated to lay bare her lying and affectation. His well-intentioned but clumsy attempt at small talk ("You were married once, weren't you?") triggers a faint polka strain, the play's first use of the music Blanche hears in her mind when she is reminded of the one she married at sixteen. Scene 1 ends with her line: "The boy – the boy died. I'm afraid I'm – going to be sick!" (268).

Scene 2, the following evening, comprises two sequences, both "duets," one between Stella and Stanley, followed by one between Stanley and Blanche. When Stanley comes home at six o'clock, Blanche is in the bathroom, "soaking in a hot tub to quiet her nerves" (269). The bathroom will be Blanche's habitual retreat throughout the play, and her constant bathing evokes a purification ritual. While Blanche uses the bathroom as a place of renewal, Stanley's annoyance is expressed in simple physical terms: ". . . it's my kidneys I'm worried about!" (364).

Learning that Belle Reve had to be "sacrificed or something," Stanley becomes concerned that Stella must have been swindled out of her share of the property, "and when you're swindled under the Napoleonic code I'm swindled *too*" (273). He roots through Blanche's trunk looking for legal papers and pulling out clothes and jewelry that to him represent a fortune, whereas Stella sees them as mere costume pieces. His crude violation of Blanche's possessions might be weighed against Blanche's intrusion into his domestic kingdom, where she swills his liquor and hogs the bathroom, but it also presages his violation of her person in Scene 10. The social class distinctions that inform much of the action are pithily acknowledged by Stanley: "The Kowalskis and the DuBoises have different notions" (275).

Stella retreats to the porch, but Stanley waits inside for Blanche's emergence from the bathroom. Blanche is in a flirtatious mood and refuses to be baited by him, apart from a momentary loss of self-possession over his clumsy handling of a packet of love-letters from "a dead boy . . . my young husband" (282–3). She gives Stanley the legal papers, saying, "I think it's wonderfully fitting that Belle Reve should finally be this bunch of old papers in your big, capable hands!" (284). She repeats the idea to Stella when she rushes out to the porch upon learning that Stella is going to have a baby: " . . . maybe he's what we need to mix with our blood now that we've lost Belle Reve" (285). Robert Bray, in his Marxist reading of the play, sees this transfer of papers/merging of bloodlines as a key concept in the evolution of the social system from the old agrarian South, burdened by its past, as represented by Blanche, to the postwar urban-industrial society in which Stanley's class has gained leverage.[16] Stanley's friends begin to arrive for an evening of poker as Stella and Blanche leave for an evening out. Scene 2 ends on a note that suggests Blanche has won this round.

Scene 3 stands out from the others in several ways. It has its own title, "The Poker Night." Its pictorial atmosphere of "lurid nocturnal brilliance, the raw colors of childhood's spectrum" is inspired by "a picture of Van Gogh's of a billiard parlor at night" (286), which Henry I. Schvey has identified as *All Night Café* (1888).[17] It is one of few ensemble scenes in a play composed largely of two- or three-character sequences. And most importantly, it is the scene in which Blanche and Stanley truly begin to see each other as a threat. The opening line, spoken by one of the men at the card table, serves as a pointer: "Anything wild in this deal?"

Stanley has been losing at cards and displays a volatile irritability even before Stella and Blanche come in. Mitch sets himself apart from the other card-players by his anxiety over his sick mother. The association with sickness and the dread of loneliness in his comment that "I'll be alone when she goes" (288) convey a subtle thematic linkage with Blanche, to whom he is introduced by Stella. Blanche quickly senses that Mitch is a prospective conquest. When she changes out of her dress, she deliberately stands in the light so the men can see her through the portieres. When Stella exits into the bathroom, Blanche turns on the radio and sits in a chair (Blanche's chair in the moon?) as if confident of her power to attract Mitch to her. First, however, it is Stanley who crosses to the bedroom and turns off the radio, but "stops short at the sight of Blanche in the chair. She returns his look without flinching" (295), and he returns to the poker table. Thus with great economy of means, by a simple dramatic gesture, Williams demonstrates the staking out of territory.

Mitch soon leaves the card game to chat with Blanche. He shows her the inscription on his silver cigarette case, given to him by a girl who knew she was dying. Blanche homes in on his vulnerabilities: "Sick people have such deep, sincere attachments" (298). She asks him to cover the light bulb with a paper lantern she bought on Bourbon Street: "I can't stand a naked light bulb, any more than I can a rude remark or a vulgar action" (300). Her equation of the naked bulb with vulgarity implies its opposite: the soft glow of filtered light as the refined sensibility by which she identifies herself. It recalls her comment to Stanley in Scene 2: "I know I fib a good deal. After all, a woman's charm is fifty per cent illusion . . ." (281). Blanche's desire for illusion in opposition to the harsh realities that surround her is probably the play's most obvious thematic value. It is significant that Mitch is the one who both installs the paper lantern and, in Scene 9, removes it, for these actions define the period during which he sees Blanche as she wants him to see her, under the spell of an illusion she creates. A number of critics have analyzed Blanche in metatheatrical terms: she is an artist who dramatizes herself as if she were a stage character, playing roles detached from the reality of her situation, costuming herself from the trunk containing fake furs and costume jewelry, designing the lighting effects that will show her to advantage. With Mitch as her enthralled audience, she adds musical underscoring: she turns on the radio and "waltzes to the music with romantic gestures" (302).

The radio galvanizes Stanley into aggressive action, though the actual source of his anger undoubtedly lies deeper. Here in his own home, where he is cock of the roost and host of the poker party, the intruder Blanche has lured both his wife and his best friend into her orbit. She has appropriated his radio for her kind of music. In a drunken rage, he throws the radio out of the window. "Drunk – drunk – animal thing, you!" (302), Stella cries, and this provokes him to attack her. While the men subdue Stanley, Blanche leads Stella upstairs to Eunice's and Steve's flat. The men put Stanley under the shower and leave hurriedly. When he emerges, dripping wet, he tries telephoning uptairs, but Eunice apparently hangs up on him. This abortive phone call at Stanley's lowest point in his fortunes, when he is actually reduced to sobs, parallels the unsuccessful attempt to telephone a rescuer that Blanche will make in Scene 10, at *her* lowest point. Stanley stumbles outside and calls up to Stella, but Eunice threatens to call the police: "I hope they do haul you in and turn the fire hose on you, same as the last time!" (306). Her mention of a fire hose juxtaposes the fire and water imagery that pervades the play. A thorough examination of the many interrelated symbolic references to fire, heat, and the color red has been published by Philip C. Kolin.[18] The fact that Stanley and Blanche both have associations with fire and water is indicative of the complexity of their characterizations and the fallacy of any attempt to reduce them to simple opposites.

Stanley howls "with heaven-splitting violence": "STELL-LAHHHHH!" The lament of a clarinet wells up as Stella descends the stairs. She and Stanley "come together with low, animal moans" (307) and he carries her into the darkened interior. This sequence is particularly powerful in the 1951 film version of *A Streetcar Named Desire*, directed by Elia Kazan and featuring Brando, Kim Stanley (Stella), and Karl Malden (Mitch) from the Broadway cast. (Vivien Leigh replaced Jessica Tandy as Blanche.) Scene 3 of the play ends in a brief dialogue between Blanche and Mitch. He has returned to make sure that all is well and reassures her that the incident was not serious. Blanche's last line in Scene 3 not only plants the key word, "kindness," which will resurface in her last line in the play, but also packs into a few words the social context of the times as well as her fragility and yearning: "There's so much – so much confusion in the world . . . Thank you for being so kind! I need kindness now" (309).

The next morning, Scene 4, Blanche descends the stairs to the Kowalski flat where Stella is lolling contentedly in bed. Stella resists Blanche's efforts to demonize Stanley. She accepts him as one who has "always smashed things," and, besides, "only one tube was smashed" in the radio (312–13). Stella's passivity is countered by the frantic twists and turns of Blanche's search for solutions to what she perceives as Stella's predicament. She decides to contact a former beau, a Texas oilman named Shep Huntleigh, but the irrationality of the idea becomes clear when she tries to compose a Western Union message with an eyebrow pencil on a Kleenex. This scene strongly invites feminist criticism: although Blanche regards Stella's husband as a brutal predator, her first impulse is to turn to another man as savior. There is a subtle irony in her reflexive reversion to the Southern belle's habits of thought – that is, emotional dependence on a patriarchal system of male protection for the helpless female – just moments after she has said, "I'm going to *do* something. Get hold of myself and make myself a new life!" (313). Stella, on the other hand, may be trapped in marriage to a man who makes messes for her to clean up, but it is a situation she has chosen for herself and one in which she chooses to remain. The scene culminates in Blanche's *tour de force* speech opposing Stanley's ape-like behavior to the finer things of the spirit. The noise of a passing train covers Stanley's entrance into the outer room where he overhears Blanche's description of him as a "survivor of the Stone Age!" (323). Another passing train allows him to exit unobtrusively. He calls from outside, and Stella runs to embrace him. Stanley grins over Stella's head at Blanche. He now knows beyond a doubt that he is engaged in a war with Blanche for Stella's heart and mind, and that he has won this round.

Blanche's past begins to catch up with her in Scene 5, making her situation increasingly serious while the comedic elements move into minor key: a humorous running fight sequence between Eunice and Steve punctuates Blanche's conversations with Stella and Stanley. Stanley hints that he has been hearing from "somebody named Shaw" (329) about Blanche's reputation back in Laurel. After Stanley leaves, Blanche tells Stella: "I wasn't so good the last two years or so, after Belle Reve had started to slip through my fingers" (331). She expresses nervousness about her ability to hold Mitch's interest, and – touching on a frequent theme in Tennessee Williams's plays, the ravages of time – confides her fear of losing her attractiveness as she grows older.

Stella goes off to meet Stanley, leaving Blanche alone to wait for Mitch. A Young Man comes to collect for the newspaper, and Blanche draws him inside to light her cigarette. She kisses him on the lips and then sends him away, saying: "It would be nice to keep you, but I've got to be good – and keep my hands off children" (339). While the sequence with the Young Man does nothing to advance the action, it does serve other dramatic functions. It demonstrates what up till now has been only a matter for speculation: Blanche has a psychological problem. It prepares the way for the story she tells in Scene 6, recounting the key formative event in her past. As details are added in subsequent scenes, a pattern will emerge of obsessive desire for boys half her age.

The importance of Blanche's story is suggested by its placement in the very middle of the play, in Scene 6, which takes place when she and Mitch return late that evening from their date. Less animated than usual, Blanche is undoubtedly preoccupied with what Stanley may have learned about her and what he might tell Mitch. Mitch's sick mother is never far from his mind, so the conversation turns to death and loneliness and love. This cues Blanche's reminiscence of Allan Grey, the boy she married at sixteen, whom she loved deeply without understanding the kind of help he sought from her – until she discovered in a room together "the boy I had married and an older man who had been his friend for years . . ." (354). Pretending that nothing had changed, they went dancing at Moon Lake Casino. On the dance floor, Blanche suddenly could not avoid blurting out, "I saw! I know! You disgust me . . . " (355), upon which Allan ran from her to the edge of the lake and shot himself. Her story is underscored by the music of the polka that was playing during their last dance, an effect that tells us we are in the world of Blanche's memory, not merely witnessing another performance designed to impress Mitch. This may be the first sincere moment she has spent with Mitch, and it gains her what she has not been able to achieve in two months or so of artful deceit: a proposal of marriage. "You need somebody. And I need somebody, too. Could it be – you and me, Blanche?" Her brief response carries a rush of pent-up desperation, gratitude, and the hope of redemption: "Sometimes – there's God – so quickly!" (356).

Stella's preparations for Blanche's birthday tell us that Scene 7 takes place on September 15, a date Blanche has earlier announced in a discussion of astrological signs (hers is Virgo, the virgin, and Stanley's is Capricorn, the goat). While Blanche warbles in the bathroom, Stanley tells Stella what he has learned about her sister. Not only was "Dame Blanche" a disreputable resident of the Flamingo Hotel in Laurel, but she was fired from her teaching position at the high school for getting "mixed up with" a seventeen-year-old boy. "On the question of what attracts Blanche to adolescent boys – the newsboy and the high school student who get her fired," Roxana Stuart recalls: "It seemed obvious to me that their innocence and purity are cleansing to her. Then it occurred to me that perhaps they remind her of Allan Grey, her young husband who killed himself. When I mentioned it to Mr. Williams he said, 'No, in her mind she has become Allan. She acts out her fantasy of how Allan would have approached a young boy.'"[19]

For the birthday supper in Scene 8, only three of the four places at the table are occupied. Blanche tries to keep up a brave front even though she says, "I've been stood up by my beau" (369). Stanley's crude table manners provoke Stella's criticism. Stanley reacts by throwing dishes on the floor: "That's how I'll clear the table!" (371). After the candles on the cake are lit, Stanley gives Blanche a birthday present: a bus ticket back to Laurel. Overcome, Blanche runs to the bathroom. Stella reproaches him for being "so cruel to someone alone as she is," but Stanley can think only of regaining sovereignty in his home, of recapturing nights with Stella when he can pull her "down off them columns" (377) and "get the colored lights going with nobody's sister behind the curtains to hear us!" (373). Suddenly, Stella apparently begins going into labor and asks to be taken to the hospital.

The polka music plays in Blanche's head as she sits drinking alone in the dark several hours later. Mitch arrives, unshaven and bolstered by a few drinks. Blanche does her best to maneuver the relationship into its familiar patterns, but is forced to relinquish her pretenses when Mitch removes the paper lantern, stares at her under a glaring light, and confronts her with the names of men who knew her at the Flamingo in Laurel. Cornered, she lashes out with dark humor: "Flamingo? No! Tarantula was the name of it! I stayed at a hotel called The Tarantula Arms! . . . Yes, a big spider! That's where I brought my victims" (386). This surprising turn in her outburst exemplifies dramatic dialogue at its best; no wonder Scene 9 was Williams's own favorite.[20] Blanche goes on to bare her soul to Mitch, telling of the deaths in her family and of death's opposite, desire, which she gratified with soldiers from the training camp near Belle Reve. The sequence is intercut by the faint cries of a Mexican street vendor, a blind woman in a dark shawl selling "flowers for the dead." Mitch does not seem to hear or understand what Blanche tells him. Or perhaps he hears it as a justification for attempting to take from her "what I been missing all summer" (389). Perhaps nowhere else in the play does she say anything as direct and unadorned as her final plea to him, "Then marry me, Mitch!" When he refuses because she is "not clean enough to bring in the house with my mother," she switches back to hyperbole. If all her bathing has not made her clean, she will invoke the opposite of water: "Fire! Fire! Fire!" (389). Her cries send Mitch away. She falls to her knees.

The water imagery recurs a few hours later as Blanche, wearing a white satin evening gown and diamond tiara, prattles to herself about swimming in the old rock-quarry. She is still in touch with reality, however, as demonstrated by her first questions to Stanley when he enters: she asks about her sister and the baby. He tells her that the baby is not due until morning, and questions her in turn about her "fine feathers." Fire and water imagery recur in his suggestion that she is going to "a fireman's ball" (392) and her claim that she has been invited to cruise the Caribbean on a yacht. Stanley is not taken in by her face-saving story of a telegram from Shep Huntleigh, but he does invite her to "bury the hatchet" (395). In a buoyant mood, with his baby on the way and the prospect of Blanche's departure within the week, he can be generous. But Blanche makes the mistake of echoing the theme she had developed in Scene 3, when Stanley overheard her likening him to an ape. Now focused on reconstructing her self-image – an ideal of womanhood that depends not upon transitory physical attractiveness, but "beauty of the mind and richness of the spirit and tenderness of the heart" – she mentions "casting my pearls before swine!" (396). And "swine" is the word Stanley hears. Like the "ape" speech of Scene 3, this speech turns him into an adversary. He taunts Blanche for her "lies and conceit and tricks!" (398). Stanley's abuse of her might yet remain on the verbal plane except that Blanche's ensuing hysteria ultimately provokes him to physical aggression.

As her irrational fear mounts, the scene moves into an expressionistic mode; that is, reality becomes distorted by Blanche's subjective vision of it. Lurid reflections and grotesque shadows appear on the walls around her, while "the night is filled with inhuman voices like cries in a jungle" (399). Significantly, it is during her futile attempt to telephone for help that the walls become transparent, so that the sordid life on the street (an encounter between a drunkard and a prostitute) can be seen simultaneously. As interior and exterior menace mingle in her perception, so also is the distinction blurred between subjective and objective reality. She latches onto the telephone as her lifeline to illusion, but she cannot escape the reality of her entrapment in the small flat with Stanley. For Mary A. Corrigan, Scene 10 "depicts the total defeat of a woman whose existence depends on her maintaining illusions about herself and the world."[21] While Blanche and Stanley symbolize for most critics an opposition of spirit and flesh, Corrigan sees also that "the conflict between Blanche and Stanley is an externalization of the conflict that goes on within Blanche between illusion and reality."[22] At the end of Scene 10, her illusion of Shep Huntleigh to the rescue succumbs to the physical reality imposed on her by Stanley when he rapes her.

From Stanley's point of view, it is Blanche who provokes the attack, first when she imagines a threat where none had existed, virtually planting the suggestion that he might "interfere with" her (401), and then when she smashes a bottle in order to "twist the broken end in your face!" (402). This is a challenge he cannot ignore. He catches her wrist to force her to drop the bottle, and she sinks to her knees, as she did after Mitch left. (She will fall to her knees for the third time just before her final exit at the end of Scene 11, a scene in which Henry Schvey has signalled a cluster of religious references.[23]) With Blanche in her soiled white satin gown and Stanley having changed into his silk wedding pajamas, his picking her up and carrying her to the bed takes on, according to Thomas P. Adler "the aura of a desecrated marriage."[24]

Scene 11 takes place some weeks later. Stanley is winning at the poker game in progress. Stella, packing Blanche's things while Blanche bathes, tells Eunice, "I couldn't believe her story and go on living with Stanley" (405). However, Stella expresses doubt about whether she has made the right decision, which she has described to Blanche as making "arrangements for her to rest in the country" (404–5). Blanche has taken this to mean that Shep Huntleigh is coming for her. When she dresses, Blanche describes her jacket as "Della Robbia blue. The blue of the robe in the old Madonna pictures" (409). This calls up an association with her sign, Virgo, while the religious connotation is reinforced by the sound of cathedral bells. Eunice has brought her some grapes from the French Market, which leads Blanche to imagine that she will die of eating an unwashed grape. However, the death she fantasizes is couched in images of purity: sea, air, noon sunlight, white, blue, soul, and heaven. She also invokes her "first lover" and, by extension, the young pure love she has been yearning to recapture.

A very institutional-looking Doctor and Matron ring the bell, which

Eunice answers. Blanche asks if it is the gentleman she has been expecting from Dallas, and Eunice implies that it is, thus sparing Stella from having to lie to her sister. The poker players rise as Blanche passes through – except for Mitch, who cannot bring himself to look at her. Seeing that the man is not Shep Huntleigh, Blanche runs back into the bedroom. Her subjective perception of reality at this moment is theatricalized in the lurid reflections on the walls, a distorted rendering of the polka music accompanied by jungle noises, and the echoing reverberation of the voice of the Matron who has followed her in. Stanley moves in toward Blanche and taunts her cruelly, while Stella runs outside uttering prayers for Blanche's safety, finally blaming herself: "Oh, God, what have I done to my sister?" (416). Stanley tears off the paper lantern that had been put back on the light bulb, and Blanche "cries out as if the lantern was herself." In symbolic terms, this may pinpoint Blanche's definitive retreat from reality into her world of illusion. Despite her clinging to the notion of a rescue by Shep Huntleigh, she has hitherto remained lucid enough to react to Mitch's presence in the outer room, to speculate about her own death (as Big Daddy says in *Cat on a Hot Tin Roof*, "the human animal" is "the only living thing that conceives of death, that knows what it is . . . " III. 87, 91), and to have apparently told Stella what Stanley did to her. After the tearing of the paper lantern, she does not speak again until she decides to accept the Doctor as her rescuer.

Although most critics seem to accept the premise that Blanche goes mad, it is possible to interpret the action otherwise. Just as the boundary between illusion and reality has constantly fluctuated for Blanche, so is the line between sanity and madness a tenuous one. Indeed, a dramaturgical analysis that takes Blanche as the protagonist would logically place her crisis not in Scene 9, as Kazan did (making her a passive figure who is acted upon in the last two scenes), but in Scene 11, when (as the active agent of her own destiny) she finds a way to salvage her dignity in spite of everything and to be the lady she has been striving to be. Blanche is correct in perceiving the Doctor as a gentleman who knows how to treat a lady with respect. From there, it is a simple step to see him as the protector upon whom the Southern belle has been conditioned to rely.

Others have been putting their hands on Blanche and her things throughout the play. When Stanley handled Allan Grey's letters in Scene 2, she exclaimed, "The touch of your hands insults them!" (282). In Scene 6, Blanche gaily tells Mitch, "I said unhand me, sir" (348). At the birthday party, she responds to Stella's sympathetic gesture: "Oh, keep your hands off me, Stella" (375). In Scene 9, her rupture with Mitch is precipitated by his placing his hands on her waist. In Scene 11, the Matron "pinions her arms."

But when the Doctor smiles and sees her as an individual, Blanche extends her hands toward him. She holds his arm for her exit, as she says: "Whoever you are – I have always depended on the kindness of strangers" (418).

Stella cries out as Blanche disappears around the corner. Then Eunice brings Stella her baby, wrapped in a blue blanket. Stella begins to sob with total abandon. Stanley comes out to the porch. He "kneels beside her and his fingers find the opening of her blouse," as the blue piano music swells. At the poker table, Steve speaks the curtain line: "This game is seven-card stud" (419). That line, along with the music and the "holy family" visual grouping, seem to say that life will continue as Stanley would have it. However, it means that Stella will now have to live with illusion, as Blanche did. We know also that Stella and Mitch have been irrevocably changed by Blanche's passage; perhaps they will find it in themselves to stand up against the hegemony of the apes.

The ambiguity of the ending became an issue in Kazan's 1951 film version. The screenplay was subject to pressure from the Legion of Decency as well as from its own producer, Warner Brothers, and this resulted in a number of cuts and changes.[25] According to Maurice Yacowar, Williams and Kazan won the case for keeping the rape scene on condition that "the rapist would not go unpunished." Thus the film ended with the impression that Stella would take her baby and leave Stanley.[26] In 1994 a new print of the film was released with restored footage at the end suggesting that Stella's retreat to Eunice's flat may be only temporary. Another treatment of the ending is discussed in June Schlueter's analysis of the 1984 television film version directed by John Erman.[27] R. Barton Palmer's essay in this volume explores in further detail the film's ending.

Among the many accounts of the original Broadway production, two are particularly useful, Brenda Murphy's book *Tennessee Williams and Elia Kazan: A Collaboration in the Theatre* and Susan Spector's article in *Modern Drama* (December 1989), "Alternative Visions of Blanche DuBois: Uta Hagen and Jessica Tandy in *A Streetcar Named Desire*." The play's perennial popularity has led to New York revivals in 1956, 1973, and 1992. The latter production became the basis for a three-hour CBS television broadcast on October 29, 1995, with Jessica Lange and Alec Baldwin recreating the roles of Blanche and Stanley.

It seems fitting in conclusion to give the last words to those who are particularly equipped to appreciate the art and the craft of this play; that is, to those who themselves write plays. Philip Kolin's 1989 "Playwrights' Forum" on *A Streetcar Named Desire* is an excellent collection of commentaries from which superlatives may be drawn. Horton Foote, who saw the original production, asserts: "The theatre, to my mind, was given new life when the play was produced that first time, and though we have rarely lived up to that kind of excellence, it certainly remains there for all of us to strive for" (181). "There are very few nearly perfect plays," writes Robert E. Lee. "*Streetcar* is one of them" (188). Calling it "a perfect organic entity – seamless, fluid, soaring," Dennis J. Reardon declares: "The search for the Great American Play can stop with *A Streetcar Named Desire*. It's the genuine article. I know this to be true because even after all these years, the thing still takes my breath away" (193). Alfred Uhry: "I believe that *A Streetcar Named Desire* contains the finest dialogue ever written for an American play" (200). Wendy Wasserstein: "Stella and Blanche are among the best written women characters in any dramatic literature" (201). Paul Zindel: "*Streetcar* for me will always be a poetic, brutal, thrilling lesson in how a single brave playwright let his demons and angels dance with every ounce of truth he could know" (202). Megan Terry: "What I love best about the play is the poetry. Not the words, but the motion, the way the play moves, sweeps in and out of time and forward into our consciousness forever. *Streetcar* was a necessary addition to the national consciousness, emotionally, economically, and politically. *Streetcar* is a feminist play . . . Also it has the properties of the great classics of all time" (199). And according to Garson Kanin, "Tennessee Williams was the best, and *A Streetcar Named Desire* was *his* best" (186).

NOTES

1 Richard Watts, Jr., "Streetcar Named Desire is Striking Drama," *New York Post* (December 4, 1947) in *New York Theatre Critics' Reviews* 8 (1947), 249.

2 Ward Morehouse, "New Hit Named 'Desire'," *The Sun* (December 4, 1947) in *New York Theatre Critics' Reviews* 8 (1947), 250.

3 Louis Kronenberger, "A Sharp Southern Drama By Tennessee Williams," *PM* (December 5, 1947) in *New York Theatre Critics' Reviews* 8 (1947), 250.

4 Harold Clurman, "Streetcar," *The Collected Works of Harold Clurman* (originally published in *Tomorrow*, February 1948; New York: Applause Theatre Books, 1994), 131.

5 C. W. E. Bigsby, *Modern American Drama, 1945–1990* (Cambridge University Press, 1992), 51.

6 Thomas Postlewait, "Spatial Order and Meaning in the Theatre: The Case of Tennessee Williams," *Assaph: Studies in the Theatre*, no. 10 (Tel Aviv University, 1994), 45–73.

7 Philip C. Kolin, "*A Streetcar Named Desire*: A Playwrights' Forum," *Michigan Quarterly Review* 29 (Spring 1990), 173–203.

8 Some of these are laid out schematically in terms of the opposition between Stanley and Blanche in Thomas P. Adler, *"A Streetcar Named Desire": The Moth and the Lantern* (Boston: Twayne Publishers, 1990), 32–33.

9 Vivienne Dickson, "*A Streetcar Named Desire*: Its Development Through the Manuscripts," Jac Tharpe (ed.) *Tennessee Williams: A Tribute*, (Jackson: University Press of Mississippi, 1977), 155–57.
10 Audrey Wood, with Max Wilk, *Represented by Audrey Wood* (Garden City, NY: Doubleday, 1981), 150–51.
11 Dickson, "*A Streetcar*," 157–58.
12 Roxana Stuart, "The Southernmost DESIRE," *Tennessee Williams Newsletter* 1, 2 (Fall 1979), 5.
13 Elia Kazan, "Notebook for *A Streetcar Named Desire*," Toby Cole and Helen Crich Chinoy, (eds.) *Directors on Directing* (Indianapolis: Bobbs-Merrill, 1963), 364–79.
14 *Ibid.*, 366.
15 *Ibid.*, 366.
16 Robert Bray, "*A Streetcar Named Desire*: The Political and Historical Subtext," Philip C. Kolin (ed.) *Confronting Tennessee Williams's "A Streetcar Named Desire": Essays in Critical Pluralism* (Westport, CT: Greenwood Press, 1993), 189–90.
17 Henry I. Schvey, "Madonna at the Poker Night: Pictorial Elements in Tennessee Williams's *A Streetcar Named Desire*," Harold Bloom (ed.) *Tennessee Williams's A Streetcar Named Desire: Modern Critical Interpretations* (New York: Chelsea House Publishers, 1988), 104.
18 Philip C. Kolin, "'Red-Hot!' in *A Streetcar Named Desire*," *Notes on Contemporary Literature* 19 (September 1989), 6–8.
19 Stuart, "Southernmost," 6.
20 Stuart, "Southernmost," 6.
21 Mary A. Corrigan, "Realism and Theatricalism in *A Streetcar Named Desire*," *Modern Drama* 19 (December 1976), 391.
22 *Ibid.*, 392.
23 Schvey, "Madonna," 107–9.
24 Adler, *A Streetcar Named Desire*, 45.
25 Some of these points in the film are discussed by Linda Constanzo Cahir, "The Artful Rerouting of *A Streetcar Named Desire*," *Literature/Film Quarterly* (1994), 72–77.
26 Maurice Yacowar, *Tennessee Williams and Film* (New York: Ungar, 1977), 22–23.
27 June Schlueter, "Imitating an Icon: John Erman's Remake of Tennessee Williams's *A Streetcar Named Desire*," *Modern Drama* 28 (March 1985), 146.

BIBLIOGRAPHY

Adler, Thomas P. "*A Streetcar Named Desire*": The Moth and the Lantern. Boston: Twayne Publishers (Twayne's Masterwork Studies, no. 47), 1990.
Bloom, Harold (ed.). *Tennessee Williams's "A Streetcar Named Desire"*. New York: Chelsea House, 1988.

Bray, Robert. "*A Streetcar Named Desire*: The Political and Historical Subtext," in Kolin (ed.), *Confronting Tennessee Williams's "A Streetcar Named Desire,"* pp. 183–97.

Chesler, S. Alan. "*A Streetcar Named Desire*: Twenty-five Years of Criticism," *Notes on Mississippi Writers* 7 (1973), 44–53.

Corrigan, Mary A. "Realism and Theatricalism in *A Streetcar Named Desire*," *Modern Drama* 19 (December 1976), 385–96.

Cahir, Linda Constanzo. "The Artful Rerouting of *A Streetcar Named Desire*," *Literature/Film Quarterly* (1994), 72–77.

Dowling, Ellen and Nancy Pride. "Three Approaches to Directing *A Streetcar Named Desire*," *Tennessee Williams Newsletter* 11, 2 (Fall 1980), 16–22.

Fleche, Anne. "The Space of Madness and Desire: Tennessee Williams and *Streetcar*," *Modern Drama* 38 (1995), 496–509.

Harris, Laurilyn J. "Perceptual Conflict and the Perversion of Creativity in *A Streetcar Named Desire*," in Kolin (ed.), *Confronting Tennessee Williams's "A Streetcar Named Desire,"* 83–103.

Kolin, Philip C. "*A Streetcar Named Desire*: A Playwrights' Forum," *Michigan Quarterly Review* 29, 2 (Spring 1990), 173–203.

"'Red-Hot!' in *A Streetcar Named Desire*," *Notes on Contemporary Literature* 19, 4 (September 1989), 6–8.

Kolin, Philip C. (ed.). *Confronting Tennessee Williams's "A Streetcar Named Desire": Essays in Critical Pluralism.* Westport, CT: Greenwood Press, 1993.

Miller, Jordan Y. (ed.). *Twentieth Century Interpretations of "A Streetcar Named Desire": A Collection of Critical Essays.* Englewood Cliffs, NJ: Prentice-Hall, 1971.

Murphy, Brenda. *Tennessee Williams and Elia Kazan: A Collaboration in the Theatre.* Cambridge University Press, 1992.

Nordon, Pierre. "Le Jeu des stéréotypes dans *Un Tramway nommé désir*," *Etudes anglaises* (April–June 1979), 154–61.

Porter, Thomas E. "The Passing of the Old South: *A Streetcar Named Desire*," Chapter 7 in *Myth and Modern American Drama.* Detroit: Wayne State University Press, 1969.

Postlewait, Thomas. "Spatial Order and Meaning in the Theatre: The Case of Tennessee Williams," *Assaph: Studies in the Theatre*, no. 10 (1994, Tel Aviv University), 45–73.

Riddel, Joseph N. "*A Streetcar Named Desire* – Nietzsche Descending," *Modern Drama* 5 (February 1963), 421–30.

Schlueter June. "Imitating an Icon: John Erman's Remake of Tennessee Williams's *A Streetcar Named Desire*," *Modern Drama* 28 (March 1985), 139–47.

Spector, Susan. "Alternative Visions of Blanche DuBois: Uta Hagen and Jessica Tandy in *A Streetcar Named Desire*," *Modern Drama* 28 (December 1989), 545–60.

Stuart, Roxana. "The Southernmost DESIRE," *Tennessee Williams Newsletter* 1, 2 (Fall 1979), 3–7; 11, 1 (Spring 1980), 5–10.

Tharpe, Jac (ed.). *Tennessee Williams: A Tribute.* Jackson: University Press of Mississippi, 1977.

Williams, Tennessee. *The Theatre of Tennessee Williams*, 1: *Battle of Angels, The Glass Menagerie, A Streetcar Named Desire.* New York: New Directions, 1971.

The Theatre of Tennessee Williams, III: *Cat on a Hot Tin Roof, Orpheus Descending, Suddenly Last Summer.* New York: New Directions, 1971.

Wood, Audrey, with Max Wilk. *Represented by Audrey Wood.* Garden City, NY: Doubleday, 1981.

Yacowar, Maurice. *Tennessee Williams and Film.* New York: Ungar, 1977.

4

JAN BALAKIAN

Camino Real: Williams's allegory about the fifties

During the fifties Williams's plays were eclectic. His two great box-office successes, *Cat on a Hot Tin Roof* (1955), which grapples with greed, mendacity, and homosexuality, and *Sweet Bird of Youth* (1959), an indictment of Southern bigotry, demonstrated his facility with naturalism. On the other hand, he wrote several non-naturalistic plays: *The Rose Tattoo* (1950), inspired by his relationship with Frank Merlo, a carnival-esque comedy celebrating the Dionysian; *Camino Real* (1953), an allegory about being trapped in a fascist state; *Orpheus Descending* (1957), a tragic love story set in a racist, brutally materialistic, dying South, Williams's version of the myth of Sisyphus; and *Suddenly Last Summer* (1958), in which Williams depicts the destructive nature of the writer and of homosexuality.[1] Of the latter plays, *Camino Real* seemed the most egregiously misunderstood.

Williams's idea for *Camino Real* first came to him when he was sick in a desolate corner of Mexico. Ill, friendless, penniless, he felt as though he would never escape. He also thought that he would never be able to write a great play again:

> I thought . . . that those "huge cloudy symbols of a high romance" that used to lift me up each morning . . . had gone like migratory birds that wouldn't fly back with any change of season. And so it was written to combat or to purify a despair that only another writer is likely to understand fully.[2]

Moreover, his fears recalled terrifying visions he had had as a child, which came like a pageant before his eyes. Accordingly, he wrote *Camino Real* in the form of pageant and a dream. Before falling asleep in the prologue and awakening in the final scene, Don Quixote tells Sancho, " . . . my dream will be a pageant, a masque in which old meanings will be remembered and possibly new ones discovered, and when I wake from this sleep and this disturbing pageant of a dream, I'll choose one among its shadows to take along with me in the place of Sancho . . ."[3] The action moves surrealistically

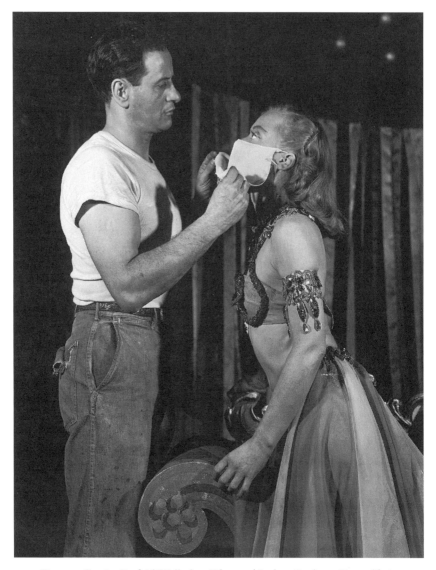

Figure 4 *Camino Real*. Eli Wallach as Kilroy and Barbara Baxley as Esmeralda in
Elia Kazan's March 19, 1953 New York production, produced by Cheryl Crawford at
the National Theatre

the way dreams do, and it contains elements of melodrama, farce, pagan ritual, romance, satire, tragedy, and comedy. Never before had the American theatre seen a play that exploded realism in this fashion.

Characters from Dumas, Proust, and Cervantes, along with the archetypal World War II American soldier, Kilroy, settle down into Williams's pageant, which is set in a Latin-American police state, an archetypal hell. Quixote's dream consists of a pair of old lovers, Jacques Casanova and Marguerite Gautier; a declining artist, Lord Byron; a homosexual Frenchman, Baron de Charlus; a wealthy couple, Lord and Lady Mulligan; and the American hero, a former champion boxer, Kilroy, who has left his faithful wife because of his enlarged heart (he was afraid he would have a heart attack while sleeping with her). These Romantics are trapped on the oppressive Camino Real with a gypsy and her daughter, bums and drunks, a loan shark, and street cleaners, who dispose of dead people. In addition, Gutman rules the camino tyrannically and acts as narrator, announcing the blocks and events to come and brings down the final curtain. Williams used Gutman as a theatrical device because he "wanted the regular announcement of the blocks as they come along to have the whiplike quality of time."[4] The trapped travellers can escape from Gutman and his Camino Real in only three ways: death; being lucky enough to take a plane called the Fugitivo, which crashes in Elizabeth, New Jersey; or to jump from the high wall that may lead them across a great desert to distant mountains.

Williams originally wrote *Camino Real* in 1947 as a one-act play called *Ten Blocks on the Camino Real* and set it in a Mexican locale. As an exercise at the Actor's Studio, director Elia Kazan wanted to work on fantasy and staging, so he chose the whorehouse scene with the Gypsy's daughter. When Williams saw the scene, "he was devastated by its impact and decided to enlarge and elongate it to make it a complete play."[5] Since his initial draft, he "had been back and forth to Europe and Africa . . . and . . . added touches from Fez, Tangiers, and Casablanca" (Brown, *Saturday Review*, 1953). His revisions also reflected the reduction of human liberties in the world that deeply disturbed him. Furthermore, in making the play longer, he added the character of Lord Byron and expanded the roles of Jacques Casanova and Marguerite Gautier (Brown, *Saturday Review*, 1953). Eli Wallach, who played Kilroy in the original production, wrote "when Kilroy finally made his bid to escape, and then 'competes by dancing,' the stage was set for Act Three. Originally we did it as a two-act play, but by New York it was split into three parts – with the third act beginning in the Gypsy's place."[6] Wallach saw, however, a structural weakness in the initial three-act script, because his character's story dominated Act one, but was then dropped in order to investigate Casanova and Camille (Wallach, letter, 2).

His most personal play, *Camino Real* affirms Williams's own philosophy that romanticism is absolutely essential. By romanticism, he means "the ability to feel tenderness toward another human being, the ability to love," a capacity achieved by not allowing the dehumanizing experiences on the Camino Real to brutalize one's spirit (7). Don Quixote, the romantic, has the two key speeches in the play. In the prologue he arrives in the midnight plaza of this nowhere, everywhere place and hears all about him the whispering of the word "lonely" from beggar and outcast people asleep on the pavement. He seems oddly comforted by it: he turns to the audience and observes: "In a place where so many are lonely, it would be inexcusably selfish to be lonely alone" (5). Indeed, desperation is the price of admission to the Camino Real. The other key speech conveying Williams's idea of romanticism appears at the end of the play: "The violets in the mountains have broken the rocks" (100). Williams decided to give these words to Quixote in his revised, published version for the following reason:

> I do truly believe, that the human coat-of-arms can and must, finally, bear such romantic mottoes as these, at least in the later stretches of our Camino Reals.
> What the play says through this unashamed old romanticist, Don Quixote, is just this, "Life is an unanswered question, but let's still believe in the dignity and importance of the question. "   (Williams, *New York Times*, 1960)

Williams insisted on pronouncing "camino" (road) in the accepted Spanish style, but Anglicized the second word as "real" instead of "reh-al," as it should be in Spanish. He meant the phrase to be a hybrid Spanish-American one to convey the ideal of a real, actual, road rather than a royal road. Like Dante's *Inferno*, *Camino Real* is a mythic and poetic allegory about characters who find themselves in the middle of the journeys of their lives where the straight way is lost. Williams captures his characters in that middle realm between life and death where everyone gathers at the end of their life's journey. While they are already dead, they have not forgotten their lives; their memories pain them, and they want to return to their lives, but the way back is barred.[7] Therefore, he appropriates the first canto of Dante's *Inferno* for his epigraph, and he imitates Dante by using historical and literary figures as symbols.[8] Moreover, like Dante, Strindberg, and Blake, Williams's vision in *Camino* is theological and apocalyptic; he foresees the end of humanity (Jackson, *Broken World*, 110). As he explains:

> The people in my play are romantics confronted by very real situations as
> they come to the end of the road. It is a real road. The play . . . is about the
> indomitability of the romantic spirit. I approve of romantics. They fascinate
> me.   (Williams, *New York Times*, 1960)

Williams's romantic characters, who are in conflict with a harsh material
world, were nothing new in 1953. He had established his apocalyptic and
romantic sensibility in *A Streetcar Named Desire* and in *The Glass
Menagerie*, in which the collapse of Blanche and Laura also represented the
collapse of a culture and its myths. Like Kilroy, they are romantics caught
in a culture on the brink of collapse. And, like the earlier plays, *Camino
Real* also concerns itself with surviving appalling experiences gracefully.
Moreover, it looks forward to his later play, *Secret Places,* in which the fear
of death provokes the theatrical impulse. Always writing about dispossession and alienation, he continued in *Camino Real* to dramatize characters
at the moment when they feel their world begin to slip away from them.

Williams's romantic sensibility attracted him to the writing of Hart
Crane, F. Scott Fitzgerald, D. H. Lawrence, and Keats, whose "Ode to a
Nightingale" was his favorite poem (Bigsby, *Modern American Drama* 33).
But *Camino Real* even seems to reach back to Wordsworth's and Coleridge's idea of Romanticism in that Williams was using colloquial language,
exploring the realm of the supernatural, employing the persona of a poet-prophet who writes in a visionary mode, and charging his dramatic world
with poetic symbolism. In addition, *Camino Real* has the kind of spontaneous form that Wordsworth advocated in his Preface to the *Lyrical
Ballads*. And, Romantic subjects were often outcasts, solitary figures
engaged in a long, elusive quest, just as Kilroy and Don Quixote are in
Williams's play. Finally, Romantic writers firmly believed that the imagination could create new beginnings and infinite possibilities; similarly,
Williams placed his faith in the imagination's ability to resist the harshness
of the public world (Bigsby, *Modern American Drama,* 34). In *Camino
Real,* the romantics ultimately escape the road of reality, and Don
Quixote's dream *is* the play, the imagination that redeems the world of
Gutman.

Camino Real was Williams's response to the fifties in America, a time
when "the spring of humanity [had gone] dry" (5), when the romantic
ideals of nobility, truth, valor, and honor gave way to desperation.
According to him, the play represented "my conception of the time and
world that I live in, and its people are mostly archetypes of certain basic
attitudes and qualities with those mutations that would occur if they
continued along the road to this hypotethical terminal point in it."[9] In this

context, *Camino* denounced "the fascist demagoguery then spreading over the country in the voice of Joseph McCarthy."[10] In an interview, Williams explicitly said that the play presented the dilemma of an individual caught in a fascist state and was an expression of his belief in the difficulties of romanticism in a predominantly cynical world.[11] Indeed, it is no co-incidence that both Arthur Miller's *The Crucible* and *Camino Real* appeared in 1953. In fact, Williams wrote to the State Department to protest the withdrawing of Miller's passport, and he attacked the simple-mindedness of Cold War politics (Bigsby, *Modern American Drama*, 38). For Williams, the Red Scare became analogous to the "real road" in his play, where fascism crushes outcasts and rebels: homosexuals, prostitutes, panderers, thieves, starving peasants, dreamers, writers, and those who are lonely, weak, or emotionally disturbed. Eli Wallach attributes the play's failure to the conservatism of the fifties:

> 1953 in the U.S. was the worst anti-art, anti-intellectual assault since the prudishness that preceded WWI. Williams wanted to investigate Death, the young dreamers, the innocents abroad, the cruelty and injustice of the innocents. But the play upset people . . . *Camino* will be done again – it should be – it was born a little early. Kilroy pre-dated the Beatnik, the wanderer, the bearded-travelling folk singer. Today he would be the Jimmy Dean, the lost-soul, the innocent. (Wallach, letter, 3)

Moreover, Barbara Baxley, who played the Gypsy's daughter, recalls that "Walter Winchell and Ed Sullivan attacked the play as anti-American. They accused it of being a leftist manifesto" (Spoto, *Kindness of Strangers*, 187). All references in the play to fascism in America, and to brotherhood and lover were cut, since they were thought to be ringing cries of Communist sympathy. She remarks, however, that the earlier version of the play was an unwaveringly anti-imperialist play. While it was certainly not anti-American, it was anti-fascist (187). But when he revised the play, he restored some of the cuts demanded by Winchell's political objections, insisting that his politics were humanitarian, not partisan (184).

Whether or not Williams considered *Camino* political, he could not deny its allegorical quality. Accordingly, he set it in an unspecified Latin-American country, and the plaza bears resemblance to ports like Tangiers, Havana, Casablanca, and New Orleans. Indeed, Williams may have had the 1942 film *Casablanca* in mind, because, like the play, *Casablanca* captures characters in crisis, in frustrated relationships, stranded in a distant port, trying to escape fascism. Moreover, he divides the "real road" into three metaphoric parts: the luxury side, the Sietes Mares, and Skid Row – consisting of the Gypsy's place, the Loan Shark's, and the flea-bag hotel called Ritz Men Only. Terra Incognita, beyond the Archway, is a wasteland between the walled town and the distant mountains, where there is "nothing . . . and then more nothing. And then snow covered mountains" (45). Similarly, the characters who inhabit the camino represent a microcosm of society: the outcasts – bums, drunks; the Street People, who dance, sing, prostitute themselves, and steal; the historical romantics – Marguerite Gautier, the "Lady of the Camellias," Jacques Casanova, Lord Byron, and Baron de Charlus; the wealthy – Lady and Lord Mulligan; the impoverished – A. Ratt; the tyrannical authorities – Gutman, who reports to an absent Generalissimo, and his soldiers, the Street Cleaners, who collect and dispose of the dead, and the Medical Team; the capitalists – the Gypsy, her son, and the Loan Shark; the idealists – Don Quixote, Kilroy (and Byron). Within this microcosm, Williams reviews Western history through a literary glass by recalling Marguerite Gautier, the "Lady of the Camellias," Jacques Casanova, the "great lover," Lord Byron, the poet, Baron de Charlus, the "homosexual masochist from Proust,"[12] and Lord Mulligan, a twentieth-century tycoon. In addition, everything he drew from Dumas's *Camille* and Casanova's *Memoirs,* he reshaped according to his poetic ideal (Spoto, *Kindness of Strangers,* 177).

While Williams appropriated a good piece of the early European literary tradition for his allegory about America in the fifties, he also reached to T. S. Eliot for his American literary influence. As Alice Griffin points out, Williams's symbols, stream of consciousness, themes of desire, death, resurrection, destruction of cities, sterility, and life-giving water, his allusions, and even choice of characters and settings reveal the influence of T. S. Eliot's *The Love Song of J. Alfred Prufrock* and *The Waste Land* on his imagination.[13] It is no coincidence that *The Waste Land* grabbed Williams because it is a kind of a play in its own right, a symphony of voices. And like Eliot's poetry, *Camino Real* uses colloquial cadences to create poetic diction. Moreover, Williams's choice of Marguerite, Casanova, and Byron as characters reflects Eliot's interest in the contrast between a heroic past and an ineffectual present. In addition, A. Ratt, who leans out of the window of the Ritz Men Only, to shout the word "lonely," echoes the lonely men who lean out of windows of one-night, cheap hotels in *Prufrock.* And, Eliot's images of sterility in *The Waste Land* become Williams's actual fountain in the square, dry until Don Quixote restores it at the end, symbolically reviving "the spring of humanity" (11). Furthermore, Gutman's cry in Block Seven – "it's like the fall of a capital city, the destruction of Carthage, the sack of Rome by the white-eyed giants from the North! I've seen them fall! I've seen the destruction of them!" (100) echoes Eliot's destruction of the cities in "What the Thunder Said."

Williams even takes an actual line from Eliot's "Burnt Norton," of his *Four Quartets,* when La Madrecita, holding the dead body of Kilroy in her arms near the end, remarks that "Humankind cannot bear very much reality" (150). The resurrected Kilroy rises to his feet when she says, "Rise, ghost! Go! Go bird!" (150) paraphrasing the closing lines of "Burnt Norton," which interrelates past, present, and future (Griffin, 129–130). Both Williams and Eliot were writing about the destructive impact of time and about a spiritual waste land.

In *Camino Real,* each character exemplifies the way that time has betrayed them or that they have betrayed themselves. Quixote is an old desert rat; Byron has lost his integrity as a poet; Kilroy is a former boxing champ, who had to retire because of his failing heart; Casanova is an impoverished, seedy rake, and Gautier, a former prostitute, is a frightened and lonely woman. As James Coakley notes, the decadents, the transients of the expensive tourist hotel are, like the romantics, terrified of time. But they are morally no better than their counterparts across the plaza; although they have more money, they have the same fears, viewing their existence as a series of way stations towards death. In short, each has lost his honor.[14] Kilroy, for instance, has to sacrifice his ruby-and-emerald-studded belt with the word CHAMP in order to survive on the camino: "sometimes a man has gotta hock his sweet use to be in order to finance his present situation" (32). Therefore, Williams concludes his play with a prayer for the return of honor to the world. But the idealists retain symbols of past achievements: Byron's pen, Kilroy's gold gloves, and Quixote's blue ribbon. Moreover, each chooses to defy life's betrayals and start anew. Any hope for redemption from the road of reality lies in the violets breaking the rocks. In other words, beauty, imagination, and love ultimately triumph over cruelty, ugliness, and fascism.

Williams's title reflects the desolate quality of the enervating Camino Real, where desperation is the price of admission, and everyone is "confused and exhausted" (15–16). On the "real road" characters must confront the cold-hearted ruler, Gutman, and get "stewed, screwed, and tattooed" (157) "baptized with the contents of a slopjar," robbed, beaten, turned into a patsy, and have their heart stolen, becoming an undistinguished member of a collectivist state, as Kilroy is. To put it another way, Williams's fugitive characters have arrived at the end of a royal road of imagination to meet with reality in the form of age, disease, cruelty, disillusionment, and death.[15] The Camino Real was an actual highway that existed during Spanish rule in southwest Mexico and Central America, and Williams is playing with the Spanish meaning of Camino Real, "Royal Road," and the English denotation, "the way of reality." In this double meaning lies

Williams's interest in the idea that the road of the Spanish knights who conquered the land is also the road upon which Christianity came to the West Coast of America. Accordingly, the play's division into sixteen stations represents missionary stations. In twentieth-century America, however, the old missionary way has become a street of commerce (Jackson, *Broken World*, 121). The final station, where the play is set, is the plaza, a place of entry and departure, "with no permanent guests" (15).

Martial law protects the only never dried-up spring under the Siete Mares, and as Casanova explains to Kilroy, "the exchange of serious questions and ideas, especially between persons from opposite sides of the plaza, is regarded unfavorably here . . . " (42). With the loss of democracy is the obliteration of individualism on the camino, especially if one is poor:

> If its [the stiff's] pockets are empty . . . the "stiff" is wheeled straight off to the Laboratory. And there the individual becomes an undistinguished member of a collectivist state. His chemical components are separated and poured into vats containing the corresponding elements of countless others. If any of his vital organs or parts are at all unique in size or structure, they're placed on exhibition in bottles containing a very foul-smelling solution . . . There is a charge of admission to this museum. The proceeds go to the maintenance of the military police. (43)

The government exploits not only those who are poor, but also those who are unique. Kilroy, the ruggedly individual American, refuses to take orders from Gutman, who wants to turn him into a patsy. Here, Williams draws on the *commedia dell'arte*, a sixteenth-century Italian form which used improvised comedy and always had a buffoon called the Pulcinella. Typically, the actors, playing stock characters, improvised the dialogue around a given scenario; usually a pair of young lovers outwit a rich old father, "Pantalon," aided by a clever servant, "Harlequin," in a plot enlivened by the buffoonery of "Punch" and other clowns.[16] Williams plays with this genre when Kilroy tosses the patsy dress into Gutman's face and leaps into the aisle of the theatre, exclaiming, "Kilroy's a free man with equal rights in this world!" (51). While Esmeralda cheers him on, the officers capture and beat him. Block Six closes ominously as the guard presses the button at the end of a cord and Kilroy's nose goes off and on like a firefly. Casanova explains that Kilroy is Gutman's prime target because he has "a spark of anarchy" in his "spirit . . . and nothing wild or honest is tolerated here!" (57). Clearly, *Camino* protests oppressors of the human spirit.

Given Williams's concern with diminishing human values on the camino, it makes sense that he employs expressionism, which grew up in Germany during and after World War I, when artists were concerned about the loss of individual integrity in the face of frighteningly rapid technological progress. There is a rebellious and subversive quality to expressionist plays, and, while Williams is not specifically attacking technology, he was clearly pointing a finger at the oppressive conservatism of the fifties in America. Accordingly, in the *New York Times* article, he wrote that if *Camino Real* were a product being promoted on a television commercial and he were the spokesman for it, he would present it in the following theatrical terms:

> Are you more nervous and anxious than you want people to know? Has your public smile come to resemble the grimace of a lion-tamer in a cage with a suddenly untamed lion, or that of a trapeze performer without a net beneath him and with a sudden attack of disequilibrium coming on him as he's about to perform his most hazardous trick near the top of the big-top?
>
> And do you have to continue your performance betraying no sign on your face of anxiety in your heart?
>
> Then here is the right place for you, the Camino Real, its plaza and dried-up fountain, at the end of it. Here is where you won't be lonely alone, bewildered alone, frightened alone, nor desperately brave alone either.
>
> (Williams, *New York Times*, 1960)

The play addresses a profound existential despair of the kind that later expressionist plays dramatized when they moved from attacking the family to questioning the whole cosmic order. The expressionists typically represented the individual by an Everyman-like protagonist, just as Williams uses Kilroy. Kilroy, a former boxer, represents the archetypal, innocent, trusting, good-natured American soldier in World War II, who would leave his message, "Kilroy was here," one step ahead of everyone else. As C. W. E. Bigsby points out, he was a gesture of resistance, both heroic and anti-heroic. The essence of Kilroy was that he could never be seen because he was always in the vanguard. He could never be caught (Bigsby, *Modern American Drama*, 52).

Moreover, just as intense subjectivism – the externalization of the writer's inner feelings – characterizes expressionist plays, *Camino Real* takes the form of Don Quixote's dream. Expressionist drama also has a lyricism of language, which takes precedence over stage technique. Therefore, the technique of expressionist plays often seems clumsy and untheatrical, as many critics complained about *Camino Real*. Finally, the primacy of language over plot and action in the expressionist drama results in removing all psychological verisimilitude from the plays. Only the author-hero is psychologically delineated. The subsidiary characters are always types, impersonal and frequently grotesque because they are inimical to the other characters, who are often representatives of the authoritarian social order. Williams employs this technique in his depiction of the Street Cleaners, Nursie, the Gypsy, the Bum, A. Ratt, and Gutman. They are merely marionettes with unthinking devotion to society's ideals. As Williams says, "more than any other work I've done, this play has seemed to me like the construction of another world, a separate existence . . ." (Williams, *Where I Live*, 63). Some critics even liken it to a comic strip (Bigsby, *Modern American Drama*, 51). Thus, *Camino Real* confirmed the fact that Williams had never been interested in realism, that he always resisted an art of surfaces. It was his attempt to liberate the American theatre from its conservatism once and for all.

Accordingly, Jo Mielziner's poetic, nonrealistic set design seemed most appropriate for Williams's poetic vision. Mielziner wanted the set in the 1955 production to take the form of a pit, as though Kilroy were trapped in a place where there were no obvious physical escape. In this "labyrinth," he sought ways of using projected images, patterns, and colors to fulfill Williams's suggestion of constant changes in the various blocks.[17] For various reasons, however, Lemuel Ayers, a friend of Williams from the University of Iowa, designed the set, costumes, and lighting. Ayers's heavily realistic set differed greatly from Mielziner's fluid, imagistic sketches that called the audience's attention to the stage as a performance space and created a subjective realm unrelated to time and place (Murphy, *Williams and Kazan*, 69). It clashed with the play's timeless fantasy, stylized costumes, and choreographed movement. Another difficulty was that the actors had been trained by Stanislavsky's Method, which proved too realistic for the demands of *Camino*. Director Elia Kazan's aesthetic challenge was to attempt to interpret the subjective fantasy of the play through the stylized but naturalistic psychological realism of Stanislavsky.

But the subjective quality of the play did not mean that Williams had written whimsically. With meticulous attention to form, he had achieved an extraordinary degree of dramaturgic freedom:

> When it began to get under way I felt a new sensation of release, as if I could "ride out" like a tenor sax taking the breaks in a Dixieland combo or a piano in a bop session . . .   (Williams, *New York Times*, 1960)

> My desire was to give these audiences my own sense of something wild and unrestricted that ran like water in the mountains, or clouds changing shape in a gale, or the continually dissolving and transforming images of a dream. This sort of freedom is not chaos nor anarchy. On the contrary, it is the result of painstaking design, and in this work I have given more conscious attention to form and construction than I have in any work before. Freedom is not achieved simply by working freely.   (Williams, *Where I Live*, 65)

Camino's freedom and mobility of form attracted Elia Kazan to the play. Williams recalls, "we kept saying the word 'flight' to each other, as if the play were merely an abstraction of the impulse to fly" (Williams, *Where I Live*, 65). Both were infected with the wild spirit of anarchy within the play, the dynamic and organic qualities that Williams most values (Williams, *Where I Live*, 69). Exploding the fourth wall, *Camino* was the first time on Broadway that actors ran down the aisles, spilled into the audience, and invaded the balcony.[18] Kazan explained his direction of the play in the following way:

> It's Tennessee speaking personally and lyrically right to you. That's one reason we've pulled the audience inside the fourth wall by having the actors frequently speak directly to the spectator and by having some of the exits and entrances made throughout the aisles of the theatre. This device also gives a feeling of freedom.[19]

Similar to Thornton Wilder's *Skin of Our Teeth,* the play's narrative stretches time and place, and its emotional truth is the poetic truth of dream and fantasy. The action is a kind of theatrical circus, a festival dance, with vaudevillian routines. Each time a legendary character in the play appears, a hunchback Mummer somersaults through his hoop of silver bells, springs up, and shakes it excitedly toward a downstage arch, which begins to flicker with a diamond-blue radiance. Moreover, Williams notes in his stage directions that the Fiesta is a sort of serio-comic, grotesque-lyric "rites of fertility" with roots in pagan culture. During the Fiesta, the Coronation of the King of Cuckolds, Casanova is crowned King of the Cuckolds. Kilroy snatches Casanova's antlers, while Casanova removes Kilroy's wig and electric nose. When the gong sounds, the Gypsy announces that the moon has restored the virginity of her daughter, Esmeralda. Then, Esmeralda and Kilroy woo each other, both professing their sincerity. They symbolically consummate their relationship when Kilroy lifts her veil. But the whole event is anti-climactic for Kilroy because Esmeralda is not the true woman for whom he had hoped, nor does she provide the salvation he sought. Disillusioned, he exclaims, "I pity myself and everybody that goes to the Gypsy's daughter. I pity the world and I pity the God who made it" (133). Furthermore, Williams stages a kind of melodrama when Kilroy challenges the Street Cleaners, who kill him. On the camino, death is not the symbol of finality and grandeur that it is in romantic literature. Represented by the Street Cleaners, it is simply absurd. Indeed, *Camino* is perhaps his most obviously absurdist work, produced the same year that Beckett's *Waiting for Godot* opened in Paris. Unlike naturalistic plays in which heredity and environment shape character, his protagonists' conflicts in *Camino Real* are more metaphysical than social (Bigsby, *Modern American Drama*, 39).

La Madrecita magically resurrects Kilroy. He retrieves his golden heart, refusing to surrender it to the state, where it will be displayed in a museum whose proceeds will support the military police. He then pawns his heart for jewelry and furs to offer Esmeralda. In a farcical moment, Kilroy pounds on the Gypsy's door, the door is thrown open and the sordid contents of a slop jar are thrown at him. Just as Kilroy is convinced that "the deal is rugged," Quixote awakens, advises him not to pity himself, and invites him to venture with him into the Terra Incognita. Thus, Williams subverts the original *Don Quixote*, which satirizes chivalric romances. Here, Quixote is anything but quixotic; his zeal for adventure is not only a matter of survival, but it is the way out of hell. In the comic tradition, the play ends affirmatively. Quixote and Kilroy are united; together they walk through the arch into the Terra Incognita. Marguerite pays Casanova's bills, and Quixote announces that the violets in the mountains have broken the rocks.

CRITICAL RECEPTION/LANDMARK PRODUCTIONS
Elia Kazan's 1953 New York production

Whether it was *Camino Real*'s eclectic mixture of theatrical conventions and forms, or Broadway audiences' plain resistance to anything political, let alone nonrealistic, or both, *Camino* failed on Broadway after sixty performances (Spoto, *Kindness of Strangers*, 225). John Mason Brown called it

> A sorry mixture of Gehenna (Hell), the Kasbah (a section in North Africa containing nightclubs and houses of prostitution) seen and inhaled at noon, the inferno as rewritten by Mickey Spillane and *Paradise Lost* in translation by Sartre.[20]

Williams recalled that the opening of *Camino Real* on March 19, 1953 was the worst night he had ever spent in his life. Most of the audience had walked out, demanding their money back.[21] He was so depressed by the failure of both *Camino Real* and *Summer and Smoke*, that he even considered abandoning his career (Bigsby, *Modern American Drama*, 52). Perhaps he should have been prepared for this resistance; when he wrote the original sketch in two months, his agent, Audrey Wood, advised him "not to go on with it. It was too fantastic" (Murphy, *Williams and Kazan*, 64). Watching the Broadway audience leave, Williams remarked, "Well, I don't think they're really taking the play to their hearts" (Spoto, *Kindness of Strangers*, 177). But even Elia Kazan, the director, and Williams himself were confused about the play; neither realized that *Camino* was really a romantic pageant,[22] with roots in a medieval literary tradition, the pageantry of the miracle plays, as well as in *commedia dell'arte* and expressionism. It also drew from the profane mimicry of festival days, and many of the play's images, such as the Street Cleaners, are grotesques, drawn from the plastic arts (Jackson, *Broken World*, 110–11).

Kazan recalled that Williams was more tense than he had been about *Streetcar* because of "the nature of *Camino*. It was a risky thing. He knew that, and we all knew it" (Spoto, *Kindness of Strangers*, 177). There were frantic, late meetings between Williams, producer Cheryl Crawford, and Kazan about sets, costumes, and script revisions. Williams wrote a revised draft of the play during a period of increasing use of alcohol and pills for sedation and alertness (Spoto, *Kindness of Strangers*, 177), convinced that the play would never seem "obscure and confusing to anyone who was willing to meet it even less than halfway" (Williams, *Where I Live*, 65). *Camino* was so different from traditional kinds of drama that some critics called it "anti-drama," "comic-tragedy," "anti-theatre," "grotesque mime," and "magic theatre" (Jackson, *Broken World*, 110). Indeed, it established Williams as a writer whose idea of form derived from recent developments in philosophy, theology, politics, dance, cinema, literature, and the plastic arts – those three-dimensional, visual arts such as painting, sculpture, which are usually distinguished from written art forms. Making use of gesture, sound, music, dance, light, color, action, and design, *Camino* illustrates Williams's concept of plastic form, of multidimensional design in motion.

In addition, it seems ironic that the Chrysler Corporation invested heavily in Elia Kazan's 1953 New York production of *Camino Real,* produced by Cheryl Crawford, at the National Theater,[23] a play that derided the ethics of capitalism. Despite the talent of Eli Wallach as Kilroy, Jo Van Fleet as Marguerite Gautier, Frank Silvera as Gutman, Barbara Baxley as Esmeralda, and Lemuel Ayers's exotic set, surrounded by a high and crumbling stone wall, studded with phrenology charts, window dummies, and illuminated pawnshop signs,[24] the play had a short life. As Eli Wallach wrote, "people began coming two or three times, but with the large cast, the staggering cost of production – we didn't even have enough money for posters or pictures out front" (Wallach, letter 2).

Along with financial problems, the play suffered from an overwhelming misunderstanding. Eric Bentley had trouble with the play's lack of realism, which he considered Williams's strength.[25] Similarly, Walter Kerr argued that

Mr. Williams is attempting to apply the methods of lyric poetry – the images made of illogical and unexpected combinations, the processes of free association, the emphasis on mythology – to the spoken stage. But the poetic imagination must have something realistic to exercise its imagination on, some actuality to serve as a point of departure. *Camino Real* is all departure and no point. (Kerr, *Herald Tribune*, 1953)

Richard Watts said it was "full of sound and fury, signifying very little . . . *Camino Real* is an enigmatic bore."[26] Robert Coleman recognized *Camino* as Williams's most ambitious play, but argued that it was "burlesque for PhD's . . ."[27] Other critics called it "decadent, avant-garde pretentiousness," complained that it was not "about anything," and that Kazan's direction "obscured the play," because it was "too fast, too dazzling, too brilliant."[28] On the other hand, John Gassner praised Williams's "fascination with the underworld of the id."[29] But, in discussing the historical characters who escaped from the infernal world of Williams's imagination, Gassner remarked that "these escapes are not worked out dramatically; . . . his ideas suffer as mere ideas or symbols and literary allusions. The play is at once too badly abstruse and too strenuously theatrical" (Gassner, *Literary Criticism*, 499). Still, Gassner acknowledged that only exceptional dramatic talent could have written *Camino Real* because it says so much about the state of the world. John Chapman called it "a welter of extravagance, vulgarity, bombast, excruciatingly fancy writing, pretentious philosophy, half-baked symbolism." He further complained that it lacked "the singleness of purpose and of viewpoint which are absolutely necessary to any work of art." Yet, he admired Lemuel Ayers's setting of a street – the Camino Real, "which seems to be somewhere between heaven, hell and earth, is beautifully imagined and visually brilliant" – and he complimented Kazan's combination of "spoken drama, pantomime and ballet."[30] Joseph Shipley said that "Williams sees futility even beyond the grave," and that "Williams has given us symbols without story."[31] Moreover, the London theatre critic wrote deridingly about Williams's obscure language.[32] *The New Yorker* claimed that the play had Kafka's nightmarish quality.[33] A more interesting response came from the *Herald Tribune*, which called *Camino Real* the theatrical counterpart of the art of Breughel, Bosch, Callot, Goya, and others in its dark view of the world, but argued that art does not necessarily make a good play.[34] Similarly, John Mason Brown compared Williams's approach to theatre to Salvador Dali's approach to canvas (Brown, *Saturday Review*, 1953). A Philadelphia reviewer called *Camino Real* "a sort of male Alice in a sorry wonderland."[35] Russell Rhodes, however, remarked that "it is quite unorthodox, a bit muddled, a bit corny and a bit vaudevillian as some characters rush about the audience, but it's a stimulating experience in theater that you cannot afford to forgo."[36] Only William Hawkins and Brooks Atkinson appreciated the play entirely. Hawkins called it a "brilliant and riotous adventure," which he said, "succeeds in making tangible for all your senses the delirious pains and ecstasy of a wild dream" (Londré, *Tennessee Williams*, 118). Atkinson wrote, "as theatre, *Camino Real* is as eloquent and rhythmic as a piece of music."[37] In addition, Eli Wallach was convinced that the production "was fast and strong – filled with a throbbing urgency as only Kazan could do" (Wallach, letter 2). While Peter Hall in London also saw talent in *Camino Real* and chose it to launch the International Playwrights' Theater in 1957, starring a stellar cast of Diana Wynyard, Harry Andrews, Denholm Elliott, Freda Jackson, and Elizabeth Seal, in America Walter Kerr summed up the prevailing response to *Camino Real*: it was "the worst play yet written by the best playwright of his generation. Mr. Williams is hopelessly mired in his new love – symbolism" (Kerr, *New York Herald Tribune*, 1953).

José Quintero's 1960 New York production

For many critics, José Quintero made *Camino* a success at the Saint Marks Playhouse in 1960, with a production starring David Doyle as Gutman, Collin Wilcox as Esmeralda, Clifton Kimbrough as Kilroy, Addison Powell as Casanova, Lester Rawlins as Byron, Charlotte Jones as the Gypsy, and Nan Martin as Marguerite Gautier. In contrast to the play's reception in the fifties, a New York critic commented as follows:

> This wild, dark-hued poetic fantasy is one of the most exciting, fascinating scripts Williams has ever done. And this off-Broadway production is infinitely superior to the 1953 premiere. Director José Quintero, himself an ardent Panamanian poet, is more simpatico to the special brand of Williams anguish than the jazzier, less subtle Elia Kazan.[38]

Although Quintero went even further than Kazan "to visualize the black phantasmagoria of *Camino*, which meant muting the note of hope," the liberalism of the sixties made the play more acceptable (Tischler, *Rebellious Puritan*, 377). Brooks Atkinson praised Williams's mastery of language, his exploration of the meaning of our lives, "his own private inferno," and Williams's restraint from cynicism.[39] In 1960, some critics were calling *Camino Real* an "exercise in surrealism . . . closer to Saroyan than to Williams."[40] Whitney Bolton applauded Quintero as a shrewd and surgical director: "Quintero has brought some light into the murkier areas [of the play] and gives the cast more cohesion than it first had." Still, however, he had trouble understanding the play, as critics did in the fifties.[41] Judith Crist thought that Quintero's production was better than the play: he and his company lent "sporadic fascination to a hodgepodge of symbolism, giving momentary meaning to a jargon that aspires to poesy but stumbles on prose, and making the Turkish-bath atmosphere of the St. Marks Playhouse intermittently bearable."[42] Other critics, along with actor Eli Wallach, thought Quintero's production was tedious or blurred[43] (and Bogdnovich). In particular, George Oppenheimer found Quintero's staging "inept and the cast, for the most part, inadequate." He attributed the weak production to the confining space of the Saint Marks Playhouse, insisting that Williams's plays achieved "elegance and brutality" when "his stage world is enshrouded in an unreal mist that softens the outlines of its violence." Quintero, unlike Kazan, he argued, made the fantasy of Camino "too real."[44] Conversely, John McClain thought that the compressed production at the Circle in the Square made the play less pretentious and that the cast was exceptionally gifted.[45]

Milton Katselas's 1968 Los Angeles production

In 1968 at the Mark Taper Forum in Los Angeles, Milton Katselas directed Earl Hillman as Kilroy, Victor Buono as Gutman, Sylvia Syms as the Gypsy, Lee Meredith as the Gypsy's daughter, and Nancy Wickwire as Camille. Peter Wexler's "forbidding abstract set projected the hot, dry desert beyond the city."[46] Some critics called the play "a delightful excursion,"[47] while others continued to ask, "Where is the play going?"[48] Most agreed, however, that the production was superb, that it was brilliantly and imaginatively staged and directed.[49] Critics attributed the creative production to the rich resources of The Center Theatre Group at the Mark Taper Forum.

Milton Katselas's 1970 Lincoln Center production

In 1970, just as Williams was emerging from a long and critical hospital stay, Camino Real was being revived at the Vivian Beaumont Theater.[50] Milton Katselas again directed the production, this time starring Al Pacino as Kilroy, Philip Bosco as Baron de Charlus, Jessica Tandy as Marguerite Gautier, Susan Tyrrell as Esmeralda, Patrick McVey as Don Quixote, and Jean-Pierre Aumont as Jacques Casanova. Some critics continued to denounce the play, calling it "sprawling, self-indulgent, often obtuse."[51] John Simon claimed that "dredging up Camino Real is an indecent act."[52] Walter Kerr wrote that Camino Real "doesn't happen. The poem doesn't rise. Because no true people are there, no true event takes place,"[53] and the Wall Street Journal critic argued that Camino "is the most painfully autobiographical of Mr. Williams's plays," that it "drifts into hazy banalities of self-pity and sentimentality."[54]

On the whole, however, audiences were more receptive about the Lincoln Center's Vivian Beaumont Theater production in 1970 than they were to the original production. In 1970, most agreed that *Camino Real* was Williams's most ambitious play. Although several critics thought that Al Pacino was not accurately cast as Kilroy because he did not convey Kilroy's genuineness and vulnerability, they applauded Jessica Tandy's performance as "a splendidly refined, sad, and desperate" Marguerite Gautier.[55] Moreover, some critics admired Katselas's direction of the play: in the scene where Marguerite frenziedly attempts to persuade the guards to let her board the Fugitivo, for which she has no ticket, Katselas amplified her sobbing with a loudspeaker, making her pleading larger-than-life, which suited well Lincoln Center's thrust stage.[56] Katselas gave the performance a carnivalesque quality, with action over and around the stage, up and down the aisles, and had one character make his entrance by being lowered from the ceiling over the audience.[57] Others thought that Katselas "mounted a misty, mannered, and ponderous production with no apparent point of view."[58] In addition, Peter Wexler's multi-level scenery was "boldly abstract," but some critics felt that the play "needed a more specific set" (Hewes, *Saturday Review*, 1970). Nevertheless, critics became convinced that the play was written for "an open stage. Free of a picture-frame stage's fetters, the play is opened up to provide the illusion of great space." The spare setting and "a kind of Man of la Mancha stairway to the sky, are all that the play needs."[59] Marjorie Gunner remarked, "*Camino Real* is staged dreamily by Milton Katselas like a fiendish night-mare."[60] Carolyn Dutton called *Camino Real* "one of Williams's most engrossing, introspective plays, and the Repertory Theater of Lincoln Center nurtures every intended nuance." And in the seventies, some critics began labeling *Camino* a "baroque fantasy."[61] Clive Barnes noted the change in America's aesthetic sensibility. Calling it "a play of genuinely poetic vision . . .' he remarked that "our standards of obscurity, like our standards of obscenity, have escalated . . . since those dark days of theatrical innocence . . ." (Arnott, *Williams on File*, 32). "At the Vivian Beaumont, it seems almost a model of clarity." But he was not entirely accurate when he said that the play was more about Williams's life than it was about his view of the world (Arnott 42). Indeed, Williams had managed to achieve both. Although Richard Watts agreed that the play was at its best at Lincoln Center, he continued to be troubled by it, arguing that "there is something pretentious, disordered and almost self-consciously obscure about its poetic imagery that stands in its way." Brendan Gill of *The New Yorker* called the Lincoln Center production "attractive and ingenious" and "one of the most entertaining shows in town . . ." The director and designer "have struck . . . the note of extravagance, mingling death and fiesta; gestures and accents are exaggerated, colors bedazzle, and pranks of stage craft abound."[62] By and large, the reception of the play changed dramatically from its first off-Broadway production, done under extreme pressure, with no money, and put together in twenty-one days prior to opening in New Haven.[63] Seventeen years after its original production, Williams's "ode to losers" drew much praise from Broadway critics.

Nikos Psacharopoulos's 1979 production at Williamstown

In 1979, the Williamstown Theater Festival launched their twenty-fifth season with a highly successful production of *Camino Real*, directed by Nikos Psacharopoulos, starring William Burns as Kilroy, Richard Woods as Gutman, Richard Kneeland as Casanova, and Caris Corfman as Esmeralda. (The production is on video at Lincoln Center's Library for the Performing Arts.) Critics praised the director's "courage, imagination and delight"[64] and Williams, who was in the audience, regarded it as the finest production he had seen. The Williamstown set was especially unique: John Conklin constructed a crumbling tropical town divided between plaza and hotel terrace. The stage was large, and Conklin created a sense of great depth by making the plaza run uphill and putting an arch at the back that suggested great distances beyond.[65] Psacharopoulos chose to have the airplane, called the Fugitivo, land in the lobby. Similarly, a 1992 Lafayette College production pulled the audience into the lobby of the performing arts center, where students enacted an airplane as they ran up the stairs, using their arms as wings. Psacharopoulos described his set as "Fellini-esque," and critics agreed that the production had the energy and oddities of a Fellini movie, along with the Italian director's love of strange costume and gaudy color.[66] Moreover, in the seventies, some critics were likening the sensibility of *Camino Real* to Bob Dylan's "Desolation Row," claiming that even though Dylan's song was written long after *Camino*'s opening in 1953, its form, meanings, and poetry seemed rooted in the play. And it was not until the seventies that critics began to see the play as absurdist.

Camino was not only aesthetically difficult for Americans at first, but its moments of darkness contradicted an intrinsic American optimism. Marguerite Gautier (Camille) crystallizes the apocalyptic vision of the play. While Casanova insists that love is our only defense against betrayal, Marguerite claims that distrust is the better protection. After having missed the Fugitivo, the unscheduled plane out of the camino, she explains her relationship with Casanova with cynicism:

We're lonely. We're frightened. We hear the Street Cleaners' piping not far away. So now and then, although we've wounded each other time and again – we stretch out hands to each other in the dark that we can't escape from – we huddle together for some dim-communal comfort – and that's what passes for love on this terminal stretch of the road that used to be royal. What is it, this feeling between us? When you feel my exhausted weight against your shoulder – when I clasp your anxious old hawk's head to my breast, what is it we feel in whatever is left of our hearts? Something, yes, something – delicate, unreal, bloodless! The sort of violets that could grow on the moon, or in the crevices of those far away mountains, fertilized by the droppings of carrion birds. Those birds are familiar to us. . . . But tenderness, the violets in the mountains – can't break the rocks!   (96–97)

For Marguerite, love has become a habit born out of necessity. In fact, "brother" is the forbidden word on the camino because, according to Gutman, a brother is "someone to get ahead of, to cheat, to lie to, to undersell in the market" (22). Marguerite maintains that the feeling between her and Casanova is as precarious as violets growing between rocks. Similarly, when Kilroy is trying to woo Esmeralda, she is resistant because she believes that no one is "sincere" (131). On the other hand, Casanova contradicts this idea when he tells Marguerite, "I'm terrified of the unknown country inside or outside this wall or any place on earth without you with me!" (71).

While relationships seem tenuous on the camino, they are the only source of solace and protection against the collapse of integrity when, as Marguerite puts it, there is "nothing but the gradual wasting away of everything decent in us!" (72). In Williams's revised version for New Directions, he added a prologue in which Quixote laments that " . . . the singing words Truth! Valor! Devoir! [have been] turned into the meaningless mumble of some old monk hunched over cold mutton at supper!" (3–4). Esmeralda's mother, the Gypsy, describes the dissolution of tradition in another way:

There's nobody left to uphold the old traditions! You raise a girl. She watches t.v. Plays be-bop. Reads *Screen Secrets*. Comes the Big Fiesta. The moonrise makes her a virgin – which is the neatest trick of the week! And what does she do? Chooses a Fugitive Patsy for the Chosen Hero!   (108)

On the contrary, Kilroy has the compassion that the camino robs. Because he has died believing in his inherent worth, he has earned his salvation and resurrection by the kind, blind singer, La Madrecita, despite the coldly analytical doctors who dissect him. Accordingly, early in the play, Williams calls for a banner with a "phoenix painted on silk" to be "softly lighted now and then" during the play, "since resurrections are so much a part of its meaning" (1). Kilroy's redemption is complete when the old knight, Don Quixote, awakens and chooses him as his companion to voyage into Terra Incognita. Thus, Williams again reaches back to the medieval morality play, which sought to discover a mode of human salvation on the journey from life to death to resurrection (15). Kilroy's soul, like Everyman's, is saved, not because of his unshakeable belief in God, but because his honor prevents him from being corrupted by the temptations on the camino. As he says, he fought many hard fights to win his golden gloves, "and the fixers never got to me" (25). Gutman chooses him as the "patsy," the anti-hero, because he possesses the virtues of courage, honor, and sympathy. He embodies Odyssian courage as he tries to make his way past the Scylla, Charybdis, and Cerberus of Gutman, the Gypsy, and the Street Cleaners. Former hero, lover, and conqueror, he is also humanity with a heart of gold. The Street Cleaners come to take his life, but he heroically challenges them: "Washed up! – Finished! [piping] . . . that ain't a word that a man can't look at . . . Come on, you sons of bitches! Kilroy is here! He's ready!" (147). While Casanova, Marguerite and Byron lack heroic stature because of their moral weaknesses, Williams finds in the anti-heroic Kilroy a possible savior of humanity (Jackson, *Broken World*, 123).

Kilroy's resurrection and escape from the camino with Don Quixote represent the return of honor for which Esmeralda prays in the play's most poetic moment:

> God bless all con men and hustlers and pitch-men who hawk their hearts on the street, all two-time losers who are likely to lose once more, the courtesan who made the mistake of love, the greatest of lovers crowned with the longest horns, the poet who wandered far from his heart's green country and possibly will and possibly won't be able to find his way back, look down with a smile tonight on the last cavaliers, the ones with the rusty armor and soiled white plumes, and visit with understanding and something that's almost tender those fading legends that come and go in this plaza like songs not clearly remembered, oh, sometime and somewhere, let there be something to mean the word honor again! (156)

Esmeralda recollects all of the marginalized characters on the camino, those who have lost their hearts, their loves, their fidelity, their talents, and their nobility by the time they arrived on the real road. In her ode to losers, Esmeralda asks for a New Testament kind of grace, pleading for a romantic attitude toward life, which Don Quixote, Lord Byron, and Kilroy finally reattain. Elia Kazan was the one who recommended that Williams list these romantic outcasts in Esmeralda's prayer because he saw the play as a defense of this fast-disappearing breed (Murphy, *Williams and Kazan*, 72). In fact, Kazan's directing concept for *Camino* derived from his view of

Gutman, who preys on society's last surviving romantics. For Kazan and Williams, the play expressed their feelings about the fate of the romantic in the repressive world of America in the fifties (Murphy, *Williams and Kazan*, 72–74). For Williams, *Camino* expressed much the same idea as his 1941 play, *Stairs to the Roof*. It was "a prayer for the wild of heart kept in cages," "a picture of the state of the romantic nonconformist in modern society," stressing "'honor' and [our] own sense of inner dignity which the Bohemian must reachieve after each period of degradation he is bound to run into." Williams insists that "the romantic should have the spirit of anarchy and not let the world drag him down to its level."[67] Don Quixote, who appears at the end of the play, exemplifies the "obstinate knight, gallant in meeting ultimate degradation and unashamed at being the victim of his own romantic follies" (Hewes, *Saturday Review*, 1970). In this context, Kazan had considered *Camino*'s thematic statement neither social nor universal, but personal and subjective; he and Williams were speaking for themselves. If the play's hero were the arch-romantic, the misfit, the antagonist was Gutman, the archetypal American businessman who was out to exterminate the romantics and the rebels. And the complement for Gutman was the Gypsy. While Gutman preyed on people facing death, the Gypsy exploited love and the future. But touched with the romantic spirit of anarchy, she too had her attractive side. In illustrating the destruction of romantics, then, *Camino* presents the collapse of moral values by holding up to scrutiny the traditional romantic values of love, power, success, and death. As Esther Merle Jackson notes, each of these poetic ideals progressively disintegrates on the camino (Jackson, *Broken World*, 117).

Byron best exemplifies the frustrated romantic as he desperately seeks to retrieve his poetic integrity that has been corrupted by worldliness:

> That was my vocation once upon a time, before it was obscured by vulgar plaudits! – Little by little it was lost among gondolas and palazzos! – masked balls, glittering salons, huge shadowy courts and torch-lit entrances – . . . all these provided agreeable distractions from the rather frightening solitude of a poet . . . There is a passion for declivity in this word! And lately I've found myself listening to hired musicians behind a row of artificial palm trees – instead of the single – pure-stringed instrument of my heart . . . (77–8)

Sailing to Athens, Byron hopes that he will recover his ability to write, that "the old pure music will come to [him] again" (78). In response to Casanova, who says that the human heart is meant to be twisted, torn, crushed, or kicked, Byron retorts that "the poet's vocation is to influence the heart in a gentler fashion . . . purify it, lift it above its ordinary level; for him, the heart translates noise into music, chaos into order" (76). In effect, he seeks to do what Williams does in the play, and he has the writer's transcendent vision: "Make voyages! Attempt them! There's nothing else" (78). When he leaves, he takes the caged birds of the camino with him. As in *Streetcar*, Williams concerns himself with the brutes who crush the aesthetes and the dreamers. Yet, the poet is dangerous because of the power of his words to transform people's lives. As Gutman tells the Generalissimo, "Revolution only needs good dreamers who remember their dreams . . . " (20). The play is not only the dream of Don Quixote, which results in rebellion against Gutman and the whole Camino Real, but in a larger sense, Williams is talking about the subversive power of art, the power of the imagination to overcome tyranny. Benjamin Nelson, however, questions the purpose of the romantic revolt of the play, asserting that "the affirmation is our ability to rebound from ultimate degradation, but the possibility of going forward after this initial effort is lacking." "Williams," he argues, "is not really confronting his situation with true moral energy."[68] On the contrary, the moral energy derives from the romantics' courage to leave the camino and venture into the unknown territory beyond it, into Keats's negative capability.

The romantic spirit is especially important on the Camino Real as a means to resist the spiritual dislocation in a post-atomic, post-industrial, godless world that the camino represents. The Gypsy makes this clear in the jargon of advertising. Here, Williams demonstrates his talent with popular diction and humor in a play also full of poetic language and an apocalyptic sensibility:

> Are you perplexed by something? Are you tired out and confused? Do you have a fever? Do you feel yourself to be spiritually unprepared for the age of exploding atoms? Do you distrust the newspapers? Are you suspicious of governments? Have you arrived at a point on the Camino Real where the walls converge not in the distance but right in front of your nose? Does further progress appear impossible to you? Are you afraid of anything at all? Afraid of your heart beat? Or the eyes of strangers! Afraid of breathing? Afraid of not breathing? Do you wish that things could be straight and simple again as they were in your childhood? Would you like to go back to Kindy Garten? (28)

Williams casts the Gypsy's announcement in the language of capitalism; she is selling her services as counselor to the alienated and confused on the camino. Because of Gutman's tyranny and lack of compassion, people suffer from intolerable fear and anxiety, which Williams describes in terms of a profoundly ontological and existential malaise. Alienation, fear of nuclear war, and of politics make the camino like an inescapable inferno, and there is no God to alleviate that emptiness. Later in Block Twelve,

Esmeralda asks Kilroy, "Do you think they've got the Old Man [God] in the bag yet?" (123). In fact, the camino has replaced God with the Gypsy, like T. S. Eliot's Madame Sosostris in *The Waste Land*, the famous clairvoyante with "a wicked pack of cards." When Gutman confronts his own existential despair, asking, "Can this be all? Is there nothing more? Is this what the glittering wheels of the heavens turn for?" (55), he wants to seek the advice of the Gypsy. But she is incapable of helping anyone.

Camino seems to say that some of the lostness on the camino has its roots in American politics of the fifties, in America's paranoia about and ignorance of things un-American. Completely misunderstanding Marxism, Esmeralda humorously asks Kilroy how he feels about the class struggle: "Do you take sides in that? . . . Neither do we because of the dialectics. Languages with accents, I suppose. But Mama don't care as long as they don't bring the Pope over here and put him in the White House" (122–23). When Kilroy asks who would put the Pope in the White House, Esmeralda responds, "Oh, the Bolsheviskies, those nasty old things with whiskers! . . ." (123). Confusing Marx's theory of dialectics with language dialects, religious figures with political ones, and ignorant about who the Bolsheviks really are, Esmeralda conveys America's confused politics.

In *Camino Real*, then, Williams creates an expressionistic, political, and mythic allegory about the need for romantics. For those trying to impose realism on the play's dreamlike fabric, it will in fact seem "a funny paper read backwards," as the Gypsy describes it. Williams's versatility as a writer enables him to write in the tradition of the medieval morality play, of farce, satire, comedy, and tragedy. And while he has one foot in the European literary tradition, alluding to Proust, Cervantes, Dumas, and Dante, he has the other in America. Williams's pageant is not only steeped in T. S. Eliot's modernism, but in American street language and advertisements. His characters' cultural touchstones are Jean Harlow, *Screen Secrets*, Ovaltine, Western Union, and Greyhound Bus terminals. Despite its American fabric, however, *Camino Real* has mythic and allegorical dimensions. Gutman could be Hitler as much as he could be Joseph McCarthy. The play dramatizes a time of spiritual crisis when the romantic values of nobility, truth, valor, and honor have been lost. Quixote advises Kilroy about how to survive the camino's "rugged deal": "Don't! Pity! Your! Self!" He further tells Kilroy to embrace life's betrayals:

> The wounds of the vanity, the many offenses our egos have to endure, being housed in bodies that age and hearts that grow tired, are better accepted with a tolerant smile . . . Otherwise what you become is a bag full of curdled cream attractive to nobody, least of all to yourself! (159)

Camino is ultimately an affirmative play because the violets break the rocks, and imagination and love triumph over cruelty and tyranny. Indeed, Williams's most crucial metaphor is Kilroy's retrieval of his heart from the state because this is a play about reclaiming one's heart. Furthermore, it affirms Quixote's conviction that "the time for retreat never comes!" (155), and that when the straight way is lost, as Casanova tells Kilroy, we will find a way out, as long as we have "patience and courage" (57).

NOTES

Many of the reviews at Lincoln Center's Library for the Performing Arts did not have page numbers. I have used the abbreviation, n.p., for no page number.

1 C. W. E. Bigsby, *Modern American Drama 1945–1990* (Cambridge: Cambridge University Press, 1992) 54.
2 Tennessee Williams, "Reflections on a Revival of a Controversial Fantasy," *New York Times*, Sunday, May 15, 1960, section 2, 1.
3 Tennessee Williams, *Camino Real* (New York: New Directions, 1953), 7.
4 John Mason Brown, "Broadway Postscript," *Saturday Review*, March 23, 1953, 27.
5 Tennessee Williams, "Reflections on a Revival of a Controversial Fantasy," *New York Times*, May 15, 1960, section 2., n.p.
6 Eli Wallach's letter to Dan Isaac on file at Lincoln Center, 1966.
7 Esther Merle Jackson, *The Broken World of Tennessee Williams*, (Madison: University of Wisconsin Press, 1965), 121–28.
8 Signi L. Falk, *Tennessee Williams* (New Haven: Twayne Publishers, 1961), 120.
9 Tennessee Williams, "Foreword to *Camino Real*," in *Where I Live – Selected Essays*, ed. Christine R. Day and Bob Woods (New York: New Directions, 1978), 63.
10 Donald Spoto, *The Kindness of Strangers: The Life of Tennessee Williams* (Boston: Little, Brown and Company, 1985), 187.
11 *Variety*, "Camino Real," January 14, 1970, page number missing.
12 Henry Hewes, "Tennessee Williams – Last of Our Solid Gold Bohemians," in Albert J. Devlin (ed.) *Conversations with Tennessee Williams* (Jackson: University Press of Mississippi, 1986), 31.
13 Alice Griffin, *Understanding Tennessee Williams* (University of South Carolina Press, 1995), 128.
14 M. H. Abrams, *A Glossary of Literary Terms* (Fort Worth: Holt, Rinehart and Winston, Inc., 1988), 113.
15 James Coakley, "Time and Tide on the Camino Real," in Harold Bloom (ed.), *Modern Critical Views, Tennessee Williams* (New York: Chelsea House Publishers, 1987), 95.

16 Nancy M. Tischler, *Tennessee Williams: Rebellious Puritan*, (New York: The Citadel Press, 1961), 191.

17 Brenda Murphy, *Tennessee Williams and Elia Kazan* (Cambridge University Press, 1992), 68.

18 Tennessee Williams, *Memoirs*, (New York: Doubleday & Company, 1975), 16.

19 John Mason Brown, *Saturday Review*, March 2, 1953, n.p.

20 George Oppenheimer: "'Camino Real' Loses Luster With Age," *Newsday*, Friday, January 9, 1970, n.p.

21 Arthur Gelb, "Williams and Kazan and the Big Walk-Out," in Devlin, *Conversations*, 67.

22 Charles Ruas, "Tennessee Williams," in Devlin, *Conversations*, 285.

23 *Variety*, March 16, 1953, n.p.

24 Walter Kerr, *New York Herald Tribune*, in *New York Times Theater Reviews*, March 20, 1953, 331.

25 Catherine M. Arnott, *Tennessee Williams on File* (London: Methuen, 1985), 31.

26 Richard Watts, Jr., *New York Post* in *New York Times Theater Reviews*, March 20, 1953, 330.

27 Robert Coleman, *Daily Mirror*, in *New York Times Theater Reviews*, "Camino Real Will Please Some, Anger Others," March 20, 1953, 330.

28 Peter Bogdnovich, "Did Quintero Botch It?" *The Village Voice*, August 21, 1960, 7.

29 John Gassner, *Contemporary Literary Criticism*, 498.

30 John Chapman, *Theater Arts*, 1953, n.p.

31 Joseph T. Shipley, "Royal Road to Despair," April 20, 1953, 27.

32 W. Macqueen Pope, "Williams's *Camino* Presented," *London Theatre*, 1957, n.p.

33 Ere Whon, *The New Yorker*, March 28, 1953, 69.

34 Emily Genauer, *Herald Tribune*, April 5, 1953, n.p.

35 Jerry Gaghan, "*Camino Real* in Forrest Bow, New Tennessee Williams's Play," *Philadelphia Daily News*, March 5, 1953, 11F.

36 Russell Rhodes, "Make Mine Manhattan," on file at Lincoln Center, 66.

37 Brooks Atkinson, *New York Times Theater Reviews*, "Tennessee Williams Writes a Cosmic Fantasy Entitled *Camino Real*," March 20, 1953, 333.

38 *Cue*, May 28, 1960, n.p.

39 Brooks Atkinson, "Camino Real," *The New York Times*, May 29, 1960, section 2, n.p.

40 Thomas R. Dash, "Off-B'way *Camino Real* Engrosses Only Fitfully," *Women's Wear Daily*, May 17, 1960, n.p.

41 Whitney Bolton, "*Camino Real* Still Has Spotty Flavor," *Morning Telegraph*, May 16, 1960, n.p.

42 Judith Crist, "Revival of *Camino Real* at Saint Marks Playhouse," *Herald Tribune*, May 17, 1960, n.p.

43 Frances Herridge, "Controversial *Camino* is Back," *New York Post*, May 17, 1960, n.p.

44 George Oppenheimer, "Bedlam Revisited," *Newsday*, May 25, 1960, n.p.
45 John McClain, "'Camino Real' Still Has Power," *New York Journal-American*, May 17, 1960, in *New York Times Theater Reviews*, 332.
46 Cecil Smith, "'Camino Real' Opens at Forum," *Los Angeles Times*, May, 1968, n.p.
47 *Variety*, "Camino Real," August 5, 1968, n.p.
48 Lawrence DeVine, *Herald Examiner*, 1968, n.p.
49 Hal Bates, "*Camino Real* Given New Life", *The News*, August 9, 1968, n.p.
50 Edward Sothern Hipp, "A Playwright's Second Chance," *Newark Sunday News*, 1970, E4, Sec. 6.
51 Richard Watts, Jr., "Two on the Aisle," January 9, 1970, 61.
52 John Simon, *New York Magazine*, January 26, 1970, vol. 3, 64.
53 Walter Kerr, *New York Times*, January 18, 1970, D1, 1, 3.
54 John J. O'Connor, "The Theater," *Wall Street Journal*, January 14, 1970, 10.
55 Carol Dutton, *Park East*, January 15, 1970, 8.
56 Henry Hewes, "Errant Knightmare," *Saturday Review*, January 24, 1970, 24.
57 *Variety*, "Camino Real", January 14, 1970, 84.
58 John Crother, "'Camino Real' Sags in Leaden Revival," *Morning Telegraph*, New York, January 10, 1970, n.p.
59 Edward Sothern Hipp, "New *Camino Real*," *The Evening News*, Newark, January 9, 1970, n.p.
60 Edward Sothern Hipp, "New *Camino Real*," *The Evening News*, Newark, Friday, January 9, 1970, n.p.
61 Marjorie Gunner, *Bronx Home News*, January 23, 1970, 7.
62 Helen Kruger, "Camino Real," *Chelsea Clinton News*, February 5, 1970, 6.
63 Brendan Gill, *The New Yorker*, January 10, 1970, vol. 45, 50.
64 Mike Steen, *A Look at Tennessee Williams*, (New York: Hawthorn Books, Inc., 1969), 296.
65 Richard Eder, *The New York Times*, July 4, 1979, n.p.
66 Rob Woolmington, *Bennington Banner*, June 29, 1979, n.p.
67 David Frost, *Conversations with Tennessee Williams*, 142.
68 Benjamin Nelson, *Tennessee Williams: The Man and His Work* (New York: Ivan Obolensky, 1961), 177–78.

BIBLIOGRAPHY

Arnott, Catherine, M. *Tennessee Williams on File*. London: Methuen, 1985.
Bigsby, C. W. E. "Valedictory," in Harold Bloom (ed.), *Tennessee Williams*, Modern Critical Views, New York: Chelsea, 1987.
American Drama 1945–1990, Cambridge University Press, 1992.
Bloom, Harold (ed.). *Modern Critical Views: Tennessee Williams*. New York: Chelsea House, 1987.
Boxill, Roger. *Macmillan Modern Dramatists: Tennessee Williams*. London: Macmillan, 1987.

Devlin, Albert, J. (ed.). *Conversations with Tennessee Williams*. Jackson: University Press of Mississippi, 1986.

Falk, Signi L. *Tennessee Williams*. Boston: Twayne, 1961.

Griffin, Alice. *Understanding Tennessee Williams*. Columbia: University of South Carolina Press, 1995.

Hayman, Ronald. *Tennessee Williams: Everyone Else Is an Audience*. New Haven: Yale University Press, 1993.

Hirsch, Foster. *A Portrait of the Artist. The Plays of Tennessee Williams*. Port Washington: Kennikat, 1979.

Jackson, Esther Merle. *The Broken World of Tennessee Williams*. Madison: University Press of Wisconsin, 1965.

Londré, Felicia Hardison. *Tennessee Williams*. New York: Frederick Ungar, 1979.

Murphy, Brenda. *Tennessee Williams and Elia Kazan*. Cambridge University Press, 1992.

Nelson, Benjamin. *Tennessee Williams: The Man and His Work*. New York: Ivan Obolensky, 1961.

Spoto, Donald. *The Kindness of Strangers: The Life of Tennessee Williams*. Boston: Little, Brown, 1985.

Stanton, Stephen, S. *Tennessee Williams. A Collection of Critical Essays*. Englewood Cliffs: Prentice-Hall, 1977.

Steen, Mike. *A Look at Tennessee Williams*. New York: Hawthorn Books, 1969.

Tischler, Nancy, M. *Tennessee Williams: Rebellious Puritan*. New York: Citadel Press, 1961.

Williams, Dakin and Mead, Shepherd. *Tennessee Williams: An Intimate Biography*. New York: Arbor House, 1983.

Williams, Tennessee. *Memoirs*. Garden City, New York: Doubleday, 1975.

Where I Live: Selected Essays, eds. Day, Christine R., Woods, Bob. New York: New Directions, 1978.

"Playwright Seeks Creation of a World," *New York Times*, 1953.

5

ALBERT J. DEVLIN

Writing in "A place of stone": *Cat on a Hot Tin Roof*

Cat on a Hot Tin Roof was a great critical and financial success for Tennessee Williams. The play opened on Broadway on March 24, 1955, ran for nearly 700 performances, and won all the major awards, including Williams's second Pulitzer Prize for Drama. The MGM film adaptation in 1958, although deplored by Williams, was lucrative and made the playwright financially secure for the rest of his life. Major New York revivals in 1974 and 1990 confirmed the appeal of *Cat* to successive generations of theatregoers. To give the dimension of a Broadway career to these bare facts of success is my intention in the pages that follow. The inner story of *Cat on a Hot Tin Roof* begins with Williams's need to reverse a pattern of failure that became alarming with the early closing of *Camino Real* in 1953. But writing in this "place of stone," to quote the original epigraph of *Cat*, occasioned the practice of a deceptive realism that satisfied both the economic law of Broadway and the artistic prompting of Tennessee Williams's endangered career. In this work of mediation, the realistic conventions of the Southern literary plantation were used to obscure Williams's skepticism for the theatre of "de-monstration." Examining the origins of this aesthetic, and its testing as well, leads to a consideration of the fictive sources for *Cat on a Hot Tin Roof*, and in turn leads to a discussion of the famous third-act controversy between Williams and the director, Elia Kazan. At issue was preserving "'the poem of the play' – the poetry of the man who is not competing," as Williams described it. How this core of silence was compromised and guarded by Williams is the inner story of *Cat on a Hot Tin Roof*. It led him to "Be secret and exult," as Yeats's line from the original epigraph advised.

On March 25, 1955, Tennessee Williams wrote a customary note of thanks to Brooks Atkinson for his "lovely notice" of *Cat on a Hot Tin Roof*. There was, however, an urgency in this letter. He "would have just died," Williams said, if Atkinson "hadn't liked and praised 'Cat,'" and then he went on to describe an exceptional case of first-night jitters:

Figure 5 Ben Gazzara as Brick stumbles into the arms of Burl Ives as Big Daddy, in *Cat on a Hot Tin Roof*, directed by Elia Kazan

I can't explain to you or myself or anybody why the reception of this play meant so damnably much to me, why I was so disgustingly craven about it, why the wait for the morning notices to come out was the most unendurable interval of my life . . . It must stem from some really fearful lack of security, some abysmal self-doubt. Also it takes such ugly, odious tangential forms, such as my invidious resentment of Inge's great success[.] Despite my friendly attitude toward Bill and his toward me, I was consumed with envy of his play's [*Bus Stop*] success . . . Hideous competitiveness which I never had in me before! But after 'Camino' I was plunged into such depths, I thought I would never rise from. I love writing too much, and to love anything too much is to feel a terror of loss: it's a kind of madness.

Williams's supply of envy predates the mid-1950s by at least two decades, but otherwise the letter to the *Times* critic is a reliable starting point for a much needed contextualizing discussion of *Cat on a Hot Tin Roof*. The issue so little addressed – or addressed so often with little information and much hostile intent – is the periodic disrepair of Williams's career and efforts to save it from breakdown or oblivion. The original epigraph for *Cat* summarized this problem as Williams approached his seventh Broadway production in ten years. "Amid a place of stone, / Be secret and exult, / Because of all things known / That is most difficult."[1] Addressed by Yeats "To a Friend whose Work has come to Nothing," the lines counsel Irish cunning and reserve in a poem whose menacing title captured the fear that had been stamped down by admiring reviews of *Cat on a Hot Tin Roof*. But as Williams said in writing to Atkinson, it was an abiding fear, and it had struck cruelly in the aftermath of *Camino Real*. In rising from these "depths," from "a place of stone," as it were, Williams distilled into *Cat* the tensions of his apparently faltering career. Did he succeed in wearing the Yeatsean mask? If so, it was one that did not come easily to Williams, for as the director Margaret Webster once said, he tended to wear his heart on his sleeve "'for daws to peck at.'"[2]

The success of *Cat on a Hot Tin Roof* begins with the failure of *Camino Real* in March 1953. Williams predicted the terms of this failure in a letter to his friend Maria Britneva in the preceding December. Fearful of reading the script to prospective backers, he worried that "not many people seem to understand what it's about, and just reading it does very little good as most of its values are so plastic, pictorial and dynamic, that just listening to it or reading it is almost useless unless the listener or reader has a trained theatrical mind" (*Angel*, December 3, 1952, p. 62). With very few exceptions, the reviewers fervently rejected Williams's foray into "Mexican poetic-fantasy."[3] To them, *Camino Real* was "an enormous jumble of five-cent philosophy" (Chapman), a "self-consciously poetic stew" (Kerr), "pompous nonsense" (Watts), "overall bushwah" (Chapman). To Williams's artistic pretension, the more bumptious reviewers played the role of the offended common man invited to a "'burlesque for PhD's'" (Coleman). As befitting a Timesman, Brooks Atkinson wrote a more dignified review, but it was a temporizing piece whose evasive tone Williams did not miss.[4] He wrote a rather uncustomary note to Atkinson shortly after opening night and asked plaintively, "Were you pulling your punches?" (March 24, 1953).

The fear that Williams expressed to Maria Britneva in December 1952 had come to pass with these decisive first-night reviews: no one knew where or when the play was set, much less what it was "about." Williams by contrast knew all too well that domestic realism was the master discourse of Broadway, and thus neither he nor the director, Elia Kazan, was surprised by the early verdict or by the closing of *Camino Real* after only sixty performances. Its "grotesque comedy," as Williams described the play's "dominant element" in a second post-mortem letter to Atkinson, had "violated the boundaries of audience acceptance." But in this letter of April 3, 1953, Williams also implied that personal motives had hastened the play's demise. He attributed his present isolation in Key West to a "feeling of being shut out and the door barred against me" by "the arbiters of that vocation to which I have completely committed myself and my life for the past fifteen years or more." Williams went on to identify himself with "'the lower depths', which are a large strata of society," and to claim that "only the upper levels" have "rejected" him. He recalled being "kicked out of a Roman country-club last summer" after behaving with "the most fastidious propriety." He was banished, he thought, for having libeled Rome itself in *The Roman Spring of Mrs. Stone* (1950), and for having as a "guest one afternoon . . . a poor young Italian painter." Rough trade, no doubt, or so Williams felt he was accused. He concluded this remarkable letter by explaining to Atkinson what his work was "really about": "It is mostly the animation that comes from the finding in people of those expressions of sensibilities and longings that were in Blanche and Alma and Serafina and Kilroy and Marguerite and Jacques, and that is what my work is really about, and when it stops being about those things it will be finished. (Me, too)."

Williams may have derived two lessons from his mid-career crisis. By 1952, he was so well versed in the economic law of Broadway that he could glibly summarize its logic for Carson McCullers, whose own play, *The Member of the Wedding*, had recently completed a long run. "A few years ago," he wrote in August 1952, "I could have anything I wanted in the theatre, now I have to go begging. Two plays that didn't make money and, brother, you're on the skids!" (August 7, 1952). *Summer and Smoke* (1948) and *The Rose Tattoo* (1951) were the guilty plays, but Williams also said implicitly, and in silent warning to McCullers, that little lasting capital in tolerance or understanding had accrued to him from the long-running productions of *The Glass Menagerie* (1945) and *A Streetcar Named Desire* (1947). Now in 1953 he had a third successive failure to record. In writing to Brooks Atkinson in April, Williams shunned the economic and made instead a reprobate argument to rationalize both the mean-spirited tone of the first-night reviews and his own vigorous protest against "hypocrisy and brutishness,"[5] as expressed in his work. He may have remembered Walter Kerr's gratuitously harsh review and its smug tally of the "not quite human fragments" in *Camino Real*, including "homosexuals" shot down by the police. By the early 1950s, a pious critique of Tennessee Williams had started to form in the theatre world, at the same time that each new production of his was eagerly awaited for its commercial value. It drew upon a perception of Williams's self-importance and ambition, cruelty to friends and colleagues, and his moral deviance. Williams, it appears from correspondence, read this critique between the lines of the *Camino* criticism – one of the first of many censures that he would receive from the "arbiters" of his vocation.

The second lesson that Williams may have derived is one that measured anew "the boundaries of audience acceptance." In *Camino Real* Williams assembled a trans-historical cast of hysterics, whose "sensibilities and longings," or so he thought, were companionable with those of the time-bound "Blanche and Alma and Serafina."[6] Josh Logan, a well-known director of Williams's acquaintance, doubted this assumption. He had seen an early version of *Camino Real* at the Actors Studio and wrote to Williams on January 12, 1949, to express his fascination, and doubt, about the project. The "Kilroy part" he found to be "very, very exciting and . . . easy to understand," but Marguerite Gautier and Casanova were "more confusing"[7] and not so easily staged. Now in February 1953, he apparently saw *Camino* in tryout or rehearsal and wrote to Williams and Kazan with advice for the play's final tuning: "'Work through Kilroy,'" he repeated.

This World War II graffito, with his eyes peering over a fence, was "so immediately recognizable" that Logan thought he might help to fix the trouble spots in the show, which still lay with Casanova and Gautier. A more visible Kilroy would lend dramatic presence to these exotic conjurors of thwarted dreams, but when he was dressed in the patsy's costume in Block Six, Williams seemed to have disarmed his most potent character. Logan's friendly critique could not have been unfamiliar to Williams or Kazan.[8] Both realized that the art-world connections of Casanova and Gautier and the other old-world misfits were vague, if not unknown, and must be grounded in a more popular mythology. Kilroy was a perfect icon.

After finishing a draft of *Camino Real* in 1946, Williams explained to his agent, Audrey Wood, that Kilroy could be seen everywhere "nowadays," and that his appeal resembled "the American comic-strip transposed into a sort of rough, colloquial poetry." Could not this "common young transient's affair with longing and disappointment" (March 12, 1946) give the missing familiar touch to his ghostly peers on the Camino Real? In Block Fifteen, La Madrecita faces the audience with the body of Kilroy spread across her knees: "This was thy son, America," she intones. Hers would have been a moving chant if its force had not been squandered by Kilroy's disappearing role as the patsy. Bereft of his "colloquial poetry," Kilroy could not bring the other defeated visionaries within "the boundaries of audience acceptance."

In the aftermath of *Camino Real*, it was some consolation to Williams that a "passionate minority" (*Angel*, April 22, 1953, p. 75) had cherished this unusual Broadway play. But such a select company was not Williams's natural or desired constituency, and it was not the audience that he intended for *Cat on a Hot Tin Roof*. In drafting *Cat*, Williams gave evidence of having absorbed the painful lessons of *Camino Real*. He renewed his covenant with Broadway, but it was a cunning conformity that he practiced, as he had in *A Streetcar Named Desire* – one that protected the integrity of the subject, at the same time that it appeared to satisfy the "irresistible scopic drive" (as Julia Kristeva would say) of a consumer-minded audience. In so positioning himself, Williams assumed the Yeatsean mask of secrecy and exultation described in the original epigraph. Soon it would be replaced with the familiar, uplifting lines of Dylan Thomas ("Do not go gentle into that good night"), but the original expressed far better Williams's difficult personal and professional situation and the deceptive realism that he used to relieve it. The stony place was softened for the moment by the critical and financial success of *Cat on a Hot Tin Roof*. Broadway, Williams may have thought at the time, was so impressed by the immutability of its economic laws and its intolerance for the unfamiliar that it could be outflanked by a wily "descendent of Indian-fighting Tennessee pioneers."[9]

It was with this hardy self-image that Williams had introduced himself to his agent, Audrey Wood, in 1939. An astute and weighty presence on Broadway, she knew that *Camino Real* was not commercial theatre when shown a partial script in 1946. But to a similar "work draft" of *Cat on a Hot Tin Roof*, she gave instant approval. In her memoir, she recalls being in Rome in 1954 when Williams, also living there, brought her "a large manuscript, typed mostly on odd pages of hotel stationery." "I was terribly excited," she recalls, "and . . . I immediately told him this was certainly his best play since *Streetcar*, and it would be a great success."[10] But this was not Wood's first knowledge of *Cat on a Hot Tin Roof*. Earlier in 1954, Williams had written from Key West to say that he was "pulling together a short-long play based on the characters in 'Three Players'" that he had "started last summer in Rome." Perhaps as titillating ballast, he warned his agent not to expect the new play "till you see it, as I might not like it when I read it aloud" (March 21, 1954). The later delivery scene in Rome bespeaks the author's approval, but Wood's enthusiasm also gave warning of controversy to come. The "work draft" had a very short tail – in that early version, Williams "had written a two-act play," or so Wood described it – and she encouraged him to finish the piece.[11] Williams's grudging assent would lead to the publication of alternate third acts in 1955 and strained relations with the director. But this well-known story, if it is to be told again, can be refreshed by adopting Wood's perspective upon a play-in-progress that invited comparison with *A Streetcar Named Desire*. By drawing such a firm line of descent between these Broadway vehicles, Wood placed the new play squarely within "the boundaries of audience acceptance."

The plantation legend of gentility and *noblesse oblige* that Williams had used in *Streetcar* gave domestic grounding to a play that otherwise probed the extremity of desire. The originating scene of *Streetcar*, he has said, was that of a woman in a "steaming hot Southern town, sitting alone in a chair with the moonlight coming through a window on her, waiting for a beau who didn't show up."[12] Williams projected in that original vision of Blanche DuBois the feminine ideal of fragility and dependence that lay embedded in a patriarchal society given to "epic fornications" (Scene 2). In *Memoirs*, he recalled being "mysteriously depressed and debilitated" by her solitary figure, but Williams confirmed Blanche's role as a fading Southern belle with apt stylization of dress, diction, and decorum. With reference to the columns of Belle Reve, he appealed to an American mind steeped in images of the literary plantation. What he assured his audience through this powerful symbolic language was that Blanche DuBois, for all her sexual unruliness, issued from a domestic order that had tolerated little feminine intransigence.

Williams exploited the plantation setting and ideology more systematically in *Cat on a Hot Tin Roof*. The notes of the original production stage manager indicate that "there is constantly an awareness of the living plantation just beyond the borders of the stage."[13] Williams sustained this illusion by auditory and visual codes that gave a rather predictable social history to the setting. The play opens with "a merry, old-fashioned Southern song" in the lawn area, and then solidifies the presence of "a plantation home in the Mississippi Delta" by tracking the obligatory Negro servants as they "amble" about their tasks (DPS, Act I, pp. 5–6). Thereafter the warning sounds of nature and the plaintive song of the field hands intersect with a household drama of death and succession to form an antiphonal text – one that culminates in Act III with Big Daddy's godlike view of his "kingdom": "28,000 acres of the richest land this side of the Nile Valley!" (DPS, p. 78).

Williams combined far-flung sources to realize the plantation household of the Pollitts, but pointed references to people and places in Clarksdale, Mississippi, and Williams's own familiarity with the region, suggest its formative role in *Cat on a Hot Tin Roof*.[14] Williams's maternal grandfather, the Reverend Walter E. Dakin, was the rector of St. George's Episcopal Church in Clarksdale from 1917 until his retirement in 1932. During that time, his grandson came to know the lore and gossip of the town and Coahoma County from periods of residence and visitation at the rectory, and from joining his grandfather on calls to the privileged families of his parish. The plantation culture to which he was exposed, and upon which he drew for *Cat*, was of fairly recent origin and possessed few of the elegant reiterations of antebellum Natchez to the south. Its growing of premium staple cotton was a business rather than a social ritual steeped in courtly tradition. This is a key distinction for Williams's attempt to write within the Broadway canons of domestic realism.

In September 1982, Williams advised a British company planning a revival of *Cat* to observe degree: "Please avoid the mistake made by [Laurence] Olivier who conceived the part of Big Daddy as that of the Southern planter gentleman. Big Daddy is a former overseer who struck it rich through hard work."[15] It was fitting in *A Streetcar Named Desire* that the plantation be given a more refined and lengthy heritage in the memory of Blanche DuBois. Her metonymical trunk is stuffed with the family history of Belle Reve – "thousands of papers, stretching back over hundreds of years" (Scene 2). As a spiritual Southerner, Williams was family proud and revered the "elegance" of a bygone South that he was "just old enough to remember."[16] But in drafting *Cat on a Hot Tin Roof*, he knew that he must suppress this romantic memory so that material relations, and the "mendacity" they engender, could form the economic crux of the play. Considered ideologically, *A Streetcar Named Desire* and *Cat on a Hot Tin Roof* summarize the ambiguity of the Southern plantation. Was it formed on a precapitalist model, as the Marxist historian Eugene Genovese has argued; or did it resemble a factory in the field as Kenneth Stampp and James Oakes have surmised? In effect, Tennessee Williams said it was both, given the dramatic needs of the text. In *Cat on a Hot Tin Roof*, the capitalist model that Clarksdale had perfected was chosen.

In the antics of the Pollitt family, Williams had packed enough deviance, or at least strangeness, to satisfy a prime requirement of Southern writers in addressing the nation: that the South be cast as a problematic region – or, as Allen Tate said in 1945, "backward and illiberal," with "a unique moral perversity." Williams had satisfied this national requirement before, would do so again spectacularly in *Baby Doll* (1956), and would continue to be resented by his Southern peers, who had run "the New York gauntlet," or so they thought, with less craven fear and capitulation than Tennessee Williams. Flannery O'Connor, for example, called *Baby Doll* "a dirty little piece of trash," and when Faulkner was asked to write some publicity stories for the film version of *The Sound and the Fury* in 1959, he sneered, "Have Tennessee Williams write them." Williams knew that the market paradoxically held in mind images of a "sunny" and benighted South, and that its minions in the New York press had often denounced him for slighting the former. *Cat on a Hot Tin Roof* was no exception to this rule. If only in naming the Pollitts – Big Daddy and Big Mama, Mae and Gooper and their "no-neck monsters," and of course Maggie the Cat – Williams seemed to address an audience well accustomed to the bizarre ethnicity of the South. Their expectations of "a unique moral perversity" in Dixie would help them to find the familiar and invidious social critique within the so-called "Southern grotesque." Williams and every other major Southern writer, including Faulkner and O'Connor, exploited this paradox in pursuing national fame.

A similar process was at work in Williams's treatment of generational strife and dynastic succession. The domestic core of *Cat on a Hot Tin Roof* was mediated by the rhetorical extremes of Big Daddy's *ore rotundo* style and his younger son Brick's existential silence and mourning. Neither speaker was entirely plausible in view of his social and intellectual origins, and neither was reassuring to an audience that preferred a clear statement of the bottom line. But if the rhetoric of *Cat on a Hot Tin Roof* may have decentered the play's emphasis upon family continuity and the bestowal of property, the domestic plot emphasized again and again the economic tenor of modern plantation life in the Delta. Big Daddy was no avatar of the old plantation philosophe, whose addiction to leisure and contempt for wealth, or so the story went, bespoke a contemplative frame of mind. He is, instead, economic predation untouched by any communal ethos. Big Daddy's cancer, which is diagnosed as fatal in the course of the play, has drained some of the old-time fervor; but in a brief abatement of his impending death, Big Daddy restates his control to an abashed wife, who has been "Bossin', talkin', sashayin' [her] ole butt aroun' this place," in a way calculated to replace the founder.

I made this place! I was overseer on it! I was the overseer on the ole Straw and Ochello plantation . . . I quit school at ten years old an' went to work like a nigger in th' fields. An' I rose to be overseer of the Straw an' Ochello plantation. An' ole Straw died an' I was Ochello's partner an' the place got bigger an' bigger! I did all that myself with no goddam help from you, an' now you think that you're just about to take over. Well, I'm just about to tell you that . . . you are not just about to take over a goddam thing. (DPS, p. 38)

In Big Daddy Pollitt, Williams found the exemplar of a rather crude domestic order that had pioneered for wealth since launching its economy after the Civil War. Onto this American stock he grafted a plantation imagery, including suggestible columns done in "velour" (DPS, p. 5), that could not have failed to captivate a national audience. Expectations of a benighted and quaintly attractive South were not slighted in *Cat on a Hot Tin Roof*, nor was the allegiance of the audience to a masterful discourse of capitalism subverted by Big Daddy's business ethic or the domestic theme of inheritance. It is this amalgam of the familiar that one hears in the reviews of *Cat on a Hot Tin Roof*. To be sure, there was squeamishness about the play's blue language and steamy situations, but nothing in the notices said that Williams had sinned against current prescriptions of genre, race, class, or economy. Even Brick's complaint about the "mendacity" of modern life strikes the familiar note of the American jeremiad, and the peculiar literary South itself did not seriously raise a New York eyebrow. It was Brooks Atkinson, of course, who gave Williams the perfect absolution for the old exotica of *Camino Real*. The new play, he said in review, "seems not to have been written. It is the quintessence of life. It is the basic truth."[17] No softer words could have been spoken in the "place of stone," and we know from Williams's letter of thanks how timely and consoling they were. But by no means was this the most astute review. In calling *Cat* a "stunningly acted play of evasion,"[18] Walter Kerr heard in Brick Pollitt the aberrant silence that Williams had so cunningly preserved. In all probability, it was this core that was negotiated by Williams and Kazan in 1954 as the script was readied for production. Precisely when Kazan conveyed his thoughts about revision is not known; but as Williams told Maria Britneva in late October, he had kept him as "busy as a 'Cat on a Tin Roof!'" (*Angel*, October 29, 1954, p. 103) through his well-known practice of urging revision upon playwrights who sought his prized direction.

When he came to publish *Cat on a Hot Tin Roof* in 1955, Williams took the unusual (and Kazan thought provocative) step of printing the so-called "original" and "Broadway" versions of the third act, and with them a mischievous "Note of Explanation." Any dictatorial culture of revision was self-imposed, Williams said, by virtue of his fear that Kazan would lose "interest" if he did not "re-examine the script from his point of view." In the absence of Kazan's own phrasing, we are dependent upon Williams's listing of the director's three main "points" of revision, the last being the most unappealing to Williams: a more sympathetic treatment of Maggie the Cat, the reappearance of Big Daddy in Act III, and a loosening of Brick's "moral paralysis."[19] Over the years, the glare of theatre politics has obscured the terms of Williams's resistance to Kazan's energetic Broadway style. It was, however, strong and principled, as Williams wrote to Audrey Wood in November 1955. With plans maturing for a new production of *Orpheus Descending*, he was "determined to express just me, not a director or actors," even if it "means giving up the top-rank names as co-workers" (November 18, 1955). To the list of usurpers he could have added agents as well, for with *Cat on a Hot Tin Roof* the first serious strains appeared in his relation with Audrey Wood.

Precisely how had Williams failed to express himself during the enforced revision (if it was that) of Brick's character? Sources for his name and history connect this figure with the University of Missouri, that Williams attended in Columbia from 1929 to 1932, and with the childhood world of Clarksdale, Mississippi.[20] But in a more personal way, Brick is an unforgiving mirror of Williams's artistic identity and his own besetting career. "It was Williams," Kazan said of their collaboration on *Cat*, "who wanted the commercial success, and he wanted it passionately."[21] Williams never denied this motive. But he was also drawn by "failure"; and this alluring release from competition was sewn into the character of Brick Pollitt, as it was Blanche DuBois. Their subversive wish to fail entailed a dramaturgy that reflects Williams's skepticism for Broadway and its commodified exchange of meaning between playwright and audience. Was not Kazan an astute director to attack the privacy of Brick Pollitt as hostile to his own flamboyant expressiveness?

Something of the evolution of the Pollitt character can be found in several tributary sources, and with it a better grounding in the aesthetics of Williams's evasive dramaturgy. In Oliver Winemiller, the "unforgettable youth" of the story "One Arm" (1948), Williams made an early and discerning study of mutilation. The loss of his arm in a motor accident transforms the eighteen-year-old boxer into a homosexual hustler, whose murder of a corrupt patron leads to his execution by the state. But Williams was more intrigued by psychic than legal effects. Oliver's brush with time isolates his being: "He never said to himself, I'm lost. But the speechless self knew it and in submission to its unthinking control the youth had begun . . . to look about for destruction" (*CS*, p. 176). By turns indifferent and "disgusted with all the world," Oliver is "a personality without a center." If only this "insularity" were absolute, final, his death would have been "easier"; but he is brought back to life by a "torrent of letters" from nameless men "who couldn't stop thinking of him." "Too late, this resurrection" (CS, p. 182), Williams intones, in patent imitation of D. H. Lawrence, who taught him the modernist language of "the speechless self."

In *The Roman Spring of Mrs. Stone* (1950), Williams treated a woman's aging and loss of beauty as a more refined mutilation. At fifty, a widow, and retired from her cold "career-existence" on the Broadway stage, Karen Stone has started to "drift" after failing in the miscast role of Shakespeare's Juliet. Her "posthumous existence" brings "the speechless self" to uncanny realization:

> Mrs. Stone knew, in her heart, that she was turning boldly inward from the now slackened orbit . . . She knew it in her heart without consciously knowing it. And being a person of remarkable audacity, she moved inward with her violet eyes wide open, asking herself, in her heart, what would she find as she moved? (p. 103)

To this universal dilemma, Williams added elements of his own unique anxiety. Karen Stone was insecure in her talent, ruthless with other competing actors, and depressed by the "vast ritual of nothingness" in New York City. She was also beginning to find, as Williams had in the late 1940s, a diminishing exilic return from the "gold weather" of Rome. Resurrection, the Lawrentian stamp that is borne by novel and story alike, is ill-timed again, coinciding as it does with menopause – or "moon of pause."

Williams completed "Three Players of a Summer Game" in May 1952 and perhaps started *Cat* as early as the following summer in Rome. The story repeats the basic design of "One Arm" and *The Roman Spring of Mrs. Stone* with the seizure of Brick Pollitt by abstract forces not of his making. Two years after his marriage, the former athlete and Delta planter is besieged by "self-disgust [that] came upon him with the abruptness and violence of a crash on a highway" (CS, pp. 305–6). His mutilation is neither accidental nor organic but deliberate: "It was as though [his wife Margaret] had her lips fastened to some invisible wound in his body" and "drained . . . the assurance and vitality that he had owned before marriage" (CS, p. 306). In the summer of the story's title, Brick drinks to obscure this violation. The game that he plays in vain hope of resurrection is croquet; its requirement that each wicket and stake be carefully aligned is a discipline, but it teaches Brick only the treachery of time and space. Triumphant at the end of the story, his wife leads Brick through the streets of Meridian,

Mississippi, "as Caesar or Alexander the Great or Hannibal, might have led in chains through a capital city the prince of a state newly conquered" (CS, p. 325).

If any single literary source informs these stories, it is certainly D. H. Lawrence, to whom Williams paid tribute, both in open declaration (as in the plays *You Touched Me!*, 1943, and *I Rise in Flame, Cried the Phoenix*, 1951), and in silent adoption of his epistemology and social critique. Lawrence wrote especially in his later years in bitter protest of the mendacity of postwar culture, as did Williams in the aftermath of the next great war. For each, the themes of mutilation and resurrection clothed a biting social critique, but it was Lawrence's modernist poetics that held a greater attraction and lesson for Williams. The inability of "words" to express the "primordial silences," the "deepest secrets," and the urgent complaints of those who require that "mystery" be formulated, were addressed by Lawrence in an early manifesto, "Art and the Individual: A Paper for Socialists" (1908). "They should know," he said of such materialists, "that they are purposely led to the edge of the great darkness, where no word-lights twinkle."[22] This warning of oblique aesthetic intention is the point where Williams's evasive dramaturgy can be connected to the originating Pollitt stories, which culminate in *Cat*, and to the abiding problematic of Williams's relations with the Broadway theatre. In effect, their evolution charts the periodic debilities, addictions, breakdowns, and writing blocks that besieged Williams after the great success of *A Streetcar Named Desire*. But the stories have still greater potential for defining the issues and positions taken by Williams and Kazan in the third-act controversy, and perhaps meeting the challenge that Williams issued to the reader (in the "Note of Explanation") to "make up his own mind about it." Underlying the local controversy over *Cat on a Hot Tin Roof* is a century-long discussion about the possibilities of theatre itself.

In "The Sociology of Modern Drama" (1909), Georg Lukács defined "the heroes of the new drama" as "more passive than active." Their heroism, he observed, was one "of anguish, of despair, not one of bold aggressiveness." The dramatic conflict generated by such a retiring kind of hero was that of "man as merely the intersection point of great forces, and his deeds not even his own."[23] To this perceptive Marxist critic, such an attenuation of tragic man gave further evidence of modernist subjectivity undermining the social basis of art. With his talk of "silences" and "mystery" and frail "words," Lawrence had also blurred the contours of the world, and his paper, we should recall, was addressed to "Socialists." There is a line to be drawn from Lukács's early concern for the faltering "equilibrium between man and the external world," where the source of dramatic conflict lies, and the declaration of its collapse in the contemporary writing of Julia Kristeva.

Kristeva's analysis cites the destabilizing effect of modern history upon the traditional "place" of theatre.

> Since no set or interplay of sets is able to hold up any longer faced with the crises of State, religion and family, it is impossible to prefer a discourse – to play out a discourse – on the basis of a scene, sign of recognition, which would provide for the actor's and audience's recognition of themselves in the same Author.[24]

Thus "Modern Theater Does Not Take (A) Place," as Kristeva's 1977 essay is entitled, and as it declares in banishing the old "theater as de-monstration." Governed by an "irresistible scopic drive," this drama "can do nothing but chain itself to the normative ideologies to which the failure of contemporary social sets, and perhaps, even the failure of the human race, affixes itself." Only in "the silent theater of colors, sounds and gestures," in which the semiotic "encompasses" the symbolic, can the more advanced playwrights and actors "develop a technical arsenal of 'alienation'" and demolish "an antiquating society's antiquating fantasies." In such silent space, Kristeva thinks, "a new subject" can be born.

The analyses of Lukács and Kristeva describe a continuous line of drama theory that is pertinent to Williams (and Kazan too) as he approached the production of *Cat on a Hot Tin Roof*. The writing of the originating Pollitt texts released Williams from the "normative ideologies" of the stage and allowed him to test strategies of "alienation" in media more conducive to such experiment. In "One Arm," Williams not only purged great anger by the murder of the boy's unholy patron, but he also made of Oliver Winemiller a writer of letters – "crudely eloquent" replies to his former trade that amended their crass sex. With this textualizing of desire, Williams modeled a wish for purity and impersonality that arose periodically from the wreckage of his precarious literary career. A similar retreat from the cold exchange of Broadway informs the transgendering poetics of *The Roman Spring of Mrs. Stone*. As biological metaphor, menopause reconstituted the maimed writing subject in surcease from desire and productivity – in a word, competition – and it was an organic, necessary condition to which Williams could give vicarious assent. In "Three Players of a Summer Game," Williams found a consolidating metaphor of creativity to assuage the human chaos of the story. The chaste game of croquet he thought "composed of images the way that a painter's abstraction of summer or one of its games would be built of them" (*CS*, p. 303). With such dehumanizing strokes of the artist could the volatile personal histories of Brick and Margaret Pollitt be rendered as spatial form. It was this aesthetic desire, hallowed by the practice of Oliver Winemiller and Karen Stone, that Williams distilled into *Cat on a Hot Tin Roof*, as a secret, exulting reply to the stony marketplace of Broadway.

Shortly after he replaced Ben Gazzara in the New York production of *Cat*, Alexander Nicol received a note of thanks from Williams for having played Brick "precisely as I had conceived his character. You had the quality which I think of as 'the poem of the play' – the poetry of the man who is not competing."[25] There is no visual record of Nicol's performance, but Kristeva's advice to actors and writers to develop an "arsenal of 'aliena-tion'" is integral no doubt to this performative virtue and to Williams's own attempt to preserve "'the poem of the play.'" From the originating Pollitt stories the structural habits of this "'poem'" are clear, and so too are their relations with the uneasy covenant that Williams made with Broadway, including his ritualistic courting of Kazan to direct each new play. Coming at a time of crisis, the writing and production of *Cat* added poignance to Williams's unforgiving fate as a dramatist. His tools, ideology, and audience were those of the old "theater as de-monstration," but "the poetry of the man who is not competing" seemed to imply a variant "Theater [that] Does Not Take (A) Place," or at least one that has severely trimmed its expressiveness. Especially in Act I of *Cat on a Hot Tin Roof* did Williams use his skill and resolve to frame this urgent writer's dilemma.

To Maggie's passionate arias, Brick's speech is usually terse, mocking, and phrased in a wry interrogative mood: "What are they up to, Maggie?" "Don't they have any necks?" "Did you *say* something, Maggie?" (ND, pp. 2–6). With such measured, alienating speech, Brick deflects the family politics, economic aspiration, and sexual allure that Maggie would use to recenter her husband's interest in his patrimony. His broken ankle, devout drinking, and mocking self-detachment repeat the now familiar pattern of the originating Pollitt stories, and here they display Williams's skill in producing in his protagonist the intense and surprising effect of silence and reserve. In Act I Brick's discipline is unassailable until Maggie picks the "sore" of his friendship with Skipper. It was "one of those beautiful, ideal things . . . that never could be carried through to anything satisfying or even talked about plainly," Maggie says. But talk she does, and with Williams's brilliant verbal investment in the advertisement of her ego. Finally it leads Maggie to the same rational discourse of accommodation that Eunice voices in *A Streetcar Named Desire*. "Life," says Maggie, "has got to be allowed to continue even after the *dream* of life is – all – over . . ." (ND, p. 41).

Act I ends by forcing Brick to "play out a discourse," which does indeed "provide for the actor's and audience's recognition of themselves in the same Author." What they all meet to "de-monstrate" are the "antiquating fantasies" of the Southern literary plantation, whose rites of death and succession overwhelm Brick's early reserve and govern the second act as well. However reluctantly, Williams is complicit in this development, as he is in revealing "the speechless self" of Brick in his ensuing talk with Big Daddy. To substitute a homosexual identity (however well closeted) for an ontological self that cannot "be talked about plainly" is not, however, to cast the sexual Other as a normalizing identity, as some hold; but to place "the *dream* of life" in socio-historical rather than pure subjective space, as the commercial theatre always requires. But precisely where does this accommodation leave Tennessee Williams in the famous third-act controversy with Elia Kazan?

Nearly twenty years later, Williams could speak with composure about *Cat on a Hot Tin Roof*. Of the alternate third acts, he said in a 1972 interview that "I still prefer the one that I wrote first. But the thing is, I worked longer on the third act as Kazan wanted it, and, consequently, it is texturally the better written of the two, the more fullbodied." This is accurate and so too is Williams's "doubt" that *Cat* would have succeeded on Broadway with "the original ending."[26] The return of Big Daddy, Maggie's bold lie of fecundity, and Brick's admiration for his wife carry through the imperatives of the domestic plot and amply satisfy the "scopic" needs of the mass audience. The dynamics of resurrection, nearly devoid of resolution in the originating Pollitt stories, are readjusted as well in the Broadway version of Act III to reassert passion and productivity and thereby revoke "the moon of pause."

In effect, Williams repeated Maggie's truism that "life has got to be allowed to continue even after the *dream* of life is – all – over . . . " This is a constant refrain in Williams's work and to blame Kazan for its sudden imposition in *Cat on a Hot Tin Roof* is naive. Still, Williams took the unusual step of publishing alternate third acts in the first edition of *Cat* (New Directions, 1955), and he invited the reader to "make up his own mind about it." Williams had the kind of vivid theatricality that overshadowed his prose. But in "One Arm" he endowed prose, specifically letters, with the power to redeem the tainted marketplace of sex with countervailing values of purity and impersonality. In printing alternate third acts, Williams attempted a similar purification by proposing a "book-theatre" that would bypass the semiotics of performance and assert the primacy of the dramatic text – of language abstracted from the traditional place of theatre and its outmoded communal exchange of meaning. This would entail a more impersonal relation with a reader who could then share the solitude of Williams's writing – his "mornings at the Olivetti" (*Angel*, April 27, 1955, p. 113) – and by extension, "the poetry of the man who is not competing." It is this studied confinement of *Cat* to literature – to the sparse writing of the original third act after the vivid "levitation" of Act II – that Williams envisioned as the new locus of "'the poem of the play.'"

As Brick hears the *"click"* of liquor at the end of Act III, Williams no doubt felt a similar protection from the allure of "lights, theatres, city glitter and excitement," as he described a nascent Broadway career in 1940. The writing and production of *Cat on a Hot Tin Roof* some fifteen years later confirm the temptations that Williams anticipated in a career in the commercial theatre, and they also suggest the heroism with which he resisted them. In 1940, in a letter to Joe Hazan, Williams feared that he would always be "casting" himself "against the stones of the world in an effort . . . to escape from aloneness. I pray for the strength to be separate, to be austere."[27] Yeats's call to "Be secret and exult" was surely recognized by Williams in this light as a modernist aesthetic of impersonality that he had embraced at the beginning of his career. To the "city glitter" would soon be added a "highly imaginative director," but even his substantial and enduring talent did not deter Williams from austerity. By textualizing their third-act controversy, which seems mild indeed after nearly fifty years, Williams had the last word – until, that is, he recalled how instrumental Kazan was to his success in the theatre, and sought his direction for *Orpheus Descending*. Perhaps only in the gesture could Williams reconcile the anxieties of an artistic career with a keen interest in success.

NOTES

1 Brenda Murphy identified the original epigraph from Yeats in her study, *Tennessee Williams and Elia Kazan: A Collaboration in the Theatre* (Cambridge University Press, 1992) 108. Yeats's phrase "a place of stone" served as a provisional title for *Cat*.

2 Quoted by Tennessee Williams in *Memoirs* (Garden City, NY: Doubleday, 1975) 62.

3 Unpublished letter, TW to Wood, February 27, 1946.

4 See reviews of *Camino Real* by Richard Watts, Jr., "An Enigma by Tennessee Williams," *New York Post*; John Chapman, "Symbols Clash in 'Camino Real,'" *New York Daily News*; Walter F. Kerr, "'Camino Real,'" *New York Herald Tribune*; Robert Coleman, "'Camino Real' Will Please Some, Anger Others," *New York Daily Mirror*; Brooks Atkinson, "Tennessee Williams Writes a Cosmic Fantasy Entitled *Camino Real*," *New York Times* – all printed on March 20, 1953.

5 Unpublished letter, TW to Atkinson, April 3, 1953.

6 *Ibid.*

7 Unpublished letter, Logan to TW, January 12, 1949, The Papers of Joshua Logan, Library of Congress, Manuscript Division.

8 Unpublished letter, Logan to TW and Elia Kazan, February 26 [1953], The Papers of Joshua Logan, Library of Congress, Manuscript Division.

9 Unpublished letter, TW to Wood, May 5, 1939.

10 Audrey Wood (with Max Wilk), *Represented by Audrey Wood* (Garden City, NY: Doubleday, 1981) 165.

11 *Represented by Audrey Wood* 165–66. Williams's defense of his "short full-length play" was made in an unpublished letter to Wood, received on September 7, 1954. Curiously, on October 15, 1953, as dated by Maria St. Just, TW said that he had received from Wood "a devastatingly negative reaction" to a manuscript mailed to her from Rome. In *Angel* (pp. 79–80), Maria identifies the ms. as *Cat*.

12 Williams, *Memoirs* 86.

13 Robert Downing, "From the Cat-Bird Seat: The Production Stage Manager's Notes on *Cat on a Hot Tin Roof*," *The Theatre Annual*, 14 (1956), 48.

14 See Linton Weeks, *Clarksdale & Coahoma County: A History* (Clarksdale, MS: Carnegie Public Library, 1982). Although local references (Moon Lake, the Clarksdale *Register*) in *Cat* suggest Clarksdale as setting, the play's plantation space is generalized.

15 Unpublished letter (copy/unsigned), TW to Royal Shakespeare Company, September 2, 1982, Tennessee Williams Papers, Harvard Theatre Collection. TW refers to an NBC-TV production of *Cat* on December 6, 1976.

16 Quoted by Louise Davis in "Nashville Was a Streetcar Named Happiness," *Nashville Tennessean Magazine*, March 10, 1957, 13.

17 Brooks Atkinson, "Theatre: Tennessee Williams's 'Cat,'" *New York Times*, March 25, 1955.

18 Walter F. Kerr, "'Cat on a Hot Tin Roof,'" *New York Herald Tribune*, March 25, 1955.

19 See "Note of Explanation," in *Cat on a Hot Tin Roof* (New York: New Directions, 1955), 152.

20 See Allean Hale, "How a Tiger Became a Cat," *Tennessee Williams Literary Journal*, 2 (1990–91), 33–36; Lyle Leverich, *Tom: The Unknown Tennessee Williams* (New York: Crown Publishers, 1995) 55, 417, 460; and Brenda Murphy, *Tennessee Williams and Elia Kazan: A Collaboration in the Theatre*, 97–98.

21 Elia Kazan, *A Life* (New York: Alfred A. Knopf, 1988), 544.

22 D. H. Lawrence, "Art and the Individual: A Paper for Socialists" (1908), in Bruce Steele (ed.), *Study of Thomas Hardy and Other Essays, The Cambridge Edition of the Letters and Works of D. H. Lawrence* (Cambridge University Press, 1985), 140–41.

23 Georg Lukács, "The Sociology of Modern Drama" (1909), *Tulane Drama Review* 9 (1965), 149–51.

24 Julia Kristeva, "Modern Theater Does Not Take (A) Place," *Sub-Stance*, 18/19 (1977), 131.

25 Unpublished letter, TW to Alexander Nicol, October 28, 1955.

26 Quoted by Jim Gaines in "A Talk about Life and Style with Tennessee Williams" (1972), in Albert J. Devlin (ed.), *Conversations with Tennessee Williams* (Jackson: University Press of Mississippi, 1986), 216–17.

27 Unpublished letter, TW to Joseph Hazan, August 18, 1940, Tennessee Williams Papers, Harry Ransom Humanities Research Center, University of Texas, Austin.

BIBLIOGRAPHICAL NOTE

The unpublished correspondence of Williams to Audrey Wood, Brooks Atkinson, and Carson McCullers is to be found, respectively, in the Tennessee Williams Papers, Harry Ransom Humanities Research Center, University of Texas, Austin; the Brooks Atkinson Papers, Billy Rose Theatre Collection, New York Public Library at Lincoln Center; and the Carson McCullers Papers, Duke University, Special Collections Library. Dates are cited in the text. This copyrighted material is quoted with the permission of New Directions Books.

Quotations of Williams's published works follow the texts as cited: *Cat on a Hot Tin Roof* (New York: New Directions Books, 1955); *Cat on a Hot Tin Roof* (New York: Dramatists Play Service, 1958); *The Roman Spring of Mrs. Stone* (New York: New Directions Books, 1950); *Tennessee Williams: Collected Stories* (New York: New Directions Books, 1985); *Five O'Clock Angel: Letters of Tennessee Williams to Maria St. Just, 1948–1982* (New York: Alfred A. Knopf, 1990). In quotations of *Cat*, the abbreviations ND and DPS identify the 1955 and 1958 versions. The abbreviations *CS* and *Angel* refer, respectively, to *Collected Stories* and *Five O'Clock Angel*. Pagination is cited in the text.

6

THOMAS P. ADLER

Before the Fall – and after: *Summer and Smoke* and *The Night of the Iguana*

> Another decent thing about me is my tolerance and my love of people and my gentleness toward them. I think I have acquired that through suffering and loneliness.
>
> Tennessee Williams, unpublished journal

I

Perhaps because he wrote verse even before he turned to short fiction and drama (his poems, in fact, began to appear in little magazines as early as 1933, prior to his first plays being given amateur productions), Tennessee Williams often used poetry – his own and that of others – as *intertext* in his works for the stage. Over a dozen of his full-length plays in their printed versions feature epigraphs from writers as various as Sappho, Dante, Rimbaud, Yeats and, an especial favorite of his, Hart Crane. Both *Summer and Smoke* (1947) and *The Night of the Iguana* (1961) incorporate a poem that provides a key to the drama. In the former, the Southern parson's daughter, Alma Winemiller, recites William Blake's "Love's Secret," albeit in altered form, at her literary club gathering, not only foreshadowing the course the action will take as she loses Dr. John Buchanan to another, but also hinting at the rejection that may be visited upon a somehow forbidden " 'Love that never told can be.' "[1] In the latter, the 97-year-old minor poet Jonathan Coffin (called Nonno) exuberantly declaims his final poem – only slightly revised from one the playwright himself wrote on a visit to Mexico in 1940 – about the decay that inevitably follows the ripening of all things living, pleading for the "courage" necessary to endure in the face of awareness of mortality.[2]

Dissolution and decline – purity giving way to corruption, a sanctuary or safe harbor invaded by harsh judgment and condemnation – these are, indeed, recurring motifs in the verses from his own pen that Williams includes in his plays. In, for example, *Something Cloudy, Something Clear* (1981), the autobiographical retelling of his affair forty years earlier with the dancer, Kip, the authorial character August implores: "God give me death before thirty, /Before my clean heart has grown dirty, /Soiled with the dust of much living, /More wanting and taking than giving."³ Or, in *The Mutilated* from *Slapstick Tragedy* (1966), the Carollers and Jack In Black alter and expand upon Williams's "Poem for Paul," a deeply personal lyric composed twenty-five years previously, wherein all society's outsiders and marginalized ("the strange, the crazed, the queer"; "the lonely and misfit"; "the brilliant and deformed") will be proffered pity before oblivion: "I think for some uncertain reason, /mercy will be shown this season . . . / before, with such a tender smile, /the earth destroys her crooked child."⁴

If, as the Reverend T. Lawrence Shannon asserts in *Iguana*, "we – live on two levels" (317), so also must Nonno's poem about the cyclical nature of existence be read on multiple levels: on the literal one, the golden orange reaches its height of perfection ("zenith") only to plummet to the ground in the dark of night and then mix with the earth and decay, without the least tremor of regret at nature's elemental and immutable process; on an allegorical level, however, humankind, conscious of change and loss, finds it deeply fearful and unsettling to contemplate leaving the pristine world of green and gold to commence "A second history," "An intercourse" with the earthly, "A bargaining with mist and mould" that occasions disillusionment and despair (371). All of these poetic statements – as is true of Gerard Manley Hopkins's "Spring and Fall" about "grieving/Over Goldengrove unleaving . . . It is the blight man was born for,"⁵ with which they resonate – consider our torturous growth from innocence to experience and the need for finding a way to live in the ruined Eden of the present.

II

Always aware of what he called the "plastic problems" inherent in utilizing theatrical space – which he often treated as a painter or a sculptor would – Williams conceives of the stage setting for *Summer and Smoke* as an altarpiece-like triptych positioned against a cyclorama of sky, blue as in Renaissance "religious paintings." Dominating the slightly elevated central panel is a crouching stone angel with "hands held together to form a cup from which water flows": she is intended as "a symbolic figure (Eternity) brooding over the course of the play" (120). One side panel is the Episcopal rectory (its American Gothic architecture merely hinted at by Victorian tracery), with "a romantic landscape in a gilt frame"; the opposite (similarly suggested by just a framework) is the doctor's office, with its "chart of anatomy" (120). Although the categorization "morality play" has frequently implied a derogatory judgment because of the way in which, within the allegorical mode, abstract concepts tend to be foregrounded at the expense of subtle analysis, it can still be applied revealingly to Williams's play, as several critics have demonstrated.[6] Yet the binary oppositions he sets up early on – eternity/time; soul/body; purity/carnality; winter/summer; ice/fire; religion/science – far from establishing a hierarchy of values are intended, rather, to demonstrate how an either/or dissociation results in fragmentation and incompletion instead of in a healthy intermingling. In this play, finally, the spiritual can only be reached via, in union with, the physical; the body cannot, however much Alma might wish otherwise, be completely bypassed or ignored in the search for what lies beyond. The angel's timeworn name, inscribed on the statue's base, can only be read tactilely, by touch. The issue of reading signs, and of whether the visible sign can communicate the invisible substance or essence, becomes a crucial issue in *Summer and Smoke*. When John, for instance, looks through the microscope he sees "a mysterious [universe]," rightly perceiving its complexity as "Part anarchy – and part order!" (141). Alma, on the other hand, wants to take the physical evidence as proof of something more, "The footprints of God!" – though John's skeptical rejoinder, "But not God" (142), questions that leap.

Later on, when John reads the anatomy chart, he approaches the task as a literalist would: the body pictured on it (brain, belly, genitalia) hungers to be fed with truth, food, sex. Alma rejects this reading unequivocally; she insists, too narrowly as she will learn, that *only* the soul, which her name means in Spanish and which the chart cannot show – "But it's there, just the same" (221–22) – and *not* physical sexuality can be the source of love and its expression. Although Alma nowhere in the play "reads" the meaning of the romantic painting in the rectory parlor, she does interpret the architecture of the Gothic cathedrals (arches, vault, spires all straining heavenward) as a symbolic representation of "the principle back of existence – the everlasting struggle and aspiration for more than our human limits have placed in our reach" (197). John immediately deflates Alma's clichéd sermonette about "gutter" and "stars" by identifying Oscar Wilde as the source of her quotation, while she remains blithely ignorant of the phallic connotations that her description shares with the Roman candles exploding across the sky on Independence Day. Both John and Alma *misread* with disastrous consequences: he by refusing to admit the possibility of any level of existence beyond empirical data; she by ignoring the surface level in order to escape too quickly into the metaphorical realm, with the consequence that neither one knows, until very late in the play, what it means to be a fully integrated human being.

Alma's immature "reading" and understanding belong more appropriately to the prelapsarian world of the play's Prologue when she was still chronologically a child; the hymn entitled "The Voice That Breathed O'er

Eden" which she is preparing to sing at an upcoming wedding hints, in fact, at her attempt to hold on to a morally uncomplicated and thus unreal world. Williams gives the name "Glorious Hill" to his "garden" locale in the Mississippi Delta during the innocent decade or so before World War I – a more idealized designation than the actual Clarksdale where he spent part of his early youth in the home of his maternal grandfather, who was rector of St. George's Episcopal Church. Perhaps precisely because Williams himself lived during his formative years in "the shadow" of a church he felt a special kinship with Alma Winemiller, who he thinks "may very well be the best female portrait [he has] drawn in a play. She simply seemed to exist somewhere in [this] being and it was no effort to put her on paper."[7] The play, admittedly stronger in its delineation of character and demonstration of ideas than in its minimal and somewhat flaccid plot, was first staged by Margo Jones at her regional arena theatre in Dallas in 1947. It only really came into its own as a major work with José Quintero's triumphant direction of Geraldine Page in her first starring role at the Circle-in-the-Square in 1952 – an event that some critics have singled out as virtually beginning the modern off-Broadway movement.[8]

During the Prologue in the park, the stone angel serves as a ministering figure, a source of refreshing and cleansing water; the ten-year-old Alma at one point even assumes the attitude of the angel, hands cupped "in a way similar to that of receiving the wafer at Holy Communion" (125). Yet the stone figure, cold and lifeless, quickly assumes a synchronous iconographic association with the angel in Genesis who guards the entry to Eden after the Fall, preventing reentry. And if paradise has been lost in this play, the "original sin" according to this duplicitous society seems to be sexual in nature, insofar anyway as the woman is concerned. Alma's hysteria, her palpitations and "nervous breathless laughter," are symptoms of the restraints and unreal expectations that repressive social mores have placed upon her, especially as a parson's daughter. The playwright described her as "caged by her inhibitions";[9] and John diagnoses this woman who has always been forced to keep "her true nature . . . hidden even from herself" (135) as suffering from a "badly irritated" Doppelganger. It is a tension that Williams himself, when he was similar in age to Alma, had felt over his own unresolved sexuality; he expressed his frustration in his journal, by writing: "'If only I could realize I am not 2 (sic) persons. I am only one. There is no sense in this division. An enemy inside myself!'"[10] Alma's tendency to anorexia (John observes that she has "fed . . . maybe [her] body a little – watery subsistence" [221]) signifies her desire to deny the body, to somehow escape from and transcend it. In spurning John's sexual advances out at Moon Lake Casino, as she had run from his childhood kiss in the garden-like park, she suffocates the flame of passion within herself, appearing henceforward to John as so icily frigid that he no longer feels decent enough to touch her. From that point on, she can be only a rarefied angel of mercy to him, a source of maternal tenderness like "a stone Pieta," but never a potential wife.

Although John may appear at first to have a more balanced perspective on life, by excessively feeding the physical (for him, as Donne would say, "the soul is sense") he actually exaggerates, rather than integrates, one side of our humanity at the expense of the other. Sowing his wild oats through drinking, gambling, and whoring, he hardly fulfills Alma's sentimentally elevated image of him as a Prometheus in an otherwise stagnant society; furthermore, she accuses him of "desecrate[ing]" the sacred calling of a doctor to relieve the "suffering – and fear" endemic to being human. John's indolence and indulgence of the senses result in a progressive "slide down-hill," so pronounced that he sentences himself to an unnatural punishment, claiming he "should have been *castrated*," his masochistic outburst under-lined by "fling[ing] his wineglass at the anatomy chart" (212). But after the father of Rosa, his fiery lover, shoots and kills John's father, the young doctor undergoes a reformation which he attributes in part to Alma's influence. Lionized for his medical discoveries in helping wipe out infec-tious diseases, he becomes engaged to Alma's former music pupil, Nellie. More importantly, he comes to believe that there indeed does exist "an immaterial something" not visible to the eye or capable of being repre-sented on an anatomy chart. Williams strongly intimates, however, that if love and sex truly will be more easily fused and balanced in the marriage between John and Nellie, it will be so precisely because John had never bifurcated his identity in the first place by denying the flesh, as Alma did. As a sign of his own redemption and as a little act of kindness to thank Alma, John prevents Nellie, who feels only joy, from seeing the tears of hurt and loss on Alma's face.

If one charts the plot's progress as forming an hourglass pattern, in the way that several commentators have, John begins in the flesh and ascends to the spirit, while Alma begins in the spirit and descends to the flesh. As Marlon B. Ross, for example, expresses it: "in the tragic irony of *Summer and Smoke* that Williams makes movingly persuasive, these two characters need each other to be whole, but instead each is transformed into the other, John sacrificing his capacity to revel for Alma's earnestness, Alma sacrifi-cing her belief in the soul for John's capacity to experience the passion of flesh."[11] Yet even that oversimplifies; these two characters do, it is true, pass by one another in the night without ever experiencing any physical consummation, though they do, in the process, achieve a meeting of minds.

For Alma, too, comes to admit a fragmentation or division within herself, recognizing that a spiritualized angel like the figure named Eternity is a creature of unearthly existence, not of the here and now, for, in words that intimate a severely diminished rite of communion, "Her body is stone and her blood is mineral water" (237).

The final scene of the play, in which Alma – who has always felt troubled by the "wide stretches of uninhabitable ground" and "the enormous silence" (198–99) that characterized her few earlier attempts to connect with someone of the opposite sex – gives herself physically to the lonely traveling salesman, has prompted the most divergent interpretive comments. Whereas Durant da Ponte, for instance, judges this "a tawdry assignation – presumably the first of what will become an endless succession of such casual immoralities,"[12] Jack Brooking argues from an existentialist perspective that "It is unimportant to theorize about Alma's future and wrong to moralize upon the direction her life has taken [for] it has neither good nor evil connotations to her but reflects her new life where vague nostalgias and longings have been replaced by the fresh examination of experience."[13] Williams's choice of imagery emphatically hints that this action should not be seen as a descent into a life of profligacy but as a necessary antidote to human need, marking Alma's initiation into integrated personhood. Alma herself had expressed a surprisingly magnanimous acceptance (given how harshly she responded to John's conduct) of Nellie's mother, known as "the merry widow of Glorious Hill" for her assignations, foreshadowing Alma's own, with traveling salesmen, explaining: "I always say that life is such a mysteriously complicated thing that no one should really presume to judge and condemn the behavior of anyone else" (148). This, as we shall see, comes close to encapsulating Williams's own ethic as he expresses it most clearly through Hannah in *The Night of the Iguana*.

When, earlier in *Summer and Smoke*, John gave Alma the pills to calm her nerves, the "box rest[ed] in the palm of her hand" (187) as if she were – reminiscent of the stone angel's cupped posture – holding a communion wafer. Now, at the close, Alma offers to share one of her pills with the salesman, which he places "on his tongue" and washes down with water from the angel fountain, so that it becomes a kind of secular sacrament. The pills provide one of life's "little mercies" so that these two people "are able to keep on going": "The prescription number is 96814. I think of it" Alma remarks, "as the telephone number of God!" (254). Physical sexuality to assuage loneliness is also a part of that grace. Alma had always possessed spirituality. But now, as must become true of a creature of the earth after the Fall, she begins to experience her full humanity. When she gives her "valedictory salute" to the angel and then to the audience, it is a valediction forbidding mourning either for her or for her innocence that is well lost.

III

If the scene of the paradisal garden – both well lost and then, in a peculiarly Williamsesque and to some observers almost heretical (because sexual) way, regained – is never far from the audience's consciousness in *Summer and Smoke*, the garden imaged visually as well as verbally in *The Night of the Iguana* is more Golgotha and Gethsemane than Eden. True, for Nonno the luxuriant Mexican hilltop forest surrounding the Costa Verde Hotel returns him, near the end of his days, to the archetypal source of life, the sea. Yet this is not the age of innocence but of Hitler on the march, and this garden has been invaded by a German tank manufacturer and his family parading around nearly naked, "pink and gold like baroque cupids in various sizes – Rubenesque, splendidly physical" (261). Fueled by the erotics of power upon hearing a shortwave radio broadcast of the Battle of Britain, they burst into a rousing rendition of a "Nazi marching song." (Significantly, the communal songs of the female teachers on tour from the Baptist college echo the patriarchal pieties of the Germans.) In Act III, after the Germans have taunted the aged Nonno over his faltering memory when he tries to recite one of his verses, Shannon passes the playwright's own unassailable judgment upon them as they cheer the news that London is burning: "Fiends out of hell with the . . . voices of . . . angels" (351). Yet this almost inexplicable coexistence of culture with evil, the fact that supposedly highly civilized societies countenance and even become complicitous in inhuman acts, is nothing new to a colonized Mexico "caught and destroyed in its flesh and corrupted in its spirit by its gold-hungry conquistadors that bore the flag of the Inquisition along with the Cross of Christ" (305).

Iguana opened on 28 December 1961, starring Margaret Leighton and Bette Davis, and achieved a run of 316 performances, making it the dramatist's last Broadway success. Several things link what Williams himself thought of as a summative work with the play from almost fifteen years earlier, particularly the emphasis – a recurring one for Williams who early on adopted as his personal motto *"En avant!"* – about the need for tenacity and endurance. A profound and reflective work, *Night* arrives ultimately at a sense of tranquillity, perhaps more Eastern than Western in its sensibilities. Both Alma Winemiller in *Summer* and Hannah Jelkes in *Night,* in fact, are described in terms of Japanese and Chinese imagery. The former claims to "feel like a water lily on a Chinese lagoon" (255) during her encounter with the traveling salesman, while the latter at one point dons a Kabuki robe and is twice addressed by Shannon as "Miss Thin-Standing-Up-Female Buddha" (346–47).

Though the most realistically conceived among the dramatist's major plays, *The Night of the Iguana* still depends heavily upon symbolism for its meaning. In a preproduction article, Williams described the work as "more of a dramatic poem than a play [and so] bound to rest on metaphorical ways of expression" and justified more generally the visual poetry that is one of his distinctive hallmarks as a dramatist by commenting: "Some critics resent my symbols, but let me ask, what would I be without them? . . . Let me go further and say that unless the events of a life are translated into significant meanings, then life holds no more revelation than death, and possibly even less."[14] Set on the verandah of a hotel like the one where Williams himself had stayed in 1940, the design features "a line of small cubicle bedrooms" (253) across the back wall. Visually, these cell-like rooms concretize the universal human condition of locked doors and walls of incommunication, whereas "broken gates" between people constitute what we "know of God." The play's epigraph from Emily Dickinson speaks to this urgent effort, unallayed even by death and extending beyond time, to break through walls and talk "Until the moss [reaches] our lips" (247) and obliterates the names engraved on stone. Alma, too, as we have seen, had spoken of silence and spatial separation between individuals; the task Williams sets for himself in *Night*, however, involves broadening his inquiry to examine even more insistently the building of human community.

Arriving at the Costa Verde is the Reverend T. Lawrence Shannon, a defrocked Episcopalian priest – though he was locked out of his church for fornication and heresy, Hannah kindly refers to him as "A man of God, on vacation" (315) – now functioning as tour guide to the Baptist women led by Judith Fellowes, who is, perhaps out of sexual jealousy as much as from moral outrage, especially irate over Shannon's physical intimacies with the teenage Charlotte Goodall. Like the iguana caught and tied under the verandah for much of the play, Shannon, who has "cracked up," feels desperate, "at the end of [his] rope," but "still has to try to go on, to continue" (272). He fantasizes about achieving peace through a bottle or, if that fails, through a long suicidal swim to China. Undergoing a dark night of the soul, he yearns not for any mystical union but simply for human communion. Williams believed that in Shannon he "was drawing a male equivalent almost of a Blanche DuBois,"[15] who sought a similar surcease from isolation in an incessant search for an individual or a community that would accept and protect her.

Shannon's problem has always been an obsession with darkness and evil, a too-vivid sense of his fallen humanity, an excess of guilt, and an inability to forgive himself or believe in himself as redeemed. Being human means to be flawed, but not so flawed as to despair, which may be the worst evil of all – the unforgivable sin. His life, beginning from the time when his mother caught him masturbating and promised that if she did not exact punishment on him for finding pleasure, then God most certainly would, has been a recurring cycle of weakness, sin, guilt, and prayer to a "senile delinquent" and "angry, petulant old" God of vengeance who "blame[s] the world and brutally punish[es] all he created for his own faults in construction" (303–4), rather than to Hannah's Good Shepherd of calm who leads his creatures through "still waters." At one point, the gold cross that Shannon wears around his neck, no longer a sign of loving self-sacrifice and atonement, has become so much an albatross to him that he violently tries to tear it off. Although not always as explicit textually, the religious symbolism in *Night* is hardly less pervasive than in *Summer and Smoke*. A slightly delirious and self-destructive Shannon speaks of spiking Hannah's proffered poppyseed tea with hemlock and consecrating it in a kind of black Mass, and then effects a "voluptuous" and "painless atonement" restrained in a hammock, arms spread as if crucified. When he stretches out his hands to be washed in the rain, as his own God of "oblivious majesty" and dazzling power reveals himself in the "majestic apocalypse" of thunder and lightning, Shannon's body could well assume a cruciform position, since Hannah at one point labels his self-indulgent histrionics as a "Passion Play performance" (345).

Hannah – together with her aged grandfather, who admittedly appears as a loving homage to Williams's own maternal grandfather and who is attempting to complete one last poem before death – is another of the Costa Verde's transient guests, but one who must plead for a welcome. A middle-aged spinster painter of portraits, she has an "androgynous-looking" quality and possesses the air of an "ethereal . . . medieval saint" or "guardian angel" about her. As Jacob Adler remarks, "Here, for the first time [in Williams], is a central character who has *not* fallen, who is neither neurotic nor depraved, but who retains the virtues of vitality, sanity, kindness, faith, and courage, and who has resolved the problem of sex through virginity without prudery, intolerance, or psychological instability."[16] Hannah, too, has undergone her personal dark night – whether it involved coming to terms with her solitary sexual condition or an awareness of her limited artistic talent Williams leaves ambiguous – but she successfully "stared down" and beat back her own "blue devil," which is how the playwright himself referred to the terrors and fears he faced throughout his life.[17] To Shannon's way of thinking, one is particularly prone to torment by such a "spook" when faced with the tension between wanting to exist on some "fantastic level" that admits the unexplainable, but always being forced instead to operate on the more mundane "realistic" plane. Hannah, who understands full well that belief in something, or preferably "someone," outside of the self is essential to one's sense of wholeness or completion, acts as a catalyst, leading Shannon to rediscover in himself some spark of human-ness that will restore his confidence in his innate decency and worthiness of being saved. Yet precisely because he understands that there can never be any physical, in the sense of sexual, meeting between them, Shannon remains suspicious of her ability to help him. Only through her agency, however, can he finally escape from solipsism and perform some good act that will affirm his renewed faith.

Hannah and Shannon each articulate what might be broadly termed an artistic credo, and both these testaments reflect certain aspects of Williams's own hermeneutic as a writer. Hannah, as a quick-sketch portraitist, says that she "observe[s]" people but she does not "judge" them; though this does not necessitate being totally dispassionate, it does require that the artist move away from his or her own prejudices and grant to the work's subject its own integrity. Shannon's credo speaks, on the other hand, of the need to probe deep and plumb life in its totality, revealing its dark underside – and in so doing perhaps to shock the observers: "I always allowed the ones that were willing to see, to *see*! – the underworlds of all places, and if they had hearts to be touched, feelings to feel with, I gave them a priceless chance to feel and be touched. And none of them will ever forget it, none of them, ever, never!" (338). This latter strategy, indeed, is the one that Williams most often employed (to the dismay of his moralistic critics), and it echoes the playwright's own comments about opening up subjects and vistas that may previously have remained closed or off-limits to artistic representation: "I dare to suggest, from my POV [point of view], that the theater has made in our time its greatest artistic advance through the unlocking and lighting up and ventilation of the closets, attics, and basements of human behavior and experience."[18]

Both Shannon and Hannah go on to narrate a story. In his, Shannon admits not only to his frequent seduction of the ladies in his tour parties, but tells of deliberately exposing the women to such "horrors" as seeing the starving natives "creeping and crawling about this mound of [excrement] and occasionally stopping to pick something out of it, and pop it into their mouths. What? Bits of undigested . . . food particles" (369).[19] Tonally similar to the tale Catherine tells about cannibalism in *Suddenly Last Summer*, Shannon's episode causes the normally fastidious Hannah to retch. Hannah's own story, though more delicately told, is really equally shocking in its own way in its unvarnished expression of what she regards as an almost unbearable depth of loneliness, seldom encountered. In answer to Shannon's question of whether she ever had a "love experience," Hannah almost wistfully tells of two events in her life: of fleeing as a young girl from an unwanted hand upon her leg in a movie theatre; and much later in her life, at the expense of moving beyond her normal reticence, of accommodating the desire of the underwear fetishist out in a boat for a piece of her clothing he could hold while achieving orgasm. In response to Shannon's critical limitation that (mis)interprets this as a "sad, dirty little episode" (363), Hannah insists on the *loving* nature of the act, by which she responded compassionately and non-judgmentally to human need. And then she utters what is perhaps the most explicit statement to be found anywhere in his plays of Williams's own moral code and of the ethical lens through which his characters must be seen: "Nothing human disgusts me, unless it's unkind, violent" (363–64). Williams intended Hannah, he says, "almost as a definition of what I think is most spiritually beautiful in a person and still believable."[20]

In the almost intuitive kindliness and sympathy that the defrocked minister, who claims to "love nobody," has all along shown for her grand-father, Hannah recognizes the seeds for a potential renewal of Shannon's sense of dignity and worth. She urges him to build upon that remaining spark of goodness by releasing the caught and struggling iguana who, like themselves, is "one of God's creatures" (373). Shannon, in "a little act of grace" (Williams's original title for the play was *Two Acts of Grace*) akin to Hannah's unselfish acquiescence to the lonely man, cuts the rope setting the iguana free – somewhat like Coleridge's Ancient Mariner who "blessed [the watersnakes] unaware." Only then can Nonno complete his poem about living beyond despair, which alludes directly to Shannon's moral and emotional predicament.[21] So the result is art, and art seen almost in sacramental terms, of making whole a previously ruptured community. In fact, the names of the three central characters in *Iguana* underscore the dramatist's point about human interconnectedness, since "Shannon" con-tains all the letters needed to spell the other two, "Hannah" and "Nonno." And the listeners, like the Creator in Genesis, see that the poem "is good." Nonno's triumphant assertion, "It is finished," is, like the *consummatum est* of the cross, a sacrifice of self to years of toil to bring forth the saving word. For the completed poem recapitulates the central visionary statement of the play, of humankind's need to live after the Fall without succumbing to a stultifying spiritual malaise, even when the literal facts of existence would seem to preclude any hope. As Williams himself articulated it, "*The*

Night of the Iguana is a play whose theme, as closely as I can put it, is how to live beyond despair and still live."[22]

The mutuality that is key to the ethic affirmed by Hannah (and by Williams himself) extends to Maxine and Shannon as well and, in fact, provides the necessary clue to putting into proper perspective their relationship at play's end which, like Alma's with the traveling salesman, has been much misunderstood. If Hannah is ethereal, the hotel proprietress Maxine is earthy, making them somewhat akin to the contrasting Alma and John in *Summer and Smoke*. Maxine, a gutsy and "rapaciously lusty" recent widow, whose deceased husband Fred was given the Hart Crane-like burial at sea that Williams always wanted for himself but was finally denied, might seem all body to Hannah's all spirit. Williams is not, however, setting up a Manichean duality, but rather insisting once again on the need for accepting and embracing, rather than denying or outrightly condemning, the "unlighted side" of human nature: not everyone is capable of transcending to and existing upon the otherworldly plane of a Hannah. Maxine claims to "know the difference between loving someone and just sleeping with someone" and understands that "we've got to settle for something that works for us in our lives – even if it isn't on the highest kind of level" (329). What "mattered" in her marriage to Fred was satisfying sexual need; when that stopped they were able to reach an accommodation about her frequent infidelities that, far from destroying, actually solidified the mutual respect that they always felt for one another. In another of his intertextual poems – this one more jaunty doggerel than lyrical profundity – Williams has Nonno validate, even celebrate, this notion of *carpe diem*, urging his listeners to: "Dance to the candle while lasteth the wick, / . . . Gaze not before and glance not behind, / . . . But laugh with no reason except the red wine" (310–11). Maxine, albeit on the level of physical sexuality, will be able to keep Shannon from rotting and sustain him in a relationship that will enable him to reaffirm what remains of his life. Just as Hannah had to push the wheelchair-bound Nonno up the hill, so, too, Maxine, whose face now "wears a faint smile . . . suggestive of . . . the carved heads of Egyptian or Oriental deities," will "get [Shannon] back up the hill" (323–24) after their swim, something he feels unable to accomplish alone. The physical, so long as it is not predatory ("violent, unkind"), is never denigrated in Williams. So Shannon is able, through the grace of what might be seen as another variation on Alma's little pills, to rest in the bed of Maxine.

The focus at play's end remains on Hannah, and the Mexican hilltop that has become her Garden of Gethsemane. Alone now with the dead grandfather whose need for care had given her purpose, all that is left for her is to plaintively utter "can't we stop now?" (375) – her contemporary version of Christ's biblical plea, "if it be possible, let this cup pass from me: nevertheless not as I will . . ." Her going on, in a kind of Beckettian endurance beyond endurance, serves Williams well as a potent image of humankind's condition after the Fall.

NOTES

1 Tennessee Williams, *Summer and Smoke*, in *The Theatre of Tennessee Williams*, vol. II (New York: New Directions, 1971), 117–256.

2 Tennessee Williams, *The Night of the Iguana*, in *The Theatre of Tennessee Williams*, vol. IV (New York: New Directions, 1972), 247–376. Lyle Leverich reprints Williams's original version of the poem in *Tom: The Unknown Tennessee Williams* (New York: Crown, 1995), 379.

3 Tennessee Williams, *Something Cloudy, Something Clear* (New York: New Directions, 1995), 23.

4 Tennessee Williams, *The Mutilated* from *In the Bar of a Tokyo Hotel and Other Plays*, in *The Theatre of Tennessee Williams*, vol. VII (New York, New Directions, 1981), 82, 102, 119. A holograph copy of the poem, signed "Tenn" and dated "August 1941," is housed in the manuscript collection of the Butler Library at Columbia University, New York City; Leverich includes this previously unpublished poem in *Tom*, 419.

5 Gerard Manley Hopkins, "Spring and Fall: To a Young Child," Norman H. Mackenzie (ed.) *The Poetical Works of Gerard Manley Hopkins*, (Oxford: Clarendon Press, 1990), 166–67.

6 For the most extensive discussion of the play as allegory both of mankind and of the South, see Jacob H. Adler, "The Rose and the Fox: Notes on the Southern Drama," in Louis D. Rubin, Jr. and Robert D. Jacobs (eds.), *South: Modern Southern Literature in Its Cultural Setting*, (Garden City, New York: Doubleday, 1961), 353–60.

7 Tennessee Williams, *Memoirs* (Garden City, New York: Doubleday, 1975), 109.

8 For an extended review of the 1952 production, see John Gassner, "*Summer and Smoke*: Williams's Shadow and Substance," in *Theatre at the Crossroads: Plays and Playwrights of the Mid-Century American Stage* (New York: Holt, Rinehart, 1960), 218–23.

9 Tennessee Williams, quoted in "Studs Terkel Talks with Tennessee Williams," in Albert J. Devlin (ed.), *Conversations with Tennessee Williams*, (Jackson: University Press of Mississippi, 1986), 80.

10 Tennessee Williams, quoted in Leverich, *Tom*, 169.

11 Marlon B. Ross, "The Making of Tennessee Williams: Imagining a Life of Imagination," *Southern Humanities Review*, 21: 2 (Spring 1987), 131.

12 Durant da Ponte, "Tennessee Williams's Gallery of Feminine Characters," *Tennessee Studies in Literature*, 10 (1965), 19.

13 Jack Brooking, "Directing *Summer and Smoke*: An Existentialist Approach," *Modern Drama*, 2: 4 (February 1960), 385.

14 Tennessee Williams, "A Summer of Discovery," in Christine R. Day and Bob Woods (eds.), *Where I Live: Selected Essays*, (New York: New Directions, 1978), 142, 146.

15 Williams, quoted in "Studs Terkel," in *Conversations*, 80.

16 Jacob H. Adler, "*Night of the Iguana*: A New Tennessee Williams?" *Ramparts*, November 1962, 66.

17 Leverich, *Tom*, 174.

18 Tennessee Williams, "Tennessee Williams Presents His POV," in *Where I Live*, 116–17.

19 As Alice Griffin notes in *Understanding Tennessee Williams* (Columbia: University of South Carolina Press, 1995): "His story . . . is countered by Hannah's travel story of human 'acts of grace,' in the House for the Dying in Shanghai, in which relatives of the dying poor ease their last moments through small tokens of kindness" (225).

20 Williams, quoted in "Studs Terkel," in *Conversations*, 83.

21 For an extended explication of Nonno's poem as an encapsulation of "Shannon's spiritual history in 'timeless' form," see Ferdinand Leon, "Time, Fantasy, and Reality in *Night of the Iguana*," *Modern Drama*, 11: 1 (May 1968), 93–96.

22 Tennessee Williams, quoted in "Williams on Williams," interview by Lewis Funke and John E. Booth, in *Conversations*, 104.

BIBLIOGRAPHY

Adler, Jacob H. "*Night of the Iguana*: A New Tennessee Williams?" *Ramparts*, November 1962, 59–68.

"The Rose and the Fox: Notes on the Southern Drama," in *South: Modern Southern Literature in Its Cultural Setting*, ed. Louis D. Rubin and Robert D. Jacobs. Garden City: Doubleday, 1960, 349–75.

Boxill, Roger. *Tennessee Williams*. New York: St. Martin's Press, 1988, 94–107, 139–44.

Brooking, Jack. "Directing *Summer and Smoke*: An Existentialist Approach," *Modern Drama*, 2: 4 (February 1960), 377–85

Embrey, Glenn. "The Subterranean World of *The Night of the Iguana*," in Jac Tharpe (ed.) *Tennessee Williams: 13 Essays*, Jackson: University Press of Mississippi, 1980, 65–80.

Fritscher, John J. "Some Attitudes and a Posture: Religious Metaphor and Ritual in Tennessee Williams's Query of the American God," *Modern Drama*, 13: 2 (September 1970), 201–15.

Griffin, Alice. *Understanding Tennessee Williams*. Columbia: University of South Carolina Press, 1995, 81–104, 217–40.

Thompson, Judith J. *Williams's Plays: Memory, Myth, and Symbol* (University of Kansas Humanistic Studies vol. 54). New York: Peter Lang, 1987, 151–81.

7

JOHN M. CLUM

The sacrificial stud and the fugitive female in *Suddenly Last Summer*, *Orpheus Descending*, and *Sweet Bird of Youth*

CATHERINE: I tried to save him, Doctor.
DOCTOR: From what? Save him from what?
CATHERINE: Completing! – a sort of! – *image!* – he had of himself as a sort of! – *sacrifice* to a! – *terrible* sort of a –
DOCTOR: – God?
CATHERINE: Yes, a *cruel* one, Doctor!

Suddenly Last Summer

Tennessee Williams's Val Xavier, the itinerant sexual magnet of *Orpheus Descending* (1957), is immolated with a blowtorch on the night before Easter. Chance Wayne, the hustler hero of *Sweet Bird of Youth* (1959), is castrated on Easter Sunday. In between these two plays and acting as a queer gloss on them is the grotesque parody of the Eucharist in Sebastian Venable's crucifixion and consumption by the street urchins he has tasted in *Suddenly Last Summer* (1958). These three martyrs, Sebastian Venable, Val Xavier, and Chance Wayne, are sacrificed for violating their proscribed roles in the patriarchal sex/gender system. The possibility of a new sex/gender system is seen through the two central female characters in each play, one mutilated, the other healed. These plays, then, make a kind of trilogy, developing themes and characters seen in earlier plays and resolving in Williams's next dyad of quasi-religious acceptance, *The Night of the Iguana* (1961) and *The Milk Train Doesn't Stop Here Anymore* (1963–64). I want to focus here on the beautiful male as sexual martyr in these three plays, on the dynamics and erotics of the martyrdoms, and on the ways in which his relationship to the fugitive woman suggests a liberating possibility. To discuss Williams's depictions of the sex/gender system, one must also examine the relationship of homosexuality and heterosexuality in Williams's work.

THE TRAFFIC IN WOMEN / THE TRAFFIC IN MEN

In her groundbreaking essay, "The Traffic in Women: Notes Toward an Anthropology of Sex," Gayle Rubin defines the way in which gender (socially constructed masculine/feminine as opposed to the biological male/ female) is determined (by heterosexual men, of course) and the ways in which women's roles are determined by negotiations between men.[1] For instance, women are married to allow men to form tribal or national alliances. This system makes the woman the currency of masculine transactions. The system of heterosexual marriage also ensures the policing of compulsory heterosexuality by means of official homophobia, which never succeeds at the impossible task of eliminating homosexual desire or behavior. It may even find a limited space for such behavior within a system so long as heterosexual marriage is privileged.

Eve Kosofsky Sedgwick goes a step further than Rubin to show that the homosocial bonds between men – what is often called male bonding – for which women are the currency – contain elements of homophobia to "protect" them from the very real potential of homosexual desire often denied but inherent in such bonds.[2] Recently critics have been writing about the ways in which women forge potentially subversive bonds within this system and the ways in which those bonds are subverted by marriage.

In Williams's work, there is from the outset a different formulation. Instead of the woman being the apex of a triangle, with a bond between two men at its other poles, a man is at the apex, with a tentative bond or conflict between two women negotiated by them in order to establish a bond with the man. We see this in the scenes between Blanche and Stella in *A Streetcar Named Desire*. There the two sisters argue about Stanley. His sexual attractiveness is not questioned, but his worthiness as a marriage partner is. The conflict here is between Blanche's romantic, essentially asexual view of marriage, which may have led her to marry a homosexual but is hardly consonant with her subsequent promiscuity, and Stella's understanding that marriage is one avenue for sexual fulfillment, a channel for her healthy sexual appetite. Ostensibly Stella and conventional heterosexual marriage win, but only through Stella's denying the truth about Stanley's rape of Blanche. For all Stanley's macho posturing, it is Stella's denial that sends Blanche to the asylum, not Stanley's rape. When Blanche goes, so also goes the possibility of homosexuality which she brings into the play through the story of her husband and through her own camp behavior. At the end, Stanley does not stand triumphant. Rather, he kneels before Stella in a final tableau which shows her as the powerful figure in this heterosexual unit.

In *Suddenly Last Summer, Orpheus Descending*, and *Sweet Bird of Youth*, two women form a triangle with a man who is martyred, yet no relationship between a man and either of the women can be sustained. While the martyred men represent some violation of the socially acceptable principle of masculinity – that is, they are threats to marriage and patriarchy – it is the women who define the meaning of the martyrdom and who really offer the potential for change in the sex/gender system. In essence, as in the epigraph from *Suddenly Last Summer*, the women voice and define the men.

Though the focus is on the violence done to the male figure, the women are also in danger of mutilation and death. Catherine in *Suddenly Last Summer* is in danger of being lobotomized, Lady in *Orpheus Descending* is killed, and Heavenly in *Sweet Bird of Youth* has her womb surgically removed. Yet, for one of the women, there is also a healing process.

MARTYRS, HOMOSEXUALITY, AND ATONEMENT

Of these three martyrs, Sebastian Venable is the one who is most closely related to characters in earlier Williams plays. Like Blanche DuBois's husband, Allan Grey, in *A Streetcar Named Desire*, and Brick Pollitt's friend, Skipper, in *Cat On a Hot Tin Roof*, Sebastian is a dead gay man whose story is relegated to exposition, but he is the focus of the play from its first line, "Yes, this was Sebastian's garden" (350)[3] to Catherine's description of his gruesome death and its aftermath. Sebastian is another invisible homosexual, impossible to show on stage in the 1950s, though from the very beginning of his career, Williams insistently forged a space, however tentative, for the presentation of the homosexual. But these homosexuals in Williams's plays and stories always die a grotesque death, not so much as the expected punishment for their proscripted desire, but as the victim of rejection by those closest to them. Allan Grey shot himself after being publicly exposed and humiliated by his wife. Skipper drank himself to death when he became convinced of his homosexuality and when his best friend deserted him. One has to remember that *Cat On a Hot Tin Roof* takes place in the bedroom of a gay couple (dead, of course) who represent the play's only model for a long-term loving relationship.[4]

Sebastian Venable does not kill himself as Allan and Skipper do. In an aria of violence worthy of Euripides, his cousin Catherine relates how he was killed, stripped, and partially devoured. Understanding this primal scene is crucial to understanding the meaning of martyrdom in these plays of the late 1950s. As usual in Williams, the starting point for such an understanding is in Williams's stories, where we often find the first sketches of some of the plays and the crucial themes of the plays presented in more openly homosexual terms. Sebastian's bizarre death has its roots in Williams's short story, "Desire and the Black Masseur" (1946).

Anthony Burns, thirty years old, but still with the unformed face and body of a child, had a lifelong desire "to be swallowed up" which was only realized at the movies "where the darkness absorbed him gently so that he was like a particle of food dissolving in a big hot mouth" (205).[5] Anthony's life becomes devoted to attaining his desire.

In the story written just before *A Streetcar Named Desire*, Williams defines that favorite word of his – desire – more cogently than he does in any of his other works and relates it to Christian notions of guilt and atonement. We are told in one paragraph that "Desire is something that is made to occupy a larger space than that which is afforded by the individual being" (206), and in the next paragraph that "the sins of the world are really only its partialities, its incompletions, and these are what sufferings must atone for" (206). Man's weakness is that he is too small for his overwhelming desire. Atonement, the "surrender of self to violent treatment by others with the idea of thereby clearing one's self of his guilt" (206), is one compensation for one's smallness, one's inability to contain one's desire.

Anthony Burns discovered his sought-for compensation, atonement, in the baths. There a giant Negro masseur, who hated white men for their assaults on his pride, provided Anthony with violent massages which provided both sexual release and atonement. This transaction, like the transaction between hustler and john, seems to place desire in a loveless, materialistic framework, but Williams is always aware of the slippages in such a rigid formulation. For him, love can be found in any sexual connection, however brief or ostensibly cynical. In Williams's world, money is usually a factor in sexual transactions. If the ideal is a passion which transcends a world in which "there's just two kinds of people, the bought and the buyers," that is seldom and only briefly attained. The violent, paid transactions between Anthony and the masseur allowed both to enact their deepest desires and became for both, acts of love: "The giant loved Burns, and Burns adored the giant" (209). When Anthony's cries of pleasure/pain became too loud and the manager discovered his bruised, broken body, the Black masseur was fired. He carried the battered, but sated Anthony to his house in the Black section of town to continue their passion. The move from the place of business to the masseur's home is a move from a system of cash exchange to another system of consumption and a move into the world of the racial other.[6] Their final week together was at the end of Lent, Passion Week, within earshot of the services of atonement from the church across the street: "Each afternoon the fiery poem of death on the cross was repeated. The preacher was not fully conscious of what he wanted nor were the listeners groaning and writhing before him. All of them were involved in a massive atonement" (210), but none so massive as that of Anthony Burns, who died willingly and contentedly at the hands of his Black masseur. His last wish was also enacted when the giant masseur ate his body: "Yes, it is perfect, he thought, it is now completed" (211), a parody of Christ's last words on the cross, "Consumatum est."

Peace, perfection, serenity, completion, from this violent communion and literal consumption of the flesh. "Take, eat, this is my body which is given unto you," Christ said at the Last Supper, but he only spoke metaphorically. Always the pagan, Williams believed that true fulfillment of desire will come only from such a complete communion as that of Anthony Burns and his Black masseur. It is typical of Tennessee Williams that this story offers such a multiplicity of meanings. Here, unlike his plays, he can openly offer his vision in its original homosexual terms, though homosexuality only offers release in a brutal, final masochistic relationship. Here is not Blanche's belief that "The opposite of death is desire"; rather the fulfillment of desire is death and the only total relationship is a literal enactment of the Eucharist. Christianity offers a pale, symbolic approximation of the Dionysian sacrifice at the heart of real passion. But this passion also has a racial dimension, a joining of undeveloped white self with the gigantic, overwhelming Black other, yet this was love. Here is an allegory of race relations where perfection, communion, can only come through ritual violence, where cultures meet and atone. Here also is Williams's vision of religion, of guilt, and the need for atonement at the heart of our most basic needs. Sex and atonement are inextricably linked in a perversion of *imitatio Christi* which no one can escape. Those who act on their sexual desire contain their own policemen.

Anthony Burns and the Black masseur connected through simultaneous fulfillment of their separate desires, not through a romantic, spiritual joining. This idea is central to Williams's work: love, insofar as it exists at all, is the transient joining of two different desires contained in individuals who will always remain isolated, separate. This is why romantic love and marriage, straight or gay, seem to be impossibilities in Williams, or, at best, uneasy compromises. Williams's stories and dramas are sagas of solipsism. People may occasionally and briefly break through and connect with others, but their real dramas, passions, are enacted within. People may be the victims of awful violence, but they are often willing victims. This is why in Williams liberation can only come with death. One's self – body, mind, desires – is a turbulent drama from which one only exits through death.

Religion is one language for defining this combination of isolation, desire, and atonement. This formulation supports the idea that for Williams, despite his vaunted revolutionary politics, politics is contained within the individual, not in the relationship of individual to others and to the body politic.

While these principles are basic to all of Williams's work, we see them dramatized most vividly in this homoerotic, if not consistently homosexual, trilogy of male sacrifice and martyrdom written in the late 1950s. The aristocratic poet Sebastian Venable in *Suddenly Last Summer* is, like Anthony Burns, devoured by "the other" with whom he has been engaged in paid acts of sex. While Anthony Burns has desired anonymity, Sebastian has carefully, with the help of his doting mother, maintained an image of aristocratic superiority and artistic sensibility. When mother can no longer serve as policeman of the image, denying the homosexual reality underneath, Sebastian runs amok with starving Mediterranean urchins, revealing the underside of the image of old world pomp he and his mother have nurtured. When he decides he will no longer sexually consume these hungry boys, they literally consume him.

Suddenly Last Summer offers Williams's version of meaningful martyrdom. Its violence is tied up in complex ways with homosexual desire, which is described as voracious appetite: "Fed up with dark ones, famished for light ones: that's how he talked about people, as if they were – items on a menu" (375). It is far too easy to see, as some have done, Sebastian's death as poetic justice, the queer consumer consumed. Or, in a sexy replaying of the French Revolution, the predatory aristocrat torn asunder and eaten by the exploited peasantry. However, nothing in Williams is as simplistic as poetic justice, nor would Williams ever present a story so supportive of Puritan policing of desire. Sebastian's death is a working out of the connection of hunger and desire. Clearly Williams connected sex, at least homosex, and feeding, sating of appetite. As I have noted elsewhere, he was known to talk like this himself.[7] Here this connection of feeding and desire is clearly connected to religion, to Sebastian's search for God. *Suddenly Last Summer* is another expression of Williams's paganism in Christian terms, another blasphemous Eucharist. Sebastian's garden, the true expression of his vision of the fallen world, is filled with carnivorous plants. His vision of God is of birds of prey devouring the baby turtles as they rush toward the sea on the Galapagos Islands. His death is consonant with his own vision: the human birds of prey feast on his corpse as he sexually feasted on their bodies. Not divine justice, but divine economy. Hunger – hungers – desire – the operative principle. Nor is the sating of desire without its consequences. Sebastian does not seek atonement, but he gets it nonetheless. We are to see the cosmic meaning in this violent act as we see the inevitable failure of policing and silencing it.

INTERSECTING TRIANGLES

Suddenly Last Summer is structured as two conflicting narratives of Sebastian which represent the conflict between Catherine, who has seen "the truth" of Sebastian's life and death, and Sebastian's mother Violet (the color of penitence, atonement), who ruthlessly protects the eternally young, eternally chaste, image of her too-beloved son. To allow his image to age would be to admit age and mortality exist. To allow him sexuality would be to lose her primacy in his life. To acknowledge the ramifications and consequences of his vision would be to acknowledge an unbearable truth. Violet Venable wants her son to be a work of art, carefully tended like his carnivorous garden. Yet the "real" story Catherine tells is far richer, more interesting, more terrifying, than Violet's chaste version of Sebastian. To protect her version of Sebastian, Violet will order an act of violence as brutal as anything her son could conceive of: the destruction, the literal cutting apart, of a mind.

The competing agents of truth in this story are both women, the Solomonic arbiter an agent of the ultimate thought police, psychiatrists, who in America have a particularly bleak record in the immoral, impossible policing of homosexual desire. The blond, handsome "Dr. Sugar" is offered a large bribe to keep Violet's memory of Sebastian sweet. Catherine, who admits she "came out" sexually in the bohemian French Quarter before she "came out" as a debutante in the aristocratic Garden District, cannot deny what she has seen and experienced, despite the wishes of her poor family, desperately in need of Violet's largesse, or the threat of mental castration, lobotomy. Nor can Dr. Sugar honestly fulfill his function of denying what Catherine has seen. The ultimate, religious truth of Sebastian's death and devouring, as voiced by Catherine, is too powerful to be denied even by a psychiatrist.

While Dr. Sugar, both alien to this aristocratic hothouse through his Polish origins and rendered ineffectual by his sweet nickname, decides the outcome of the conflict between the two women, he is little more than a plot device. The women dominate the play as even Sebastian only exists as voiced by them. One question intrigues me: why must the "young, blond" Dr. Sugar be "very, very good looking"? Why couldn't Dr. Sugar look like . . . Sigmund Freud? Is the "glacially brilliant" doctor with his "icy charm" potentially homosexual? In fifties dramas, very good looks are often a sign of homosexuality. The only sign of Mr. Harris's homosexuality in Robert

Anderson's *Tea and Sympathy* is that he is described as "good looking." The beautiful blond man, Rodolpho, in Arthur Miller's *A View From the Bridge* is accused of being homosexual. Being too good looking, thus being looked at, was a sign of being not totally masculine, thus homosexual. Dr. Sugar is neither responsive to Mrs. Venable's steel magnolia charm nor to Catherine literally throwing herself at him: "*She crushes her mouth to his violently. He tries to disengage himself*" (403). This hint of a remaining homosexual potential after Sebastian's death means that there is no realistic closure to homosexuality in the play. Sebastian is not killed to remove homosexuality from the scene – only a heterosexual writer could maintain that formula – rather the narrative of his death keeps his vision and his sexuality alive, aided visually by the presence of that very, very good-looking man in a white suit just like the one Sebastian was wearing![8]

In "Desire and the Black Masseur" and *Suddenly Last Summer*, we see the daring of Williams that makes him our greatest playwright, the willingness to go to extremes beyond even the absurdities of melodrama to share his frightening vision with his reader and his audience. Like the mad extremes of Euripides' *The Bacchae*, these works offer a Dionysian vision of human experience, made more vivid by the contrast with the mundane "reality" of modern American life and the futile attempts to deny those acts which are most human and most godlike. But to what end? At the conclusion of *Suddenly Last Summer*, Catherine's story has freed her from the threat of a lobotomy, but the characters move off in different directions, disconnected. The truth of Sebastian's story is also the truth of isolation. At the end of the play Violet and Catherine leave the stage separately and alone with their memories of Sebastian.

THE MARTYRDOM OF THE PASSIVE STUD

In Williams's early plays, the sexually transgressive figure was the woman. In *A Streetcar Named Desire* (1947), Blanche DuBois can play the prim Southern belle, but her proudest moment is ravishing the soldiers from the nearby base, leaving them spent on the grass where "later the paddy wagon would gather them up like daisies" (389). Blanche is a wild card in the seven card stud game that is the sex/gender system. For that the men in the play must humiliate and punish her, but Williams is on the side of queer, if not gay, Blanche. The parodic image of the heterosexual family that ends the play does not provide a final resolution. The Blanches of the world endure if they do not yet prevail. Alma Winemiller in *Summer and Smoke* (1948) moves from being a prim, hysterical, preacher's daughter to a sexually liberated woman willing to find her transient fulfillments in occasional sex –

the kindness of strangers – but Alma is not punished. Her liberation is her triumph, her cavalier's plume. It is her beloved John, who moves from wildness to conventional marriage, who is crying when we last see him.

There are three sexually transgressive figures in *Orpheus Descending*: Carol Cutrere, Val Xavier, and Lady Torrance. Carol, the wayward daughter of the richest family in town, is a self-confessed exhibitionist and "lewd vagrant." Strangely made up like a punk before her time, Carol is the only true rebellious spirit in the small Southern town in which the play takes place. Like her predecessors in Williams's plays, she asks for the pleasure she craves. She sees herself as a remnant of an earlier, less civilized time: "This country used to be wild, the men and women were wild and there was a wild sort of sweetness in their hearts, for each other, but now it's sick with neon, it's broken out sick with neon, like most other places" (327).[9] Carol is often accompanied by an old Black Conjure Man whom she pays to give a wild Choctaw Indian cry from another place and time. The sexual energy, the wildness of the past, is heard in the cry of racial otherness, Native American and Black. But Carol's wildness is no threat to the Southern patriarchal order. She is a remittance relative, paid to get out of town, but not in danger when she breaks her contract and appears. She is an embarrassment to her family and an outrage to the women, but nothing more. Yet only Carol understands the threat Val represents to the community, and his mythic status as well as his sexual attraction. It is she who warns him of the danger he is in and it is she who remains to define him at the end of the play.

Val Xavier is mutilated and sanctified for his sexual potency, which is a threat to other men because the sexual free agent is a magnet, drawing women outside the boundaries of patriarchal authority and marriage. Val first appears as if summoned by the Conjure Man's wild Choctaw cry. The stage directions tell us that Val "*has the kind of wild beauty about him that the cry would suggest*" (240). He wears a snakeskin jacket, a kind of Dionysian remnant of his link with the wildness of nature and human desire, but also connoting the Judeo-Christian notion of temptation. He also carries with him a guitar, his version of Orpheus's lyre, but Val's guitar connects him to the blues, and through them to the racial other, the Black. On his guitar are inscribed the names of great Black musicians: Leadbelly, Bessie Smith, King Oliver, and Fats Waller.

Val has lived the life of a vagabond, singing and playing in New Orleans bars, but the day he appears in this small-town general store is his thirtieth birthday, "and I'm through with the life I've been leading. I lived in corruption but I'm not corrupted" (261). Val does not lament the loss of youth as many of Williams's characters do, but he wants to retain the freedom of youth. He wants to remain "uncorrupted" which for him means remaining outside the materialistic system of ownership. He tells Lady Torrance:

VAL: Lady, there's just two kinds of people, the ones that are bought and the buyers! No! – there's one other kind . . .
LADY: What kind's that?
VAL: The kind that's never been branded. (265)

The only way to remain uncorrupted is to be like "a kind of bird that don't have legs so it can't light on nothing but has to stay all its life on its wings in the sky" (265). Such freedom may be an impossible goal, but the free bird is also isolated, as all beings are: "We're all of us sentenced to solitary confinement inside our own skins, for life!" (271). The impossibility of the freedom Val so eloquently describes, and the inevitability of the isolation he laments are borne out by the action of the play.

Val takes a job working in the general store Lady runs for her terminally ill husband. Lady, the other figure in this female-dominated triangle, is an Italian-American whose father ran a wine garden where young couples came to have sex. The garden was burned down and Lady's father burned up when a Ku Klux Klan-like group discovered that he sold liquor to Blacks. Eighteen-year-old Lady had been left by her lover, David Cutrere, Carol's brother, who married for money to save the family home. David and Lady had had an extraordinarily passionate relationship, "Like you struck two stones together and made a fire! – yes – fire" (230). Broke and bereft, Lady is "sold cheap" to Jabe Torrance who, unbeknownst to her, led the gang that killed her father. Now Lady lives for the moment she turns part of the general store into a recreation of her father's wine garden, recreating the sexually free past the men in the town destroyed and the site of her moment of passion and happiness.

We are told by the women who form a kind of Greek chorus – while patriarchy may be conditionally restored, women have the dominant voices in this play – that Lady's marriage is sexless and barren, that she and her husband live in separate rooms on opposite sides of the dark second floor of the general store, that her only previous passion was with David Cutrere. David had to give up their relationship for economic survival and Lady had to marry, to sell herself, for economic survival. The store represents the barren world of commerce, of people bought and sold, that Val tries to rise above. The minute he literally moves into that store, he places himself at great risk, for he makes himself vulnerable to a dehumanizing system. The system, itself barren, will not allow Lady fertility. Twice she is robbed of motherhood.

Val may be able to resist Carol Cutrere, but his sexual magnetism is still his undoing. Val becomes the one person who will listen to the blind visionary sheriff's wife, Vee, but twice the sheriff catches them in moments of innocent physical contact, a result of their spiritual understanding. The sheriff delivers an ultimatum to Val: "Boy, don't let the sun rise on you in this county" (321), an echo of a common Southern threat, "Nigger, don't let the sun go down on you in this county" (320). Val's perceived threat to a powerful man's property – his wife – turns him into a "Nigger." Val has also, somewhat reluctantly, slept with and impregnated Lady Torrance. There is no conventional love scene. Like Blanche, Alma, and Carol Cutrere, Lady takes what she wants and needs to bring herself back to life. Once Lady realizes that she is pregnant, that she has life within her, she can let Val go. The man who wants to avoid being seen merely as the stud has been just that.

However strong the women are, the men of the town provisionally restore the sex/gender system. On Easter eve, Lady's dying husband comes down the stairs from his bedroom with a gun, shoots Lady and shouts that Val has killed his wife and robbed his store. The townsmen, probably the same ones who killed Lady's father and burned down his wine garden, take a blowtorch and incinerate Val.

The primary images in *Orpheus Descending* are heat and fire. Val's body temperature is two degrees warmer than most humans, a reflection of his sexual energy. In a strange sex reversal, Val is in heat and arouses all the females who come near him. But Val's heat is countered by the fire that destroys all signs of sexual energy, the orgiastic wine garden and Val himself. The fire is the fire of a human hell and Val, like Orpheus, has the power to bring the woman he loves out of the abyss: "I guess my heart knew that somebody must be coming to take me out of this hell! You did. You came. Now look at me! I'm alive once more!" (333). But, like Orpheus's Eurydice, Lady's rescue is temporary. Characteristically, Williams mixes pagan mythology with Christian. This Orpheus is killed on Easter eve. Val is Christ, Dionysus, and Eros combined, the spiritual principle and the sexual principle, or rather the sexual principle made spiritual, seeking an impossible freedom.[10]

In essence, Val is killed for bringing life to the town. He literally brings life to the imprisoned, embittered Lady. He also enables the visions that inspire Vee's religious paintings. He is killed by men who can only bring death and destruction. Val, the disseminator of Black culture through his music, the rebel who will not conform to patriarchal order, threatens the social order by bringing life and a measure of autonomy to the women. The men do not win, however. At the end, Carol has Val's snakeskin jacket:

"Wild things leave skins behind them, they leave clean skins and teeth and white bones behind them, and these are tokens passed from one to another, so that the fugitive kind can always follow their kind"(341). Carol refuses to obey the sheriff's order to stop and walks past him as if she hasn't seen him. The old Black Conjure Man is alone on stage as the curtain falls. The victory of the white patriarchy is temporary at best. The spirit embodied in Val still exists and prevails, but through the body and voice of a transgressive, isolated woman.

Ironically, Val, the reluctant stud, is a relatively passive character. He attracts women but tries to resist their attempts to take what they want from him. Freedom for him means freedom not only from the world of people being bought and sold, but freedom from women. He will not have sex in the graveyard with Carol Cutrere (another mix of death and desire), and he tries to leave when he realizes that Lady wants to set him up as live-in lover as well as employee: "A not so young and not so satisfied woman that hired a man off the highway to do double duty without paying overtime for it . . . I mean a store clerk days and a stud nights, and – " (304). When Lady cries out her need for him, he walks into the alcove where he sleeps. Lady must be the aggressor and go in and take him. The sheriff may see Val's hand on his wife's bosom, but she put it there.

Williams transfers to his heterosexual redeemer the qualities of his earlier homosexual martyrs: Oliver Winemiller, the beautiful one-armed hustler who is electrocuted with the letters of his male admirers shoved between his legs; the beaten and eaten Anthony Burns (note the last name!). As these beautiful men, straight or gay, are erotic fantasies for Williams, so their mutilation is an erotic fantasy, the ultimate communion with them. There is a book to be written on physical mutilation as a sign of homosexuality in gay drama, the mark of a vindictive heterosexist society. In some of Williams's plays, the mutilation is a sign of a potential gay reading of the straight body.

Why the move from the homoerotics of the stories to the heterosexuality of *Orpheus Descending*? One could make a case that this is Williams presenting what he thinks his audience will tolerate, but there were references to homosexuality all through the highly successful *Cat on a Hot Tin Roof*. Moreover, as Rory B. Egan points out, "The homosexuality of Orpheus is a feature of several ancient versions of the story, including Ovid's, and it is usually a concomitant of his attractiveness to women and their resentment at his hostility or indifference."[11] Is Val necessarily exclusively heterosexual? He has bummed around the French Quarter, and throughout the play he tries to avoid sexual contact with the women who pursue him. Williams came out at a time when there was less delineation between straight and gay, when the secrecy surrounding homosexuality made it possible for men to have sex with other men without fear of being branded as homosexual. Seeing a straight "stud" as sexually attractive and available was a reality as well as a fantasy in the pre-Stonewall years in which Williams spent his young manhood.[12] Indeed, Val's reluctance and passivity suggest a sexually ambiguous figure. This is not the aggressive stud, a cousin of Stanley Kowalski. Val is more akin to Doctor Sugar. It is the women who are active, taking what they want from the men.

The world of *Orpheus Descending*, like that of *Suddenly Last Summer*, is one of powerful women and sexually ambivalent men. The patriarchs seem impotent, capable of killing but not of creating life. There is no place for marriage in this Amazon society in which the man's basic function is to be, however reluctantly, "stud at bay." In killing Val and Lady, the men kill part of the potential for a new, non-patriarchal gender order. But at the final curtain, there is still Carol, Val's snakeskin jacket, and the wild Choctaw cry. Carol represents freedom and isolation in a play that denies all human connection except brief sexual encounter. As Val declares: "Nobody ever gets to know *no body!* We're all of us sentenced to confinement inside our own skins, for life!" (271).

THE STUD CORRUPTED

In all three plays of male martyrdom, we are in symbolic landscapes: from the carnivorous creation of a malevolent God in *Suddenly Last Summer*, to the Southern Hades of *Orpheus Descending* where fire reigns, to the heavenly world of St. Cloud on the "gulf of misunderstanding," the setting of *Sweet Bird of Youth*, where impotent men emasculate those who threaten their power. *Sweet Bird of Youth*, like its companion pieces, is comprised of intersecting triangles: Chance, Heavenly, and Heavenly's father, Boss Finley; but far more important, Chance, Heavenly, and Alexandra del Lago. The two women never meet, but offer the two sexual and emotional possibilities Chance experiences in the play. Heavenly is a mirage, the shell of the girl Chance loved, but Chance, denying the power of time, believes that regaining her is regaining his youth and his purity. The aging star Alexandra del Lago is very real, complete with grand neuroses and the means to temporarily forget them. She is also, like many of Williams's heroines – Alma, Maggie the Cat, Catherine – an agent of truth forcing a weak man to confront reality.

Chance, figuratively, is the black-sheep brother of Brick Pollitt in *Cat on a Hot Tin Roof*. Like Brick, he wants his world to be what it was when he was a teenager, but Brick had real athletic ability while Chance never had

Figure 6 The bar scene in *Sweet Bird of Youth*, showing Mielziner's use of lighting in combination with Kazan's composition. Madeleine Sherwood as Miss Lucy, Paul Newman as Chance, Charles McDaniel as Scotty

much more than his looks to depend on. Brick's one experience of ideal beauty was his asexual friendship with Skipper. His desire to live stopped when he realized that friendship was not as ideal as he thought. Chance had one glorious moment of beauty in bed with Heavenly on a speeding train and lives to recreate that moment. There is purity in Chance's futile dream, but Chance's link with reality is more tentative than that of most Williams characters, male or female.

If Val Xavier resists entering the world of buyers and bought, Chance is totally absorbed into that world. Chance is a gigolo, a man who lives off the money of the women who hire him for sex and companionship. The gigolo is the most fascinating case of reversal of the sex/gender system. The woman is in financial control and pays the financially dependent man to service her physically and emotionally. His looks and his sexual prowess are his most important assets. Williams, no stranger to hiring men for sex, used the related (sometimes identical) figures of the male hustler in a number of works, particularly the story "One Arm," the novel *The Roman Spring of Mrs. Stone*, and the plays *Sweet Bird of Youth* and *The Milk Train Doesn't Stop Here Anymore* in which the paid companion, Christopher Flanders, functions symbolically as the angel of death.

To the men in power in St. Cloud, Chance is a "criminal degenerate," a phrase usually applied to homosexuals. *Sweet Bird of Youth* is one instance of a Tennessee Williams play which was first intended to present a homosexual relationship, then "heterosexualized." In his study of the sketches and manuscripts of *Sweet Bird of Youth*, Drewey Wayne Gunn explains:

> In most early versions, including the ones which led directly to Act I of *Sweet Bird*, "she" is Artemis Pazmezoglu, a plump but spiritually attractive man vaguely connected in Hollywood. In some drafts, Art is in retreat in Phil's [the early name for Chance] home town, and Phil searches him out for help with his faltering acting career. But in the most important draft of this series, Art has picked Phil up in Miami, fallen in love with him on a nonphysical basis (he is too old for sex, he says), passed out drunk, and been driven by Phil to his home town to search out the old girlfriend. . .the daughter of Boss Finley.[13]

Williams was right: a sexual relationship with a woman had more dramatic interest than a one-sided nonsexual homosexual crush (all the 1950s would allow). Yet, oddly, Chance considers himself metaphorically "castrated" for being treated as what he is, a gigolo (120). When in the first scene Alexandra del Lago scoffs at his attempts to blackmail her and orders him to perform in bed, Chance turns puritan:

> PRINCESS: Chance, I need that distraction. It's time for me to find out if you're able to give it to me. You mustn't hang onto your silly little idea that you can increase your value by turning away and looking out a window when somebody wants you . . . I want you . . . I say now and I mean now, then and not until then will I call downstairs and tell the hotel cashier that I'm sending a young man down with some traveler's checks to cash for me . . .
>
> CHANCE [*turning slowly from the window*]: Aren't you ashamed a little?
> PRINCESS: Of course I am. Aren't you?
> CHANCE: More than a little . . .   (44)[14]

What should the Princess be ashamed of? That she wants what she has paid for? Why should Chance feel ashamed and later claim that this is a moment of castration? The Princess is doing what Williams's strong women do – claim their right to sexual satisfaction – but she places it within a material economy. It is this commodification that unmans Chance. Chance is the male version of the whore with the heart of gold, a loving romantic at heart, who is redeemed by voicing patriarchal judgments on his relinquishment of masculine power. His corruption is caused by his entrapment within a materialistic system. He is, in Val Xavier's formulation, one of the bought. He tries to gain power over Alexandra by blackmailing her, but he is no match for such a ruthless pragmatist: "When monster meets monster, one monster has to give way, AND IT WILL NEVER BE ME. I'm an older hand at it . . . with much more natural aptitude at it than you have" (43). Chance is also unmanned by his conventionality, his futile insistence on conventional masculine prerogatives.

Unlike Alexandra del Lago, Heavenly is an impossibility. Her father will never let Chance take her away and she is nothing but a "dream of youth," broken and rendered sterile by the venereal disease Chance gave her, now forced to marry the doctor who cut out her diseased womb.

Alexandra offers Chance a way to get out of town and avoid the impending very real castration that has been ordered for him. He can remain in her employ:

PRINCESS: You'd better come down with my luggage.
CHANCE: I'm not part of your luggage.
PRINCESS: What else can you be?
CHANCE: Nothing . . . but not part of your luggage.   (122)

When his dream of youth is gone, Chance has nothing left but his pride. He would rather face castration than be Alexandra's toyboy.

Chance is castrated, not killed, but in Williams's world in which sex is life, castration *is* death. His castration is ordered by Boss Finley, the ruthless politico who "can't cut the mustard." It will be enacted by his sexually profligate son and his friends. Boss Finley is campaigning for castration of Blacks who commit miscegenation, and Chance is to have the Black man's punishment for corrupting and polluting his too-beloved daughter. While castration links Chance to the racial other and the term "criminal degenerate" links him to a sexual other, impotence and castration seem to be the way of the world. When Chance tells Alexandra that her forcing him to perform sexually was a form of castration, she counters, "Age does the same thing to a woman" (120). The surgeon's knife does it to Heavenly, but indirectly Chance has castrated her by giving her "the whore's disease."

Sweet Bird of Youth takes place on Easter Sunday, suggesting a redemption the play doesn't allow for. Easter is used ironically here, for there is no escape from time or mortality: "Time – who could beat it, who could defeat it ever? Maybe some saints and heroes, but not Chance Wayne." There is no heaven, only the half-dead Heavenly and the corrupt St. Cloud. The church bells ring at the beginning of the play, but the bell does not toll for the likes of Chance or Alexandra del Lago who live in a world of the body. Anyway, religion is depicted in the play as hypocrisy, the tool of megalomaniacs like Boss Finley.

The play celebrates the endurance of Alexandra del Lago, capable of honesty with herself and others and capable of shining moments of compassion, even love. Yet Alexandra also knows that one is always, essentially, alone in beanstalk country. Alexandra prevails because she is, like her creator, "artist and star!": "Out of the passion and torment of my existence I have created a thing that I can unveil, a sculpture almost heroic, that I can unveil, which is true" (120). Alexandra's acting, recorded on film, can fight time. Only art can, and one can not finish discussing these three plays without considering the importance of art. Sebastian was an artist remembered, unfortunately, for the way he died rather than for his poems of summer. Val was a singer, carrying the legacy of great singers. That legacy remains. Alexandra's triumphs still exist even if her career is almost over. Sex, too, momentarily transcends time, but only momentarily. It is odd that a gigolo wouldn't understand that. But how many American heroes are prized precisely for their lack of understanding?

Perhaps the oddest moment in *Sweet Bird of Youth* is its end in which Chance steps before the audience: "I don't ask for your pity, but just for your understanding – not even that – no. Just for your recognition of me in you, and the enemy, time, in us all." Donald Spoto calls this "the single most jarring interruption of dramatic structure in Williams's work."[15] Williams has seldom been so concerned with giving his leading man the last word, and what a strangely qualified utterance it is. Are we to feel more for the feckless, deluded Chance, the loser, than we feel for Alexandra del Lago, who faces her situation and moves on? Chance only gives up his futile illusions when Alexandra confronts him with the truth about himself and Heavenly. What does he gain by submitting to castration? Is not living with the fact of "the enemy, time," more heroic than giving up because of it? The ending is jarring and weak because, for once, Williams does not understand that the woman, Alexandra, is the core of the play, not Chance. Alexandra's last words to Chance offer the philosophy of adaptability and endurance that are the positive counter to the mutilation of Williams's martyrs: "So come on, we've got to go on" (124). Like many of Williams's heroic women, Alexandra has the strength to face an uncertain, potentially bleak future. Chance, the passive stud, frozen in time, incapable of compromise, can only submit to the completion of his emasculation.

NOTES

1 Gayle Rubin, "The Traffic in Women: Notes Toward a Political Economy of Sex," *Toward an Anthropology of Women*, ed. Rayna Reiter (New York: Monthly Review Press, 1975), 157–210.

2 Eve Kosofsky Sedgwick, *Between Men: English Literature and Male Homosocial Desire* (New York: Columbia University Press, 1985).

3 Tennessee Williams, *Suddenly Last Summer*, *The Theatre of Tennessee Williams*, vol. III (New York: New Directions, 1971), 343–423.

4 For a full discussion of homosexuality in *Cat on a Hot Tin Roof*, see my *Acting Gay: Male Homosexuality in Modern Drama*, revised edn. (New York: Columbia University Press, 1994), 156–62. David Savran also has an excellent, extended discussion of homosexuality in Williams's works in *Communists, Cowboys, and Queers: The Politics of Masculinity in the Work of Arthur Miller and Tennessee Williams* (Minneapolis: University of Minnesota Press, 1992), 76–174.

5 Tennessee Williams, "Desire and the Black Masseur," *Tennessee Williams: Collected Stories* (New York: New Directions, 1985), 205–12.

6 David Savran points out that in Williams's work, "With a remarkable consistency, desire is provoked by differences in race, ethnicity, social class, and age. Almost inevitably, subject and object are configured as antitheses that are congruent with a series of binary oppositions – white/black, wealthy/poor, old/young. Almost inevitably the first in the pair is granted the priority of the desiring subject, while the second is objectified and exoticized, and thereby endowed with the power to arouse sexual desire." *Communists, Cowboys, and Queers*, 125.

7 "While in Italy in 1948, Williams wrote Donald Windham: '[Frederick Prokosch] says that Florence is full of blue-eyed blonds that are very tender hearted and 'not at all mercenary.' We were both getting an appetite for blonds as the Roman gentry are all sort of dusky types.' Sebastian's unfeeling sexual exploitation is as much a dramatization of the playwright as is Sebastian's pill-popping and confused sense of private and public personae." "'Something Cloudy, Something Clear': Homophobic Discourse in Tennessee Williams," in Ronald Butters, John M. Clum, and Michael Moon (eds.), *Displacing Homophobia: Studies in Gay Male Literature and Culture*, (Durham, N.C.: Duke University Press, 1989), 157–58.

8 I am aware that Dr. Sugar claims to have a girlfriend he cannot afford to marry, but does this excuse ring true for a doctor even in a state hospital in 1935? He would be better off than much of the Depression-era population who did get married.

9 Tennessee Williams, *Orpheus Descending*, *The Theatre of Tennessee Williams*, vol. III (New York: New Directions, 1971), 217–342. This line also appeared in *Battle of Angels* (1940), Williams's disastrous first "Broadway" play (actually the Broadway production was scuttled after the Boston tryout), which he rewrote extensively and retitled *Orpheus Descending*. The latter made it to Broadway, but closed after sixty-eight performances. It was made into a movie entitled *The Fugitive Kind* (screenplay by Williams, directed by Sidney Lumet) with Anna Magnani and Marlon Brando. *Battle of Angels* appears in volume I of *The Theatre of Tennessee Williams*.

10 I will not recount all the Orphic and Christian parallels that can be mined out of a careful reading of *Orpheus Descending*. For the fullest account, see Rory B. Egan, "Orpheus Christus Mississippiensis: Tennessee Williams's Xavier in Hell" in *Classical and Modern Literature: A Quarterly*, 14 (1993), 61–98.

11 Egan, "Orpheus Christus Mississippiensis," 81. Orpheus is, in the myth, brutally murdered by a band of women, not by men, as in Williams's play.

12 In his recent memoir, *Palimpsest*, Gore Vidal recounts the postwar world of New York's Astor Hotel bar, before what he calls "the ghettoization of 'gay' and 'straight.'" There Alfred Kinsey interviewed male subjects for his revolutionary study of sexual behavior in the human male: "I like to think that it was by observing the easy trafficking at the Astor that he figured out what was obvious to most of us, though as yet undreamed of by American society at large: perfectly 'normal' young men, placed outside the usual round of family and work, will run riot with each other." (New York: Random House, 1995), 102.

13 Drewey Wayne Gunn, "The Troubled Flight of Tennessee Williams's *Sweet Bird*: From Manuscript through Published Texts," *Modern Drama* 24 (1981), 29.

14 Tennessee Williams, *Sweet Bird of Youth*, *The Theatre of Tennessee Williams*, vol. IV (New York: New Directions, 1972), 44.

15 Donald Spoto, *The Kindness of Strangers: The Life of Tennessee Williams* (New York: Ballantine, 1986), 257.

8

NANCY M. TISCHLER

Romantic textures in Tennessee Williams's plays and short stories

> I believe in Michelangelo, Velásquez and Rembrandt; in the might of design, the mystery of color, the redemption of all things by beauty everlasting and the message of art that has made these hands blessed. Amen.

This, Tennessee Williams proclaimed to be his own creed as an artist.[1] Like his "Poet" of the short story by that name, Tennessee Williams was a natural romantic whose very existence was one of "benevolent anarchy" ("The Poet," 246). His artistic *creed* (a term of some significance to a man nurtured in theology) signals the primacy of the artist, not God. He was dedicated to: (1) the power of "design" or artistic control over the material world; (2) the "mystery" of color or the non-rational, supernatural gift of beauty, affecting the artist and the audience; (3) the "redemption" of all things by "beauty" – an act of salvation by means of created and experienced splendor; (4) the "message" of art, the need to communicate the artist's vision of reality to the audience; and (5) the "blessedness" of his hands – his conviction that he is the chosen vessel for this important work.

CREDO: "I BELIEVE IN . . ." WILLIAMS'S ROMANTIC INFLUENCES

Thomas Lanier Williams, also known as Tennessee, was born to be a visionary. He gathered ideas, images, themes, and phrases as he wandered through life and wove colorful romantic pictures onto the dark background of his increasing realism to form grand designs and vivid contrasts. He lived his life as a peripatetic poet, one of the everlasting company of fugitives who discover their vocation in their art, transforming experience and giving shape to visions.[2]

Descended from colonial settlers and pioneers, he was quintessentially American, but never a typical pragmatic middle American. He saw himself as the archetypal outsider: a poet in a practical world, a homosexual in a heterosexual society. Living in the "Century of Progress," he preferred candlelight to electricity. A Southerner who lamented the loss of a dignity,

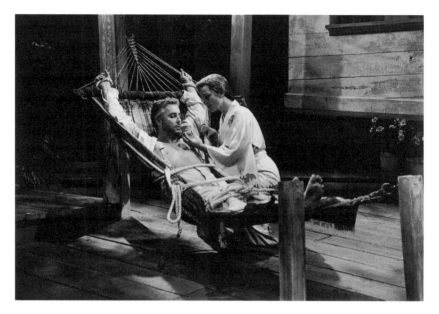

Figure 7 Hannah (Cherry Jones) feeds Shannon (William Petersen) some calming poppy seed tea in *The Night of the Iguana*, directed by Robert Falls, The Goodman Theatre, Chicago, 1994

elegance, and sense of honor, he was never satisfied with the dreary present and its flat speech. Williams yearned for "long distance," for "cloudy symbols of high romance," or what romantics called the "yonder bank."[3] His characters love a lost, idealized past ("Blue Mountain"), and they live for a dangerous, problematic future ("Terra Incognita"). From beginning to end, Williams's theatrical struggle was also a romantic quest for Parnassus. It was romantic dreamers – quixotic and tattered old warriors, fragile young poets, frightened misfits – whom he celebrated in his poems, stories, novels, and plays. Romanticism was the very fabric of his life and work – woven throughout. In his early self-descriptions for Audrey Wood, his longtime agent, he presented a persona deliberately crafted as the romantic loner.[4] This portrait of the peripatetic, penniless writer was then polished and repeated in many articles, interviews, and biographies which followed. (Note especially *Conversations with Tennessee Williams*[5] and *Where I Live*.)

In a statement for the press, developed at the time *The Night of the Iguana* was premiering in New York, he showed that he was aware of his obsession with what he called "the Visionary Company": "This new play, *The Night of the Iguana*, and the one to follow, off-Broadway, which is presently titled *The Milktrain Doesn't Stop Here Anymore*," he explained, "both contain major characters who are poets, and this was not planned, it just happened." He then continues: "In *Suddenly Last Summer* the chief topic of discussion and violent contention was also a poet. So obviously the archetype of the poet has become an obsessive figure, a leit-motif in my recent work for the stage, and possibly was always, since Tom Wingfield in *The Glass Menagerie* was a poet, too, and so was Val Xavier in *Orpheus Descending* essentially a poet, for a singer is a kind of poet, too, just as a poet is a kind of singer."

He then explains that "the idea, the image, of a poet has come to represent to me, as a writer, an element in human-life that put up the strongest resistance to that which is false and impure, in himself and the world . . ." Such a person is "always a tragic antagonist."

Finally, waxing eloquent about this figure, Williams announces that, "If he is really a poet, by vocation, not affectation, his sword Excalibur or his Holy Grail, is truth as he himself conceives it, and he believes in it as an absolute, as many non-practicing poets in the world also do."[6] Here, most clearly we have the romantic imagery of the chosen vessel for divinely inspired activity.

Williams's letters, his early drafts, his short stories, and his plays often signal the particular artists whose lives captured his attention: D. H. Lawrence, Vachel Lindsay, William Wordsworth, and George Gordon, Lord Byron in the early days; F. Scott Fitzgerald, Mishima Yukio, Jane Bowles, and Jackson Pollock later on; and Hart Crane always.

This whole inclination to observe the world and its people through the eyes of the romantic came as naturally to Williams as writing did. He was related to both Sidney Lanier, the nineteenth-century poet, and to John Sharp Williams, one of the more eloquent of the Southern political orators.[7] To have spent his early youth in the Mississippi Delta, in the home of an Episcopal minister, in the midst of people speaking rich Southern dialects, would be adequate to establish his taste for purple prose and romantic thoughts. It also fixed his identification of youth, Eden innocence, and the bucolic South.

He spent many hours of his childhood in the well-stocked library of his grandfather, a classically educated man. (A portion of this library is currently held in the Tennessee Williams Collection at Washington University in St. Louis.) Among the earliest reading for the young boy were "The Lady of Shalott" and the novels of Sir Walter Scott, the poetry of Coleridge and Poe. Tom Williams's early flowery style derived originally from this saturation in such lyric poets as Sara Teasdale and Edna St. Vincent Millay. In the "Frivolous Version" of a "Preface to My Poems," he noted that he "began writing verse at about the time of puberty," and that his earliest success was an "apostrophe to death" which named a number of the lyric women poets, ending with a tribute to "glorious Millay."[8]

In *Summer and Smoke*, Williams parodies these memories of his adolescent self and his fellow poets of the women's club, portraying the typical genteel Southern poetry club gathering in the manse for lemonade and uplift. The scene reflects Williams's changing preferences among romantic poets. Miss Alma, like her creator, finds the atmosphere of the gathering vaguely oppressive. Her selection of the "dangerous" poet – William Blake – for her topic, foreshadows her sexual rebellion. Without fully realizing that Blake's vision violates her tidy Puritan world, she is drawn to his lyrics because they speak to her own love and frustration. (In another scene, she quotes Oscar Wilde, before she realizes her embarrassing source.) Blake does hold the key to the hidden tiger lurking almost out of sight in the forest of Miss Alma's nature.[9] The short story out of which this play grew, "The Yellow Bird," is even clearer in its rejection of rigid Puritanism. For Williams, it became clear that the art he cherishes is rude, violent, outrageous. He believed he was called to live and think like Cassandra (in *Battle of Angels*), his early social rebel and Val Xavier, his vagrant sensualist.

Tennessee Williams believed that he could never discover his own richest potential until he rejected the anemic romanticism of his repressive, conformist home for the full-bodied romantic life of *Sturm und Drang*. In the months prior to college in 1929, he immersed himself in the biography of "Mad Shelley" and was, as Lyle Leverich tells us, "fascinated that the poet had been wild, passionate and dissolute" (99). His first escape from home came with his enrollment at the University of Missouri at Columbia, where he had a taste of independence. There, as a journalism major, he expanded his understanding of the literary romantics. We know that he read and wrote extensively, finding himself drawn to the nineteenth-century French and Russian writers.

While at Missouri, in 1930, he wrote *Beauty Is the Word* for Professor Ramsay's one-act play contest. Lyle Leverich, in *Tom: The Unknown Tennessee*[10] notes that the play is significant "not only because its Shelleyan fervor reflects Tom's own enthusiasm for the poet but also because the theme, while not a restatement of Shelley's atheism, was Tom's first attack upon the inhibitions of Puritanism and its persecution of the artist . . ." In short, he was depicting "the heroism of the freethinker" (113). In a stirring speech, the heroine announces: "Fear is ugliness. God – at least *my* God – is Beauty" (Leverich, 113). Going even beyond Keats's Grecian Urn, by proclaiming that beauty is God, Williams aligned himself with the aesthetes.

The sudden conclusion to his studies at the University of Missouri in 1932, when his father angrily brought him home and put him to work in the shoe factory, reinforced his hatred of St. Louis, factories, and the industrialized world of work. The years 1932 to 1935 were a nightmare for him, the basis for numerous of his later stories and plays about life trapped in a stultifying home situation and a dead-end job. These years fixed permanently in his psyche his recurring themes of claustrophobia and the hunger for "romance." From this torturous time, he forged his image of the Poet climbing out of the factory to the roof, where he can see the sky, the stars, and the distant world. This autobiographical image, which appeared in the early play *Stairs to the Roof*, was to find its richest expression in *The Glass Menagerie*.

Working among intellectual strangers, living at home in the midst of constant hostility also reinforced his sense of loneliness. A decade later, he wrote to Audrey Wood, "Sometimes the solitary struggle of writing is almost too solitary for endurance!"[11] For him, writing was not a pleasant pastime, but an emotional hunger. It was this life of quiet desperation that demanded "redemption" by "beauty everlasting."

It was in 1936, having begun evening classes at Washington University in St. Louis, that he found companions in his quest. At the university, he was an active member of the College Poetry Society, with Clark Mills and William Jay Smith, two poets who were also dedicated to the literary life.

In addition, he found the Mummers, a small theatre group in St. Louis that provided him both company and left-wing orthodoxy typical of the thirties. Working with them, he had some of his earliest – if ephemeral – theatrical successes (*Candles to the Sun* and *The Fugitive Kind*,[12] as well as an anti-war curtainraiser for Irwin Shaw's play *Bury the Dead*, were his main contributions).

At Washington University Williams was also continuing his reading and thinking about the English romantics. There, from the distinguished Professor Otto Heller, he must have learned something of the Germanic philosophic background of the romantic movement, which Coleridge especially had found useful in the development and explication of his ideas.

Though he did frequently quote both Wordsworth and Coleridge, Williams had a pronounced inclination toward the second wave of English romantics. To have preferred not only the poetry, but also the morality of Byron, Keats, and Shelley to the more conservative Wordsworth and Coleridge would have been considered an act of rebellion at the time. (Irving Babbitt, in his famous book on Rousseau, had condemned the younger romantics as "diseased.") Others agreed that their ideas were dangerous, their lives depraved. Byron had boasted publicly (and outrageously) of having slept with two hundred women in two years. Shelley was a wife-swapper who founded a free-love colony.[13] In his twenties and beyond, Williams came to accept the romantics' rejection of "obsolete standards of family life and morality." Such celebrations of the "Cavalier" spirit delighted this rebellious puritan.

The young Tom Williams explored the bohemian world in college (after Washington University, a year at the University of Iowa, where he majored in theatre), and later in New Orleans. In 1939, having finally graduated from college, he left home for good, though he was never entirely free of the cords of love, need, and duty that continually drew him back. The young writer joined the company of fellow bohemians in New Orleans. (Later he spoke affectionately of the cities in America which were home to artists, noting Key West and San Francisco as meccas for writers and painters.[14]) There, trading his old image of the choirboy lyric writer for his new persona as the vagabond poet, Williams changed his nom de plume to "Tennessee."

In these early days, Hart Crane became his mythic hero. In the character and poetry of this modern American romantic he found a perfect mirror for his own experience:[15] the poet on the wing, hungry for the deepest experiences of life, in love with beauty and with poetry, seeking to express the ineffable. Additionally, in the outcast D. H. Lawrence, he found echoes of his own passions. (He visited Lawrence's widow, Frieda, and wrote a play about Lawrence, "I Rise in Flame, Cried the Phoenix," which pictures his unquenchable spirit.) Such latter-day romantics appealed to his faith in his art and his image of the poet as the outsider. They also helped him to define his own experience, give form to his very real passions.

Decades later, having embraced the "Bitch Goddess Success," he found he was increasingly disgusted with himself and his world. He explored authors who had always interested him and who gave voice to his disillusionment: Proust, Baudelaire, and Rimbaud – French neo-romantic symbolists.[16] Plays such as *The Night of the Iguana, Suddenly Last Summer*, or *Sweet Bird of Youth* have clear ties to these artists. His defrocked priest, decadent poet, and obsolescent artist are painful reminders of the fierce romantics he had celebrated earlier. Far more decadent than the English romantics, these *fin de siècle* French writers mirrored Williams's own declivity. Rimbaud, a recent critic commented, was noted for: "Furiously hallucinogenic imagery (fueled by hashish and absinthe), bourgeoisie-skewering rudeness, mysticism, proud bisexuality and an adolescent taste for despair."[17] By 1969, Williams himself had sunk into the world of drugs, writing fragments of stories that tended toward fantasy. This trend was foreshadowed as early as the 1948 story of "The Poet," when the vat of mysterious fermented drink fuels the poet's ecstasies and the young followers' orgiastic celebration (246).

Williams's influences became increasingly eclectic. In love with the exotic, he was enamored of Eastern mysticism and Asian dramatic forms. This astonished Williams's fans when they saw *The Milktrain Doesn't Stop Here Anymore*, with Flora dressed in a ceremonial Kabuki costume and the final spotlight on the Angel of Death's mysteriously lighted mobile. The Japanese writer Mishima Yukio was a friend and an especially important influence.[18] He and Williams first met in the sixties, discovered they shared a publisher and tastes in life and art; they considered themselves soul mates. In 1970, Williams traveled to Asia, visiting with Mishima (though not with his traditional family in his home) and saw him shortly before his suicide.[19]

Other neo-romantics, like William Butler Yeats, added to Tennessee Williams's allusions, his worldview, and his imagery. He was an aesthetically adventurous writer who read voraciously and traveled constantly, exploring many regions and ideas. Even those he chose to designate or quote are by no means the only ones who inspired him. To the very end of his life, he was insatiable – reading the latest books, seeing the new plays, experimenting with new styles. Some of his most experimental pieces are yet to be published. Tennessee Williams's early love of romantic poetry was to leave a deep mark on his plays and stories: poetic speech became his signature. Critics were regularly impressed by the lyricism of his drama.

THESE "BLESSED HANDS": WILLIAMS AS AN INSPIRED WRITER

The poet distilled his own liquor and had become so accomplished in this art that he could produce a fermented drink from almost any kind of organic matter. He carried it in a flask strapped about his waist, and whenever fatigue overtook him he would stop at some lonely point and raise the flask to his lips. Then the world would change color as a soap bubble penetrated by a ray of light and a great vitality would surge and break as a limitless ocean through him. The usual superfluity of the impressions would fall away so that his senses would combine in a single vast ray of perception which blinded him to lesser phenomena and experience as candles might be eclipsed in a chamber of glass exposed to a cloudless meridian of the sun.

("The Poet," 246)

This visionary poet's experience parallels Wordsworth's "spots of time" in "The Prelude." In this extended autobiographical poem, Wordsworth also described himself as "the Poet." He thought that his writing was "emotion recollected in tranquillity" – an idea Williams frequently quoted and occasionally experienced. As he said, his writing was rarely a result of tranquil recollection. He was far more inclined to the "spontaneous overflow of powerful feeling." In any case, inspiration is essential to the true romantic. Although Williams used real details of his individual experience and dreams, he could not create without this mysterious gift from the muses. This explains Williams's assertion that writing was a *vocation* for him. He had no choice, as his biography clearly demonstrates. During his prolonged apprenticeship in writing, he borrowed, begged, and sponged off friends and family; he signed on for one subsistence-level job after another, rarely holding any for more than a few months – long enough to allow him to survive. Any other work seemed irrelevant in the face of this calling to be a writer. Even writing for the films, in 1943, when he spent six months with MGM, was too artificial and claustrophobic for this free spirit.

Perhaps as a result of spending his first years intimately connected with the Episcopal Church, hearing the language of spiritual leadership, he believed that poetry was a high calling. Over and over, he said that "work" was his favorite four-letter word. It was certainly central to his concept of integrity. He thought no sexual or contractual violation so corrupt as the betrayal of his art or the abandonment of his writing.

Like Coleridge, Tennessee Williams sensed this power of inspiration rushing through him. His references to the wind and his love of wind chimes[20] blend romantic with Pentecostal wind imagery. (Consider "Ode to the West Wind" and "Aeolian Harp" as romantic precedents.) When this inspiration faltered, he followed the path of Hart Crane, Coleridge, and de Quincey, using sex, drugs, and alcohol to induce an artificial ecstasy.

Tennessee Williams was a latter-day incarnation of Plato's Poet-as-Inspired-Madman. Biographies and character sketches note the artist writing with a frenzy that astonished visitors. He laughingly said he was not a writer but a compulsive typist. His letters testify to his demonic attack on typewriters, which frequently broke under his constant pounding. Landladies were reluctant to disturb the piles of crumpled paper they found littering the floor where he worked. Scholars find themselves puzzling at the various pages on different papers, unnumbered, often written on different machines.[21] He could work on several pieces at a time, blending in his fertile imagination bits of experience, remembered poetry, phrases he had heard on the street, and images from his reading. Like Coleridge, as described in *The Road to Xanadu* (by John Livingston Lowes), Williams read widely, especially when considering writing about actual people. For example, when working on the life of Lindsay, he read E. L. Masters's life; he spent a long time reading about D. H. Lawrence for a long Lawrence play he finally abandoned. As a result of reading the latest books on Zelda

Fitzgerald, which Andreas Brown, the owner of the Gotham Book Mart, had sent him along with other books, knowing of his interest in the Fitzgeralds and Hemingway, Williams was inspired to write *Clothes for a Summer Hotel*. But the magic moment of creativity came not in an intellectual mixing of notes into a coherent thesis, but in the powerful act of chemical fusion that took place in the "deep well" of the unconscious.

Also, in the mode of the true romantic spirit, he never considered a work completely finished. He would attend rehearsals, watch the movement, listen to the sound of the lines delivered on stage, and then revise whole sections, crossing out scenes, revising movement, adding dialogue. Many of his plays exist in variant editions; even when published, they were not complete – largely because they were not satisfactory copies of the Platonic image in his mind. ("The Yellow Bird," then *Summer and Smoke*, evolved into *The Eccentricities of a Nightingale*; *Battle of Angels* metamorphosed into *Orpheus Descending*; *Confessional* grew into *Small Craft Warnings*; and "Three Players of a Summer Game" became *Cat on a Hot Tin Roof*, which had at least two possible third acts.)

The real drive of the romantic is to give form to the individual God-given vision. Like most romantics, Tennessee Williams wrote most powerfully when he worked "inside out." Whether describing his own adventures as a young artist, his mother's pain, his sister's tragedy, or his father's incomprehension, Williams was at his best when his subject was the Dakin/Williams family. He knew that the written words always fell short of the noetic experience; thus his ideal poet avoided freezing his ideas by fixing them on paper, preferring to keep them fluid ("The Poet," 247). Later, he was able to expand this family circle to include theatre people and homeless wanderers, all of whom shared his own values and anguish.

Like the Wandering Jew or the Ancient Mariner, the Williams hero is the lonely stranger who bears a mark setting him apart from other men – a special hunger, an unsatisfied need. Handsome and cursed, he dominates the stage as he does the community. He is the sun to their moons of desire ("One Arm"). A non-conformist, he must speak his outrageous Truth, facing turmoil, expulsion, and death. The Poet (of the short story) is washed by the sea and bleached by the sun until he is finally free of the corrupting flesh.

Tennessee Williams, a child of the Church, born during Passion Week, readily commingled aesthetic and religious mysticism, eroding barriers between art and faith. His imagery of the Poet is frequently laced with references to Christ. Sometimes disciples, the "women," the Pharisees, the Sanhedrin, and the mob elaborate this Williams Christology. Variants on the Crucifixion are common in his work. At one point, when discussing

The Night of the Iguana with Bob MacGregor, his editor at New Directions, he noted he had "Too many Christ-figures in my work, too cornily presented." He asked that MacGregor remove the extraneous one he had written into Shannon's first entrance description.[22]

Like the brooding Byron, Williams's Poet/Wanderer is a magnet to women. Whether he is the virile farmer in *Seven Descents of Myrtle* or the anguished defrocked preacher in *The Night of the Iguana*, this outcast hero marches to the beat of his own drummer. A creature of flesh, he attracts the lust of others, but needs more than the flesh for his satisfaction. Female characters too – Blanche and Alma – express this tormented dualism, hunger for sexual contact, subsequent self-loathing, and loneliness. They love poetry, cherish an impossible idealism, and despise their own physical needs.

The conflict of the spirit and the flesh is a central agony for the romantic artist: the act of creation is a mystical process of conception, pregnancy, and birth – an aesthetic Incarnation. As the Word was planted by God in the Virgin, so the Idea is the seed planted by Inspiration in the poet – e.g., Sebastian spent nine months nurturing each perfect poem. The eventual birth, after a fierce and painful time of labor, brings forth a creature separate from the bearer. It then takes on a public life of its own, over which the writer/parent has no control. The "incubus in his bosom" ("The Poet," 248) was both natural and invasive, demanding development regardless of the contrary will of the artist.

For Tennessee Williams, the "blessedness" of the artist is also his ironic source of damnation or torment. From the guitar-playing hobo of the Depression-era Delta to the contemporary All American, the Williams hero is unprotected by family, uncomfortable with companions. He inevitably draws hostility. Torn apart by dogs, blowtorched, castrated, or cannibalized, the Williams fugitive is finally chased to earth and destroyed in a catastrophic finale.

THE MYSTERY OF COLOR: THE ROMANTIC PORTRAYAL OF REALITY

Transforming human experience into art, showing the complexity of human life on stage, was the ultimate challenge for Williams. Whether named Valentine Xavier, Kilroy, Chance Wayne, or Sebastian, the Williams mythic protagonist is a romanticized persona exploring and explaining facets of the artist himself. Williams acknowledged that he never developed a character who did not contain some quality of his own personality – elaborated and developed for theatrical purposes.

Basing his dramas on his own anguished life, Tennessee Williams often portrayed the male/female attraction/conflict. The masculine/feminine identity, the need to individuate the growing personality, the love/hate conflicts of the family. Over time, he increasingly moved toward a more subtle symbolic use of multiple facets of human complexity. In *The Night of the Iguana*, for example, the virgin and the widow become spirit and flesh, as well as fully conceived characters. Shannon's good and bad angels demand he choose between two diametrically opposed visions of the future. The ending cannot be happy for him, for either choice demands the rejection of a part of his psyche.

An even more complex vision of the human psyche appears in *Out Cry* with the brother and sister, both of ambivalent gender, who appear to be two sides of a single person, the animus/anima. Williams acknowledges freely his belief in the dual nature of the artist, or at least his kind of romantic artist. Like Alma, Williams believed himself to be a double person, referring frequently to his "doppelganger" or his "blue devils," and to his double vision as "something cloudy, something clear."

In organic writing, the passionate manuscript grows naturally from the passionate life. Williams thereby felt justified in following Millay's caustic advice to burn his candle at both ends. He craved the intensely experienced moment, full of color, variety, and violence. Like Keats, he believed that he must "drink deep" in order to feel the full range of emotions. In himself and in others, Williams cherished the youthful sense of wonder that Keats characterized in "On First Looking into Chapman's Homer." Williams's central characters search for that "surprise" that leaves them "breathless upon a peak in Darien." Without this capacity for breaking out of his own body in the "rapture of vision," life is only another form of death.

In *Small Craft Warnings*, the young man from Iowa – an echo of the youthful Williams on his 1939 trip West – delights in his first view of the Pacific Ocean. The older scriptwriter – a reference to Williams in 1943, during his MGM period – sadly notes that he has lost that quality of amazement. The later works of Williams have the melancholy cast of the romantic who has outlived his childhood to become a sour stoic. The old doctor in *Small Craft Warnings* – painfully underscored by the playwright's brief appearance in the role himself – has lost even the ability to deliver the live child, much less to conceive one. In a sad letter he wrote to his friend and editor, Robert MacGregor from Key West in 1960, he said he was weary of writing but could not stop. "I am like old Aw Boo Ha, the tiger balm king of the Orient who kept building and building his palaces and gardens till they became grotesque because a fortune-teller told him that he would die when he stopped." *Small Craft Warnings, Moise and the World of Reason, Something Cloudy, Something Clear* all contain double or even triple images of the poet, the young man and the old, reflecting what Tennessee Williams called "corruption."

Over the years, as his idealism was tempered with reality, he learned to balance the lyricism with cynical descants, giving up his "early genius" for "the telling of marvelous stories" ("The Poet," 247). He found a mature voice in the subtle textures of human existence, the interplay of personalities, the "net" of words. He loved bold contrasts, startling climaxes, angry confrontations. In his delight with language, he indulged in the juxtaposition of romantic rhetoric with realistic put-down. When Blanche speaks of "Mr. Edgar Allan Poe," Stanley quotes Huey Long, a notorious Louisiana politician of the era. When Amanda refers to her skill in the "art of conversation," Tom laughingly acknowledges that she "sure can talk." Realism intrudes on the dreamer in the Williams drama, as it did in his life.

In a letter to Audrey Wood,[23] he clarified this trend for her and for himself. At the time, he was transforming *Battle of Angels* into *Orpheus Descending*. Apparently, Audrey, always a tough critic for her client/friend, did not have an immediately enthusiastic reaction. He tells her that he too was bothered by the earlier "juvenile poetics, the inflated style" and was seeking to "'bring it down to earth', to give the character "a tougher, more realistic treatment." He notes that Cassandra was too "hi-faluting" in the original: "Behold Cassandra, shouting doom at the gates!" He notes that "all that sort of crap . . . seemed so lovely to me in 1940. Unfortunately in 1940 I was younger and stronger and – curiously! – more confident writer than I am in the Fall of 1953. Now I am a maturer and more knowledgeable craftsman of the theatre, my experience inside and outside the profession is vastly wider . . ." But he still insists that some lyrical passages are justified by "heightened emotion." "It's only on rare occasions that our hearts are uncovered and their voices released and that's when poetry comes and the deepest emotion, and expression . . . I think they should have this contrast to the coarse common speech. The coarseness is deliberate and serves a creative purpose which is not sensational." (He justified the use of Kilroy in *Camino Real* in similar terms in a letter to Audrey Wood, February, 1946.) He concludes his long defense by insisting that, "Despite the coarse touches in the dialogue, I think the total effect of the play would be one of tragic purity. . ." This powerful letter reveals that Williams deliberately shifted levels of diction to match the dramatic flow of the play. He was a craftsman as well as a visionary.

The plot patterns of the plays reflect this romantic/realistic duality more effectively than do the stories and the other fiction. "Realistic" drama forced him to conform to recognizable, though exaggerated and compressed, human experience and dialogue. Even his dream visions have touches of reality when shaped for the stage. Short stories and novellas, by contrast, do not constrain the artist in the same way, freeing him to indulge his taste for magic realism. While Alma in *Summer and Smoke* is obliged to sit beneath the fountain's angel and pick up a traveling salesman, the more "magical" Alma in the short story of "The Yellow Bird" can bear a beautiful child who rides off on the back of a dolphin and returns with a cornucopia of treasure.

THE MESSAGE OF ART: COMMUNICATING WILLIAMS'S WORLD-VIEW

"We are all of us sentenced to solitary confinement in our own skins," says Val – and Tennessee. The barriers, walls, curtains in his plays signal the solitude of the individual and the difficulties of communication. Characters retreat to their cells only to meet briefly in bars or restaurants. Like Leibniz's monads, they are isolated, with minimal contact or insight.

The Poet, unable to bear this silence and solitude, is driven to communicate "the presence of something beyond the province of matter" ("The Poet," 251). Williams believed that writers are the messengers of transcendence, informing humanity that humdrum life behind the plow is not the full story. Poets help people to look towards heaven.

For Tennessee Williams, the world was the scene of epic battles – between the Flesh and the Spirit, Good and Evil, God and Satan, Gentle Jesus and Terrifying Jehovah. Unlike the more cynical post-Christian postmoderns, he insisted on the cyclorama as the background for his plays. A sweep of sky and sea, a rainforest; sounds of thunderstorms, lightning, and wind are all signals of God's sovereign power, dwarfing the human activities front and center in our consciousness. This brief moment on the stage of life is not the whole story; our choices here and now define humanity existentially.

In his multilayered creations, nothing is simple: the iguana is not just a small, ugly reptile; it represents mankind in the hands of an angry God. The turtles racing for the sea are not simply evidence of nature's prodigious wastefulness, they are symbols of humanity in the face of an avenging deity. For this child of the Church, each drama is a bit of symbolic action played out under the watchful eye of heaven. The youthful hours Tom Williams spent studying the stained glass windows of St. George's Episcopal Church in Clarksdale, Mississippi, reading the scripture passages, repeating the words of the services were not wasted. Although he rarely went into a church in his later years (even after his conversion to Catholicism in 1969), he did acknowledge that the mass at the local cathedral was more powerful drama than he could ever write. The historic bonds between the Church and the theatre were quite real to him.

Even the most bestial of people in the most superficial relationships feel the need to make connections, discovering moments of grace that are breathtaking. In *The Night of the Iguana*, Shannon and Hannah, who listen to the final lines of Nonno's sonnet have a magic moment of communication. In "The Mutilated," two old women in a seedy hotel room in the Vieux Carré discuss a vision of the Virgin and share a glass of Tokay wine and a Nabisco wafer. Such moments of grace are emanations of transcendence.

This three-storied universe gave Williams's work a remarkable range. In *Summer and Smoke*, he knew he was creating a medieval play with modern twists. In a letter to Audrey Wood he noted that it had a " . . . sort of Gothic quality – spiritually romantic – which I wanted to create. It is hard for you to use such stuff in a modern play for a modern audience, but I feel it is valid."[24]

Although both heaven and hell were part of his three-storied universe, they were romantic interpretations of the medieval cosmology. Echoing William Blake, Williams spoke of "Innocence" and "Experience" as polar opposites. He also saw that heaven was hell and hell was heaven in the topsy-turvy world of materialistic dreams. Sharing Wordsworth's concept of the innocent child ("Ode on Intimations of Immortality") Tennessee Williams fully believed that he had come into this world "trailing clouds of glory."

Like Wordsworth and Blake, he saw growing up as a process of losing innocence and joy. His poetry and stories are full of images of free children leaping over fences, gamboling in wild nature, drunk with imagination and delight – like those who follow his "Poet." Childhood for him was the halcyon age of Edenic wholeness. He was by nature a follower of Rousseau. No Calvinist, he could not believe that the loss of innocence was a result of sin. Rather it was the fault of society, which refused to allow the child to remain free of fetters. Armies and factories finally claimed the children, pulling them "home," safe from the song of the Poet. Their voices were stilled.

Living in an era bombarded with the ideas of Freud, Williams came to see the discovery of sexuality – the moment the child realized he or she was naked – as the end of innocence. In *The Night of the Iguana*, Shannon explains his own anger at his mother's furious interruption of his childish masturbation. Her assertion that she spoke for God in her unequivocal judgment was sufficient cause for the child to resent both the parent and the deity.

In innocent love scenes like those in *The Rose Tattoo, Battle of Angels,* and "A Field of Blue Children," Williams echoes Keats's portrayal of the lovers caught in the moment of anticipation in the frieze on the Grecian Urn or melting into delight in "The Eve of St. Agnes." Following their natural inclinations, untroubled by the nasty-minded puritan culture, the young lovers enjoy fully the prelapsarian spirit of joy in sharing their bodies with one another.

This world and its people are doomed to final destruction. From beginning to end, from *Battle of Angels* to *The Red Devil Battery Sign,* his was an apocalyptic vision.

REDEMPTION BY BEAUTY: ROMANTIC FORM

Like the English romantics, Williams loved lyric poetry. Like them, he adored Shakespeare, but unlike most of the playwrights of the great ages of romanticism, he did not restrict his theatre to poetic closet dramas. It is a tribute to Williams's genius that, in spite of his romanticism, he was able to craft plays that were meant for the stage.

He blended the melodramatic form of the nineteenth century with contemporary realities, counterbalancing the exuberant hyperbole with ironic litotes. Thus Blanche DuBois can wear her feather boa, but Stanley Kowalski, in his undershirt, will sneer at her pretenses at "royalty." A grand old actress, like the Princess Alexandra del Lago, can demand and command, but she knows that she is pathetic rather than tragic, pretentious rather than real. Their exotic names, their large gestures, their taste for rhetoric and overwrought scenes place them solidly in the grand style of the romantics. Yet Williams was enough of a realist to acknowledge their faults, to undercut their theatricalism with irony, but he loved to produce them for our entertainment.

In a beautiful letter to Brooks Atkinson (Key West, 2TLS, "June 7 or 8, 1953"), Williams expressed his gratitude to this faithful old critic for understanding his vision of the theatre. Atkinson, the *New York Times* reviewer, was one of the few who understood what *Camino Real* was really about and expressed his disappointment at its weak reception. Williams insisted that it was written as a "communion with people." "Preserving it on paper isn't enough," he said, "a published play is only the shadow of one and not even a clear shadow. The colors, the music, the grace, the levitation, the quick inter-play of live beings suspended like fitful lightning in a cloud, those things are the play, not words, certainly not words on paper and certainly not any thoughts or ideas of an author, those shabby things snatched off basement counters at Gimbel's." He then goes on to refer to the speech in *The Doctor's Dilemma*, of which he can no longer remember a line. But he does remember that, when he heard it, he thought, "Yes, that's what it is, not words, not thoughts or ideas, but those abstract things such as form and light and color that living things are made of." One of his most lacerating letters in response to a critic was written when Williams thought that Walter Kerr had missed all of the music, color, dance, and theatricality of *Camino Real*. He had missed "the great plastic richness" and the consequent demands on the whole troupe of performers and practitioners. (A copy of the letter, unsigned, undated, and probably unsent, is in the Billy Rose Theatre Collection at Lincoln Center.)

Given Williams's romantic rejection of traditional controls and forced conventions, it is hardly surprising that he would have espoused this dynamic form.[25] From his earliest critical comments, printed as a preface to *The Glass Menagerie*, Williams rejected the realistic theatre with its fourth-wall conventions. His letters are full of passionate pleas to actors, directors, producers not to subvert the poetry of his plays. He had a vision of the theatre as lively painting, poetry in motion; he loved color, dance, and music. Although he mentioned his admiration of Aristotelian form – especially the unities – he felt no compulsion to conform to classic or neoclassical principles of dramaturgy. He preferred to explore his own patterns. Like Pirandello, he was fascinated by the process of perception, the multiple meanings of reality. He enjoyed underscoring the primary role of the artist by showing the dreamer as well as the dream. In *Camino Real*, Don Quixote introduces his vision of the Royal Road that has become the Real Road. Tom Wingfield explains that *The Glass Menagerie* is a "memory" play and that the memory is his.

Perhaps it was an element of his basic comedic view of life that brought this doubleness to his drama. Like Shakespeare with his plays-within-plays, Williams liked to set the narrator outside the drama, thereby allowing an ironic counterpoint to the melodrama of the tale. Tom, like the artist, stands inside the story and outside it simultaneously. Inside, his voice is personal – angry and loving; outside, it is analytic – it is dry and ironic. At the beginning of *The Glass Menagerie*, the Narrator-Tom presses the audience to see the story as a part of the world picture; later he draws attention to himself as a Stage Magician; and finally, he demands our sympathy as he leaves the doomed women to blow from place to place like leaves from Shelley's "Ode to the West Wind." Like other framing devices that Williams used in early plays, the Narrator underscores the play as a play, a presentational device designed to disorient the audience.

Williams's experiments in presentational drama – *Camino Real* as Don Quixote's dream, *Battle of Angels* as a memory play set in a museum, *Out*

Cry as the fragment of a clouded memory being reconstructed as it is acted and viewed – were challenges to the popular realistic play with its fourth-wall convention. Williams pressed the artist's "God-like freedom" in the act of creation, able to destroy the illusion at will by calling attention to it as an illusion.[26] This acting-out of the role of the Promethean rebel-as-artist continued to the extent of deconstructing the play as it is being presented. This climaxed in *Out Cry*, where the characters tease out the different levels of illusion and reality as they suffer through their genuine distress.

This fiction of non-control, which is the mark of romantic irony, produces a work riddled with unresolved ambiguities, in which the artist creates a sense of his own inability to master his recalcitrant materials.[27] Thus, we watch Felice-the-actor worrying about the absence of the production crew, Felice-the-character involved in the action of the play, and Felice-the-writer arguing with Clare about the actual events from which the play derived. At the end, the deliberate decision to reenter the world-of-the-play in order to escape the world of the make-believe-theatre is painfully ironic and clearly ridiculous, but somehow right. As Furst notes, without grounding in external reality, we enter the hall of mirrors, "plunged into the persona's paradoxes, ambivalences, ironies, and schizophrenic dualisms . . ." (33) .Williams-the-relativist welcomes this opportunity to force the audience to join him in the curious quest of the romantic, ultimately a quest of the imagination. His imagery of the legless bird is a fitting symbol of the artist who rejects the solid grounding in reality. The flight ends only with death.

The life on stage was for Tennessee Williams an image of the human condition, not simply a chronicle of individual experience. His was a mythic vision, involving people with allusive names, performing ritual actions in the "circle of light." Taking his cue from the Church, he transformed the stage into an altar and the play into a ritual. He allowed no limits on the creator-artist or his claims for his prophetic role. It is no wonder he wrote of that "visionary company." For him, no human was more valuable, on earth or in heaven, than the Artist.

In those last plays, the poetry diminished, the experience of life dimmed, the characters pressed into pitiful choices. But like the Ancient Mariner, the compulsive old playwright continued to fix us with his glittering eye and tell us his compelling tale of the voyage, the violation, the pain, and the aching hunger to expiate his sin. His hands no longer seemed so blessed, his message grew blurred, he saw more of life as ugly, but he never lost faith in the redemptive power of beauty.

As the sweet bird of youth finally flew out of sight, and Williams grew to be an "old alligator," in letters to friends he insisted that he was still a romantic – though now a senile one.[28] One of the saddest pieces of writing in the Harvard Collection is an unfinished letter to the actors in what he called his "last long play for Broadway," asserting that this play was "intransigently romantic." He concluded by saying that, though now an old man, he still responded to the "cry of the players." (1TLS, N.P, N.D.)

NOTES

1 The phrasing is from Shaw's play *The Doctor's Dilemma*, quoted in Tennessee Williams, "Afterword to *Camino Real*," in *Where I Live: Selected Essays* (New York: New Directions, 1978), 69.

2 See, for example, the letter from Tennessee Williams to Audrey Wood, 2TLS, Laguna Beach, CA, June, 1939, in which he identified himself with Vachel Lindsay and provided a lengthy description of a proposed script (Harry Ransom Humanities Research Collection – hereafter HRHRC – University of Texas, Austin).

3 Lillian Furst, *The Contours of European Romanticism* (Lincoln: The University of Nebraska Press, 1979), 3.

4 Tennessee Williams to Audrey Wood, 3TLS, NP [Probably Laguna Beach, CA], May 5, 1939. HRHRC, Austin.

5 Albert J. Devlin, ed., *Conversations with Tennessee Williams* (Jackson, Mississippi: University Press of Mississippi, 1986).

6 This rough draft document entitled "The Visionary Company" is part of the Williams collection at HRHRC, Austin, Texas. I have silently corrected some typographical errors.

7 Lyle Leverich, *Tom: The Unknown Life of Tennessee Williams* (New York: Crown, 1995), 44, describes Senator John Sharp Williams, who was noted for his comic stories as well as his rhetoric.

8 "Preface to My Poems," in *Where I Live: Selected Essays*, 1 (reprinted from *Five Young American Poets*).

9 See the discussion of Blake and the other romantics in Lawrence S. Lockridge's *The Ethics of Romanticism* (Cambridge University Press, 1989), 22 ff.

10 It is interesting that Lyle Leverich constructs his impressive work in terms of a romantic search, entitling chapters: "Lodestar," "Moonward," "Outer Space," "Wanderings," and "New Harbors." All of these are images of the journey, a standard romantic image.

11 Tennessee Williams to Audrey Wood, 1TLS, Nantucket, July 29, 1946. HRHRC, Austin.

12 This is a different play from the later *Fugitive Kind*, a version of *Battle of Angels*. New Directions plans to publish several of these early plays within the next few years.

13 Alan Ehrenhalt, *The Lost City: Discovering the Forgotten Virtues of Community in the Chicago of the 1950's*. (New York: HarperCollins, 1995).

14 Tennessee Williams, "Home to Key West," in *Where I Live*, 160.

15 See *Hart Crane and the Image of the Voyage*, a work which reveals any number of parallels to Tennessee Williams's life and thought.

16 Tennessee Williams's letters to Margo Jones (in the HRHRC, Austin) in the mid-sixties already mention his regular reading of these authors. Jay Laughlin sometimes shipped him boxes of books that were his own favorites. In return, Williams sent Laughlin materials on Crane, including biographies he thought interesting. (The Laughlin letters are soon to be published at New Directions.)

17 Janet Maslin, in a review of *Total Eclipse*, entitled "Rimbaud: Portrait of the Artist as a Young Boor," in the *New York Times*, November 3, 1995, C–14. Maslin notes that Rimbaud is the source of much contemporary popular culture, including Bob Dylan, Jim Morrison, and Patti Smith.

18 For a full description of Mishima's romanticism, see Susan Jolliffe Napier's *Escape from the Wasteland, Romanticism and Realism in the Fiction of Mishima Yukio and Oe Kenzaburo* (Cambridge, MA: Harvard University Press, 1991).

19 Allean Hale has discovered a "secret" Noh play that Williams wrote as a tribute to Mishima. Williams referred to "The Mutilated" as a "Yes Play" in one typescript version in the Billy Rose Theatre Collection.

20 He thanked Donald Windham for the gift of windchimes and mentioned them in letters to others as well.

21 See, for example, Lyle Leverich's account of the room in which he lived when he first moved to Key West and lived at the Trade Winds, or Allean Hale's description of the papers she discovered to be his "Secret Manuscript," a Noh Play.

22 See letter from TW to Robert MacGregor, March 27, 1963, in the New Directions Archive.

23 Tennessee Williams to Audrey Wood, 3 TLS, from Tangiers, October 14, 1953. HRHRC, Austin.

24 Tennessee Williams to Audrey Wood, 1 TLS, from Nantucket, July 29, 1946. HRHRC, Austin.

25 René Welleck, in *Concepts of Criticism*, speaks of the romantics' use of dynamism, organic form, and change. See Furst, 8.

26 Furst, 27.

27 Furst, 31.

28 Tennessee Williams to Oliver Evans, 1 TLS, from Rome, July 10, 1971. The Houghton Library at Harvard University.

BIBLIOGRAPHY

Abrams, Mark. *The Mirror and the Lamp*. London: Oxford University Press, 1953.

Barzun, Jacques. *Romanticism and the Modern Ego*. Boston: Little, Brown, 1944.
   Classic, Romantic and Modern. Garden City, New York: Doubleday, 1961.

Bate, Walter Jackson. *From Classic to Romantic*. Cambridge: Cambridge University Press, 1946.

Combs, Robert. *Vision of the Voyage: Hart Crane and the Psychology of Romanticism*. Memphis State University Press, 1978.

Cranston, Maurice. *The Romantic Movement*. Oxford: Blackwell, 1994.

Driver, Tom. *Romantic Quest and Modern Query*. New York: Delacorte Press, 1970.

Furst, Lillian R. *The Contours of European Romanticism*. Lincoln: University of Nebraska Press, 1979.

Lovejoy, Arthur O. *The Great Chain of Being: A Study of the History of an Idea*. New York: Harper & Row, 1936.

Praz, Mario. *The Romantic Agony*. New York: The World Publishing Co. 1933.

9

GILBERT DEBUSSCHER

Creative rewriting: European and American influences on the dramas of Tennessee Williams

Though Williams expressed himself, sometimes quite candidly, about his private life, he was always reluctant to give information about his working methods. Yet he repeatedly mentioned the influence of three writers – D. H. Lawrence, Hart Crane, Anton Chekhov – and cited numerous others; from an examination of recent criticism it is possible to compile a list that includes Samuel Beckett, Bertolt Brecht, Jean Cocteau, Federico Garcia Lorca, Eugene O'Neill, Harold Pinter, Luigi Pirandello, Bernard Shaw, August Strindberg, Oscar Wilde, and Thornton Wilder. I shall examine the effect on Williams's works of his acknowledged mentors and determine the guise of their presence in the plays. A recent investigation about the significance of Oscar Wilde in this context adds a new perspective on Williams's modes of reading and borrowing and on the subtle planes of intertextuality in his work.

D. H. Lawrence's influence on Tennessee Williams was documented by Norman J. Fedder[1] as early as 1966. Fedder's analyses of thirty years ago are still persuasive but his conclusions need revising now that the respective statures of the two artists are more accurately assessed. There is external evidence that Williams had read the works of D. H. Lawrence. In 1939 already he had manifested his admiration for the English novelist by visiting Lawrence's widow, Frieda, in Taos, New Mexico and by promising her to complete a play about her husband. The outcome was the one-act play *I Rise in Flame, Cried the Phoenix* (1941).[2] A few years later, Williams's friend Donald Windham suggested that they dramatize Lawrence's short story "You Touched Me"; Williams responded enthusiastically and, as it turned out, did most of the work.

Williams's admiration for a writer often concerns the man as much as his ideas. Fedder has pointed out that Williams was attracted to Lawrence because of the Englishman's emphasis on sexuality: to him sex was a means of restoring a balance between the two antagonistic forces of the flesh and the spirit, locked in a battle in which the British writer felt the intellect had dangerously gained the upper hand. Sex was also to be a liberating force opposed to the bourgeois Puritanism of the Victorian Age and of the American Genteel Tradition. As its apostle, Lawrence was part of a larger movement of liberation – social, political as well as emotional – born in the wake of Freudianism. It is therefore entirely possible that Williams's own insistence on the importance of sex derives as much from Lawrence as from the emerging Freudian revolution of which the playwright was to become a leading proponent on Broadway.

Beyond this convergence of views rooted in the *Zeitgeist*, there are, however, in Williams's and Lawrence's particular cases, a series of striking biographical parallels which may have intensified his feeling of kinship. The family backgrounds of both writers are very comparable. They were both born to hopelessly mismatched parents: a mother that insisted on propriety and decorum, a father whose misguided vital energy expressed itself in violent and bawdy outbursts. Both boys were ill-treated by their fathers which resulted in their turning away from these male models and embracing the attitudes of their mothers who despised their husbands as socially inferior. As children, both also went through a long period of illness which left them sickly or hypochondriac and required the mother's – and in Williams's case, also the grandmother's – intensive care and thus reinforced the maternal hold on them. Both men in later years came to realize that they did not really hate their fathers; instead, they had failed to understand them, mostly because they had been forced to adopt the prejudiced view of their mothers. Both were associated through adolescence or early manhood with hypersensitive young ladies who became their closest companions: Lawrence's early love Jessie Chambers, the real-life model of Miriam in *Sons and Lovers* and, on the other hand, Rose, the playwright's sister, the prototype of Laura in *The Glass Menagerie*. Finally, both authors were confronted with the alienating aspects of industrial civilization – Lawrence amidst the collieries of the English Midlands, Williams in the sordid urban wilderness of St. Louis, Missouri, an environment which he hated the more since it contrasted starkly with that of his early childhood in rural Mississippi.

The author's note to *I Rise in Flame, Cried the Phoenix* leaves little doubt as to what attracted Tennessee Williams to the English novelist: "Lawrence felt the mystery and power of sex, as the primal life urge, and was the life-long adversary of those who wanted to keep the subject locked away in the cellars of prudery" (VII, 56). The one-act play depicts D. H. Lawrence's last day in St. Paul de Vence. The portrait of the artist is not a flattering one as Lawrence emerges as an irascible man, a neurotic given to invective and abuse, essentially antagonistic to women. His relationship with his wife is compounded in equal measure of attraction and repulsion; in his last hours, Lawrence wishes to be left to die alone because, although a convinced advocate of the power of sex, he is also frightened of it when it is used by a woman to establish control over a man. The dying writer is confronted with not one but two women: his earthy, German-born wife and Bertha/Brett who worships him like a prophet and reproaches Frieda for having kept Lawrence "so much in his body" (VII, 68). An exchange between them exemplifies the flesh vs. spirit conflict and anticipates almost verbatim conversations between Alma and John Buchanan or between Maxine and Shannon in plays as diverse and distant in time and setting as *Summer and Smoke* (1948) or *The Night of the Iguana* (1961):

BERTHA: There's more to be known of a person than carnal knowledge.
FRIEDA: But carnal knowledge comes first.
BERTHA: I disagree with you.
FRIEDA: And also with Lawrence then. He always insisted you didn't know women until you had known their bodies. You just don't know. The meaning of Lawrence escapes you. In all of his work he celebrates the body. How he despises the prudery of people that want to hide it!   (VII, 68)

Although presented as a proponent of sexual liberation, Williams's Lawrence is terrified of the destructive nature of the female in the sexual relationship. It is this fear that the play diagnoses as the cause of Lawrence's insistence upon the woman's subservience to the male and designates, unflatteringly in the prefatory note, as a "tangent obsession" (vii, 56). The accuracy with which the views of the actual Lawrence are presented has been repeatedly called into question. Williams admires Lawrence as a liberator from puritanical hypocrisy but the portrait is probably more revealing of Williams than of his real-life model. Fedder asks: "Is Williams praising or damning his hero?" (50). As in a premonitory answer, in a letter of 1941, Williams stated: "I make it primarily the story of a woman's devotion to a man of genius and a man's, a sort of modern satyr's, pilgrimage through times inimical to natural beings – a would-be satyr never quite released from the umbilicus."[3] In this startling formulation Frieda and Lawrence relate to each other not only as wife and husband but also as mother and son. This reveals the ambivalent attitude of Williams: the virile husband rejects the tender wife, yet in his helplessness the son in him craves her motherly help. The internal conflict is informed by an Oedipal love/hate relationship which Williams, more than Lawrence, sees as the basis of all male/female bonds and is as such repeatedly echoed in his plays. Therefore, when all is said, *I Rise in Flame, Cried the Phoenix* is not a document but a play and, recognizably, a Williams play: Williams is not a scholar or a literary critic but a passionate reader and an artist. His concern is not with objectivity, his aim is dramatic expressivity. His Lawrence is primarily a Williams character.

Much the same can be said, paradoxically for an adaptation, of *You Touched Me!*, the full-length play based on the Lawrence short story by the same title (without exclamation mark). The play is set in rural England during the second world war and deals with the sensual awakening of the delicate and sensitive Matilda by the returning soldier Hadrian. Their budding relationship is encouraged by Captain Rockly, the ribald father of the girl and guardian of Hadrian but it provokes the immediate hostility of his unmarried sister Emmie. The playwright incorporated material from another Lawrence story "The Fox" in which a young man similarly arouses and marries a repressed spinster in spite of the opposition of the girl's female companion. Emmie has been preoccupied with the nightly raids of a fox into the neighborhood chicken-coops. In his stage directions Williams aligns Hadrian with the marauding animal. "There is something about him which the unsympathetic might call sharp or fox-like [. . .] an alert inquisitive look . . . we will not say that he has red hair, but hair of that color would suit his kind of vital, quick awareness."[4] But, again an un-Lawrentian measure of ambiguity creeps in when the playwright further adds: "Behind that quickness is something else – a need, a sensitivity. . ."

An identical ambivalence can be traced in another fox, the one that appears in a Williams poem, appropriately dedicated to D. H. Lawrence, the title of which "Cried the Fox"[5] echoes that of the early one-act play. In the poem too the fox is the vibrantly alive creature but must, in order to preserve its integrity, keep ahead of the hunter and the pack. This is Williams's view, articulated in terms borrowed from Lawrence, of the individual threatened by materialistic, bourgeois civilization, the "wild thing" opposed to the reductive forces of conformity. But, where the Lawrence of *I Rise in Flame, Cried the Phoenix* insisted on being left alone in his final hour, the fox of the poem is said to feel lonely and desperate: Hadrian's looks also betray "a need [. . .] a sad patient waiting" (12). Williams's foxes harbour a softness, a tenderness which Lawrence would have considered contemptible weakness. There is in Lawrence an intransigence about masculinity where Williams shows sympathy and understanding for unavoidable compromise.

As Fedder aptly pointed out, the fox as representative of the flesh is opposed in Williams's bestiary to the moth, the fragile representative of the spirit. But, as in the case of the fox, an ambiguity colors Williams's conception: in the poem sympathetically titled "Lament for the Moths"[6] "the lovely, velvety moths" share the same fate as the foxes in that they too are "by mammoth figures haunted." And thus, rather than taking over a clear-cut Lawrentian triad of flesh /spirit/ bourgeois civilization, Williams rewrote it in his own terms. This modified Lawrentian existential stance can be traced in most of the plays of the middle period from *Battle of Angels* (1940) to *The Night of the Iguana* (1960). Thus Val (*Battle* and *Orpheus*), Jim (*Menagerie*), John Buchanan (*Summer and Smoke*), Stanley (*Streetcar*), Alvaro (*Rose Tattoo*) are all aligned with the vibrant foxes while Myra/ Lady, Laura, Alma, Blanche, and Serafina are their respective moths; in these successive plays the vicious forces of the establishment are represented among others by the sheriff and his lynching mob; Mr. Mendoza and the alienating factory environment; Mr. Gonzales, the violent owner of Moon Lake Casino; Mr. Graves, or Shaw and Kiefaber, the nemeses of Blanche; the Traveling Salesman who jabs Alvaro in the groin.

Beyond its general adherence to the triadic Lawrentian pattern which tends to accord greater prominence to the fox figure, an individual play may be so modeled as to recall situations from specific Lawrence works that emphasize the role of the moth instead. *Battle of Angels / Orpheus Descending* for instance can be regarded, first, as a play in which the fox, a young vagrant fiercely resisting conformity (Val) erupts into a chicken-coop (the secluded Twin River community), unwillingly awakens the emotions of "the delicate" (Myra/Lady and the other women) and is pursued and ultimately destroyed by the hunter, his companions, and their dogs (the sheriff and his men and hounds); yet, the play is also plausibly close to the plot of *Lady Chatterley's Lover* in so far as it chronicles the story of "a woman [. . .] who has made an unfortunate marriage to an invalid husband [. . .] and is awakened to the joy of life by a dark lower class lover who has been connected in the past with a neurotically possessive woman [. . .]" (Fedder, 67). Thus also *The Glass Menagerie* (1944) has been compared with *Sons and Lovers*, for both works center on the relationships between a strong mother figure, a weak or absent father, an artist son, and an aborted love-affair between a delicate girl and a sturdy young man she is infatuated with. *A Streetcar Named Desire* (1947) has been likened to the short story "The Princess" in which a delicate heroine is destroyed in a forced sexual encounter with a primitive man.

Each successive play has thus been paired off, not always with an equal degree of plausibility, with a Lawrence "model." *Suddenly Last Summer* (1958) constitutes a turning point in the evolution of Williams's relationship to Lawrence. In it, Williams recycles, in part, the Lawrence material of *I Rise in Flame, Cried the Phoenix*; in so doing, he was turning for inspiration to his own recreation of the novelist rather than to the original, a symptom of the solipsistic movement in which Williams was engaged as he entered a period marked by psychiatric treatment. With *The Night of the Iguana* (1961), Williams ironically and deliberately changed allegiances, or, as Fedder put it "got back" at Lawrence. One of the four main characters is named T. Lawrence Shannon, which a number of commentators have interpreted as "Tennessee's Lawrence," i.e. the playwright's own version of his literary forerunner. I submit that, however much Lawrence contributed to shape or confirm Williams's worldview, he was, from the start "Tennessee's Lawrence," that is a guide, an eye-opener, but that from the outset the message of the Englishman was filtered through the distorting prism of the American's personal experience; however close they may have been in their emphasis on sex as a liberating, balancing force, however similar in their outlook on the conflict between flesh and spirit and on the themes, characters and metaphors that express it, Williams always remained at one remove from simple imitation. Because they regarded Williams as merely a Broadway entertainer, and not as an artist comparable to the canonical English novelist, Fedder and others failed to notice that Williams had appropriated Lawrence in order to make a dramatic statement entirely his own.

From Williams's perspective, there was deliberate irony, although concealed in a tribute, in writing a play about Lawrence, the champion of sex as a life force, set during the last hours of his tubercular existence, thus turning it into an acknowledgment of ultimate defeat. Ironic distance is a hallmark of Tennessee Williams; it is not characteristic of Lawrence. Williams could not then, for all his admiration for the Englishman, be an orthodox Lawrentian. Where Lawrence has little patience for anything but the glorious union of the sexes, Tennessee Williams shows much greater understanding and sympathy for fragmented people, who seek temporary refuge in a fumbling embrace. Where Lawrence is the stern judge of his characters, admitting only merciless light, Williams is a smiling accomplice of his, willing to settle for the glow of a paper lantern. And he is not the lesser artist for it.

If Williams's relation to Lawrence can be described as creative misreading, his attitude towards Hart Crane is one of quasi-identification. Williams had always conceived of himself primarily as a poet. He discovered the poetry of Hart Crane in 1935 and, in 1944, in the "Frivolous Version" of his "Preface to My Poems" he associated him with "the purer voices in poetry" adding that he read him "with gradual comprehension."[7] Among the few permanent possessions Williams took with him on his constant peregrinations were a copy of Hart Crane's collected poems and a framed portrait of the poet.

More significant, however, than these two material mementoes are the evident traces of Crane's literary presence in the plays. Even in *You*

Touched Me!, seemingly his D. H. Lawrence play par excellence, Crane is mentioned in a passing reference which, Donald Spoto suggests,[8] was one of Williams's last minute additions to the text during the Boston tryouts in 1945. Around the same time Williams started using epigraphs from Crane's poems to adorn the title page of some of his plays, a custom which he will never really relinquish. Thus the one-act *The Strangest Kind of Romance* written in 1944 but published in the collection 27 *Wagons Full of Cotton* in 1945 is introduced with the final stanza of Crane's "Chaplinesque" from the collection *White Buildings;*[9] over forty years later, *The Red Devil Battery Sign*, written in 1975–76 and published in 1988, is introduced in the collected plays with a quote from "To Brooklyn Bridge" (3).

Best known perhaps is the Crane motto of *A Streetcar Named Desire* (1947) from the fifth stanza of "The Broken Tower:"

> And so it was I entered the broken world
> To trace the visionary company of love, its voice
> An instant in the wind (I know not whither hurled)
> But not for long to hold each desperate choice   (139–40)

These lines signal or emphasize meanings that may not be immediately apparent to the reader or the viewer. It must be remembered in this connection that Williams always insisted on having the epigraphs reproduced in the playbill for the production so that a spectator is not necessarily deprived of these interpretative poetic signposts. In this case they point to the dramatic career of Blanche DuBois as she "enters" the world of Stella and Stanley in New Orleans. As Thomas E. Porter noticed, they reveal the playwright's conception, surprising at first sight, of not one but two "broken world(s)," "one gone with the wind, the other barely worth having."[10] Belle Reve, the plantation, symbolizes the past, both personal and collective, that is now only a beautiful illusion; likewise, the Vieux Carré, the cramped apartment of the present, stands for the threatening reality in which Blanche feels cornered. Beyond the past-present opposition, one of the strongest polarities of the play, the choice of this motto discloses an attitude of deliberateness and detachment, as if the playwright wanted us to know that he is giving both Stanley and Blanche a fair chance or, conversely, since life is described as the making of "desperate choices," that neither of them has any chance and that their existential itineraries are, from the motto on, destined to end in catastrophe. It strongly prevents the ending from being misinterpreted: Blanche's removal to the asylum does not herald the resumption of a normal relationship between Stella and Stanley, nothing will ever again be the same.

In 1948 Williams put his new play *Summer and Smoke* under the aegis of Crane by borrowing its title from "Emblems of Conduct," the third poem in *White Buildings*. The phrase appears in the lines

> By that time summer and smoke were past.
> Dolphins still played, arching the horizons,
> But only to build memories of spiritual gates. (68)

These evoke the melancholy feeling born out of the contemplation of a past now irretrievably gone. This title then encapsulates the nostalgic message of Crane's poem and makes it expressive of Williams's theme of the Old South, familiar from *The Glass Menagerie* and *A Streetcar Named Desire*; this nostalgia is a tribute to a code of morals too strict to accommodate the legitimate claims of the flesh. Crane is here made serviceable to a thoroughly Lawrentian message.

With *Sweet Bird of Youth* (1959) Williams resumed his habit of selecting a motto, here from *White Buildings*, and the poem "Legend." It runs

> Relentless caper for all those who step
> The legend of their youth into the noon. (66)

Through these lines, Williams once again instructs his listeners as to how to receive his message about the danger of trying to maintain the fiction of juvenile love – "the legend of their youth" – into middle age – "the noon." The lines then introduce a warning tone that is far less surprising here, understated as it is in a motto, than in the ill-fitting coda of the play, the final address of Chance to the audience in which he moralizes about recognizing "the enemy, time, in us all" (IV, 124). The Crane epigraph, better than the curtain lines, establishes the play's hidden agenda – its unexpected ambition to be a modern morality play.

As mottos or titles, the quotations from Hart Crane function as indications of the material's deeper meaning as conceived, with critical perspective, by the playwright himself. Sometimes, as in the case of *Sweet Bird of Youth*, the play may not be up to the task imposed on it by the motto; more often however, the lines are reliable guides not only to the playwright's intentions but also to his achievements.

In 1961, in *The Night of the Iguana*, Crane's "presence" in the plays acquires a new guise. In it, Hannah, the spinster, talks to the defrocked minister Shannon whom she is trying to sketch:

HANNAH: . . . You're a very difficult subject. When the Mexican painter Siqueiros did his portrait of the American poet Hart Crane he had to paint him with closed eyes because he couldn't paint his eyes open – there was too much suffering in them and he couldn't paint it.

SHANNON: Sorry, but I'm not going to close my eyes for you. I'm hypnotizing myself – at least trying to – by looking at the light on the orange tree . . . leaves.

HANNAH: That's all right. I can paint your eyes open. (IV, 302)

As Joe Stockdale pointed out,[11] the formulation is startlingly similar to that in Philip Horton's 1937 biography *Hart Crane, the Life of an American Poet*. In its new context the reference prompts a comparison between Shannon and Crane, both at the end of their rope in Mexico – Crane in Taxco in 1932, Shannon in Puerto Barrio in 1940. Hannah's final words, however, leave no doubt as to Williams's verdict: Crane's suffering was so intense that it could not be adequately registered by the Mexican master; Shannon's is less life-threatening: it deserves the compassion accorded a child's histrionics and can therefore easily be put onto paper by an amateur artist.

Williams's involvement with Crane must also have proceeded from his sympathy for the poet's homosexuality, as becomes clear from the note he provided for the slipcover of his Caedmon Records reading of Crane's poems in 1965. In it, he selects a quotation from "For the Marriage of Faustus and Helen:" "There is the world dimensional for those untwisted by the love of things irreconcilable" and wonders "Could he have meant that his vocation as a poet of extraordinary purity, as well as intensity, was hopelessly at odds with his night-time search for love in water-front bars?"[12] The compulsive gay cruiser that Williams turns into in the *Memoirs* (1975) is here prefigured in that aspect of Crane's sexual preference which he traces in these lines. Nor is this the only passage in which Williams identified with Crane. Already in 1944, in the preface to *Five Young American Poets* where he mentions young artists who found "the struggle too complex and exhausting to go on with," he adds "Hart Crane wasn't the only one. I have lived in the middle of it since I was released from the comparative cocoon of schools and colleges."[13] It is interesting to notice further that, in the text of the record note, the opposition between "extraordinary purity" and "love in water-front bars" constitutes another overtone of the Lawrentian conflict between spirit and flesh and that thus the boundaries between the two tutelary figures tend to blur.

The cause of this partial merging could be biographical. Indeed, as was the case with Lawrence, Williams shares a good deal of existential similarities with Crane and, as he stated in an interview with Cecil Brown, he was aware of these remarkable parallels.[14] Crane's provincial background; his mismatched parents for whom he became a battleground; his devotion to his elegant but highly-strung mother and his doting grandmother; his early antagonism but later reconciliation with his father; his constant restlessness; his generally poor health tributary to his psychological moods; his arduous struggle for artistic integrity in spite of his constant doubts; his increasing dependence on alcohol; his homosexuality, all these must have triggered responsive sympathy in Williams, who came to regard Crane as a brother under the skin, another himself.

It is less surprising then that, although at first sight absent as motto or allusion, Crane would pervade the most autobiographical of the works, viz. *The Glass Menagerie*. In the published text, Williams hints in two stage directions at the presence of his ideal poet. As Amanda appears in her yellow dress in preparation for the visit of the Gentleman Caller, Williams adds "the legend of her youth is nearly revived" (1, 193) which echoes the passage from "Legend" that was to become the motto of *Sweet Bird of Youth*. Later in the play, when Tom speaks to Jim of his plans to join the Merchant Marine, he grabs the rail of the apartment fire-escape and, William suggests, "He looks like a voyager" (1, 201); the word evokes the "Voyages" poems of Hart Crane and fitted the poet so well that it became part of the title of the monumental 1969 biography *Voyager: A Life of Hart Crane* by John Unterecker. It is easy to imagine that in the spectacle of Tom pushing against the iron bars Williams may have projected the last minutes of the poet on the deck of the ocean liner preparing to escape from a world that he found impossible to live in. Thus, behind the face of Tom we may discern the features of Hart Crane just as, conversely, in the record note, Williams's traits could be read into Crane's portrait.

Beyond biographical similarities and instances of intertextuality, there is a strong possibility of straightforward influence of one particular poem, "The Wine Menagerie" from *White Buildings* on Williams's first commercial success. The striking resemblance of the titles may be ascribed to Williams's awareness of the similarities between the role of Tom as character and narrator and that of the poet who also appears as protagonist in the second stanza of Crane's poem. Crane's persona is that of the child, looking from the distance of childhood at the constant combat between his father and mother; this is a position comparable to that of Tom who also looks back from a distance in time on the people and events that have shaped his personality. The affinities between the two works extend to their settings: Tom's narration, set in dismal St. Louis, "in the winter of cities," is akin to the bleak early winter cityscape of the poem and contributes to the depressing mood of both works.

One of the reasons why this particular poem may have found resonances in Williams's psyche is its thematic emphasis on loss. "Loss" is a fundamental concept in Williams's view of the human condition; it is intimately linked with his conception of the destructive character of time: "the monosyllable of the clock is Loss, Loss, Loss, unless you devote your heart to its opposition,"[15] he maintained in 1947. Congruent with this feeling of decline is the mood of nostalgia that suffuses both the poem and the play: the narrator's frame in the play establishes from the very beginning that Tom has escaped, not without experiencing recurrent bouts of remorse, from the oppressive atmosphere of the warehouse and the family in order to be true to himself. This drastic move away from the child's dependency into painful young adulthood is announced in Crane's poem, where the young man is prompted to:

> Rise from the dates and crumbs. And walk away . . .
> Beyond the wall . . .
> And fold your exile on your back again . . . (94)

Equally striking is the similarity between the situations of the two speakers. In the poem, an intoxicated patron at the bar looks at the colored bottles and sees reflected in them the activities of the other customers in his back, which reenact scenes reminiscent of his past. In his last speech in the play, Tom describes the small bottles in a perfume shop window which remind him of Laura's delicate menagerie. By peering at the glass containers and aided by the vision made possible through alcohol, the poet imposes order on his conflicting emotions; by looking at the multicolored vials, Tom objectifies the events of his past and exorcizes – for the time of the play – the conflicting feelings of relief and guilt that tear him apart.

Finally, the poem may have reminded Williams of one of the most painful events in his emotional life. For the quarrel between the man and the woman in the bar, Crane establishes a number of mythic parallels – Judith and Holofernes, Salome and John the Baptist, Petrushka and his "Valentine" – all evocative of dismemberment and more precisely of decapitation. The animal central to the glass collection, the unicorn, which is absent from the short story and acquires its prominent symbolic role only in the play, is submitted to a similar mutilation when its horn is broken off. The small figurine is Laura's favorite and, more than the collection as a whole, represents her uniqueness. It is a reminder of Rose, the playwright's sister, on whom was performed early in 1943 a bilateral prefrontal lobotomy – a surgical version of decapitation – which left her maimed for life and contributed not negligibly to reactivate her brother's feelings of resentment towards the parent who had allowed it.

The presence of Crane in *The Glass Menagerie* is of a nature different from that of the other instances; it touches on deeper personal affinities. In Crane, and more specifically in "The Wine Menagerie" Williams saw a statement about the necessity for the artist to accept his predicament –

guilt, exile, aloneness – in order to be true to his calling, his "vision," in order to achieve that purity constantly associated with the poet.[16]

In 1980, Williams published a short play, "Steps Must Be Gentle" that borrowed its title from Crane's poem "My Grandmother's Love Letters" and represents a dialogue, or, more accurately parallel monologues, between Hart Crane and his mother. The play may have been written as early as 1947 but textual evidence shows that Williams reworked the original before its final publication revealing, in the additions, his sustained interest in Crane and in the scholarly literature about him, e.g. the publication of his correspondence by Thomas S. Lewis in 1974.

The short play is replete with the recriminations of the two protagonists who survey their respective pasts. Crane wants to be left in peace but cannot help reproaching his father for his miserliness and his mother for her refusal to accept his sexual preference. Grace's retort concentrates on her efforts on behalf of Hart's posthumous poetic reputation. She finally breaks through his icy distance by revealing that she worked as a scrub-woman after Hart's death. The end of the play establishes that Crane's jealously guarded rest at the bottom of the ocean is now forever disturbed: the mother has reestablished her control, temporarily lost, over her son. The text is studded with unacknowledged quotations, from poems such as "At Melville's Tomb," "Quaker Hill," "The Broken Tower." They are woven in the texture of the dialogue which they enrich with ironic overtones. "Steps Must Be Gentle" was the forerunner of *Suddenly Last Summer*. The twisted relationship of Hart and Grace can be found back in that of Sebastian and Violet, the elegant possessive mother and the reluctantly submissive son; the absent father is derided and despised; both mothers use their readiness to sacrifice themselves for the reputation of their sons to justify moral blackmail. Thus in one of his best plays, the figure of the poet-wanderer which is most often regarded to a large degree as a self-portrait is in effect modeled after Hart Crane. In *Suddenly Last Summer* as in *The Glass Menagerie*, Williams was projecting not solely his own experience but that of his favorite poet. Hart Crane, as Williams reconstructed both the man and the poet from the biographies, the published correspondence, and most of all from the poems themselves, served as another objective self which allowed the playwright the distance necessary to impose artistic order on experience. Hart Crane was the persona through whom Williams told his own story, and transmuted the raw material of his life into poetry and drama.

In his *Memoirs*,[17] Williams who was a reliable critic neither of his own work nor of that of his friends wrote that "[i]t has often been said that Lawrence was my major literary influence. Well, Lawrence was indeed a highly *sympatico* figure in my up-bringing, but Chekhov takes precedence as an influence" (41).

It is in the summer of 1935, while recuperating from one of his periodic bouts of ill health at his grandparents' home in Memphis that Williams discovered the writings of Anton Chekhov, the three volumes of letters that had been recently translated and the two plays *The Cherry Orchard* and *The Seagull*. But as often with Williams, it was the playwright rather than the dramas that first attracted him. And there was enough common ground between the Russian author and himself to hold Williams's attention: Chekhov had been – and Williams still was – a mediocre student in school seeking refuge against pressures from the outside world in the private activity of reading and writing. Williams easily pictured the small town of Taganrog, which Chekhov loathed, as the forerunner of his own hateful St. Louis. And in Chekhov's interest for creatures broken in body and mind, quietly pining away over unfulfilled dreams and unrequited passions, Williams detected a sensitivity much like his own who could explore the dark motivations of characters and their survival strategies. Above all he discovered a playwright who insisted that his apparently elegiac depictions of human frailty be considered comedies rather than dramas. This subtle blend of humor and compassion, this Chekhovian mixture of pity and derision would be for many years a trademark of Williams himself.

It is often reported that attending a performance of *The Glass Menagerie* Williams would chuckle at passages that kept the rest of the audience spellbound or moved. He was presumably seeing them through that peculiar glass which, Drewey Wayne Gunn remarked, had also contributed to shape the impressions of Louis Kronenberger, one of the reviewers of the New York premiere, who said that "in its mingled pathos and comedy, its mingled naturalistic detail and gauzy atmosphere, its preoccupation with memory, its tissue of forlorn hopes and backward looks and languishing self pities, *The Glass Menagerie* is more than just a little Chekhovian."[18] Gunn convincingly points out the similarities with the four central protagonists of Chekhov's *The Seagull*: the son (Treplev/Tom) is a would-be writer who cannot free himself from his family and social background; the mother (Mme. Arkadina/Amanda) is a self-centered woman who has dreams of her own; the frail girl (Nina/Laura) is trapped by her inadequacies; a representative of the outside world (Trigorin/Jim) destroys the hopes of the others. There is also in both plays the noteworthy absence of the father and the similar motif of the resemblance between the sons and the absent figure. Interestingly, the material for the play had already been gathered by Williams in the short story "Portrait of a Girl in Glass," but transposing it onto the stage became an arduous process. Williams tried out many possibilities[19] but finally, probably subconsciously, he found in *The Seagull* a preexisting pattern that contributed to shape his own play. There are many parallels between Tom Wingfield and Konstantin Treplev – as pointed out by Gunn – but most unexpected may be their common views on the theatre. *The Glass Menagerie* is presented as Tom's narration, i.e. a play conceived and staged in his mind. Now, in 1944 it was an innovative play which Williams introduced in his production notes as "a memory play [. . .] attempting to find a closer approach, a more penetrating and vivid expression of things as they are." And he added his belief in "a conception of a new, plastic theatre which must take the place of the exhausted theatre of realistic conventions" (I, 131). This follows closely the program spelled out by Konstantin who refuses a theatre of "tradition and conventionality" and calls for "new forms of expression."[20] Even in details of production Tom, as a substitute for Williams, seems to embrace Konstantin's rejection of a form that shows how "people eat, drink, love . . ." (153) when he requests in stage directions that "[e]ating [is] indicated by gestures without food or utensils" (I, 46).

The mothers too show many points of confluence and their relationship with their sons closely resemble each other. Irina mocks the literary efforts of her son while Amanda confiscates Tom's books in an attempt to control his literary tastes. Much of their contention also revolves around money: Irina has none to spare for her son; Amanda deems Tom responsible for the financial security of the family. Both women are accomplished actresses, one on the professional stage, the other in daily life as exemplified by her scene with the Gentleman Caller.

The two women also experience difficulties in their relationships with men: Irina professes to know how to captivate a man but is unable to prevent Trigorin from devoting his attention to Nina; Amanda too believes that "pretty girls are a trap" (I, 192) but when her turn came to select a mate for life, she made a "tragic mistake" (I, 186); when Trigorin jilts Nina, Irina takes him back; Amanda has likewise never given up on Mr. Wingfield, as witnessed by his larger-than-lifesize photograph in the living room and, pathetically, by the bathrobe she wears, "much too large for her slight figure, a relic of the faithless Mr Wingfield" (I, 162). Finally both women face the same ordeal, the loss of their son: Treplev tears himself away from life, Tom, less drastically, from the family cocoon turned emotional prison.

Although less obvious, there are equally important points of confluence between Nina and Laura. First they play a crucial role in the lives of the two men they are closely associated with: Gunn points out that one of Konstantin's last speeches to Nina – "Wherever I look I see your face, that tender smile that lighted up the best days of my life" (56) – is very similar to the closing speech of Tom in both the short story and the play. Moreover Laura is like Nina in that both are psychologically maimed and unrealistically attached to a dream, Laura to her high-school hero Jim, Nina to her favourite author Trigorin. Both give the man a souvenir before he disappears from their lives, Nina a medallion, Laura the broken unicorn; and both subsequently fall back into their imaginary private worlds.

In turning to the last of the four main characters, Trigorin and Jim, a pattern is discernible again that conforms to Trigorin's idea scribbled in his notebook, "a man comes by chance, sees her, and having nothing better to do, destroys her" (30). This program is adhered to faithfully in both plays. The two men also exert attraction over the older women: Trigorin is Irina's lover; Jim reincarnates the suitors of Amanda's past.

Since many of the dramatic elements borrowed from *The Seagull* that appear in *The Glass Menagerie* are not present in *Portrait of a Girl in Glass*, it would seem, Gunn contends convincingly, that Williams seized on the Russian play as a convenient model in the process of dramatizing his own material.

Just as *The Seagull* may have served as a forerunner of the final text of *The Glass Menagerie*, *The Cherry Orchard* presents affinities with *A Streetcar Named Desire*. In a 1981 article, John Allen Quintus explored the many parallels between the two plays.[21] Common to both he found the centrality of the theme of loss as experienced, realistically and symbolically, by Lyubov Ranevsky and Blanche DuBois. The immediate loss concerns their inherited property – the house with the cherry orchard and the Belle Reve plantation – but with the estates go their past and the values it was founded on, the tradition of elegance, aristocracy, and innocent love associated with pre-revolutionary Russia or the American antebellum South. The agents of their decline are insensitive men, Lopakhin and Stanley, the representatives of a new social order, of a callous generation that has no sense or appreciation of the former beauty of these fading creatures and their world.

Chekhov may have been Williams's forerunner in dramatic impressionism in that he uses sound, lighting, and stage effects not as redundant illustration but as elements of psychological or thematic expressivity. In both plays, the decline of the characters is accompanied by music: in the Russian play we have a Jewish orchestra that expresses growing unhappiness and disappointment; in the American, there is the Varsouviana, a formal, courtly, nineteenth-century polka specifically associated with the circumstances surrounding the suicide of Blanche's young husband and her subsequent sense of guilt. Lopakhin claims not to hear the music of the orchestra, which signals his indifference to the suffering it represents; at one point in the play his existence is justified in purely Darwinian terms: "For the same reason that wild beasts are necessary to maintain nature's economic laws, you are necessary too – each of you devours everything that gets in your way" (Quintus, 203). Stanley too is compared with animals and in particular by Blanche when she formulates her perception of him to her sister: "He acts like an animal, has an animal's habits! Eats like one, moves like one, [. . .] talks like one! . . . There he is – Stanley Kowalski – survivor of the Stone Age! Bringing the raw meat home from the kill in the jungle!" (I, 203). And it is as an animal whose territory is threatened and invaded that Stanley reacts to Blanche: he hounds her down until he manages to expel her. Although Lopakhin's tactics are less evidently violent, their aim is similar; however, where Lopakhin seeks to establish economic dominance, Stanley aims at sexual destruction. Both succeed in the end. As characters, Lyubov and Blanche have in common guilt feelings that originate in a tragic event of their past: Lyubov may have had a responsible part in her son's drowning; Blanche with good reason blames herself for Allan Grey's suicide. They both have an acute sense of sin which prompts Lyubov to exclaim "Oh, my sins! [. . .] Oh, Lord, Lord, be merciful, forgive my sins! [. . .]" (Quintus, 204), while Blanche tries in vain through constant bathing to wash away the indelible marks on her soul. They both expect against all reason to be somehow rescued, Lyubov by her family, Blanche by Shep Huntleigh. Yet both move towards their doom. In these last moments, Williams parts company with Chekhov: where the Russian playwright sends his heroine to a comparatively mild exile in Paris – his play is conceived ultimately as a comedy – the American commits her to a lunatic asylum, the anteroom of death, thus turning his play into a more dramatic, even clinical exploration of a human psyche.

As time went on and Williams's career developed, Chekhov's immediately perceptible presence dimmed but the essentials of his message to the American playwright never really disappeared. The Russian's sympathetic explorations of perturbed or deluded characters, his reaching for spiritual dimensions, his sense of the tragic nature of daily life rooted in loneliness, loss, and the absence of human contact, his formulations of mild satiric comedy interspersed with bursts of good humor or even gestures towards farce, the feeling of irresistible nostalgia that emanates from his tales, and above all, his psychological humanism, the all-encompassing understanding evidenced for even the less likeable characters, all these Williams might have articulated independently but in Chekhov he found a writer who "had been there before."

Whereas D. H. Lawrence, Hart Crane, and Anton Chekhov seem to various degrees to have influenced Williams over a long period of time, other artists may have had a hand in shaping only a few characters or a limited number of situations or plays. I have shown elsewhere how Jean Cocteau's neo-romantic play *The Eagle Has Two Heads* suffuses *The Milktrain Doesn't Stop Here Anymore* and how Christopher Flanders is a faithful copy of Stanislas, the poet figure of the French play.[22] That figure of the poet is, in Williams, often a partial self-portrait to which are added traits of Hart Crane or other "poètes maudits," predestined victims of the forces of social conformity and bourgeois hypocrisy. Oscar Wilde is one of those.

In the 1978 interview with Cecil Brown, Williams revealed his thorough knowledge of Wilde's personality and tribulations: "A sentimentalist is somebody who will not cross the English Channel to avoid going to Reading Gaol [. . .] Wilde was the biggest fool of his time. He was a wit and a fool at once, and it was this paradox that made him an important figure. But his letters are his greatest work, his masterpiece" (276). As was the case with Lawrence and Crane, Williams's sympathy went to the man as well as to the work and much was based on a feeling of existential affinity. As Emmanuel Vernadakis has pointed out,[23] a number of biographical parallels can be traced back that could have triggered Williams's interest in Wilde: Williams was the grandson of an Episcopalian minister; Wilde, whose paternal uncles were both priests, was the great grandson of an archdeacon. Both were Protestants who converted to Catholicism in later life. Originating from places that could be described as provincial, the American South or Ireland, both moved towards cosmopolitanism; both became world famous in their lifetime but were later ostracized, largely because of their homosexuality; they took to alcohol and drugs and finally died in misery, financial or emotional, in second-rate hotel rooms.

Artistically too they show affinities in that they thought of themselves primarily as poets and both were of a lyrical bent. Both of them produced plays that shocked their audiences by their propensity to concentrate on the darker aspects of human activity of which the necrophilia of *Salomé* and the cannibalism of *Suddenly Last Summer* are extreme examples. Finally they both flew in the face of received ideas: their works subverted social values and traditional Christian morality, although an unmistakable religious sensitivity is operative in them.

Williams seldom mentions Wilde in his letters and not at all in his *Memoirs* but his name appears in the identification of a quotation in *Summer and Smoke* (written in 1946 but published only in 1948) and it functions there as a textual telltale, a barely noticeable signpost to Wilde's more pervasive "presence" in the play. The genesis of *Summer and Smoke*, as that of so many Williams full-length plays, is a complex one: it is based on a short story "The Yellow Bird" and was produced on Broadway in

1947 where it was not a critical success. Williams claims to have rewritten it as *The Eccentricities of a Nightingale* for production in London instead of the play that had failed. However, the new script arrived when the original was already in rehearsal. According to Donald Windham who was very close to Williams at the time when he wrote *Summer and Smoke*, rather than a final revision, *Eccentricities* was in fact the reworking of an early draft of *Summer*.[24] If this is the case, a clear line of development can be traced which reveals the reasons for the emergence of Wilde in the final play and the intertextual nature and structural function of his presence. "The Yellow Bird" tells the story of Alma, a minister's daughter who turns to prostitution. One of her ancestors, Goody Tutweiler, got involved in the Salem witch trials and was ultimately hanged for having had dealings with the devil. The yellow bird of the title called Bobo, acted as a go-between for Goody Tutweiler and Satan. This seems to explain, in part, why the prim rectory flower turned up one day as a prostitute in the French Quarter of New Orleans where she bore a son whom she named John after her favorite lover. While growing up the child would leave the house every morning and return at night bringing jewels from the ocean. As the end of her life approaches Alma is reunited in the sea with John's father who covers her in jewels. The son erects a monument to her memory, a stone carving representing, astride a dolphin named Bobo, three figures of indeterminate sex, one carrying a cross, another a cornucopia and the third a Grecian lyre.

Starting from this half realistic, half fantastic story Williams elaborated *The Eccentricities of a Nightingale*, which centers around the Alma character who is still the daughter of a minister but is afflicted with a prematurely senile mother. Alma, who is now surrounded by a group of small-town eccentric with refined tastes, has been in love for a long time with John Buchanan, the neighborhood doctor's son, who has just grad-uated from medical school but is still very much under the thumb of his possessive mother whose ambitions for him exclude socially inferior girls like Alma. One day however, as Alma seeks medical advice and is taken care of by John instead of his father, the young man asks her out for the next evening. When they return from a visit to the local movie house, Alma declares her love for him and, although aware that her feelings are not reciprocated, she entreats him to take her to a rented room. As the midnight bells herald a New Year, Alma and John make love. In the Epilogue, years later, at a Fourth of July celebration, Alma meets a traveling salesman that she now takes to the room herself.

Clearly dissatisfied, as many critics would later be, with the seemingly troublesome material, Williams used it again in *Summer and Smoke* to give it what I deem its final shape. John is now transformed into a sensualist who has rejected the values of his family: there is no possessive mother in the picture. Alma, on the contrary, is totally dominated by the moral code of the Rectory. As the play progresses through basically the same scenes, John and Alma come to realize each for their own part that they long for the opposite of what they are and in the end they exchange their roles through a double conversion. Ironically they are "like two people exchanging a call on each other at the same time, and each one finding the other one gone out" so that Alma concludes bitterly "the tables have turned with a vengeance!" (II, 247). Of the original, determined character of Alma there are, however, obvious traces left. But, she is now split into three female figures, recalling those of the monument at the end of the short story: the sensuous part of her nature is incarnated by Rosa, the daughter of Gonzales, the local casino owner; her aspiration to matrimony is represented by Nellie Ewell, the daughter of the town prostitute and a singing pupil of Alma's. The first is John's mistress, the other will become his bride.

The revelatory textual addition appears in an exchange absent from the short story and from *Eccentricities*:

ALMA: . . . Who was that said that – oh, so beautiful thing! – All of us are in the gutter but some of us are looking at the stars!
JOHN: Mr. Oscar Wilde.
ALMA (somewhat taken aback): Well, regardless who said it, it's still true.

(II, 197–98)

Although the quote is actually from *Lady Windermere's Fan*, the play in which it is now studded owes more, as Emmanuel Vernadakis showed, to two works by Wilde, the unfinished *La Sainte Courtisane or The Woman Covered with Jewels* and the masterpiece *Salomé*.[25] In the first, the anchorite Honorius converts an Alexandrian courtesan Myrrhina to Christianity, in the process is himself converted to paganism, then rejected by his convert. In order to discover divine love the courtesan retires to a desert while the anchorite sets out for Alexandria to be initiated into the pleasures of the senses. The spiritual and emotional itinerary of the Wilde characters is, in opposite directions, that of Alma and John in *Summer* where it becomes the directing principle of the plot. Similarly, Williams may have borrowed, and for the short story first, the motif of the jewels. It disappears from *Eccentricities* but is reintroduced in *Summer* where the three women are associated with jewels made of precious stones that further individualize them: Alma with a topaz ring, emblematic of November and falling leaves, indicating that she is a prematurely autumnal figure; Rosa with earrings of emerald, a stone traditionally associated with spring and hope, a hint of her designs on John; Nellie with a diamond engagement ring whose glitter significantly hurts Alma's eyes, as its very presence on Nellie's finger hurts her feelings since it also spells John's willingness to mend his ways according to social propriety.

More obvious perhaps is the influence of *Salomé* on *Summer and Smoke*. As characters, Alma and Salomé, whose names are phonetically close, undergo a similar metamorphosis. Initially Salomé is a chaste virgin who admires the coolness of the moon, that symbolizes chastity for her; only as she hears the voice of Iokanaan does she start her transmutation into an irrepressible sensualist. Similarly, John Buchanan's return from medical school and physical nearness act as catalysts of Alma's transformation.

With the appearance of Rosa Gonzales, presumably in the last version then, Williams was able to borrow the motif of the sensuous dance substituting for the sexual act, so famously central to *Salomé*. As Verna-dakis convincingly demonstrated, the ecstatic trance-like dance of Rosa, John's Mexican hot-blooded mistress, is a near replica of the notorious Seven Veils dance. Even in the details surrounding the scene Williams seems to have followed Wilde. Thus although a cold breeze is blowing in both plays, Herod exclaims (perhaps even suggesting to Williams the name of the girl): "Il y a un vent très froid . . . Mais non, il ne fait pas froid du tout . . . ma couronne de roses. On dirait que ces fleurs sont faites de feu. Elles ont brûlé mon front" (494) and John echoes: "The Gulf wind is blowing tonight [. . .] But my head's on fire" (II, 215). Thus also when Rosa senses that "something might happen tonight" (II, 214) she may be harking back to the Wildean refrain: "Il peut arriver un malheur." Thus again when Herod promises his stepdaughter "tout ce que vous voudrez je vous le donnerai" (494), he paves the way for Gonzales's promise "Anything that she want, I get for her" (II, 214).

In reshaping the character of John, Williams may also have had Wilde's play in mind: the mother-dominated young man of *Eccentricities* is trans-muted into "a Promethean figure" (II, 132) who brings the light at least of self-awareness into Alma's life and, as such, functions as the biblical prophet whose name he almost duplicates: John is the English equivalent of the Hebraic Iokanaan whose ending in turn suggests the patronym Buchanan.

To conclude, it is evident that Wilde's presence in *Summer and Smoke* reaches well beyond the mere mention of his name. *La Sainte Courtisane* provided Williams with a strong – some critics would contend too mechan-ical hence unconvincing – structure whereas from *Salomé* was borrowed the central episode of the dance. Since both the names – Alma and John – and the motif of the jewels were already present in the short story, it seems that Williams had been previously aware of Wilde's works but only gradually grew conscious of the use he could make of them in the process of dramatizing the intractable material.

Obviously Williams was never anxious about "influences"; rather, he felt that the modern artist is heir to a long tradition that he is allowed to appropriate shamelessly. In Williams's career it appears that, with time, fewer artists or individual works shine through the canvas of the plays. It is not, I think, that Williams was growing more confident – he never really would be – but rather more preoccupied with himself, not less autobiographical but more solipsistic, turning inward, away from outside reality and previous literature. But models do not disappear completely – *Milktrain* in 1963 is Cocteau through and through; *Kingdom of Earth* in 1968 still echoes Lawrence's *The Virgin and the Gypsy* – they merely appear less organically necessary or integrated. Williams was a man of feeling rather than intellect; an artist, not a scholar. The writers that appear in filigree in and through his work are kindred spirits whose existential priorities and problems are close to his. But never are the tutelary artists allowed to overshadow the master. *The Glass Menagerie* is possibly the most paradoxical example of the writer's relationship with his forerunners. From Brian Parker we know how complex the genesis of the work was: for several years Williams worked on the material and imagined bewilderingly diverse versions of it. It is considered, and probably rightly so, as his most autofictional and yet it shows through its warp a configuration of characters similar to that of *Sons and Lovers*, a dramatization of Hart Crane's life and of his poem *The Wine Menagerie* or a transcription of *The Seagull*. Williams is not a derivative artist and his plays are nothing if not recognizably his own: he was in life as in the best of his art a devourer, a predator who seized upon his own experience and that of his literary forerunners to feed his imagination and trigger his creativity. In the process, the raw material of life was blended with that of literature, mixed and transmuted into new artefacts which, in turn, have served in subsequent years to shape, by imitation or reaction, the works of a new generation.

NOTES

1 Norman J. Fedder, *The Influence of D. H. Lawrence on Tennessee Williams*. (The Hague: Mouton, 1966).

2 Tennessee Williams, *I Rise in Flame, Cried the Phoenix* in *The Theatre of Tennessee Williams*, VII, 54–75. Unless otherwise stated, references to Williams's plays are to the eight volumes of *The Theatre of Tennessee Williams* (New York: New Directions, 1971–92).

3 Quoted in Benjamin Nelson, *Tennessee Williams: The Man and His Work*. (New York: Obolensky, 1961, 87).

4 Tennessee Williams and Donald Windham, *You Touched Me! A Romantic Comedy in Three Acts* (New York: Samuel French, 1947), 12.

5 In *In the Winter of Cities* (New York: New Directions, 1956), 16.

6 *Ibid.*, 31.

7 Reprinted in *Where I Live: Selected Essays by Tennessee Williams* (eds.) Christine R. Day and Bob Woods. (New York: New Directions, 1978), 2–3.

8 Donald Spoto, *The Kindness of Strangers. The Life of Tennessee Williams* (Boston and Toronto: Little, Brown and Company, 1985), 119.

9 *The Complete Poems of Hart Crane* (ed.) Waldo Frank. (New York: Doubleday, 1958), 77. Further references in the text are to this edition.

10 Thomas E. Porter, *Myth and Modern American Drama* (Detroit: Wayne State University Press, 1969), 176.

11 Joe Stockdale, "Taking Tennessee to Hart," *Theatre Week*, 8:30 (February 27, 1995), 25–32.

12 "Tennessee Williams reads Hart Crane", Caedmon Records, TC 1206, 1965.

13 Reprinted in *Where I Live*, 5.

14 Cecil Brown, "Interview with Tennessee Williams," *Partisan Review*, 45 (1978), 276–305.

15 In his essay "On A Streetcar Named Success" (1947), reprinted in *Where I Live*, 22.

16 For further discussion of the impact of Crane on *The Glass Menagerie* see my "'Minting their Separate Wills': Tennessee Williams and Hart Crane," *Modern Drama*, 26 (1983), 475–76.

17 Tennessee Williams, *Memoirs*. (Garden City, Doubleday, 1975).

18 Drewey Wayne Gunn, "'More Than Just a Little Chekhovian': *The Seagull* as a Source for the Characters in *The Glass Menagerie*," *Modern Drama*, 33:3 (September, 1990), 314.

19 See Brian Parker, "The Composition of *The Glass Menagerie*: An Argument for Complexity." *Modern Drama*, 25:3 (September 1982), 409–422.

20 *The Plays of Anton Chekhov*, Translated Constance Garnett (New York, 1930), 6. Further references in the text are to this edition.

21 John Allen Quintus, "The Loss of Dear Things: Chekhov and Williams in Perspective," *English Language Notes*, 18 (March 1981), 201–6.

22 See my "French Stowaways on an American Milktrain: Williams, Cocteau, and Peyrefitte," *Modern Drama*, 25:3 (September 1982), 399–408.

23 Emmanuel Vernadakis, "Tennessee Williams, Oscar Wilde, leurs courtisanes et l'acte accompli." Lecture held at Nantes University (France), March 13, 1992, unpublished. I am indebted to Professor Vernadakis, Université d'Angers, for letting me have his original text.

24 Donald Windham, *Lost Friendships: A Memoir of Truman Capote, Tennessee Williams and Others* (New York, 1989), 103. It should be noted in support of this view that in the second volume of his collected plays, Williams has *Eccentricities* precede *Summer*, in an otherwise strictly chronological arrangement.

25 Oscar Wilde, *Complete Works*, (London: Collins, 1948). Further references in the text are to this edition.

IO

BRENDA MURPHY

Seeking direction

In 1955, Williams published his now notorious "reading version" of *Cat on a Hot Tin Roof*, which contained two versions of the third act. The one that Williams called the "Broadway Version" was developed in collaboration with director Elia Kazan and the other participants in the play's original production. Williams also included an earlier version from one of his pre-production scripts. In a "Note of Explanation" that introduced the "Broadway Version," Williams went out of his way to explain how helpful Kazan's advice had been to him over the years. At the same time, he intimated that the changes he had felt forced to make in order to have Kazan direct *Cat on a Hot Tin Roof* had violated his sense of artistic integrity. Noting the influence that "a powerful and highly imaginative director" could have upon the development of a play, both before and during production, Williams asserted that he and Elia Kazan had "enjoyed the advantages and avoided the dangers of this highly explosive relationship because of the deepest mutual respect for each other's creative function: we have worked together three times with a phenomenal absence of friction between us and each occasion has increased the trust."[1] After listing the three major reservations Kazan had had about the play, and the revisions the playwright had made in response to them, Williams wrote that he had made the changes because he had wanted Kazan to direct the play, and he felt that the play's success justified the revisions: "a failure reaches fewer people, and touches fewer, than does a play that succeeds."[2] Whether Williams meant to imply it with these words or not, many critics have read the "Note of Explanation" to suggest that Kazan had asked for changes in the script just to assure the play's commercial success. Several have condemned Williams for violating his artistic integrity by giving in to what they see as a manipulation of his artistic vision for profit.[3]

In 1957, to clarify his views on the relationship between playwright and director, Williams wrote an article for *Playbill* magazine that, in the end, expressed his ambivalence about the relationship as much as the note in

Cat had. One thing he was certain about was the collaborative nature of playwriting. "Whether he likes it or not," he wrote, "a writer for the stage must face the fact that the making of a play is, finally, a collaborative venture, and plays have rarely achieved a full-scale success without being in some manner raised above their manuscript level by the brilliant gifts of actors, directors, designers, and frequently even the seasoned theatrical instincts of their producers."[4]

In the essay, Williams outlined three stages of the playwright's relationship with his artistic collaborators. The first was that of the terrified neophyte who would agree to almost anything to get his play on the stage; the second that of the "Name" playwright who, having had one notable success, now became a "great, uncompromising Purist, feeling that all ideas but his own are threats to the integrity of his work" (A&D 94). According to Williams this stage might remain as a kind of arrested development, or it might give way, after a failure or two, to a third stage in which the playwright came to understand that his own view of his work could be fallible and came to believe in "the existence of vitally creative minds in other departments of theater than the writing department." He continued, "even if, sometimes, they wish him to express, or let him help them express, certain ideas and feelings of their own, he has now recognized that there are elements of the incomplete in his nature and in the work it produces" (A&D 95). He went on to say that there was danger in this third stage: "There is the danger that the playwright may be as abruptly divested of confidence in his own convictions as that confidence was first born in him. He may suddenly become a sort of ventriloquist's dummy for ideas which are not his own at all" (A&D 95). Having said this, Williams immediately distanced himself from any anxiety on this score, adding, "but that is a danger to which only the hack writer is exposed, and so it doesn't much matter. A serious playwright can only profit from passage into the third phase, for what he will now do is this: he will listen; he will consider; he will give a receptive attention to any creative mind that he has the good fortune to work with" (A&D 95–96). Williams then went on to describe the peculiar situation of the playwright whose "work is so highly individual that no one but the playwright is capable of discovering the right key for it." When this rare instance occurred, he wrote, "the playwright has just two alternatives. Either he must stage his play himself or he must find one particular director who has the very unusual combination of a truly creative imagination plus a true longing, or even just a true willingness, to devote his own gifts to the faithful projection of someone else's vision. This is a thing of rarity" (A&D 96–97).

Here Williams was describing his own relationship with Elia Kazan, the

Elia Kazan who had directed *A Streetcar Named Desire* in 1947. Kazan had been handed a finished script for *Streetcar*, and by his own account had only been interested in creating the fullest theatrical representation of what he saw as Williams's vision in the play.[5] Again by his own account, Kazan had been less and less satisfied with the limitations of his creative role and had, with *The Rose Tattoo* (1951), *Camino Real* (1953), *Cat on a Hot Tin Roof* (1955), and the film *Baby Doll* (1956), become increasingly more involved in the shaping and even the writing of the work, encouraged by the attitude of a not only receptive but creatively and emotionally dependent playwright.[6] Both Williams's resentment of Kazan's role in this complex relationship and his keen perception of its elements were evident in his description of the inevitably ensuing conflict:

> There are very few directors who are imaginative and yet also willing to forego the willful imposition of their own ideas on a play. How can you blame them? It is all but impossibly hard for any artist to devote his gifts to the mere interpretation of the gifts of another. He wants to leave his own special signature on whatever he works on.
>
> Here we encounter the sadly familiar conflict between playwright and director. And just as a playwright must recognize the value of conceptions outside his own, a director of serious plays must learn to accept the fact that nobody knows a play better than the man who wrote it. The director must know that the playwright has already produced his play on the stage of his own imagination, and just as it is important for a playwright to forget certain vanities in the interest of the total creation of the stage, so must the director.
>
> (A&D 97)

Williams was describing a struggle for creative hegemony over his plays that he was to engage in throughout his career. Whose vision was the production, and the published scripts that were prepared from it, to express? His answer was ambivalent. The playwright's first, but the playwright's enriched by the creative minds of his collaborators. The question was, where did collaboration begin and end? When did a director, designer, actor, or producer step over the line that violated the playwright's creative hegemony? Williams never articulated a clear description of this moment, but he was absolutely certain when it happened. In the case of *Cat*, he felt that his artistic integrity had been violated, that Kazan had usurped his creative role. Although the two were to continue their collaboration with *Baby Doll* in 1956 and *Sweet Bird of Youth* in 1959, the fatal seeds of suspicion, mistrust, and resistance had been sown in the artistic collaboration. Although they remained close friends throughout Williams's lifetime, they were not to work together again after 1959.

The creative relationship between Williams and Kazan was the most significant of Williams's career. Kazan's production of *Streetcar* established Williams as one of the two most important post-war American playwrights, and their collaboration on *Camino Real, Cat, Baby Doll,* and *Sweet Bird* all resulted in enormous critical or commercial success, or both.[7] Of his relationship with Kazan, Williams wrote, "Kazan understood me quite amazingly for a man whose nature was so opposite to mine" and "I don't think anyone has ever known, with the exception of Elia Kazan, how desperately much [my work] meant to me and accordingly treated it – or should I say its writer – with the necessary sympathy of feeling."[8] Williams sought similarly close personal and artistic relationships with other directors throughout his career, relationships that tended to follow the same pattern of growing artistic confidence and emotional dependency, followed by suspicion, distrust, and an eventual rupture.

Williams showed a good deal of self-knowledge in his *Playbill* article, which is an accurate depiction of his relationship with directors up until 1957. His closest directorial collaborator during the first phase, when the playwright was "just beginning in his profession" and was "submissive mostly out of intimidation, for he is 'nobody' and almost everybody that he works with is 'somebody'" (A&D 94), was Margo Jones. Williams gave Jones the nickname "Texas Tornado" because of her awe-inspiring energy and her seeming ability to do the impossible when it came to producing a play she believed in. Although Jones's main accomplishment was the establishment of her Theatre '47 in Dallas – one of the first arena theatres in the country – and her influential articulation of her dream for a vital regional theatre in the United States, she also had ambitions as a Broadway director. Williams was introduced to her in 1942 by their common agent Audrey Wood, after Jones had been so impressed with the script of Williams's failed *Battle of Angels* that she had asked to read everything of his that Wood could lay her hands on. Jones directed several of Williams's plays in Cleveland and Pasadena, including the verse play *The Purification* (1944) and the premiere of *You Touched Me!* (1943). Her admiration and enthusiasm for Williams's work was deeply sincere and seemingly unlimited. Sharing a common bond in their Southern heritage, their family situations, and their fondness for alcohol, they became close friends, and, as Williams's biographer notes, "without his mother to hover over him, Tom now had Margo as protector."[9]

When veteran actor-producer-director Eddie Dowling bought the rights to *The Glass Menagerie* and started preparing for a production in 1944, Williams found himself in the position of the "nobody" playwright, who "is afraid to assert himself, even when demands are made on him which, complied with, might result in a distortion of his work." Under these conditions, Williams wrote, "he will permit lines, speeches, sometimes even whole scenes to be cut from his script because a director has found them difficult to direct or an actor has found them difficult to act. He will put in or build up a scene for a star at the sacrifice of the play's just proportions and balance" (A&D 94). At this point, Williams found himself in need of a protector, and Jones was more than willing to play the role. Williams fled from New York to visit his family in Missouri, and Jones, traveling around the country on a Rockefeller Fellowship to investigate the possibilities for regional theatre, arranged to be there. Williams wrote to his friend Donald Windham: "Margo met me at the train and got me to wire Dowling that she was coming and would make him a great assistant. She looked wonderful, and seems to have twice as much energy as ever before . . . It's no telling what somebody like her might get away with in this world! Supreme confidence and verbal witchcraft are useful items."[10]

In the course of the troubled production, Jones assumed greater and greater responsibility, eventually becoming co-director and co-producer with Dowling. Williams's reliance on her protection proved to be wise. Concerned that the play might be too "heavy" for its audiences, Dowling put pressure on the young playwright to insert some more humor into it, but, in her unwavering respect for the playwright's text, Jones managed to head him off. Williams wrote to his mother that "Mr. Dowling occasionally suggests changes in the script but so far Margo and I have managed to keep him in line. I am lucky to have her, as I am less effective in arguments than she is."[11] Williams was to face two major contests with Dowling. One was over the insertion of a hackneyed drunk scene that Dowling had concocted with the help of the critic George Jean Nathan. The other was over the ending, which the production's main source of money, Louis J. Singer, wanted Williams to change to a "happy" one. In the first case, Williams was ambushed by Dowling and Nathan in the absence of Margo Jones, and apparently gave in to them. Williams has described what happened next in his *Memoirs*:

> This "drunk scene," obviously composed in a state that corresponded, was given me as a *fait accompli* the next day, when I crept into rehearsals.
> I said to myself, "This is the living and dying end."
> I went into a huddle with Margo. She shared my opinion of the drunk scene. And more than that, she said she was going to confront the no longer mysterious Mr. Singer and poor Eddie with a protest of the kind that had earned her the sobriquet of "The Texas Tornado."
> As usual, in such cases, a compromise was reached. I said they would have their drunk scene but that I would accept no collaboration on it.
> I wrote it and it is still in the script and I honestly think that it does the play little harm.[12]

The scene, at the beginning of Scene Four, is an index of Williams's artistry, for it provides both insight into the relationship between Tom and Laura, and, in Tom's monologue about the magician who escaped from a coffin without removing a single nail, a vivid image of Tom's dilemma about his sister and mother. It is certainly more appropriate than the Dowling–Nathan version, in which Tom was to carry a red, white, and blue flask and sing "Melancholy Baby."

The crisis about the ending came as the company was preparing for the Chicago premiere. Becoming anxious about his investment, Singer called together Dowling, Williams, and Jones, and insisted that the play should have a happy ending, that Laura should marry Jim. Jones's biographer describes the scene:

> "Tennessee," Margo began quietly, "don't you change that ending. It's perfect." Then she looked up at Louis Singer, her cat's eyes narrowing. Making her hand into a fist, she said in a menacing tone, "Mr. Singer, if you make Tennessee change the play the way you want it, so help me I'll go around to every critic in town and tell them about the kind of wire-pulling that's going on here."[13]

The ending remained as Williams had written it.

Margo Jones's contribution to *The Glass Menagerie* and its author's peace of mind had been so great that Williams felt he could not refuse her request to stage the world premiere of *Summer and Smoke* in 1947, during the inaugural season of her Theatre '47 in Dallas. Having much greater hopes for Kazan's Broadway production of *Streetcar* that year, Williams remarked that the romantic qualities of *Summer and Smoke* expressed Margo more than they did him, and although he promised her first option on producing the play on Broadway, he wanted her to wait until the following year so there would be no invidious comparisons with *Streetcar*.[14] The Dallas production, staged by Jones in the round, with minimal set pieces and props, emphasized the play's fluidity, breaking down the scenes into a seamless whole through the use of lighting and music. As was her custom, Jones did not lay out detailed blocking, but worked improvisationally with the actors to establish their movement and stage business. The production, with Katharine Balfour as Alma Winemiller, was a success with audiences and local critics, and *New York Times* critic Brooks Atkinson gave both the play and the production a positive review when he traveled to Dallas to see it at Jones's invitation. Williams, on the other hand, "thought the production was awful," but, he has remarked, "I loved Margo and I pretended to like it." He attributed its "remarkable absence of artistry to the fact that the play was, in my opinion at that time, not a good one and the leading roles had been unhappily cast, Miss Alma Winemiller being played by a very tall, skinny girl with a Bronx accent and exceptionally large front teeth."[15]

Williams's disappointment with this production and the fact that Margo Jones had been fired as director of the Broadway production of Maxwell Anderson's *Joan of Lorraine* the previous year undermined the playwright's confidence in her as the director for a Broadway production of *Summer and Smoke*. In addition to this, Audrey Wood had soured on Jones, probably because she, as producer, had failed to offer Wood the opportunity that she expected to invest in the show.[16] Wood has written:

> I was not at all certain she was capable of both producing and directing this sensitive and lovely play. Even though she'd done it well in Dallas, that city was replete with her friends and local fans. The New York critics and audiences would be an entirely different breed.
>
> I expressed my doubts to Tennessee, but he merely shrugged them off. Margo was his friend and he would remain loyal to her. In the end, he did, as usual, the gentlemanly thing. He'd promised her she could be his director, and that was that.[17]

Williams kept his promise to allow Jones to produce and direct the play, but his doubts began to show themselves early in the rehearsal period, when he told her that he thought he should direct the play himself. She ignored him until he started getting up on the stage and showing the actors how he wanted specific scenes played. Jones erupted in typical style and sent Williams storming out of the theatre. Although they eventually patched up their friendship, the fissure in their artistic relationship would never be repaired.

As Williams had expected, the critics compared the play to *Streetcar* and found it wanting, a number of them charging him with capitalizing on his success by fishing an old play out of his desk drawer and foisting it on the public. Part of the problem was that Jones's directing style was unfamiliar to Broadway actors, who, under a great deal of pressure for time while mounting elaborate commercial productions, were used to being told more directly what to do. Jones, who was used to working improvisationally with a resident company that had plenty of time for rehearsal, came across as vague and indecisive to the New York actors. When asked for a line reading, she was apt to tell the actor to "just feel it." And, perhaps because she was used to the three-dimensional arena stage, she did not have a good eye for pictorial composition within the "picture frame" of the proscenium arch. While Jo Mielziner's set for *Summer and Smoke*, composed of delicate, symbolic images and traceries of Victorian architecture, called for carefully composed, even stylized stage pictures, movement, and gestures, Jones's actors sometimes had a haphazard, even awkward look on the stage. *Summer and Smoke* was not to come into its own until another arena production, José Quintero's revival at the Circle in the Square in 1952, was to bring out the play's poetry, which Margo Jones so keenly saw but was not able to materialize on the Broadway stage effectively.

Despite his emotional involvement in Jones's direction, Williams was able to give a shrewdly objective assessment of the production to Donald Windham:

> I am afraid Margo did a rather mediocre job. Not inspired, not vital, as Kazan would have been and as the play so dreadfully needed. Nevertheless a certain romantic and pure quality was there and a great many people, I would say about 60% of each audience – practically all women – were more or less – and sometimes to the point of tears – moved by it. All in all I am not depressed or unhappy about it but I regret that it was not converted into the exciting theatre that the best direction could have made it. I always believed it was a play that could live in production (though utterly dead on paper) and what I have seen bears out that conviction. Although what happened did not give it a fair chance.[18]

By then, Tennessee Williams had discovered Elia Kazan, and no longer felt the need for Margo Jones's protection. While he depended on Kazan emotionally, and placed a deep trust in his artistic judgment, at least at first, there was a creative tension between the two that Williams found tremendously stimulating for his work. In the late forties and early fifties, the aesthetics of both Williams and Kazan embodied deep disjunctions. Kazan juxtaposed the directing theory of Stanislavsky with that of Meyerhold, creating a naturalistic environment in which his actors addressed the audience in increasingly non-realistic ways. Williams created an illusion of objective reality into which subjective perception intruded insistently. The interaction of these aesthetic impulses made for exciting and dynamic theatre, perhaps because the art they produced was always an unstable compound.

After the success of *Streetcar* and the failure of *Summer and Smoke*, Williams wanted Kazan to direct every one of his plays, and he increasingly sought the director's involvement at the early stages of a script's development. Kazan was finally not to direct *The Rose Tattoo* in 1951, much to Williams's disappointment, but he was very much involved in its conception. Their work together on the development of the script provides a good illustration of the extent to which Kazan participated in the conceptualization of Williams's plays. As became typical of their working relationship throughout the fifties, Williams sent Kazan an early outline, and then an early draft, which he called "the kitchen sink version." Kazan responded with a long letter, beginning with his reading of the overall concept of the play, in this case that it was a grotesque comic Mass said in praise of the male force, but he told Williams that the material was not yet organized properly, and he shouldn't show it to anyone else until he had revised it. He thought the playwright had turned his conception around toward the end, and he was very surprised at the final scene, in which the two women, mother and daughter, were kneeling and gathering the ashes of the dead husband and father, Rosario. In the version Williams showed Kazan, Rosario, who appears only as the dead icon through which Serafina venerates male sexuality in the published script, had appeared as a character in the first half of the play. Kazan suggested that Williams cut out Rosario as a character because he thought he would be much more forceful as a memory or a legend. In the name of Rosario, Pepina (Serafina) would reject all other men, both for herself and for her daughter. And he suggested beginning later in the story than the first version did, with Pepina repressing her powerful sexual energy through her worship of Rosario's memory.

Kazan thought that this would give the play its thematic center. Pepina would represent the female sexual force that has been vitiated by civilization. The play would celebrate the natural and the amoral. Kazan connected this theme with a side of Alvaro that he liked in the early draft, his struggle with the social and moral system represented by the demands of his "dependents." Alvaro is forced by the expectations of this system to repress his natural desires just as Pepina's self-imprisonment in the condition of widowhood suppresses hers. Kazan suggested concentrating on these two moral people, Alvaro and Pepina, a man who is devoting his life to the traditional Italian virtue of supporting his relatives and a woman who is struggling against the violence of her sexual desire, a force that finally explodes, nearly against her will. In Kazan's view, the result would be a comic Mass celebrating the essence of human sexuality in a dynamic tension with the repressive values of civilization. In Kazan's opinion, there should be no gathering of ashes at the end of such a celebration. He also advised Williams to get rid of most of the heavy symbolism that pervaded early drafts of the play, leaving only the rose and the goat, an emblem of lusty sexuality.[19]

Williams answered that Kazan's letter had made it possible for him to go on with the play, and said that Kazan saw the play more clearly than he did. He wrote, somewhat disingenuously, that he worked more or less blindly, and, since his best work came straight from his unconscious, he often had no idea what he had done when he was finished. Williams was suggesting, of course, that Kazan play the Apollonian complement to his Dionysian creative power, and for a time, Kazan accepted this role with enthusiasm, although he was to find it more and more confining throughout the fifties, as Williams was to find his collaboration more intrusive. Williams went on in the letter to say that, although he had seen the play as Kazan did in the back of his mind, he was not able to articulate it clearly, as Kazan was. He wrote that he planned to rewrite the play with only Alvaro representing the male force and to write a new scene in which Pepina, the proud widow, is, to the delight of an envious community, humiliated by the double blows of her daughter's passion for a sailor and the revelation of her late husband's infidelity.[20] This of course is the core of what finally was produced and published as *The Rose Tattoo*. Williams went on to say, however, that he liked the effect of the ashes and he didn't see how the scene was incongruous to the praise of the male force. The ashes stayed, of course, but rather than having the two women gather them, Williams has them blow away, and has Serafina say, "a man, when he burns, leaves only a handful of ashes. No woman can hold him. The wind must blow him away."[21]

Williams was devastated when Kazan chose to work on a film project with Arthur Miller rather than to direct *The Rose Tattoo*. He continued to fret about his loss of Kazan throughout the moderately successful production of *The Rose Tattoo*, which was directed by Daniel Mann, and never fully forgave him for what he felt was a choice of Miller over him. With *Camino Real* in 1953, Williams began to resist some of Kazan's suggestions. The tension heightened with *Cat*, finally surfacing in Williams's public statement in 1955 that he felt Kazan had usurped his authority as playwright with that play, and Kazan's understandable resentment of this public rebuke. This did not deter Williams from rather desperately wanting Kazan to direct *Orpheus Descending* (1957), *Sweet Bird of Youth* (1959), and *Period of Adjustment* (1960). The personal and artistic relationship between Williams and Kazan intensified rather than diminished during the late fifties.

At work here was a fundamental dynamic in the relationship between these two men, a struggle for artistic control that is masked by the rhetoric of cooperation typically used to describe the collaborative relationship among theatre artists. Within the dynamics of Williams's and Kazan's relationship, there was a struggle between playwright and director to maintain artistic control, to own the play. Kazan has made no secret of his drive for hegemony over the productions he directed. Williams usually acceded to Kazan's ideas because he had a great faith in what he called the "Kazan magic," the director's ability to take even a shaky script and realize it powerfully on the stage. But there was a point at which Williams would dig in his heels and refuse to go Kazan's way. The struggle for ownership was there almost from the beginning of this collaboration, and it could be debilitating, but it was also part of what made the creative dynamic work. By 1960, however, the fragile dynamic of the collaborative relationship had become destructive rather than productive of the free play of creativity that had made it so successful in the beginning. Their collaboration perhaps ran a natural course that helps to explain the explosive dynamics that characterize many of Williams's relationships with his directors, and many creative collaborations in the theatre.

In José Quintero, Williams found a collaborator who desired nothing more than to create the most effective material expression of the playwright's text that was possible on stage. The two men also shared a deep sympathy as artists with similar visions and sensibilities, as homosexuals in a time of rampant homophobia, and as men who were prey to depression and alcoholism. Williams first became aware of Quintero when he rescued *Summer and Smoke* from the reputation of mediocrity with his production of the play at the Circle in the Square Theatre in 1952, a watershed in theatrical history that is credited not only with recuperating the play, but with firmly establishing the off-Broadway movement in New York. The production assured the success of the Circle in the Square as well as establishing the careers of Quintero and Geraldine Page, who played Alma. After seeing the production, Williams wrote to his friend Maria Britneva:

> *Summer and Smoke* is having a big success here in a revival at an "arena style" theatre and the girl doing it is even better than Maggie Johnston was [in the London production], which was very good indeed, and the young director, José Quintero, is my new enthusiasm in the world of drama. If Gadg [Kazan] quits the theatre, which seems likely, now, Quintero will be, at last, another director that I could work with.[22]

Quintero, who was catapulted by the production's success from the condition of a penniless member of a shoestring theatre company to a well-paid and much sought-after director, viewed Williams through a haze of admiration that never quite disappeared. He has written of their first meeting:

> Tennessee Williams . . . of whom I was terribly in awe, for I considered him and still do, the greatest living American playwright, came down to see the performance. At the end he stood up and cried, "Bravo, bravo," hitting his silver handled cane on what he thought was the floor, but unfortunately was my foot. I was so filled with his generosity and drunken with my sense of success that I almost didn't feel the pain.[23]

Quintero was to direct a revival of *Camino Real* (1959), a version of *Kingdom of Earth* called *The Seven Descents of Myrtle* (1968), and *Clothes for a Summer Hotel* (1980), as well as the film that was made from Williams's novella, *The Roman Spring of Mrs. Stone* (1961). *The Seven*

Descents of Myrtle, which was produced at the nadir of both Quintero's and Williams's periods of substance abuse, was an ill-starred venture from the first, held together essentially by David Merrick the producer's belief in Williams. When lead actor Estelle Parsons finally told Merrick she could not take direction from Quintero, Merrick told Williams he saw no option but to fire the director. According to Williams, he responded, "Mr. Merrick, if you fire poor José I'm going to withdraw the play," and he left Quintero in.[24] The production was a major flop. Of *Mrs. Stone*, Williams, who almost invariably disliked the films that were made from his work, wrote in 1975, "I think that film is a poem. It was the last important work of both Miss [Vivien] Leigh and of the director, José Quintero, a man who is as dear to my heart as Miss Leigh is."[25]

By the time he wrote *Clothes for a Summer Hotel*, Williams had entered a phase of his career that he had not foreseen when he wrote the *Playbill* essay in 1957, at the peak of his fame and recognition as America's greatest living playwright. After two decades of deterioration from drug and alcohol abuse and a string of failures in the commercial theatre, Williams was in no position to make demands of his producer or director in 1980. He turned to his now old friend Quintero, who saw the promise not only of a distinguished play but of a Broadway hit in the script Williams had written out of the lives of Scott and Zelda Fitzgerald. Quintero saw in the play an authentic expression of the relationship between the drive for artistic creativity and the destructive drives of the artist. He saw "parallels in the play to his and Williams's own careers." Like Fitzgerald, both men had been on destructive drinking binges. People had said they were through. But Quintero had conquered his alcohol addiction and gotten back to work. Williams, Quintero insisted, was "back in control" and "writing as well as ever."[26] Quintero secured the support of producer Elliot Martin and the tentative interest of Geraldine Page, who objected that the three-and-a-half hour script was too long and too fragmented, and doubted Williams's ability at this stage to make the necessary cuts and shape the play into an integrated whole for production. Page's fears proved appropriate when Williams was unable to make the cuts during the rehearsal period in New York. Quintero remembered the period as "very, very painful for Williams":

> The play touched on his own terrifying experience in the hospital. There were still some vestiges of his paranoia that clung to his psyche in that play. He knew that there were lapses in the play, parts that didn't quite connect, and he didn't know how to make them connect. He didn't blame anybody, but he wouldn't come out of his [hotel] room. I would have to go and say, "Come on, Tom. It's alright." There were sad moments, very sad moments.[27]

After a disastrous press conference, Williams fled to his home in Key West, leaving the play to open in Washington at a length of three hours and to damning reviews. *Variety,* the show business trade paper, said that, although "Quintero's staging appears to do what's possible with the material," the play "collapses under three hours of sober introspection. Flashes of insight are buried under the weight of excessively wordy but unrevealing narrative."[28] Williams flew to Washington, where, every morning for a week and a half, Quintero came to his hotel room to work on revisions, "reading possible cuts to one another, discarding the repetitious, the dull, the irrelevant, and writing new transitions."[29] Since Quintero insisted on the importance of the cast's knowing that only the author could make changes in the play, it was Williams who presented the cuts to the cast each afternoon. Together Williams and Quintero cut forty-five minutes from the play, and tried four different endings before they settled on the one that closes the published play. With the shortened script and Quintero's restaging, the production opened to much better reviews, with particularly high praise for Geraldine Page, who had overcome her skepticism about the script. As the play was about to open in New York, Quintero acknowledged in an interview that it had been "a long, long siege – the most strenuous production I've ever done." But, he said,

> I wanted it to be as right as it could be for Geraldine and Tennessee – it's my gift to them, for good or bad. Now even if it doesn't go, I have the satisfaction that I did everything I knew how. There were more than 20 years to cross over, and finally we met in the tableau of the work. We are close again.[30]

Despite Quintero's Herculean effort to shore up Williams's nearly exhausted craftsmanship, the play opened to uniformly negative reviews in New York. It closed after 14 performances, following substantial efforts by the producer and a $20,000 contribution from Williams to keep it going.[31] Harold Clurman wrote a kind of epitaph for the play and the playwright: "José Quintero directed the script handsomely – abetted by Oliver Smith's discreetly evocative scenic design – and all the other effects (lighting, costumes, etc.) caught the eye. But there was too little heart at the center."[32]

To those who knew Williams and the American theatre, it was clear that *Clothes for a Summer Hotel* would mark the end of the playwright's career on the Broadway stage, although Clurman, for one, urged him to keep writing. "Did Shaw quit, or O'Neill?" he demanded, reminding Williams that "the sound artist functions because he cannot help doing so – not because he will eventually achieve fame and fortune."[33] Williams answered Clurman that he had said more than once that "it is possible to retire from a business but not from an art . . . I can assure all concerned, whether to their comfort or distress, that the failure of my ill-advised play . . . did not in the least diminish my desire and my necessity to proceed with several other unfinished works for the theater."[34] Although he continued writing until the day he died, he knew that his dream of a "comeback" in the commercial theatre was dead after 1980. In a sense he had come full circle from his first protector in the theatre, Margo Jones, to his last, José Quintero. In between he had worked with some of the best theatre directors of the twentieth century, among them Kazan, Peter Hall, Alan Schneider, Harold Clurman, Laurence Olivier, Herbert Machiz, Guthrie McClintic, George Roy Hill, Frank Corsaro, Daniel Mann, and Keith Hack, but none of them could give him everything he desired from his directors, partly because his desires were ambivalent and contradictory. He desired both protection and control. He sought collaboration and resented it. He needed an emotional connection, and he sabotaged it. He could be the most amiable of collaborators and the most difficult. He was fortunate in finding so many talented collaborators who saw the genius in the plays and were willing to take on the playwright in order to participate in their full realization on the stage.

NOTES

1 *Cat on a Hot Tin Roof* in *The Theatre of Tennessee Williams*, vol. III (New York: New Directions, 1971), 167.

2 *Cat*, 168.

3 See, for example, Nancy M. Tischler, *Tennessee Williams: Rebellious Puritan*, second edn. (New York: Citadel, 1965), 208–9 and Eric Bentley, "Theatre," *New Republic*, 132 (April 4, 1955), 22 and "Theatre," *New Republic*, 132 (April 11, 1955), 28.

4 "Author and Director: A Delicate Situation," *Playbill*, September 30, 1957; reprinted in *Where I Live: Selected Essays* (New York: New Directions, 1979), 93. Subsequently cited as "A&D."

5 Elia Kazan, *Elia Kazan: A Life* (New York: Knopf, 1988): 329–31, 338–39.

6 *Ibid.*, 540–46.

7 For a full examination of the collaboration of Williams and Kazan, see Brenda Murphy, *Tennessee Williams and Elia Kazan: A Collaboration in the Theatre* (Cambridge and New York: Cambridge University Press, 1992).

8 Tennessee Williams, *Memoirs* (Garden City, New York: Doubleday, 1975): 134–35, 102.

9 Lyle Leverich, *Tom: The Unknown Tennessee Williams* (New York: Crown, 1995), 502.

10 Donald Windham, *Tennessee Williams's Letters to Donald Windham 1940–1965* (New York: Penguin, 1980), 153.

11 Quoted in Leverich 552.

12 Williams, *Memoirs*, 82.

13 Helen Sheehy, *Margo: The Life and Theatre of Margo Jones* (Dallas: Southern Methodist University Press, 1989), 81.

14 Sheehy, *Margo*, 135.

15 Williams, *Memoirs*, 92, 152.

16 See Sheehy, *Margo*, 165 and Dakin Williams and Shepherd Mead, *Tennessee Williams: An Intimate Biography* (New York: Arbor House, 1983), 166–67.

17 Audrey Wood, with Max Wilk, *Represented by Audrey Wood* (New York: Doubleday, 1981): 157.

18 Tennessee Williams to Donald Windham, October 19, 1948, in Windham 225.

19 Undated letter, Tennessee Williams to Elia Kazan, Harry Ransom Humanities Research Center, University of Texas at Austin.

20 Undated letter, Tennessee Williams to Elia Kazan, Harry Ransom Humanities Research Center, University of Texas at Austin.

21 *The Rose Tattoo, The Theatre of Tennessee Williams*, vol. II (New York: New Directions, 1971), 412.

22 Tennessee Williams, to Maria Britneva, May 27, 1951, in *Five O'Clock Angel: Letters of Tennessee Williams to Maria St. Just 1948–1982* (New York: Knopf, 1990), 56.

23 José Quintero, *If You Don't Dance They Beat You* (Boston: Little, Brown, 1974), 121.

24 Quoted in Dotson Rader, "The Art of the Theatre V: Tennessee Williams," *The Paris Review* 81 (Fall 1981); reprinted in Albert Devlin (ed.) *Conversations with Tennessee Williams* (Jackson: University Press of Mississippi, 1986), 336.

25 Williams, *Memoirs*, 226.

26 Frances Herridge, "Quintero Finds 'Clothes' Suitable," *New York Post*, March 21, 1980, 42.

27 Quoted in Donald Spoto, *The Kindness of Strangers: The Life of Tennessee Williams* (1985; reprinted in New York: Ballantine, 1986), 380.

28 "Paul," "Shows Out of Town," *Variety*, February 6, 1980, 132.

29 Michiko Kakutani, "Williams and Quintero Build a 'Summer Hotel,'" *New York Times*, March 23, 1980, Section 2: 1.

30 *Ibid.*, 26.

31 Michiko Kakutani, "Williams, Quintero and the Aftermath of a Failure," *New York Times*, June 22, 1980, Section 2: 1, 7.

32 Harold Clurman, "Clothes for a Summer Hotel," *The Nation* 209 (April 19, 1980), 477.

33 Harold Clurman, letter to the editor, *New York Times*, July 13, 1980, Section 2: 3, 10.

34 Tennessee Williams, letter to the editor, *New York Times*, August 3, 1980, Section 2: 4.

II

R. BARTON PALMER

Hollywood in crisis: Tennessee Williams and the evolution of the adult film

WILLIAMS ON FILM: SOME PRELIMINARY THOUGHTS

In the English-speaking world, the two principal performance arts, theatre and film, have developed together in the twentieth century. An important common element of the British and American commercial theatres is that each has enjoyed a cooperative and mutually beneficial relationship with the respective national cinema since the beginning of the sound film era. In the case of Great Britain, this relationship was eased for several decades by the proximity of the commercial film studios, most of which were once located in the Greater London area, to the West End theatrical district; such proximity made it possible, in many cases almost inevitable, for creative personnel in the theatre to work part-time on film projects, and vice-versa. The move of the American film business to California from its New York base at the beginning of the studio period (c. 1912–20) posed difficulties for actors, writers, directors, and production artists wishing to work in both fields, and yet many have done so. Indeed, in the nineties, this trend shows no sign of abating, even with the dispersal of film production into a number of regional centers outside California.

Throughout the studio period (c. 1920–70), Hollywood benefited not only from the labors of those who had been trained on and worked mainly for the commercial American theatre. American filmmakers also looked to Broadway as they looked to the bestseller list: for source materials, for "properties" whose appeal to American consumers had already been well demonstrated. A play fresh from a successful Broadway run is also "pre-sold" in the sense that many filmgoers are acquainted with it even if they haven't attended a performance, and thus, so the industry reasoning runs, may be the more easily persuaded to see a film version. The result is predictable: many successful American commercial theatre productions are very attractive to filmmakers and regularly provide the source for successful film releases.

Thus we should expect that the widespread success achieved by and critical acclaim bestowed upon Tennessee Williams during his postwar Broadway career would have made his plays and other works desirable properties for cinematic adaptation. In fact, all of Williams's stage successes have been turned into films that, on the whole, have been received well by audiences and critics alike. However, the story of the transference of Williams's plays is by no means a simple one. The film business and the commercial theatre are institutions with quite different histories, requirements, traditions, and positions within the culture industry. Thus each had quite distinct reasons for valuing Williams as a writer and vastly divergent modes of shaping for presentation the dramatic texts he wrote. The result is that the Tennessee Williams who is central to the history of the American commercial theatre is substantially different from the Tennessee Williams who played a significant role in the development of the postwar American cinema. To judge the impact of his work on American culture, a consideration in some depth of both histories or versions of the author is necessary.

The purpose of this essay is to offer a critical history of the early and most important stage of the relationship between Tennessee Williams and the Hollywood cinema. That relationship, extending for more than two decades, is complex and multileveled, much more so than in the case of other American playwrights whose popularity resulted in movie versions of their works. With Eugene O'Neill, Arthur Miller, or William Inge, or, indeed, every other American playwright, of sole importance are the films in question, the screen versions themselves, which may be plumbed for their aesthetic, sociological, and institutional values or which may be examined to determine the whys and wherefores of the adaptation process.

With Williams, in contrast, such a concentration on the films would disregard a connection between the author and Hollywood that is arguably much more important. For unlike other noted playwrights, Williams's work strongly influenced the development of the film industry itself. Indeed, it is hard to imagine the course of fifties and early sixties cinematic history without his plays as source material; and if we could imagine such a history, it would be quite different from the one that actually played out on the screen. To my knowledge, no other author through his works alone has had this kind of influence on the history of a national cinema.

From this point of view, seven of the fifteen films based on Williams's work are of major importance: *The Glass Menagerie* (1950), *A Streetcar Named Desire* (1951), *The Rose Tattoo* (1955), *Baby Doll* (1956), *The Fugitive Kind* (1960), *Cat on a Hot Tin Roof* (1958), and *Sweet Bird of Youth* (1962). Though they have been analyzed by a number of scholars, all of the film versions of Williams's plays merit further, in-depth treatment, at least in terms of discussing the adaptation process, which raises interesting cultural and aesthetic questions that would in every instance repay further examination. Regrettably, space limitations make that impossible here. Focusing on Williams's impact on the cinema means that this chapter often departs from purely textual analysis. In fact, it has proved necessary to offer here a somewhat detailed account of developments within the film industry. These may not seem at first closely connected to the issues raised by adaptation, which is often approached formally through an assessment of the changes that have been made in transferring a source text from one medium to another. However, adaptation in the case of Williams must be understood in a larger sense, as designating how one medium comes to relate to another in a process that is centered upon but certainly not confined to the generation of texts. The discussion that follows of Williams's relationship to Hollywood will, I hope, make this point clear.

A NEW TYPE OF HOLLYWOOD FILM

Tennessee Williams rose to prominence during the immediate postwar era that witnessed a revitalization, perhaps even a rebirth of the American commercial theatre. Along with other new voices and innovators, most prominently Arthur Miller and William Inge, Williams succeeded in transforming the customary themes and form of the serious Broadway drama that had held sway during the early forties. These plays often featured high-minded or politically engaged comment on the American scene expressed by somewhat predictable patterns of exposition and resolution. Audiences were afforded intellectual stimulation and "dramatic" satisfactions of a traditional kind, with clear-cut divisions between rising action, climax, and falling action. A useful example is Lillian Hellman's critically acclaimed and commercially successful *Watch on the Rhine*, where the morality play opposition of democratic patriot to opportunistic fascist fellow traveler is resolved after much suspense by the former's cold-blooded elimination of the latter. The protagonist, appropriately named Freidank ("freethinker"), agonizes over the need for such killing, thereby exemplifying both a social democratic hatred of war and a desire for peace based on international comradeship. With its timely themes and intense drawing-room dramatics, the play was quickly and easily transformed by Hollywood into a successful star vehicle for Bette Davis (1943, directed by Broadway old hand Herman Shumlin).

For Williams, breaking with this Broadway tradition meant abandoning a moralistic or political analysis of American society for an exploration of the psychosexual inner lives of the emotionally traumatized and socially marginalized, those either dispossessed of happiness or indisposed to grasp it. His main characters became tortured loners who had been bypassed by the great American dream of public acclaim and bourgeois material success, often because of some sexual crime or indiscretion that alienated them from more respectable others. The drama that entangled them was always personal, seldom political, a function of complexly intimate relations with family or with fellow travelers met by chance on the road of self-confrontation.

Williams realized the usually tragic and often violent lives of such characters through a poetically rich blend of realist and expressionist techniques. The power and emotional intensity of his dramas revealed well-made theme plays to be by comparison mistakenly committed to the portrayal of irrelevant public selves. Not surprisingly, Williams's plays required new forms of stagecraft because missing fourth-wall sets often did not suit his more fluid conceptions of time and space; his characters, in turn, could only be fully realized by a different kind of naturalistic acting capable of representing conflicted, multilayered selves: the so-called "Method" that had recently come into vogue with the founding of the Actors Studio.

Williams, perhaps most notably with his early smash-hit productions such as *A Streetcar Named Desire* and *Sweet Bird of Youth*, appealed to a sophisticated and well-educated audience of playgoers much affected by the growing fashion for psychotherapy and the widespread endorsement of Freudian theory as an explanation of the human condition. They applauded Williams for putting sex on the theatrical agenda and sympathized with the guilt-ridden vulnerability of his protagonists. Responding to a contradictory historical moment that featured an intensifying Cold War but the proclamation of the "end of ideology," these playgoers did not resent the nearly complete absence of social and political themes in Williams's work, or the pessimistic bleakness of his vision. Because Williams was committed to thematizing sex and psychological discontent in new, more central ways, his plays seemed startlingly realistic, appeared despite their poetry and intellectual schemata to move beyond the restricting decorum of the previous theatrical age and make direct contact with life as it was really lived, warts and all.

Disdainful of an American cinema devoted to happy endings and flat characters, Broadway audiences were eager for an art that provided difficult satisfactions rather than the deceptive pleasures of wish fulfillment. In short, the vein of taste mined by Williams, Miller, Inge, and others was resolutely high cultural, accommodating of tragic themes and modernist techniques, scornful of traditional pieties, including what had hitherto been a more or less tacit ban on those "adult" subjects such as homosexuality, drug addiction, sexual predation, and prostitution so central to Williams's conception of dramatically arresting character. Catering to a minority, elite culture, the Broadway stage in the immediate postwar era could (and did) readily adapt to the new vision offered by Williams and others.

In contrast, the Hollywood film industry by the late forties had established itself solidly in another, rather distant area of cultural production: providing for general audiences clean, wholesome entertainment conforming to a detailed series of protocols – the Production Code. Based on Victorian notions of uplift, the Code proclaimed, in part, that "Art can be morally evil in its effects. This is the case clearly enough with unclean art, indecent books, suggestive drama. The effect on the lives of men and women is obvious."[1] Hollywood thus was committed to banishing from significant representation or often even mere mention the themes Williams found so compelling and unavoidable. This was by no means a situation unique to Williams. Literary modernism in general, with its distaste for didacticism and commitment to the truth, however unpleasant, of human behavior, could not easily be accommodated to the demands of a medium that endorsed older, opposed theories of art and cultural production.

In 1947, when Williams was making a name for himself with the popular and critically acclaimed New York production of A Streetcar Named Desire, Hollywood films were still closely vetted by the Production Code Administration, a censorship office that had been founded by the film producers themselves in 1934 in response to intense Catholic lobbying efforts for "cleaner" films and over which a prominent Catholic layman, Joseph Breen, still magisterially presided. The Code, and the censors who put it into force, demanded not only that various aspects of human existence be avoided by Hollywood films, but that these vehicles of mass entertainment should also be structured by the central principle of nineteenth-century melodrama: evil was to be punished and good rewarded, while any sympathy for wrongdoing should be eliminated by compensating moral value (such as the unlikely reform in the last five minutes of hitherto enthusiastic sinners).

During the forties, the Hollywood studios were in general careful not to offend the more traditionally minded within their audience and eagerly promoted an idealized vision of American values and society. This was especially apparent for the duration of the war when Hollywood, in exchange for being allowed to continue to produce and exhibit films, energetically supported the aims of the government, making many morale-boosting and enlistment-encouraging films that emphasized traditional

American optimism and solidly bourgeois values. The marketing strategy of appealing to a general, undifferentiated audience while not offending the morally conservative among them proved immensely successful. By war's end box-office receipts hit an all-time high; weekly attendance almost equaled the nation's population, which was at that time almost 120 million, a truly staggering figure that indicates how central moviegoing had become for many, who must have attended religiously numerous times a week.

Though film producers were always eager for material of demonstrated popularity – stories, novels or plays – they could transform into films, such an industry would seem to have little use for most of Williams's plays, which might be unprofitably restricted in their appeal because they were too arty. Furthermore, what Williams wrote was almost certainly too adult to make into movies that would meet with the ready approval of the Production Code Administration. The one obvious exception was *The Glass Menagerie*, made into a film version that was released in 1950 and directed by Irving Rapper. Williams's first stage success featured no violence and only, by way of sexual content, the Oedipal themes conventional in *Bildungsroman* narrative, at that time a Hollywood staple. *The Glass Menagerie* dramatizes the treacherous and sometimes uncrossable passage into adult life as well as the discontents of romance for women who must await the call of sexual desire. Amanda Wingfield is eager for her shy daughter Laura to be swept away by a "gentleman caller" even as, paradoxically, this overbearing mother makes it difficult for Laura's brother Tom to grow into healthy independence and sexual maturity (the conventional sexual politics of the film version are discussed in more detail below). Yet even this play, to Williams's chagrin, offended Joseph Breen in part when a scenario was submitted to him; the zealous censor thought that the relationship between Tom and Laura bordered on an incestuous attachment. Breen demanded excision of some of the dialogue in the emotional *scène à deux* where brother and sister acknowledge their mutual affection prior to Tom's departure for the Merchant Marine.

After 1946, Hollywood's most profitable year, however, the fortunes of the studios shifted radically. And in a short time what Williams had to offer in his groundbreaking later plays seemed not only acceptable, but desirable. In fact, the somewhat surprising result is that Williams soon became the most adapted of America's dramatists, with his plays and even a novella, *The Roman Spring of Mrs. Stone* (1961), providing the source for some of Hollywood's most critically acclaimed, most popular, most financially successful films during the fifties and early sixties. Against all odds, Williams's texts became key sources in the development of an "adult" form of cinematic entertainment, one radically different from the standard studio fare of the Hollywood boom during the middle forties.

At the end of the 1940s, the American film industry experienced a number of difficulties that led to a rapid and long-term decline in attendance and profits. An essential element of Hollywood financial success had been vertical integration, with production, distribution, and first-run theatrical exhibition existing under one corporate umbrella. Such economic muscle allowed the major studios to corner screen time and hence rental returns through blind bidding (the securing of exhibition contracts before a trade show of the film) and block booking (the offering of desired films for exhibition only in a block of less desirable ones). In a 1948 case involving Paramount, the US Supreme Court ruled that these trade practices and vertical integration itself were illegal. The major studios were all subsequently forced to sign consent decrees that led to their divestiture of theatrical holdings. Without a secure market for their product, the studios could no longer function as "factories" turning out hundreds of films annually by assembly-line methods. A gradual switch was made to one-off production that emphasized blockbuster or "special" projects, with each film the result of ad hoc financial and contractual arrangements. At the same time, payrolls were trimmed and the vast studio infrastructures dismantled.

Deprived of its formula for economic success, Hollywood lost its traditional main market as well: middle-class urbanites who lived close to downtown and neighborhood theatres. Lured by suddenly cheap housing, this class of Americans moved en masse to newly built suburbs, then far from movie theatres and frequently off public transportation routes. A substitute for cinema-going that was home-centered soon appeared in the form of television, which expanded rapidly in the course of the fifties until, by the end of the decade, most families in the country owned a set and tuned in many hours a week. With the establishment of a consumer economy devoted to the production of "durables" and the emergence of entertainment alternatives, Hollywood's traditional customers increasingly chose to spend their discretionary income on washing machines, vacation travel, and do-it-yourselfing. By the beginning of the fifties, weekly attendance was down to about sixty percent of immediate postwar levels, while production costs soared in an otherwise booming economy. Thousands of movie theatres around the country closed their doors forever as it appeared that Americans after forty years had finally wearied of their fascination with the motion pictures.

Producers attempted to reverse their declining fortunes with two principal strategies, one of which was particularly important in bringing the works of Tennessee Williams to the screen. First, the competition from television encouraged a differentiation of product as filmmakers attempted to outclass the fuzzy, black and white images and tinny audio then available on the tube by impressing viewers with wide-screen Technicolor epics in stereophonic sound. With its limited budgets, television programming could offer little in the way of stars or spectacle; blockbuster films of the period, by contrast, normally featured "all-star casts," exotic location shooting, and bravura action set-pieces in an attempt to woo back paying customers. This strategy was at least a partial success as the studios managed to stay in business.

Television, however, was also limited in a second way that Hollywood hoped to exploit: by the new medium's status as a governmentally regulated industry subject to Federal Communication Commission (FCC) guidelines, including production protocols similar to, but sometimes even more stringent than Hollywood's own, which were, of course, industry generated. If television had taken over to some degree Hollywood's former function as the provider of audiovisual entertainment for a mass public of all ages and tastes, then the film industry could colonize a new area of production, one whose popularity with a segment of the filmgoing public had been established by the exhibition successes of art films, especially Italian neorealist productions like *Bicycle Thief* (Vittorio de Sica, American release 1949). Though film exhibition in general suffered greatly from the late forties through the fifties, theatres that specialized in screening art films, mostly from Europe, became much more numerous and profitable at this time, indicating that there was a loyal audience of educated adults who would pay to see a "film" even if they despised Hollywood "movies" as the mindless products of a hopelessly compromised culture industry.

Because European films were not produced with input from the Production Code Administration (PCA), they often transgressed the official standards the industry had established, especially with regard to sexual representation. In fact, the term "art film" by decade's end had become, if only in part, a euphemism for soft core pornography. Normally all films, including imports, needed a certificate of approval from the PCA in order to secure exhibition contracts. *Bicycle Thief*'s importers were refused such a certificate by Joseph Breen, who objected to two scenes: one in which a young boy pauses by the side of a wall, apparently to relieve himself; and another in which a thief is pursued into a bordello whose inhabitants, though fully clothed and otherwise decent, are obviously engaged in the world's oldest profession. Despite the film's renown as an internationally acclaimed artistic triumph and protests from the American liberal establishment, Breen stuck by his decision.

Surprisingly, *Bicycle Thief* enjoyed an immensely successful run in the teeth of Hollywood's official condemnation, eventually and improbably winning the Oscar for best foreign film in a turnabout that chagrined and embarrassed Breen. Even the Catholic Church refused to go along with the PCA and did not put the film on its forbidden list. The lesson for film producers was obvious. There was a market for films that were "artistic" and violated or at least tested hitherto generally accepted limitations on the representation of sexual themes; the PCA had lost clout in its defense of what now began to seem unnecessarily old-fashioned or prudish standards, and exhibitors could do well even with controversial films that lacked PCA approval, but only if these could be justified artistically.

A STREETCAR NAMED DESIRE: THE FIRST ADULT FILM

Conditions within the industry, in other words, were right for the production of American films on the European model, films that would be both intellectually satisfying and titillating. This was a trend to which Williams's groundbreaking plays could make an important contribution, provided that they were adapted in the proper fashion. At first, however, Hollywood only showed interest in Tennessee Williams's more conventional work. The studios' initial experience with the young author was with a play not much different from the accustomed Broadway serious drama of the period. *The Glass Menagerie* bears the marks of strong influence from the Lillian Hellman family problem play (*The Little Foxes* [1939] or, perhaps even a closer analogue, *The Children's Hour* [1934]). Interestingly enough, it had first been written as a screenplay for Metro-Goldwyn-Mayer (MGM) during Williams's uneventful employment there (it was rejected as unsuitable). After the play's outstanding Broadway success, however, the Hollywood studios (including a chagrined MGM) fought a bidding war for the rights to film it, with Warner Brothers proving eventually victorious.

The Glass Menagerie was adapted to fit a time-honored and commercially successful formula, with Williams's poignant and ambiguous memory play transformed into a straightforward melodrama that attested to the perseverance and final triumph of its sympathetically evoked female leads. Though radically different from Williams's conception of the endearing but pathetic Laura, Jane Wyman here reprised her critically acclaimed role as a handicapped but resilient young woman. In Williams's story, she is a cripple rather than the deaf mute whose portrayal won her the Oscar in *Johnny Belinda* (Jean Negulesco, 1948). Like most women's pictures of the period, Rapper's version of *The Glass Menagerie* ends happily, with family members reconciled and Laura eagerly awaiting the imminent arrival of a flesh and blood gentleman caller to rescue her from the discontents of maturation.

The tragic tone imparted by the playwright to Laura's isolation, Amanda's delusions of grandeur, and Tom's self-serving reconstructions of the familial past needed to be altered substantially in the transference to the screen if a conventional woman's picture were to be the result. And Williams was appalled at what was done to his play. Rapper's film was, in the playwright's opinion, "the most awful travesty of the play I've ever seen . . . horribly mangled by the people who did the film script."[2]

Nonetheless, the core elements of *The Glass Menagerie*, once provided with a more upbeat interpretation and resolution, were eminently suitable source material for a standard Hollywood film. Not only does the play, with its social realist perspective, make an important connection between psychological and economic hardships, a common element in many of the gritty film dramas of the period; it also, except for flashback narration by a character, then an almost standard technique in Hollywood films, avoids modernist dramatic devices and moves steadily, Ibsen-like, from exposition, through complication, to an emotion-revealing conclusion. Hollywood films depended above all else upon an unambiguous and dynamic narrative to hold audience interest. And Williams provides the basis for a strong one in this play even though, characteristically, this element of dramatic construction did not particularly fascinate him and he sometimes experienced difficulties with devising a second act that would resolve the issues raised in the first.

Though the playwright was hardly pleased, the film version of *The Glass Menagerie* was moderately successful and bears close comparison with Rapper's greatest triumph in the woman's picture genre: *Now, Voyager* (1942), a much-praised Bette Davis vehicle. That film also explores the depth of female discontents with a gender system that accommodates women, if at all, as passive objects of desire whose appearance and manner mean everything. *Now, Voyager*'s at-first hysterical main character, Charlotte Vale, successfully struggles to achieve a provisional independence and adulthood, though she is denied the satisfactions of married life. Like the film version of *The Glass Menagerie*, *Now, Voyager* offers an obviously contrived happy ending, a wish fulfillment that entertainingly transcends the tragic conclusion of such exploration, which is the developmental dead-end of lonely, barren spinsterhood. Though oppressed by mothers who refuse to stop infantilizing them, both Charlotte and Laura prove in the end able to embrace maturity – the message of uplift most common in the many woman's pictures of the period that deal with young adulthood.

In contrast, Williams's second stage success, *A Streetcar Named Desire*, though it likewise offers two sympathetic women characters, could not have been transformed even by the knowledgeable and experienced Irving Rapper into anything resembling a woman's picture. With its revelation and dramatization of sexual misconduct, its delineation of a horrifying descent into madness, its portrayal of women driven and even controlled by desire, the play, in fact, offered themes that could not be accommodated to any standard Hollywood schema. Though Williams had garnered the acclaim of the critics and a Pulitzer Prize for *A Streetcar Named Desire*, which continued to pack in standing-room-only crowds, filmmakers were for two years uninterested in pursuing the possibility of a screen adaptation – with one exception, William Wyler, one of Hollywood's most commercially successful and esteemed directors.

Correctly reading the changes in popular taste and impatient with the restrictions posed upon American filmmaking while imports demonstrated that the cinema was capable of producing sophisticated art, Wyler thought *Streetcar* would be a commercial success as a vehicle for Bette Davis, an actress he had worked with on prestigious adaptations of Lillian Hellman and Somerset Maugham. He recognized that, alone of noted American writers, Tennessee Williams had authored a text that could be the source of a film both artistic and sensational, the potent marketing combination of many European art films. Davis had played strong-minded, sexually aggressive Southern women twice in her career for Wyler, first in the Warners antebellum epic *Jezebel* (1939) and later in his acclaimed version of *The Little Foxes* (1941). By the late forties, Davis had developed a screen persona nicely balanced between sympathetic roles and more villainous portrayals, an ambiguity Wyler took advantage of when he directed Davis in *The Letter* (1940), where she is successfully cast as Somerset Maugham's most notorious heroine, a seemingly ordinary and respectable woman capable of the most outrageous sexual deception and violent crime, a character similar in important ways to Blanche DuBois.

Davis would likely have made a powerful Blanche, but Wyler was so discouraged by Breen's initial pronouncements on the project that he abandoned it, turning instead to Sidney Kingsley's Broadway hit *Detective Story* (1950) for his next film. This play dealt with, in part, an abortion doctor rather than a rapist, and Wyler more easily negotiated approval from Breen, despite the fact that many alterations were required from the PCA before a certificate was forthcoming.

Though it likewise raised strenuous objections from the censor, *Detective Story* was a very different kind of property from *Streetcar*. Kingsley's drama treats sexual subject matter that was from a PCA perspective objectionable, but it is hardly an erotic text, with its dramatic center the psychological breakdown a New York detective experiences as he tries to go about the performance of his duties. Williams's play, in contrast, not only treated sexual themes prominent on the Code's forbidden list – the homosexuality of Blanche's late husband, her evidently aggressive sexual appetite, and Stanley's violent rape of his wife's sister. It also exuded animalistic sexuality, with Stanley's attack the culmination of profound feelings of attraction/ repulsion between the two main characters.

If, as Williams has emphasized, the rape in part represents the destruction of an old-fashioned gentility by the harsher, material forces of modern life, it also fittingly resolves Blanche's suspension between manipulative illusion and self-awareness. Taken by the brutish Stanley, Blanche becomes the seducer seduced and must face up to her own compulsive, predatory sexual urges. Her madness results not only from the undeniable horror of violation, but from the recognition that she has played a role in its advent. The complexity of Williams's conception is that Stanley and Blanche are compounded equally of sympathetic and unsympathetic elements. And the dramatic power of their explosive confrontation derives from the ways in which this evolving relationship is highly sexualized, with Stella's passion for Stanley and Mitch's carefully orchestrated desire for Blanche functioning as illuminating counterpoint.

In short, *Streetcar* not only takes sex as a theme; the play represents the power and destructiveness of desire, constructing itself as an erotic object that seduces the playgoer into an eagerness for the fateful, final encounter. Despite its hard-boiled look at sex, *Streetcar*, however, is never merely crude or suggestive like much popular American fiction, especially the works of Mickey Spillane, James M. Cain, and Erskine Caldwell, all of whom were notorious at the time for treating similar themes and enjoyed a wide readership. Williams's artfully ambiguous characterizations of Stanley and Blanche, and the poignant poetry of the play's dialogue, make *Streetcar* a powerfully moving if bleak examination of the human condition. Or, as director Elia Kazan, who was quite conversant with bottom-line Hollywood thinking, told film producer Jack Warner, "1/ It is about the three Fs; 2/ It has class."[3]

Remarkably, Williams's play was transferred to the screen with even fewer alterations than the playwright had suffered through while watching a Hollywood version of *The Glass Menagerie* emerge. The successful Broadway run, helped by the blatantly steamy title, had given the play a notoriety that, with its implied promise of commercial success, appealed to talent agent Charles Feldman, who bought the screen rights with the hope of breaking into the film business as a producer. If the pessimism of Williams's vision in *The Glass Menagerie* had been judged – and probably correctly – as box-office poison by Warner Brothers, the playwright's unremitting portrayal of sexual compulsion and violence in *A Streetcar Named Desire* was seen by Feldman as the quality most potentially attractive to filmgoers, despite the tragic consequences for Blanche of enduring the journey of desire to its bitter end.

Such suffering for a less-than-virtuous female main character did not violate then-acceptable notions of a poetically just ending. In fact, a popular film series at the time, what is now known as *film noir* or "dark cinema," often featured sexually aggressive or transgressive *femmes fatales* who met with violent retribution at the hands of the men they victimized. Functioning as a cultural other to the woman's picture, *noir* films thematized a self-righteous and often unambiguous misogyny, with fatally attractive women winding up dead, imprisoned, or otherwise punished. *Streetcar*'s downbeat conclusion, in other words, would be acceptable to filmgoers used to similar portrayals of feminine misadventure. Williams's change of subject matter from his first to second play meant that as far as film adaptation was concerned his dramatic conception would be less altered.

The irony involved, of course, is that *The Glass Menagerie* was in most ways closer to the kind of films Hollywood had become accustomed to making. But by a happy coincidence of authorial vision and cultural trends, Williams had subsequently begun to write just what some within the film business correctly thought would be hugely successful. *A Streetcar Named Desire* was just similar enough to the *film noir* to be easily marketable. And yet its startling differences from the standard Hollywood movie in the representation of sexual themes eminently suited Williams's play to be the source of the first Hollywood production in a new genre: the adult art film.

Afraid, perhaps, of controversy, the major studios all passed on *Streetcar*. But with the newly emerging possibilities of independent production, a screen version could be conceived and planned outside the mainstream of the business. Williams himself took a very active part in the project, an unusual step for an author at the time. However, he was very eager that his hit play be filmed and with Feldman's help approached Elia Kazan, who had directed the stage production, in hopes of convincing him to oversee the film version as well.

Kazan's career at the time usefully exemplifies how it was possible to work successfully both in Hollywood and on Broadway. In 1950, he was Broadway's hottest director, having brought to the stage what are arguably the three most important serious plays of the immediate postwar era: Arthur Miller's *All My Sons* (1947) and *Death of a Salesman* (1949) and Williams's *Streetcar* (1947). Kazan, however, had also achieved critical and commercial success with quite different film projects, all more or less standard genre pieces with strong melodramatic elements: the most important of these being *A Tree Grows in Brooklyn* (1945), *Gentleman's Agreement* (1947), and *Pinky* (1949), the last of which was coincidentally the highest-grossing film of that year.

Kazan was at first reluctant to do the project, not foreseeing, perhaps, that he could preside over the making of a very different kind of film, one that would not be forced to conform to Hollywood's Victorian aesthetic. Kazan's eventual agreement to what Williams and Feldman proposed altered the director's Hollywood career. The film version of *Streetcar* he directed would inaugurate a commercial American art cinema to which Kazan himself, immediately thereafter abandoning more conventional melodrama, would go on to make a number of notable contributions: *Viva Zapata!* (1952), *On the Waterfront* (1954), *East of Eden* (1955), and *A Face in the Crowd* (1957).

Williams thought, and rightly so, that Kazan's participation was essential to the preservation of his vision, for the director had been in large measure responsible for the effective shaping and nuancing of the complex dramatic elements in *Streetcar*. Feldman, however, knew that Kazan was perhaps even more vital to the making of financial and technical arrangements. Kazan was not only a directorial genius, but a shrewd businessman eager for the commercial success his films had achieved. By now, he knew how to oversee a well-run production and keep financial backers happy. Persuaded by his friendship for Williams and the $175,000 fee he was offered (a huge amount at the time), Kazan undertook the job. Feldman was then quite quickly able to secure the agreement of Warner Brothers to finance a substantial part of the production costs. The studio would also loan its facilities and technicians in return for distribution rights and a profit share.

In the emerging world of fifties film production, such arrangements would soon be standard, profitable ones for independent producers like Feldman who were willing to take risks on unusual, perhaps marginal projects in the hope of turning a substantial profit. The importance of these contextual factors for the particular film version of Williams's play that eventually emerged can hardly be overemphasized. The conditions within the American film industry that resulted in large part from the studios' financial difficulties made it possible for Williams's play to be purchased and conceived as an independent commercial project, with hopes of its being adapted in a more or less "faithful" fashion. Kazan's version of *Streetcar* would have been unthinkable during the heights of studio success just a few years previously when steady profits were being made from a very different kind of product.

But more than financial arrangements were necessary if this project were to be successfully realized. The next and perhaps most difficult hurdle for Feldman, Williams, and Kazan to clear was the PCA, then weakened somewhat by the defiantly successful release of *Bicycle Thief* but still a potent force in Hollywood. The arrangement with Warner Brothers specified that the film version of *Streetcar* would have to be awarded a PCA certificate; there was to be no possibility of an uncertificated release if Williams and Feldman were to live up to their contract. Initial negotiations with the PCA resulted in objections to three aspects of Williams's play, the first two of which were settled rather easily by compromise. Blanche's husband would no longer be identified as a homosexual, but simply as a weak (read impotent) man, a change Kazan was actually in favor of since he disliked the suggestion of "perversion." Blanche's sexual hunger for young men, her "nymphomania" (in fifties terms), would have to be downplayed to make it less obvious to younger viewers but still clear enough to more experienced adults. Kazan was quite well experienced with the rhetoric Hollywood directors, writers, and actors had developed in order to represent, but only by nuance and suggestion, the facts of sexual desire and activity. He would have no problem in making sure that Blanche's disreputable sexual history was something only the more sophisticated could infer and did not think that these changes of emphasis would mar Williams's vision.

Breen also wanted the rape scene excised or somehow relieved of its terrifying significance, and this was a change neither Kazan nor Williams could agree to. Here Breen was adamant that even a nuanced treatment was objectionable, but, Williams and Kazan countered, the rape was the plot's central event, the necessary culmination of the highly charged, contradictory relationship between Stanley and Blanche that holds the spectator's interest from the outset. Were it removed in some fashion or another resolution substituted, the story, and the characters whose development it traced, would no longer make any coherent sense.

Though the Code was unambiguous on this point and Breen was personally unsympathetic to the artistic problems involved, the PCA found itself in a difficult position as it attempted to respond to a rapid evolution in popular taste and yet maintain its role as guarantor of a moralistic rationale for Hollywood films. After the *Bicycle Thief* embarrassment, Breen could ill afford another public incident that suggested his office was narrow-minded in its opposition to modern art. Williams's play, after all, had won the Pulitzer Prize. And yet any obvious endorsement of the screenplay proposed by Kazan and Williams would set a dangerous precedent for future decisions. Sensing Breen's dilemma, Kazan decided to avoid overt disagreement. The rejected script would stand. When shooting it, Kazan simply did not respond to Breen's objections that the rape scene be removed, staging and filming the sequence of events subtly if unmistakably. After viewing the completed film, Breen demanded some minor changes in the ending of the story, with the result that Stella appears to be resolved never again to trust her brutal husband, an interesting example of compensating moral value. But the core of Williams's drama remained on screen for filmgoers to enjoy and ponder, the Code that hitherto had prevented such screen treatment of sexuality having been breached. Kazan's version of Williams's play thereby inaugurated a new kind of Hollywood film, one whose increasing frankness and explicitness would demand by 1967 the abandonment of the Code altogether and the development of a ratings system to take its place.

The film's outstanding success with audiences was aided considerably by a casting throughly suited to the particular requirements of the commercial film industry. Though Jessica Tandy had created an excellent Blanche for the initial New York stage production that otherwise served as the basis of Kazan's film, Warners demanded an established film star in the featured female lead, standard industry practice at a time when marketing was based on an individual film's generic affiliations and star players. The choice of Vivien Leigh, who had appeared as Blanche in the London production, was fortuitous. More so than Broadway plays, Hollywood films depended on what we might term the "production history" of stars as well as their public images to create complex and appealing resonances of meaning.

Who better to portray the dark underside of Southern belledom than the actress famous for the screen incarnation of fiction's most famous Southern belle in *Gone with the Wind* (1939), one of the industry's most celebrated films? Who better to imitate the descent into madness of a genteel woman struggling with her sexual hunger than the successful actress whose fragile mental state and growing marital unhappiness, soon to result in adulterous misadventure, were then sensational public knowledge? It is no accident that Vivien Leigh was picked to portray an aging and mentally unstable actress who forms a liaison with a handsome young gigolo in a later Williams adaptation: *The Roman Spring of Mrs. Stone* (José Quintero, 1961); that film benefits from the same aspects of Leigh's star persona. Most important, perhaps, the casting of Vivien Leigh as Blanche effectively linked the spectator's knowledge about the sexual transgressions of film stars (i.e., Hollywood as the locus of an energizing sexual naughtiness) to the similar thematics of Williams's drama. No such effect could have been achieved with the less-than-notorious Jessica Tandy. Leigh, of course, was easily outclassed as an actress by Marlon Brando's powerful Method performance, but the way she is overwhelmed on screen by his personal magnetism and expressive abilities perfectly suits the themes and plot of Williams's play.

More important, of course, for the play's representation of sex, its arousal of desire was the casting of Marlon Brando as Stanley. It is certainly no exaggeration to say that Brando's sizzling incarnation of Stanley had much to do with the Broadway success of Williams's play. The American commercial theatre had seldom seen an actor of such raw physical magnetism. Because film, being based on photography, possesses better resources for eroticizing and idealizing the human body than live theatre, Kazan was able to make Brando's Stanley, with his complex mix of sympathetic vulnerability and terrifying aggressivity, even a more central, affecting part of the film, of which Brando became the undisputed star.

Just as Williams's play deeply affected the kind of film Hollywood thereafter would make, so Brando's performance – the first time American filmgoers had been treated to a full-blown Method characterization – transformed the traditional screen image of appealing maleness. Yet this development would have been impossible without Williams's play. A year earlier, Brando's first screen part, as a paraplegic veteran in *The Men* (Fred Zinnemann, 1950), had permitted him only to create a rather one-dimensional portrait of sympathetic Americanness – exactly the kind of role most available for handsome, young male leads at the time, and to which he would likely have been largely condemned had it not been for a film version of *Streetcar*. Even though his performance as Stanley pushed his career in a somewhat different direction, Brando was still unable to escape such parts entirely, as his conventional portrayals in such films as *Teahouse of the August Moon* (Daniel Mann, 1956) and *Guys and Dolls* (Joseph L. Mankiewicz, 1955) bear witness.

Of this there is no doubt. Williams's creation of Stanley Kowalski, as well as similar male leads such as Chance Wayne in *Sweet Bird of Youth* and Brick Pollitt in *Cat on a Hot Tin Roof*, contributed centrally to a radical transformation of what Americans had previously valued as ideal, male qualities. This transformed image of masculinity, though enhanced by the essentially theatrical techniques of Method performance, achieved cultural importance because of its dominant screen – not stage – presence in the fifties, a trend inaugurated and made possible by Kazan's *Streetcar*. The most important aspect of Williams's vision is that his male characters are less the bearers of sexual desire – the traditional male role in American theatre and film – and more its object, thereby assuming what is conventionally a female position. Such feminization is homoerotic to some degree, but it creates an appeal from which female viewers are by no means immune, especially because the plays themselves offer strong women characters, perhaps most prominently Maggie in *Cat on a Hot Tin Roof*, who play the traditional male role of desiring subject.

Through weightlifting, then an activity quite socially marginal, Brando obsessively shaped his body into an erotic object, set off in *Streetcar* by the famous white T-shirt that quite self-consciously revealed rippling biceps and powerful forearms that are often emphasized by Kazan's staging. The T-shirt is only in part a signifier of Stanley's social class. It is much more the emblem of unrestrained and unabashed sensuality, an index of the character's perpetual state of mental undress, a flimsy, easily discarded concession to civilized values. Brando should be applauded for making his Stanley so attractively brutish, the appealing id whose emergence to dominance Blanche struggles against so fruitlessly.

Williams, however, must be given credit for creating a role that would bear successfully this kind of interpretation. In any event, Kazan's *Streetcar* was a success, at least in part, because it put into play and made irresistibly appealing a different approach to the male body that, while explicable perhaps because of Williams's homosexuality, fitted into, even as it decisively shaped, a larger cultural trend that was, initially at least, largely played out on the movie screen by a group of new male stars. During the fifties and early sixties, Marlon Brando, Montgomery Clift, Paul Newman, Robert Redford, and Laurence Harvey all appeared in Williams films that effectively showcased their strong heterosexual appeal; James Dean, in all probability, was prevented only by his premature death from doing so. Once again, what Williams had to offer resonated with, but also helped transform a fundamental aspect of how the cinema had traditionally attracted viewers – by directing an erotic gaze at the idealized female body. Significantly, Vivien Leigh's body is never eroticized or glamorized in the film. Her Blanche becomes instead the bearer of a desire that, while directed at young men, finds with poetic justice its true object in the dangerous appeal of Stanley.

THE TENNESSEE WILLIAMS FILM: A SUBGENRE

A Streetcar Named Desire did extremely well at the box office and was one of the most critically acclaimed films of 1951, an otherwise fairly grim year for Hollywood. The movie received ten Academy Award nominations – in all the major categories – and three awards, for female lead Vivien Leigh and supporting players Kim Hunter and Karl Malden. The lesson of this success was not lost on Hollywood, whose filmmakers eagerly awaited the production of more Williams properties to transform into moneymaking films. After *Streetcar* had achieved, in both its forms, an international renown for the playwright, Williams did not disappoint his enthusiastic publics. He began the most prolific period of his career, penning in quick succession a number of plays, all of which with one exception (*Camino Real* [1953]) became Broadway hits. Film producers competed eagerly for production rights to these properties, hoping to emulate Kazan's triumph; in the process they made the young playwright Hollywood's hottest author. Tennessee Williams seemed destined to achieve the same kind of success on the screen as he had enjoyed on the stage.

What had made Williams appealing to a general film, as opposed to a more elite theatrical audience, however, was quite different. Broadway spectators, though certainly riveted by Williams's handling of sexual themes, could appreciate his complex articulation of tone, which often ranged from the tragic to the almost farcical; though finding themselves engaged by Williams's psychological realism, which created powerful sympathy for his suffering protagonists, they could value the less emotional and more intellectual qualities that become more prominent in the plays after *Streetcar*: the self-conscious deployment of schematized ideas, mytho-logical cadres, and expressionistic sets, among other somewhat anti-realist elements.

To judge from contemporary accounts, *Streetcar*'s screen triumph re-sulted primarily from its careful articulation of sexual, anti-romantic tension between the two leads, a tension energized and made appealing by the artful eroticization of Marlon Brando's body; moreover, in this play Williams does not stray far from the social realist aesthetic then the conventional basis for most Hollywood representation. Or, to put it another way, *Streetcar*, like *The Glass Menagerie*, is more an Aristotelian than a Brechtian play; its primary appeal is emotional, not intellectual, though it is certainly true that the playwright is here interested, as else-where, in the binary opposition of essential human qualities, roughly identifiable as "gentility" and "sensuality." Williams wrote two other plays that more or less conformed to the pattern established by *Streetcar*: *Cat on a Hot Tin Roof* and *Sweet Bird of Youth*. The film versions of both proved very popular with audiences even if critics often complained that, inevitably altered in accordance with Hollywood protocols, they were less than artistically triumphant. Together with *Streetcar*, they constitute the most significant subgenre of the Hollywood adult film during the fifties and early sixties.

What of the rest of Williams's dramatic work? Predictably, film viewers were to demonstrate a deep interest only in some of what Williams had to communicate as an artist, were enthusiastic about only those plays belonging to a certain, somewhat narrow type. Not surprisingly, the playwright was urged to return to this thematic and dramatic pattern by both his own creative tendencies and the acclaim of the filmgoing public. However, all of Williams's fifties plays (*Camino Real* again excepted), because of the playwright's fame and demonstrated commercial appeal, were adapted for the screen soon after their stage success.

The Rose Tattoo (Daniel Mann, 1956), though certainly not an artistic or commercial failure, exemplifies some of the problems involved in adapting for the movies a Williams' play that is quite different from *Streetcar* despite some obvious, even fundamental similarities. *The Rose Tattoo*, like *Streetcar*, traces the developing relationship between a woman who has experienced sexual obsession and a man she does not love and yet finds compellingly attractive even though she thinks him coarse and brutish. Again, as in *Streetcar*, the principal dramatic tension derives from the way in which the woman is forced to face the truth of her own lustful feelings, abandoning illusions about more refined versions of mutual attraction; here too the plot turns on a sexual encounter as she surrenders, after much resistance and equivocation, to the man's clumsy seduction. Even the settings of the two plays are much the same. For the raw ungentility of impoverished New Orleans, *The Rose Tattoo* offers an expressively similar substitute: a poor fishing village on the Gulf coast where a drama about elemental passions can likewise appropriately be set.

And yet *The Rose Tattoo* differs from *Streetcar* in two ways that made it difficult to adapt with the same kind of success for the screen. First, Williams's tone is here complexly seriocomic. The play offers a carnivalesque meditation on the intimate connection between the loftier and baser human elements, suggesting how the conflict between lust and propriety that destroys Blanche can be embraced and thereby transcended. Serafina Delle Rose, who feels an unquenchable desire for her husband Rosario, discovers after his death that he was unfaithful to her. His mistress, whom Serafina meets, even had a rose tattoo to match Rosario's. Serafina (whose name refers to the highest class of angels) then destroys the urn containing Rosario's ashes and succumbs to the inept seduction of Alvaro Mangiacavallo, a half-wit who ironically possesses a body almost identical to that of Rosario.

But Serafina's acceptance of an oafish lover (his name means "eat a horse") is by no means tragic. Instead, it signifies her psychologically healthy abandonment of demands upon passion that a frail human nature cannot support. Love can neither be eternal nor faithful in its object, Williams suggests. The flesh and blood rose tattooed on Rosario's chest, with its duplicate on his mistress, does not properly signify Serafina's angelic vision of love, which, of course, is always, already compounded with lust. By destroying the shrine she has made of Rosario's ashes, that is, the eternal, transmuted form of his body, Serafina is enabled to accept a mockingly ironic reincarnation in the person of Alvaro, a sexual object that must, and yet cannot be taken seriously. The angelic is brought to earth, but the descent is gently comic, in no way a tragic fall.

Thus, and here is the second and perhaps more important point, *The Rose Tattoo* decisively alters the sexual dynamics of *Streetcar*. The play debunks any serious approach to passion by refusing to allow Serafina to take her lover's betrayal as anything but a revelation of her own narrow-minded idealism. Serafina must surrender to the banality of lust, as represented by the irresistible physicality of Alvaro, even acknowledge that her daughter has the right to desire her sailor boyfriend. And so *The Rose Tattoo* is less an erotic object than a humorous, if intellectually schematic, meditation on the discontents and joys of eroticism itself. In the expressionist manner, the characters are more flat than round, more the representatives of human tendencies and qualities than psychologically complex individuals whose fate is meant to engage the spectator emotionally. The play disavows the tragic implications of passion so tellingly displayed in *Streetcar*. Thus the film version, even though it deploys the attractive bodies of Anna Magnani and Burt Lancaster in the featured roles, cannot transform them into a compellingly glamorous spectacle. Famous for her steamy roles in Italian neorealist films, Magnani, though often clad only in her underwear, cuts more a comic than erotic figure as Serafina. As a result of the notorious beach scene in *From Here to Eternity* (Fred Zinnemann, 1953), where, clad only in bathing trunks, he makes passionate love to Deborah Kerr in the surf, Lancaster became a male lead often called upon to seduce the leading lady with powerful tenderness. Yet the role of Alvaro Mangiacavallo demanded he make more use of his not inconsiderable gifts for energetic farce.

In general, Mann's film simplifies the intellectual scheme of Williams's play by melodramatizing all the dramatic encounters in the Hollywood fashion; thus the film lacks the sharply distanced comic energies of the stage version. At the same time, limited by Williams's dramatic and thematic conceptions, Mann fails to deliver the explosive eroticism of *Streetcar* despite exceptional casting obviously calculated to achieve such an effect. The screen version of *The Rose Tattoo* was a disappointment to playwright and filmgoers alike. Related difficulties insured a disappointing reception for both *Baby Doll* (Elia Kazan, 1956) and *The Fugitive Kind* (Sidney Lumet, 1960), the first of which recycles *Streetcar*'s director and the second its male lead in an attempt to duplicate the earlier film's success.

The marketing campaign for *Baby Doll* aroused a storm of largely irrelevant controversy by playing on Williams's then well-established reputation as an author of smutty stories. The film's poster featured Carroll Baker posed seductively in a crib, a gambit that along with its double entendre title falsely implied that the story was somehow concerned with the sexual predation of, if not little girls, then innocent gamines. The Catholic Legion of Decency condemned the film (probably without a viewing), while Bishop Fulton J. Sheehan of New York called from the pulpit for its suppression. Reverend James Pike, a prominent Protestant clergyman, disputed Sheehan's contention, if not his judgment of the film, declaring that adult viewers should be able to exercise freedom of choice and, if morally upright, would not be harmed by filmgoing of any kind. Williams's *Baby Doll* thus earned the dubious distinction of being the only film to spark a full-fledged and much-reported ecclesiastical debate, one that brought into focus the conflict between an older and an emerging view of how the film industry should function in American society.

Catholic protests and an attendant boycott probably did much to suppress business at the box office, but the film itself, quite different from its advertised image, undoubtedly contributed heavily to what must be counted a commercial failure. Based on two one-act plays that had not been produced on Broadway (27 *Wagons Full of Cotton* and *The Unsatisfactory Supper*) and which were stitched together mostly by Kazan, who was the creative motor behind the project, *Baby Doll* is a riotously funny black comedy treating the "love" triangle that develops between Archie Lee Meighan (Karl Malden) and his business rival Vaccaro (Eli Wallach) for the affection of Archie Lee's wife (Baker), who has refused to consummate their business-deal marriage until her twentieth birthday, on the eve of which the play's action begins. Because Vaccaro's real interest in Baby Doll is to persuade her to sign a statement attesting that Archie Lee burned down Vaccaro's cotton gin, the film does not develop its romantic triangle in an erotic fashion. In fact, the most intimate moment the two characters share is when Baby Doll spies upon Vaccaro napping in her crib. Though the performers, especially Baker, are often pictured in various states of undress (by this time a hallmark of Williams's movies), the film offers little more than innuendo and seductive teasing.

Significantly, *Baby Doll* was certificated without much dispute by Joseph Breen's successor at the PCA, Geoff Shurlock. Kazan undoubtedly constructed the most satisfactory version of this material by Williams, whose own attempt to recycle it as *Tiger Tail* proved a stage failure in the late seventies. Like Blanche DuBois, Archie Lee, Vaccaro, Baby Doll, and her Aunt Rose Comfort are all shakily rooted characters who fear dispossession even as they attempt to construct financial and emotional security for themselves. Their comic failures to do so are lightheartedly staged by Kazan, who is aided by the vibrant Method performances of Malden and Wallach. Though an undoubted artistic success, *Baby Doll* obviously did not give the filmgoing public the Williams they wanted to see and which the advertising campaign had promised them they in fact would.

In contrast, *The Fugitive Kind* (Sidney Lumet, 1960) offered film audiences what they wanted to see: a very sexy, yet sensitive Marlon Brando, who becomes the object of three women's desires. But Lumet and Williams hardly give their viewers the dramatic form they would have preferred or even one, for the most part, they would have been able to appreciate. Williams's story, with its complex reworking of classical myth, depended upon a scheme of reference unknown to most filmgoers; without it, both the relations of the characters and the direction of the plot become hard to follow if not positively opaque. Like *Baby Doll*, the film is important for students and admirers of Williams because it presents most satisfactorily material that was of great interest to him. This modern update of Orpheus's tragic end was first staged as *Battle of Angels* in 1940, in a production whose overall problems insured a quick, and for Williams heartbreaking, cancellation. For most of two decades, he rewrote, and a second stage version, entitled *Orpheus Descending*, was produced on Broadway in 1957, where it enjoyed limited success. For the film version, Williams collaborated closely with screenwriter Meade Roberts and thereby exercised a great deal of control over the screenplay's ultimate form.

In the film, Lumet and Williams opt for greater realism, an artistic decision that accords with the fundamental Hollywood aesthetic. Hence the film omits the play's two old women who function as a kind of Greek chorus, commenting on the action; likewise, the setting is opened out from the store run by Lady (Eurydice) to different, authentic exteriors. While the mode of presentation and the cadre of the play are in this way made more naturalistic, little change is made in the characters' motivations. Their actions, removed from their mythic setting and now more resolutely a part of the everyday world, thus seem irrational, confusing, unengaging. The relationship between Val (Orpheus) and Lady, played effectively by Anna Magnani, fails to generate much in the way of passion or pathos because the significance of their bond, that is, its incomplete triumph over death, has been eliminated. Though the film artfully emphasizes the sensual, androgynous appeal of Brando's body in a series of initial scenes added to the playscript, the overall result is a somewhat confusing melange of representational modes, as Williams's material is only inadequately accommodated to the requirements of screen realism. A similar problem besets

Peter Glenville's film version of *Summer and Smoke* (1961), a play with a strongly expressionistic cadre and characters who quite schematically represent a binary opposition of ideas. Though played effectively by the charismatic Laurence Harvey and beautiful Geraldine Page, the romantic pair in *Summer and Smoke* are prevented by the thesis of Williams's play – the conflict between body and soul – from generating the passionate sympathy that Stanley and Blanche had aroused.

On the screen, that aspect of Williams's thematics is only recaptured effectively in *Cat on a Hot Tin Roof* (1958) and *Sweet Bird of Youth* (1962). Both plays were directed on Broadway by Elia Kazan with the film versions overseen by Richard Brooks, who made a reputation in the fifties and sixties with well-executed adaptations of literary properties, most prominently the two Williams plays, but also works by Dostoevsky, Conrad, Sinclair Lewis, and Truman Capote. In their focus on male crisis, both films owe something to Brooks's fascination with issues of ethics and character; like the title figure in his *Lord Jim* (1964), Brooks's Brick Pollitt and Chance Wayne, played similarly by a quite kinetic and ultra-masculine Paul Newman, win through to redemption after painful self-examination and consciously chosen suffering. In each case, Williams's ambiguities and tragic realities are eliminated in favor of a life-affirming coupling, a change certainly instituted by Brooks, who, when he took on the two projects, was a commercially successful director interested in making literary films with a wide appeal. Happy endings were still an important part of the Hollywood formula, even in the late fifties and early sixties, and Brooks was well aware of this.

Like the stage versions they are adapted from, these two films, however, bear the marks of a greater influence from Elia Kazan. Specifically, they reflect strongly the interpretation of Williams that emerged from the director's close collaboration with the playwright on the Broadway version of *Streetcar*. It would certainly be incorrect to say that in these three stage and one film versions Kazan reduces the complexity of Williams's themes to something like a formula. And yet, like *Streetcar*, the films of *Cat on a Hot Tin Roof* and *Sweet Bird of Youth* emphasize sexual tensions, now viewed in a traditionally romantic way, while downplaying the questions of moral responsibility and self-understanding that are also important elements of Williams's dramatic conception in each case.

The two later films are also similar to *Streetcar* in offering a thorough-going eroticization of the male body, an eroticization that is now claimed very forcefully for heterosexuality despite the feminized nature of the two male main characters. David Thomson has observed of Kazan's stage and screen work that "he invariably needed some kind of sexual investment in a show – imaginative and actual."[4] And Kazan had no interest in the homosexual undertones of Williams's plays (witness his ready agreement to Breen's demand that Blanche's husband not be characterized as a closet gay). Except for the notorious film *Splendor in the Grass* (1961), Kazan's obsession with the erotic is nowhere more clearly evident than in *Cat on a Hot Tin Roof* and *Sweet Bird of Youth*, the screen versions of which are perhaps even more dominated by their identification of personality and sexual choice than the stage productions. Clearly, Brooks was eager to out-Kazan Kazan and succeeded in so doing. If Kazan did not turn Williams's multileveled explorations of the human dilemma into a rather narrow formula for screen success, Brooks did.

When first produced in 1955, Kazan's *Cat on a Hot Tin Roof* was a hit with audiences and critics alike, garnering Williams his second Pulitzer. It is perhaps surprising that a film version took three years to produce, but the storm of controversy that raged over *Baby Doll*, as well as that film's disappointing performance at the box office, undoubtedly played a role in the delay, as did the fact that this Williams play was even more concerned with sex, especially the impotence and possible homosexual inclinations of its protagonist, than *Streetcar*. In any event, by 1958 the Production Code had been weakened by further assault from filmmakers catering to increased audience demand for adult dramas. In particular, Otto Preminger's film version of F. Hugh Herbert's popular Broadway sexual farce, *The Moon is Blue* (1953) had been released without a PCA certificate and had profited from the notoriety; a full-scale Legion of Decency protest about the story's casual treatment of sexual liaisons failed to keep it from being one of the year's top-grossing films. Though "sexual perversions" were still officially banned from screen treatment, homosexuality could now be raised as an issue because the PCA could no longer enforce the letter of the Code; the screen version of Williams's play, in fact, would hardly be the first film to do so. In concession to public taste, however, the issue still needed delicate, indirect handling.

Williams's play, fittingly enough, leaves the issue of Brick's sexuality unresolved. Does he refuse to sleep with Maggie because Skipper's confession of love has made him face his own homosexual desires? Or is he disgusted by the "mendacity" of those around him, the deception and lying of which Maggie too is self-confessedly guilty, having betrayed her husband with his best friend? Brooks's film, in all likelihood, would not have become the biggest grosser of 1958 and one of the most financially successful films ever produced and released by MGM if the director and screenwriter James Poe had not opted clearly for the second of these explanations for Brick's declining moral and psychological state. Ben Gazzara and Barbara Bel Geddes, who had starred on Broadway, were replaced by the much more charismatic and attractive Paul Newman and Elizabeth Taylor in what proved a successful attempt to transform Williams's tragic vision of characters disgusted by mendacity who must, if they are to survive, invent a more powerful lie (i.e., Maggie's false proclamation of pregnancy). By adding a long scene between Brick and Big Daddy in which the father offers marital counsel and a vision of responsible family life that the son eventually accepts, Brooks is able to motivate Brick's eventual decision to go along with Maggie's lie in a spirit of reconciliation. Melodramatized in a typical Hollywood fashion, and accommodated to filmgoers' expectations for engaging romance, *Cat on a Hot Tin Roof* became a standard, early 1960s adult film, with its initial implications of sexual irregularity and disfunction dispelled by a plot that restored a solidly bourgeois normality to the Pollitt household. This combination had proven box-office dynamite the year before in another provocative, but ultimately conservative film: *Peyton Place* (Mark Robson, 1957).

Sweet Bird of Youth received a similar treatment from Brooks. The play version dramatizes the progressive narrowing of Chance's possibilities. Despite frantic efforts to attain a chance at celebrity through manipulation and even blackmail, he finally has no choice but to accept a horrifying death in life, a castration that is his poetically just reward for the betrayal of Heavenly and his own youth. In contrast, the film's Chance never is forced to abandon his drive toward self-fulfillment; he simply must recognize that he is more interested in having Heavenly than pursuing the fading dream of a film career with the help of the Princess. He must suffer, of course, for the error in judgment that harmed Heavenly, who must endure an abortion and damage to her reputation. Chance's girl in the film version, however, is spared the more horrible fate Williams originally imagined: a hysterectomy made necessary by the venereal disease Chance infects her with.

Williams's play uses its first-act setting in a rented hotel room to express Chance's entrapment with an equally desperate fellow traveler, the fading movie star whose life, fatally dependent like his own on transient physical beauty, is ironically enough the best he can hope for. In contrast, Brooks opens his film with a bravura sequence that establishes Chance as the very height of early sixties cool, expressed by his reflector sunglasses and arrogant, in-charge demeanor; here is a character who knows what he wants and has every intention of being successful in obtaining it. For Williams's hero, castration is the ultimate sign of his feminization, the reduction of his drive for success to a harlotry that delivers him into the power of those who would punish him for it. Brooks's Chance, because he has never completely surrendered himself to the career he so desperately wants, needs a less drastic lesson in the meaning of life. With his nose broken by Heavenly's brother, he can no longer hope to become a screen idol, for his youthful good looks were his sole acting asset. And yet he had previously rejected the Princess's offer to help him break into the business in order to make a last appeal for Heavenly, a move he knows will likely bring down the violent wrath of her family. So the disfigurement he subsequently suffers simply seals the bargain he had already agreed to. Bleeding but not dismembered, he is driven away by Heavenly in her Cadillac convertible at film's end in a scene that rhymes with the opening sequence picturing him at the wheel of the Princess's car. If Chance is now less confident, less able to direct his life, he has exchanged such freedom for the obvious benefits of a beautiful, rich woman's love, a finale that Brooks does not present with even a hint of irony. The film's Chance becomes the stock "Mr. Right" of pulp romance, a desirable catch whose selfishness must be transformed into what he himself knows is a better trait: the desire to give all in order to deserve and obtain the love of the woman who wants him.

WILLIAMS AND HOLLYWOOD: SOME CONCLUSIONS

Though audiences loved the film, critics were nearly unanimous in their disapproval, and yet Williams himself, perhaps disingenuously, said that Brooks's recasting of his tragic drama "was probably better than the play."[5] The playwright's remark, I think, is suggestive for a judgment of Hollywood's version of Williams. Undeniably, the films based on the plays, with the exception of A Streetcar Named Desire and Baby Doll, are inferior artistically to the successful stage productions that inspired them. Certainly, the adaptation process, fueled by the commercial success of the filmed Streetcar, was most successful when it confined the rich and varied œuvre of the playwright to certain narrow themes and representational modes that were in accord with film industry practice and the demonstrable desire of its consumers. Overall, Williams's plays are melodramatized in the process, that is, provided with characters able to achieve, after a purgatorial journey of self-discovery, a happy ending for themselves. And yet such melodramatization in some cases simply alters the tonality of the dramatic perspective Williams originally adopted, substituting more optimistic resolutions. Films such as Sweet Bird of Youth show how Williams's tragic figures might have escaped the horrible fates to which their own actions work to condemn them. If we are to believe the playwright, these alternative visions did not strike him, at least in every instance, as either disagreeable or dissatisfying.

This is fitting for two reasons. First, unlike many authors, notably fellow playwright Arthur Miller, Williams was eager from the beginning of his career that his stage successes be transformed into artistically significant films; in the case of *Streetcar*, for example, he worked diligently with Charles Feldman to make sure that his play had the same strong impact on filmgoers as it had on theatre audiences. In this regard, his early collaboration with Elia Kazan, who was also vitally interested in both mediums, is of great importance. Second, though this was not his aim, Williams provided Hollywood with source material that transformed the industry. *Streetcar* broke the hitherto impenetrable barrier established by the Production Code to the making of adult entertainment; this startlingly innovative production was the first in a distinguished series of American art films in the fifties and sixties, a genre to which Williams was to contribute several times more during the period. Perhaps even more important, the male roles in Williams's plays, reaching a wider audience through various film versions, popularized a different kind of masculinity, offering images of desirable, vulnerable, and yet aggressive maleness that profoundly affected American ideas about gender. Such roles, in particular, made Marlon Brando and Paul Newman the period's most acclaimed stars. Both went on to build an enduring popularity on parts often written in deliberate imitation of Williams's characters; compare, among a host of examples, the tortured, alienated loners played by Newman in *The Hustler* (Robert Rossen, 1961) and Brando in *Reflections in a Golden Eye* (John Huston, 1967), films whose way was paved most obviously by *Streetcar* and *Cat*. If the American cinema of the late fifties, sixties, and early seventies is densely populated by attractive yet emotionally sensitive men who lack decisiveness and are prone to failure, then Tennessee Williams must be credited for inaugurating what is, in part, a revolution in taste, but also, and more important, a transformation of the national character. And this would never have happened without the wholesale transference of his artistic vision from the stage to the commercial screen.

NOTES

1 Quoted in Leonard J. Leff and Jerold L. Simmons, *The Dame in the Kimono* (New York: Doubleday, 1990), 288. My account of Hollywood censorship is much indebted to the detailed history of the subject offered in Leff and Simmons.

2 Quoted in Maurice Yacowar, *Tennessee Williams & Film* (New York: Frederick Ungar, 1977), 14.

3 Quoted in Leff and Simmons, *Dame*, 174.

4 *A Biographical Dictionary of Film* (New York: Knopf, 1994), 388.

5 Quoted in Yacowar, *Tennessee Williams*, 98.

RUBY COHN

Tennessee Williams: the last two decades

In a makeshift theatre of perhaps fifty seats, on a stage shrouded by swathes of coarse white cloth, a Williams two-hander plays – *The Chalky White Substance*. To a faint sad sound, lights come up on two monk-like figures in diagonal corners of the small stage. When lights are full up, but before a word is uttered, the upstage figure moves diagonally downstage and places his hands over the eyes of the other actor: "Whoooo?" And the reply: "Youuuuuuu! – You can disguise your voice but not your hands." By the end of the play those hands grasp the vulnerable figure, not in a lover's embrace but a captor's hold. The love affair of two men cannot outlast the competitive struggle for survival in a chalky white world that is hostile to human habitation, "a century or two after our time." On stage *The Chalky White Substance* was so cumulatively harrowing that I was surprised when the performance was over in half an hour. The name of Tennessee Williams had drawn me to the production, where I was transfixed by the spare performances of two unknown but capable actors in an unfamiliar piece.

The Chalky White Substance is absent from the eight volumes of *The Theatre of Tennessee Williams*, but it is listed in the revised Gunn bibliography: "Scene of betrayal in a place of desolation" (28). That same bibliography mentions over sixty titles of unpublished Williams plays in manuscript collections, so that any overview of his late drama must at present be tentative. And the overviewer must decide where "late" begins. Most criticism of Williams's work fades after *The Night of the Iguana* (1961); the attitude is succinctly stated by John S. McCann: "It is a general critical axiom that *The Night of the Iguana* was Williams's last first-rate play. It is further generally agreed that the last twenty years show a struggling, debilitated Williams trying to fulfill what . . . he expected of himself and what he continued to believe his public wanted of him."[1] Yet directors and actors continue to discover what critics have cast aside as self-repetition. However, Williams's repetitions enfold new explorations in light, sound, stage space, plot structure, character configuration, and especially dialogue.

The Chalky White Substance is unique in its futuristic setting and costumes, but it belongs thematically with Williams's socio-political plays. In the videotape of rehearsals for *The Red Devil Battery Sign* (1975), Williams declares: "I think I'm more of a social writer than Mr. Miller, which would surprise him a great deal. He's more of a polemicist, but I think I have more deeply rooted feelings than most directors I know." Perhaps so, but he rarely foregrounds his social feelings in his most telling plays. Williams has given so many interviews, penned so many letters, Broadway introductions, and informal essays, that critics can cull quotations to further any argument. Turning to the drama itself, we see that Williams imposes symbols even on his sociopolitical plays, for the red devil battery sign is the emblem of American fascism in the play of that name, as opposed to a family business in "The Knightly Quest," its source novella. Upon the social background (diluted from the story) Williams grafts a Gothic love affair between an injured mariachi player and a Texan political refugee. More concentratedly explosive is the one-act *Demolition Down Town* (1971), in which two bourgeois wives desert their homes to offer themselves to the marauding militia. The unpublished *This Is (An Entertainment)* (1976) belies its title by intruding a revolution into entertainment in an unnamed European country. In what may be Williams's last play, *A House Not Meant to Stand* (1982), where the house is explicitly designated as a metaphor for the state of society, a redneck politician wishes to institutionalize his wife so that he can use her money to run for office. For all Williams's praiseworthy liberalism in these plays, I find his sociopolitical views naive, but not his stylistic range: the mocking rhymes and repetitions of *Demolition*, the contrasting languages of the ill-starred lovers of *Red Devil* and the effete similarities of the lovers of *Chalky*, the scenes of dream, dual focus, and direct address in *House*, and the merciless hammering of the consequently dubious *This Is*. In spite of the binary limitations of Williams's social feelings in these plays (Good Guys vs. Bad Guys), he expands his theatre languages.

Antithetical to Williams's sociopolitical plays are those of poetic regionalism, and they too exhibit dialogue variety. *Confessional* (1970), the earlier version of *Small Craft Warnings* (1972), announces its technique in its title. Each of the play's eight characters in a Pacific Coast bar is spotlit in order to address the audience directly in a "confessional." Obvious and repetitive, this device nevertheless serves to cement the bar ensemble theatrically, even though each character speaks in her/his own idiom. *Vieux Carré* (1977) shifts us to New Orleans in the late 1930s, a decade before

Streetcar. Again each character speaks in her/his own idiom, but instead of spotlit monologues, we have a nameless Writer who is both a character and a memorialist of these rooming-house inhabitants of the Vieux Carré – not unlike Tom in *The Glass Menagerie.* With *A Lovely Sunday for Creve Coeur* (1978) we move to St. Louis for Williams's rendition of four speech patterns. The ungrammatical earthiness of Bodie contrasts with the pretentious artifice of Helena; an unfortunate Sophie Gluck speaks more German than English, and the protagonist Dotty shifts abruptly from an echo of Helena to verbs of action and optimism. Williams desires our sympathy for the roommates Dotty and Bodie, whom he gently ridicules in the slapstick events of their garish apartment. Reverting again to memory in *Something Cloudy, Something Clear* (1981), Williams creates another writer–memorialist – August by name – in Cape Cod during World War II. Epiphanic moments punctuate the solitudes of the characters: literal members of the fugitive kind, Clare and her adopted sibling Kip, are so attuned to one another that they complete each other's sentences, but so, occasionally, do August and Kip, and August and Clare. Although critics have lacerated these plays of poetic regionalism, their very nostalgia seeps into my memory of the Chekhovian ironies in productions of *Vieux Carré,* and of *Small Craft Warnings* where Williams himself played Doc. Unable to evoke a kind word from critics, Williams as (subdued) actor could still fill a Broadway theatre.

Not only did Williams set himself new dialogue exercises in these late plays; he also wrote what he called "lyric plays" which incorporate dance. Kip is a dancer in *Something Cloudy, Something Clear,* and he practices in the background while his foster sister Clare and the writer August praise his beauty. Williams's "lyric plays," however, contain less plausible dancing. In *Now the Cats with Jewelled Claws,* homosexual seductions are danced. In *Youthfully Departed,* a chorus of Laments separate two lovers, rendered in dance and dialogue. In *A Cavaliar for Milady* an adolescent girl is obsessed with Nijinsky, who dances for her as an apparition. Only *Jewelled Claws* has been performed, and only a choreographer can enhance these slight texts. I mention them, however, not only as examples of Williams's theatrical exploration, but also as tributes to the most graceful art by a playwright grown increasingly portly in spite of his swimming.

Aging and ill, Williams was merciless to the aged or dying in *I Can't Imagine Tomorrow, The Frosted Glass Coffin* (1970), and ten years later in *Lifeboat Drill* and *This is the Peaceful Kingdom, or Good Luck God.* Even in these slender pieces, however, he exercised his dramatic language; the stuttering of Two in *Tomorrow,* the dialogue of the deaf in *Coffin,* the distortions without dentures of *Drill,* the black and Yiddish rhythms of

Peaceful Kingdom. Accused often of sentimentality, Williams can be cruel in these plays, and yet his cruelty is not pitiless.

I depart from these mainly thematic groupings to suggest that Williams's most consistent experimentation of the late plays leaned toward the Gothic and/or grotesque. The most striking example is *Slapstick Tragedy* (1966). Although the title is singular, it embraces two one-act plays, *The Mutilated* and *The Gnädiges Fräulein.* Either of these titles is apt for both plays. The mutilation is literally the result of a mastectomy, but all the characters in both plays are physically or spiritually mutilated, so that "the mutilated" is synonymous with what Williams earlier called "the fugitive kind." As for "gnädiges fräulein," which is German for Blessed Virgin, she is at once the protagonist in her own play and in the other a Christmas apparition to two middle-aged women in a seedy New Orleans hotel. Poverty, alcoholism, and sexual yearning dissolve in the invisible presence of Our Lady, and even Jack In Black, who is Death, delays his claim. The bickering in a shabby setting of *The Mutilated* is vintage Williams, but the playwright constantly departs from realistic dialogue: both Celeste and Trinket address the audience directly, and overlapping dialogue speeds through a momentary pandemonium. Moreover, the playwright prepares us early for the final epiphany; the thief/whore who will welcome Our Lady bears the name of Celeste Delacroix Griffin, blending her celestial Christian heritage into the mythological eagle-lion. Williams interlaces his sordid scenes with rounds of carolers who sing of a miracle "To the wayward and deformed, / To the lonely and misfit" *The Mutilated* is not likely to replace *A Christmas Carol* as holiday fare, but it is funnier and more freewheeling, with luscious roles for mature actresses.

Williams's production notes stipulate that both plays of *Slapstick Tragedy* thrive on music, but there are no carols in *The Gnädiges Fräulein.* The poverty-stricken inhabitants of the Southernmost Florida key – the Cocaloony – live on fish, which they obtain by hook or crook. Polly of the *Cocaloony Gazette* presents the background directly to the audience. Soon, however, Polly fences verbally with Molly, the landlady of a dormitory for woebegone transients, including a once-famous European singer who pays her rent by racing the giant cocaloony-birds for the fish discarded from fishing-boats. Called "gnädiges fräulein," she is almost deaf and dumb, except when she is requested to sing. Before we hear the Gnädiges Fräulein, we hear about her in the rhythmic exchanges of Molly and Polly, in their respective rocking-chairs, where they rock "with pelvic thrusts as if having sex." The slapstick element is bolstered by word-play: "Take the Gnädiges Fräulein, one instant for an instance . . ." When the Gnädiges Fräulein finally appears: "She wears a curious costume which would not be out of place at the Moulin Rouge in the time of Toulouse-Lautrec." Humble and grotesque, she is manipulated by the two rocking women as if she were a puppet. More silent than the Gnädiges Fräulein is Indian Joe, blond, blue-eyed, and dressed like a Hollywood Indian. He stands his ground against the cocaloony bird that intimidates the women, and a slapstick duel ensues, the man-sized bird screaming "Awk" and the Indian countering "Ugh!" A victorious Indian Joe utters his most eloquent sentence: "I feel like a bull," and a lovelorn mooing Polly follows him into the dormitory.

By the starlit second scene Polly is dishevelled, but the Fräulein is blind, bloody, and yet indomitable. Although we see the stumbling of the sightless Fräulein, and hear her valiant attempts at song, her plight comes to us mainly through the cruel but not unwitty dialogue of Polly and Molly: "It buggers description." When the Fräulein prepares to fry her hardwon fish for Indian Joe, Polly steals it. The two malicious vixens sit down to *their* dinner, but Indian Joe pushes them out of his dining way. The fishing-boat whistles, and the Fräulein "starts a wild, blind dash for the fish-docks."

The play's first director, Alan Schneider, called The Gnädiges Fräulein "a surrealist romp about the position of the artist in our society," and he seems to have relished it in spite of casting difficulties.[2] It was certainly a daring venture for Broadway, and its failure now seems predictable. Somewhat self-indulgent, with an obvious allegory, the play nevertheless moves through its counterpoint of two hardboiled, wisecracking crones and two physically active, fantastically garbed figures.

Another predictable Broadway failure illustrates the range of Williams's invention in his late plays. After the visual opulence and witty exchanges of Slapstick Tragedy, In the Bar of a Tokyo Hotel (1969) is spare and monochromatic. Only its dialogue is grotesque, foregrounding the incomplete sentence. Thomas Adler counts over 200 examples, which outnumber those in Williams's novel Moise and the World of Reason (1975).[3] In a revisionist comparison of Miller and Williams, David Savran devotes considerable attention to incompletion in the last plays (which he dates from Tokyo Hotel): "On average, three or four times per page (or, in performance, about every fifteen to twenty-five seconds) characters are unable or unwilling to finish a statement and their words simply come to an abrupt halt, followed in the text by an end stop."[4] For Savran the device is symptomatic of "an insistent and radical fragmentation of discourse, character, and plot that is far more aggressive and overt than that which marks even the most surrealistic of [Williams's] earlier plays" (135). Savran offers a significant and provocative interpretation: "I would like to propose that the fragmentation and incoherence that mark most of Williams's texts from the late 1960s until his death are also the result of a pivotal change in his public status: his coming out . . ." (136). "Finally empowered to speak directly after so many years of (self-)censorship, he could only stutter, only hammer out a broken and lacerated speech" (137).

This ingenious theory of a sophisticated critic seems to me untenable for prosaic reasons: (1) It is too soon to generalize about "most of Williams's texts," since many are still unpublished, and Savran makes no reference to manuscript collections. (2) Even among Williams's published late texts "fragmentation and incoherence" seem to me the exception rather than the rule. (3) Savran's statistics on incompletion flatten their actual occurrence in *Tokyo Hotel*. Incompletion is a polyvalent technique, whose dramatic function varies with the play, and with the scene in that play; sometimes it is a sign of uncertainty or even desperation, as in the utterances of One in *I Can't Imagine Tomorrow*; sometimes it is the yielding to an interruption, as in the fencing of Celeste and Trinket, or Molly and Polly of *Slapstick Tragedy* (or occasional moments in almost any drama); sometimes it denotes a symbiotic closeness, when one character completes the sentence of another, as with Clare and Kip of *Something Cloudy, Something Clear*. *Tokyo Hotel* blends all three, but emotional distress dominates.

The Japanese Barman's "I was," the play's first incompletion, might be construed as hesitancy in a foreign language, and indeed all his sentence fragments can be so rationalized. When the Barman and Miriam Conley fence in incompletions, however, motivational explanation is patently inadequate. Incompletions accelerate when the paint-spattered artist Mark Conley joins his wife in the Bar. They climax in violence, when a jealous Mark throws Miriam out of the Bar, despite his physical weakness. In Part II incompletions continue more moderately, but Mark's agent Leonard is afflicted with the same aberration. In a kind of verbal swan song, Mark the artist regains volubility just before his death, and his last few sentences are complete.

Savran is surely right when he states: "*In the Bar of a Tokyo Hotel* is a death-of-the-artist play with a difference" (137). However, he and I read that difference differently. I am not inclined to historicize it into Mark, the action painter, as an agent of American imperialism *versus* his wife Miriam, who is also his double. Ahistorically, I see in this mismatched couple far from home a critique of art. Mark has narrowed his life to his painting, which after fourteen years of marriage exacerbates Miriam's frustration, sexual and emotional. Rebuffed in her advances to the Barman, battling for independence from Mark, admonished after his sudden death to show grief, Miriam closes the play's dialogue with two complete sentences: "I have no plans. I have nowhere to go." She flings her bracelets to her feet with a violence that Savran calls suicidal, since she has verbally linked that gesture with death. What the play seems to me to suggest brokenly is that one cannot live with art, nor without it, and that inability is mirrored in sentence incompletion, a syntactical inability. Of all artists, actors are conversant with this difficult-to-impossible dedication to art, including its incompletions. Williams's multi-functional fragments heighten tension, but the action is never incomprehensible. By foisting the device upon all four characters of Tokyo Hotel, however, Williams dilutes its dramatic functionality.

In spite of this dilution, however, the play's sentence incompletion served to prepare Williams to manipulate the device meaningfully in his novel Moise and the World of Reason, which Savran examines masterfully. In that fiction claimed by a fictional writer in a fictional Blue Jay notebook, Williams not only deploys sentence fragments adroitly, but he also has his writer comment knowingly upon them: "There are some sentences that a distinguished failed writer must be ashamed to complete, as if telling a secret which has been publicly published in yesterday's paper" (129). A tendency to incompletion becomes a talismanic sign of character kinship, often but not only sexual. Near the end of the novel, the "I" who writes quotes the arational painter Moise before each of them couples with a different cameraman: "I think [God] knows that the violence of reason must wait upon the soft annealments of love, at least till" (189). The fragment would resonate poorly on the stage, and two couples making love – one heterosexual and one homosexual – would be theatrically tedious. But in fiction Moise soars.

Before and after Tokyo Hotel, Williams dramatized the tyrannies of art in theatrical rather than painterly terms, exploring other avenues of the grotesque. "Before" in that Out Cry was, according to Gunn, "written 1959–75 (or later)" (166). And further: "Three versions of this play were published [1969, 1973, and 1976 in vol. v] (and more produced). In general those entitled The Two-Character Play are among the most interesting of Williams's final period; that entitled Out Cry is among the worst." Under either title, professional productions were enthusiastically trounced. Yet some version of the play continues to attract actors and directors – perhaps more than any other late Williams play.[5]

As in no other Williams play – early or late – Out Cry dramatizes the theatre as theatre. A brother and sister, Felice and Clare Devoto, playwright/actor and actress, are abandoned by their company in an unnamed theatre of an unnamed foreign country. Without resources, they are reduced to performing the only two-hander in their repertory, "The Two-Character Play," an unfinished creation by Felice, which may reflect their nontheatre life. Within "The Two-Character Play" they use their own names, and they recall a violent heritage in a small town of the American

South. Their astrologer father, threatened by their mother with confinement to a state asylum, has shot her and then himself. The orphan siblings, deprived of insurance money, bereft of supplies, cut off from communication, fear to venture outside their house. In an illuminating study Thomas Postlewait states: "Williams regularly portrays the interior thematically as a realm of entrapment and confinement."[6] In "The Two-Character Play", however, the interior seems to the siblings a refuge.

Williams, whose sensitivity to lighting has been praised by the designer Jo Mielziner, differentiates the dusky violet of the frame play from the benign amber of the inner play. The frame contains "unassembled pieces of scenery," including a mysterious papier-mâché statue, and the inner play presents "The incomplete interior of a living room in Southern summer," through whose window tall sunflowers are visible. The double focus of the set remains constant, however Clare and Felice may cross the boundary between frame and inner play. And both sets are fragmented.

When Felice appears, in an incongruous costume, he engages in writing, a dangerous stage activity because it is inherently untheatrical. Yet Williams mitigates the danger by dressing Felice flamboyantly and offering a playful first sentence, which couples "fear" with its near-homonym "fire" (309). Felice's monologue stumbles through hesitations and incompletions, which are plausible in the process of composition. Introducing Clare, Felice speaks either to himself or directly to the audience. Both are venerable Williams techniques, and yet they achieve patina in a theatre setting.

Clare's appearance is also theatrical, donning a damaged tiara in her first gesture – a tiara that recalls Blanche in *Streetcar*. Later she will sit momentarily on a stage throne. She too suffers from the fear apostrophized by Felice, and the siblings recite two quatrains about fear, one line each in perfect balance. In initiating Clare into their plight, Felice overlaps her speech. As the action progresses, Felice and Clare occasionally complete, occasionally repeat, occasionally interrupt, and occasionally balance each other's sentences. However they bicker, they are in tune.

Since the frame play is set in a theatre, the siblings' vocabulary brims with theatrical terms – the audience, rival notices, drying on stage, "Line," improvisation, makeup, curtains, and a C-sharp on the piano to signal a cut. Both in the frame and the inner play Williams allows the siblings to indulge in the word slippage that tempts him throughout his career, but, as part of a script penned by Felice, such word-play is plausible:

CLARE: Sometimes notices aren't – noticed.
FELICE: I mustn't start counting things that can't be counted on.   (325)

The inner play, with its Southern setting, sexual suggestion, and background violence, is at once a summary and a parody of the plays that made Williams famous, replete with residual cablegram and gun. Apparent interruptions alert us to the makeshift quality of the performance, as does Felice's knocking on the table to denote intruders at their door. Before the interval both siblings betray their intimacy: Clare telephones an outsider, and Felice, wresting the phone from her, utters the forbidden word "Confined." When she repeats the word again and again, Felice thrusts a pillow over Clare's mouth. It is not clear whether the violence is in the frame or the inner play.

Act II eschews violence as they resume the inner play, ostensibly with improvisations. Within the inner play, they rehearse a plea for financial credit, each completing the other's phrase. Instead of daring to go out and make that plea, however, they accuse each other of cowardice in overlapping sentences. Then Clare mimes helping Felice into an invisible jacket and tie; they gain a little distance by speaking of their characters in the third person. Clare blows a soap bubble, and Felice touches her hand to signal a new line: "And then I pick up the property of the play which she's always hated and dreaded [a gun], so much that she refuses to remember that it exists in the play" (355). This time the third person pronoun provides no distance, and tension mounts when Clare declares the performance "*over*" (357); the audience has left. The siblings fling mutual recriminations at each other. Although they are locked into the theatre, Clare leaves unspoken "the prohibited word" confined. Above or below the fear that has threaded thematically and theatrically through inner and outer play, they return to their performance. The opening lines of "The Two-Character Play" are respoken "very fast" (368), and after a fast-forward to the sunflower lines, each sibling in turn picks up that stock prop, a loaded revolver, and aims it at the other. Incapable of firing, however, they close both plays simultaneously, "their hands lifting toward each other" (370). Sentimental though that joint gesture may be, it has been perfectly prepared by the contrasting lights, the balanced sets and symbols (statue and sunflower), and the complementary speeches of Clare and Felice.

Comparable balance between wife and husband, Zelda and Scott Fitzgerald, would have improved *Clothes for a Summer Hotel* (1980), but it nevertheless remains a considerable achievement. In this "ghost play" Williams's Gothic element is the setting – Zelda Fitzgerald's asylum "which is entered through a pair of Gothic-looking black gates, rather unrealistically tall." Williams takes liberties with chronology, since the actual Scott Fitzgerald died in Hollywood seven years before his wife Zelda in her Asheville, North Carolina asylum. Williams, however, who hinges so many of his plots on a visit, imagines that Scott flies in his flimsy California clothes to visit Zelda in her asylum. Scott waits outside the Gothic gates, whose sinister quality is enhanced by the wide-sleeved black robes of the nursing sisters, and by the sound of a chill wind.

Scott's old friend Gerald Murphy seeks to prepare him for a changed Zelda: "She's taking insulin; it's put a good deal of weight on her, and, well, regardless of what the doctors – " (208). The two men have not seen each other lately, and they speak hesitantly, sometimes interrupting each other, as in any reunion. Zelda, grotesque in a tutu, is dismayed by Scott's appearance; she has to shout to be heard above the incessant wind. After a perfunctory kiss, husband and wife fence verbally, Zelda charging Scott with cannibalizing her creativity. Although Scott complains of her "cold, violent attitude," affection seeps through her recriminations while the two catch up with one another's present. This conversation is balanced and realistic, except for the wind's moan. When the Murphys return to the stage, Zelda hallucinates that she is dancing for Diaghilev, and Scott calls for a doctor. As Clare of *Out Cry* is obsessed with the word "confined," Zelda fixes on "salamander," which Scott alone recognizes as "a mythological creature that can live in fire and suffer no hurt . . ." (226). Zelda's obsessive word is a prophecy of her death by fire. By the end of the first scene a frustrated Scott, suffering a heart attack, is considered drunk; a hallucinating Zelda mistakes the asylum Intern for her French lover Edouard. The scene ends with her polite bow to the audience.

By Scene 2 we are in 1926, Zelda interrupting Scott as he writes, and the words of husband and wife interrupt each other as well. In rebellion against Scott's idea of a "dreamy young Southern lady" (240), Zelda takes a lover, Edouard, and their conversation sports occasional French phrases. Act II opens on the lovers' post-coital scene, love rendering Zelda verbose and rhetorical. This loquacity is not implausible in a hallucination, but the past is pierced by the present, when Edouard confesses that he "*grew old*"(251). Gliding back into the past, Zelda is at a star-studded Murphy ball on the Riviera, with Scott jealous of Edouard. Then Scott is in the present, discussing Zelda with her doctor, who prefers Zelda's novel to his own. A change of light, and we are back at the Murphy party, its guests witty or drunk, but not both. Hemingway and Fitzgerald, often interrupting one another, discuss their craft and their sexuality. In a Williams footnote to Hemingway's *A Moveable Feast*, that writer denies that he was attracted to Scott, and he informs Scott that he "chose to blast my brains out for no reason but the good and sufficient reason that my work was finished"(272).

For the last scene of *Clothes* we are back in the asylum, and Zelda is back in her grotesque tutu. She is more loquacious than ever, philosophizing about fate as well as blaming Scott for repressing her creativity:

"Between the first wail of an infant and the last gasp of the dying – it's all an arranged pattern of – submission to what's been prescribed for us unless we escape into madness or into acts of creation . . . The latter option was denied me, Scott, by someone not a thousand miles from here"(274). They hurl insults at one another, sometimes overlapping, and Zelda enters the Gothic gates with a last taunt to Scott: "*I can't be your book anymore! Write yourself a new book!*"(280). Through the gates Scott forlornly urges the replacement wedding band upon Zelda, before he recedes into wind and mist.

In *Clothes* Williams expands his light and sound effects: a projection of Scott in drag precedes his scene with Hemingway; fire seems to erupt from a stage bush and Zelda's third-story room; in no other Williams play does the wind whistle so cruelly. Music and dancing nourish Zelda's hallucinations. Dialogue ranges from the nurses' brief injunctions to the rhythmic exchanges of Scott and Zelda, of Scott and Hemingway, of Zelda and Edouard, sprinkled with French. At the Murphy party guests banter in trivialities; at the asylum the staff speak authoritatively. Repetitions are meaningful, particularly Zelda's: "What about *my* work?" Unfortunately, Williams does not sufficiently trust his functional dialogue, and he weakens the drama in such scenic directions as: "*the present words given [Zelda] are tentative: they may or may not suffice in themselves: the presentation – performance – must*" (230).

It is a pathetic direction from one who has never permitted words alone to suffice. Williams always explores the physical elements of theatre as well, and very inventively in this play. Perhaps the most skillful element of this late play is the fluidity of temporal transitions. Tom of *The Glass Menagerie* and the Writer of *Vieux Carré* frame their dramas in memory, but *Clothes for a Summer Hotel* moves seamlessly back and forth between the 1920s and 1940s to dramatize the abrasions of "a storybook marriage." It is unnecessary for Zelda to spell it out for us: "Neither of us is cruel, but we're hurting each other unbearably" (278).

In these "failures" of two decades Williams expanded both his visual and sonic repertory: soap bubbles, iron gates, spotlights, dancing, and manipulation of props; the noise of knocks, rattles, sea, wind, and giant wings. Verbally, Williams's expressive dialogue embraces rhyme, alliteration, repetition, overlap, soliloquy, word-play, colloquialism, and incompletion. Almost always, these devices function dramatically, even when the plays are slim. Without exception, these late plays, like the earlier ones, provide opportunities for passionate acting.

I am not so naive as to think I will convert critics to the qualities of these late plays, but I do hope that actors or directors will reach for their wealth.

NOTES

1 John S. McCann, *The Critical Reputation of Tennessee Williams: A Reference Guide* (Boston: G. K. Hall, 1983), xiii. Of the many overviews of Williams's drama, only that of Alice Griffin seems to me sensitive to his restless explorations.

2 Alan Schneider, *Entrances: An American Director's Journey* (New York: Viking, 1986), 370.

3 Thomas P. Adler, "The Dialogue of Incompletion: Language in Tennessee Williams's Later Plays," *The Quarterly Journal of Speech* 61 (February 1975), 49.

4 David Savran, *Communists, Cowboys, and Queers: The Politics of Masculinity in the Work of Arthur Miller and Tennessee Williams* (Minneapolis: University of Minnesota Press, 1992), 133.

5 My comments are based on the last published version in volume v of *The Collected Plays*, where it appears as *The Two-Character Play*. To avoid confusion, I use *Out Cry* for the whole play and "The Two-Character Play" for the play within the play.

6 Thomas Postlewait, "Spatial Order and Meaning in the Theatre: The Case of Tennessee Williams," *Assaph: Studies in the Theatre*, n. 10 (Tel Aviv University, 1994), 64.

BIBLIOGRAPHY

Adler, Thomas P. "The Dialogue of Incompletion: Language in Tennessee Williams's Later Plays," *The Quarterly Journal of Speech* 61 (February, 1975).

Gunn, Drewey Wayne. *Tennessee Williams: A Bibliography*. Metuchen, N.J.: Scarecrow Press, 1980.

Griffin, Alice. *Understanding Tennessee Williams*. Columbia: University of South Carolina Press, 1995.

Hemingway, Ernest. *A Movable Feast*. New York: Scribner's, 1964. "The Sea Change," in *The Short Stories of Ernest Hemingway*. New York: The Modern Library, 1942.

Postlewait, Thomas. "Spatial Order and Meaning in the Theatre: The Case of Tennessee Williams," *Assaph: Studies in the Theatre*, n. 10 (Tel Aviv University, 1994).

Savran, David. *Cowboys, Communists, and Queers: The Politics of Masculinity in the Work of Arthur Miller and Tennessee Williams*. Minneapolis: University of Minnesota Press, 1992.

Schneider, Alan. *Entrances: An American Director's Journey*. New York: Viking, 1986.

Williams, Tennessee. *The Chalky White Substance*, in *Antaeus* 66 (Spring, 1991).
A House Not Meant to Stand in manuscript at the Harry Ransom Humanities Research Center, Austin, Texas.
Moise and the World of Reason. New York: Simon and Schuster, 1976.
Something Cloudy, Something Clear. New York: New Directions, 1995.
This Is (An Entertainment) in manuscript at the Harry Ransom Humanities Center.

13

JACQUELINE O'CONNOR

Words on Williams: a bibliographic essay

BIOGRAPHIES

The publication of the long-awaited first volume of Lyle Leverich's biography of Williams, *Tom: The Unknown Tennessee Williams*, makes 1995 a year of important contributions to Williams studies. Leverich, the biographer authorized by Williams in 1979, relies heavily on Williams's early journals to sketch a portrait of a man divided between the public "Tennessee" and the private "Tom." The first volume ends with the success of *The Glass Menagerie* in 1945, so the student interested in Williams before fame will find much of interest here. Leverich's book offers detailed documentation for all his sources. Documentation is what is missing from Bruce Smith's account of Williams's last years, *Costly Performances. Tennessee Williams: The Last Stage* (1990). Smith seems more intent on proving the importance of his own friendship to Williams than on providing new information about the playwright's last years. Those interested in the first production of *Clothes for a Summer Hotel* might find Smith's book useful, centering as it does on the difficulties Williams encountered in staging his last full-length play.

Two other biographies that have recently been added to the dozen or more books devoted to Williams's life both appeared in 1993. The first, Nicholas Pagan's *Rethinking Literary Biography: A Postmodern Approach to Tennessee Williams*, is an attempt to speculate about the relationship between "the Tennessee Williams studied throughout America" and "the texts, whether literary or nonliterary, to which he has affixed his name." While the work is overburdened by the theoretical framework that informs the approach, Pagan's detailed discussions of individual plays are insightful. The reader should be cautioned, however, that he uses the Signet editions of some plays, with page rather than scene or act numbers, and this makes locating his quoted material difficult when using the more standard New Directions texts. Probably the best recent volume to combine biographical and textual criticism is Ronald Hayman's *Tennessee Williams: Everyone Else is an Audience*. Proceeding chronologically, Hayman divides the book into thematic chapter headings that point to the connections he makes between Williams's life and work. His sources are well documented, making this a useful biography for critics.

In 1987, Williams's long-time friend and occasional collaborator Donald Windham published *Lost Friendships: A Memoir of Truman Capote, Tennessee Williams, and Others*. The section on Williams is entitled *As If . . . A Personal View of Tennessee Williams*, originally printed privately by Sandy Campbell in Italy. Windham brings together his views on Williams and Capote to offer a different perspective than what he believes the biographers of each writer can present: he claims that he does not look back to see them, as their biographers do, but forward, and that he "cannot but see the unlikeliness of what Tennessee and Truman became in the light of what they were." Like most of the other biographies written about Williams by a friend or family member, Windham's account is necessarily colored by his personal opinions and feelings about Williams.

Harry Rasky's *Tennessee Williams: A Portrait in Laughter and Lamentation* (1986) is in some ways a portrait of collaboration, and like Smith's book, it covers a limited time span. The account is structured around Rasky's experience working with Williams while making the 1973 documentary film *Tennessee Williams's South*. The conversations included, however, cover a wide range of familiar Williams topics, and the book reads like an extended interview, much of it consisting of Rasky probing Williams on work past and present, family, and the South. Rasky also recounts his experience directing *Tiger Tail*, a play adapted from the screenplay *Baby Doll*, in Atlanta in 1978.

The most complete and detailed biography available remains Donald Spoto's 1985 *The Kindness of Strangers: The Life of Tennessee Williams*. One of the book's biggest advantages for the student or scholar is its strict adherence to chronological structure, so it is useful for checking dates or establishing Williams's whereabouts during a given period. Unlike the first volume of Leverich's biography, however, Spoto's account lacks a clear-cut thesis, and the documentation style is awkward. 1985 marked the appearance of another biographical work, this one in the form of a memoir. Dotson Rader's *Tennessee: Cry of the Heart* is an informal and personal account of the author's friendship with Williams from 1969 (soon after the playwright's release from Barnes Hospital) until his death. It provides little information that cannot be found elsewhere with more ease.

The Dictionary of Literary Biography, Documentary Series devotes the entire volume IV to Williams. Published in 1984 and edited by Margaret A.

Van Antwerp and Sally Johns, the book offers an extensive collection of information on Williams's life and work. Perhaps its greatest strength as a reference work is visual, for it is packed with photographs and facsimiles of playbills, advertisements, newspaper articles, book covers, letters, and manuscript pages; the volume provides the student entrance to Williams's theatrical world rather than his literary world. Another collection of photographs, playbills and posters, *The World of Tennessee Williams* (1978) edited by Richard Leavitt, proves that less text and more pictures is not necessarily an advantage, however, for this less comprehensive pictorial has little value as a reference book.

Mike Steen provides *A Look at Tennessee Williams* (1969) through interviews with an assortment of people who interacted personally and/or professionally with Williams; actors who embodied his characters make up the majority of the interviewees. Steen probes his subjects for personal reminiscences about Williams, and in doing so provides a nice counterpoint to the playwright's anecdotes about these friends and peers, many of which have been published in collected letters and other forms.

Portraits by two family members and another of Williams's many friends round out the list of biographies on the playwright. Dakin Williams, the playwright's brother, is the author of *Tennessee Williams: An Intimate Biography* with Shepherd Mead, published in 1983, the year of Williams's death. Gilbert Maxwell's *Tennessee Williams and Friends* (1965) is the earliest book-length memoir of Williams's social circle during the first two decades of his professional life. There are now more complete, better documented sources for the material found in both these books. The very first biography on Williams, *Remember Me to Tom* (1963) was written by his mother, Edwina Dakin Williams, as told to Lucy Freeman. Since Williams's relationship with his family was crucial to his development as a writer, this account from Mrs. Williams's perspective is enlightening, albeit subjective. She documented carefully the family's life and collected materials into a series of scrapbooks (the scrapbooks are part of the massive collection of Williams papers at the Humanities Research Center at the University of Texas in Austin), and she reprints much of this material in the biography.

BIBLIOGRAPHIES

1995 marks the year that a fully descriptive bibliography of Williams's primary work appeared. George Crandell's *Tennessee Willliams: A Descriptive Bibliography*, is the most complete attempt to date to list and categorize the sum of Williams's work. Each section proceeds chronologically to describe various kinds of published documents written by Williams: plays, collections, pamphlets, poetry, essays, reviews, letters. The later sections of the bibliography list titles set to music, sound recordings of Williams reading his works, and translations. It will no doubt prove essential to scholars who seek to trace the intricate development of most of Williams's extensive *œuvre*.

Drewey Wayne Gunn has published a revised second edition of his *Tennessee Williams: A Bibliography*. This 1991 revision is more thorough and comprehensive than the first edition, published in 1980. One of the newer edition's most useful features is a section that identifies the location of manuscripts and papers divided among various research libraries. The book is very helpful in providing production information and a list of reviews. Although the organization of the general criticism section, alphabetically by author, makes items difficult to locate, the plays and screenplays section provides a short list of criticism within each play listing. Gunn's bibliography also provides a section on translations of Williams's works.

Pearl Amelia McHaney's bibliographic essay published in Matthew C. Roudané's *American Dramatists: Contemporary Authors Bibliographic Series*, vol. III (1989), is thorough and useful in identifying the range of studies available on Williams. McHaney divides her essay and her bibliography into types of works available on Williams, and moves mostly chronologically through each type. The essay complements and expands significantly on Alan Chesler's bibliographic essay "Tennessee Williams: Reassessment and Assessment," published in Tharpe's massive tribute collection (1977). Chesler organizes his essay by play and, after briefly surveying Williams's critical reception from *Battle of Angels* (1940) through *Out Cry* (1973), spends the bulk of his essay discussing five major plays: *The Glass Menagerie, A Streetcar Named Desire, Cat on a Hot Tin Roof, The Night of the Iguana,* and *Suddenly Last Summer*.

File on Tennessee Williams (1985), compiled by Catherine M. Arnott, is part of the Methuen series on modern dramatists, and provides the student with a quick chronological overview of the plays that lists approximate time of composition, premiere dates, and excerpts from reviews. John McCann's *The Critical Reputation of Tennessee Williams: A Reference Guide,* consists of secondary material through 1981. The book is organized chronologically, which provides a nice contrast to Gunn's system, and McCann provides annotations.

Various checklists and a selective international bibliography are printed in the *Tennessee Williams Newsletter* and the *Tennessee Williams Review*, both published in the early 1980s. However, these short-lived journals are not readily available in libraries, and the checklists are fairly selective in their approaches. The *Tennessee Williams Literary Journal*, edited by W. Kenneth Holditch, has been published by Word Catering Publishers semi-annually since Spring 1989, and is a source for information about The Tennessee Williams Literary Festival, a gathering of scholars and performers held each March in New Orleans.

CRITICAL STUDIES: BOOKS

Published in 1995, Alice Griffin's *Understanding Tennessee Williams* is an excellent introduction to the major plays for the student or beginning scholar. Griffin's approach combines literary and theatrical analysis with ease, and offers readers a useful overview of the most prevalent critical approaches as well as a sense of the initial reception of each play. The book devotes one chapter to each of nine major dramas through *The Night of the Iguana*. A brief but useful annotated bibliography completes the study.

Brenda Murphy's *Tennessee Williams and Elia Kazan: A Collaboration in the Theatre* (1992) is the first full-length study of the most significant collaboration of Williams's career. In individual chapters, Murphy discusses the four plays directed by Kazan, arguing that the playwright and director combined their talents and vision with Jo Mielziner to create what became known in the fifties as "the American Style." Murphy argues that while Kazan directed *A Streetcar Named Desire* from a finished script, his later collaborations with Williams were marked by the director's interest in shaping parts of *Camino Real*, *Cat on a Hot Tin Roof*, and *Sweet Bird of Youth*. The result was a struggle for creative hegemony that strained their relationship at times, but produced dynamic theatre in a unique combination of styles.

Also published in 1992, *The Faces of Eve: A Study of Tennessee Williams's Heroines* is a traditional study that covers familiar territory without offering much original insight. Gulshan Rai Kataria uses Jungian analytical psychology to explore the feminine in Williams's plays, and divides his female characters into mothers, hetairas, Amazons, and mediums. Kataria does acknowledge the debt her discussion owes to previous scholars who have written on Williams's women.

Two works, each devoted to a single play, appeared in 1990. *The Glass Menagerie: An American Memory* by Delma E. Presley, and *A Streetcar Named Desire: The Moth and the Lantern* by Thomas P. Adler, are both part of the Twayne's Masterwork Studies and share common organizational properties. The introductory sections, that place the plays into historical, theatrical, and literary contexts, are helpful for recreating the mood of the times. Here the two volumes diverge, with Presley's book retaining the historical emphasis in its choice of chapter topics ("An American Memory," "Tradition and Technique"), while Adler's reads *Streetcar* primarily through character analysis. Similar in their level and range to Alice Griffin's book, these works provide students with a thoughtful overview. Complete with thorough chronologies and annotated bibliographies that direct readers to other treatments of the play in question, these volumes accomplish much in a small space.

Three books devoted to character study appeared within a three-year span. The first, *Cats on a Hot Tin Roof: A Study of Alienated Characters in the Major Plays of Tennessee Williams* (1990), by Dharanidhar Sahu, is a character study of the traditional literary kind. The approach is dated and the work suffers from multiple errors. In the second, an overview called *Tennessee Williams* (1987), Roger Boxill writes from a theatrical perspective and classifies the characters from Williams's plays as either "wanderers" or "faded belles"; like too many other critics before him, Boxhill uses the plays to conjecture about Williams's psychological make-up. The book is useful in its analysis of play productions.

Judith J. Thompson adopts a more sophisticated approach to character in *Tennessee Williams's Plays: Memory, Myth, and Symbol* (1987). Thompson explores classical and archetypal allusions in eight major Williams plays from his most successful years. In doing so, she uncovers a recurrent structural theme present in the plays through which the mythic characterization of particular characters results in the reconstruction of a memory or event that "invests both tale and teller with mythic significance." Although she perceives traces of this pattern in no less than seventeen of Williams's plays, she restricts her discussion to the works in which this pattern is "most fully realized": *The Glass Menagerie, A Streetcar Named Desire, The Rose Tattoo, Cat on a Hot Tin Roof, Orpheus Descending, Suddenly Last Summer, Sweet Bird of Youth*, and *The Night of the Iguana*.

In the 1987 book *Tennessee Williams on the Soviet Stage*, Irene Shaland explores "the problems involved in staging his works in the Soviet theatre." Her four chapters discuss productions of *A Streetcar Named Desire, The Glass Menagerie, Orpheus Descending, Sweet Bird of Youth*, and *Kingdom of Earth*. She argues that Williams has been popular on the Soviet stage because the playwright shares with the Soviet people an "innate interest in the life of the human spirit," and an acknowledgment of "people's eternal need for one another." In her chapter on *The Glass Menagerie*, Shaland reviews in chronological order five Soviet productions of the play, attempting to chronicle the audience's changing attitude towards Western theatre. This is a book for those interested in international interpretations of Williams, and for those interested in production-based rather than text-based study.

Because so many Williams plays were adapted for the screen, his influence on American filmmaking in the 1950s was significant. Two important books that analyze the film adaptations of Williams's work were published within three years of each other. The most recent, *The Films of Tennessee Williams* by Gene D. Phillips (1980), is a thorough treatment of the technical challenges directors faced in filming Williams's work. Phillips argues that despite necessary changes, most of the films succeed in translating Williams's dramatic works to the screen. *Tennessee Williams and Film* by Maurice Yacowar (1977) focuses more on the theoretical implications of play adaptation, and does more analysis of the films as such. Since student access to Williams's plays depends to a large extent upon these filmed versions, the books are invaluable for providing direction in this area.

Foster Hirsch, in his book *A Portrait of the Artist: The Plays of Tennessee Williams* (1979), concentrates on the various configurations of sexuality in Williams's plays, concluding that "Williams is a confused moralist, and his continuing battle with his puritanical impulses frequently complicates the dramas in interesting ways. The plays are filled with tantalizing ambiguities." Unfortunately, the work's examination of the reasons for and results of this confused morality fails to move beyond a preoccupation with the sexual exploits or frustrations of both the play-wright and his characters. To Hirsch's credit, he is among the few critics from this period who attempts a study of plays after *The Night of the Iguana*, although his criticism is mostly disparagement. A more sympathetic study from the same year is Felicia Hardison Londré's *Tennessee Williams*. Useful for plot synopsis and critical quotations from the reviews, the book offers the reader an accurate picture of the state of Williams's reputation during the mid 1970s.

The 1978 revision of Signi L. Falk's *Tennessee Williams* (first published in 1961) shares with Hirsch's book a condemnation of the plays written after 1961. Falk divides Williams's characters into types: gentlewomen, Southern wenches, desperate heroes, and deteriorating artists. Chronologically, Falk's revised edition marks the publication of the first full-length work devoted to Williams in roughly a decade; not since 1966 had any such work appeared. *The Influence of D. H. Lawrence on Tennessee Williams* by Norman J. Fedder (1966) is a study that establishes the nature and extent of Lawrence's literary influence on Williams. Fedder is unusual among the first generation of Williams's critics for his analysis of Williams's poetry and fiction. Fedder argues throughout that Williams shares with Lawrence the concern for "the duality of flesh and spirit, of the fox and the moth; and with the destructive tendencies of bourgeois civilization, of the mammoth figures." Finally, however, Fedder concludes that Lawrence's worldview is greater in scope.

Published in 1965, Esther Merle Jackson's *The Broken World of Tennessee Williams* represents one of the first attempts to place Williams into the context of American dramatic development. Jackson's emphasis on the formal qualities of the plays is revealed in chapter headings such as "Williams and the Lyric Moment," "The Plastic Theatre," and "Camino Real: The World as Spectacle." She concludes that Williams's drama "represents a significant level of achievement in the total movement of Western theatre toward a distinctively contemporary form." Her concentration on the playwright's dramaturgy rather than his biography remains refreshing. Gerald Weales, in yet another book entitled *Tennessee Williams* (1965), provides a brief overview of the plays through *The Milk Train Doesn't Stop Here Anymore*. Although later books provide this service more completely, Weales is one of the first to suggest useful groupings of early Williams characters.

Full-length studies on Williams began to appear about the time that many would mark the end of his Broadway success. Benjamin Nelson's *Tennessee Williams: The Man and His Work* remains useful as a means of measuring Williams's reputation prior to the 1960s, for the book closes with a discussion of *Period of Adjustment,* produced in 1960, and makes references to *The Night of the Iguana,* incomplete at the time of Nelson's writing. The book discusses Williams's life in the first three chapters, and then picks up a discussion of the plays with *Battle of Angels.* The book is an accurate assessment of the playwright's popular reception. Nancy M. Tischler's *Tennessee Williams: Rebellious Puritan* (1961) is the first book to develop a full-scale argument of the connection between the plays and Williams's psychological make-up, drawing on Williams's much-publicized assertion that his contradictory nature resulted from warring strains: the puritanical and the cavalier.

CRITICAL STUDIES: ESSAY COLLECTIONS

The most recent collection of original essays on Williams is a collection published in 1993 and devoted in its entirety to *Confronting Tennessee Williams's "A Streetcar Named Desire."* Edited by Philip C. Kolin, the book contains fifteen original essays written from a variety of critical/ theoretical perspectives. As Kolin suggests, these contemporary essays explore "the theoretical underpinnings of the play, revealing it to be a work that does not shrink from the philosophical interventions/social commitments of a Kristeva, Foucault, Lacan, or Jameson."

Harold Bloom has edited three collections of previously published material on Willliams. The first, a 1987 collection entitled *Tennessee Williams: Modern Critical Views*, reprints what Bloom considers the best criticism available on Williams. The collection is arranged in the chronological order in which the essays first appeared. Half the essays deal with a single play, while the remainder survey the plays over a period or discuss a feature common to a number of plays. The following year, two other Chelsea House collections edited by Bloom appeared, each devoted to a single play. They are intended to offer a representative selection of critical views on *The Glass Menagerie* and *A Streetcar Named Desire*, respectively. Clearly, these plays from the 1940s have been chosen for their sustained reputation as Williams's "best work," for Bloom speaks in the introduction of both books about the playwright's "long aesthetic decline . . . from 1953 to 1983." Both of these single play collections draw heavily from *Modern Drama*, reprinting essays that originally appeared there, and the collection of essays on *A Streetcar Named Desire* selects others from *Tennessee Williams: A Tribute*, the massive collection edited by Jac Tharpe a decade earlier. The reprints are essentially unchanged, but these collections are helpful nonetheless for students and scholars who are concentrating their work on one of the two plays, for they offer a short survey of the kind of critical material available. All three collections include a cursory chronology.

Other collections of reprinted articles on a single play are available, such as R. B. Parker's edition, *The Glass Menagerie: A Collection of Critical Essays* (1983). Parker's collection is an eclectic combination of textual and theatrical studies, and provides a good overview of the variety of ways that critics have approached the play. Jordan Miller's *Twentieth Century Interpretations of A Streetcar Named Desire: A Collection of Critical Essays* (1971) contains a varied collection of reviews, book sections, journal articles, even an excerpt from Elia Kazan's director's notebook. Many of the entries are abridged, however, so the student should recognize that this book be used as an introduction only.

Jac Tharpe edited two collections in 1977, one a radically abridged version of the other. *Tennessee Williams: 13 Essays* borrows its material from the massive volume *Tennessee Williams: A Tribute*. The latter, a vast collection of original material written from a variety of critical perspectives, is organized into sections that broadly reflect the subject matter: "European Contexts," "Themes," "Prose and Poetry," and "Techniques" are a few of the classifications. The "Assessment" section at the end of the volume is still useful in its attempts to articulate the state of the playwright's reputation and to forecast his professional future at a time of renewed interest in his work. That renewal is evident by the appearance of another volume of essays published the same year: *Tennessee Williams: A Collection of Critical Essays*, edited by Stephen S. Stanton. This collection of fifteen reprinted articles reflects thematic approaches originally printed from the mid 1960s through the mid 1970s.

CRITICAL STUDIES: BOOK SECTIONS

No book about twentieth-century American drama would be complete without a chapter (or two) on Williams, and two books published in the 1990s, which begin their study with plays of the 1940s, offer enlightening perspectives on Williams's contributions to what is now considered a classic period in American theatre. Thomas Adler's *American Drama 1940–1960: A Critical History* devotes two chapters to Williams, dividing his discussion by decades: the first chapter covers the plays of the forties and fifties; the second, "Tennessee Williams in the 1960s and 1970s: Death and the Artist," pushes against the limits imposed upon Adler's study by reaching beyond 1960 to encompass most of the second half of Williams's career. C. W. E. Bigsby's *Modern American Drama, 1945–1990* devotes a chapter to Williams that is less an overview of the plays than it is a focus on the "theatricalising self" in Williams's life and plays. Bigsby begins by placing Williams within the sociopolitical context of the postwar period, and then proceeds to argue that the central metaphor underlying his work proposes "the self as actor, society as a series of coercive fictions." Bigsby had already proven himself a provocative Williams critic in *A Critical Introduction to Twentieth-Century American Drama, Volume Two: Williams, Miller, Albee*, first published in 1984. That three-volume work remains the most thorough study of its kind, and the 120 pages on Williams is particularly useful for its analysis of early unpublished plays.

While Bigsby and Adler place Williams's work in a historical context in their books, David Savran presents the politically radical Williams in *Communists, Cowboys, and Queers: The Politics of Masculinity in the Work of Arthur Miller and Tennessee Williams* (1992). Savran argues that Williams "produced a new and radical theater that challenged and undermined the Cold War order." Both Miller and Williams explore conflicts between the political and the sexual, the public and the private, says Savran, but while Miller polices these binarisms, "Williams insistently delights in their precariousness." Savran devotes the bulk of the book to his critique of Williams, and the study is noteworthy for its extensive analysis of *In the Bar of a Tokyo Hotel*, a play not often valorized by critics.

Other books that devote less space to Williams but that might prove useful to students or scholars seeking to survey the field are too numerous to discuss: the following titles are no more than a sampling of the single-author or collected works with a chapter or essay on Williams, or studies in which his plays figure prominently in the thesis. Recently published are June Schlueter's *Dramatic Closure: Reading the End* (1995); Marc Robinson's *The Other American Drama* (1994); Julie Adam's *Versions of Heroism in Modern American Drama: Redefinitions by Miller, Williams, O'Neill and Anderson* (1991); and *Lesbian and Gay Writing* (1990), edited by Mark Lilly. *Feminist Rereadings of Modern American Drama* (1989), edited by June Schlueter, includes two essays on Williams, and the *Themes in Drama* series, edited by James Redmond, contain essays on Williams in the following volumes: *Madness and Drama* (1993), *Violence in Drama* (1991), and *Drama and Symbolism* (1982). An older book whose discussion of Williams is packed with insights on language in his plays is Ruby Cohn's *Dialogue in American Drama* (1971). Other earlier single-author works that include discussions of Williams and his place in American drama are Thomas E. Porter's *Myth and Modern American Drama* (1969) and W. David Sievers's *Freud on Broadway: A History of Psychoanalysis and the American Drama* (1955).

14

JACQUELINE O'CONNOR

The Strangest Kind of Romance: Tennessee Williams and his Broadway critics

Tennessee Williams's reputation as one of the greatest playwrights of the twentieth century seems secure. Now just over a dozen years after his death, his plays are frequently revived, he continues to provoke critical inquiry, and he is one of the few American dramatists still taught in undergraduate literature surveys. Considering his prolific output, however, he is renowned for only a handful of plays, all dating from the first fifteen years of a forty-year professional career. Indeed, one might surmise that Tennessee Williams's critical reputation during his life soared, then plummeted, and that his later works were produced and tolerated only because of the early masterpieces; moreover, that his stature is entirely dependent upon a few well-wrought dramas: *The Glass Menagerie*, *A Streetcar Named Desire*, *Cat on a Hot Tin Roof*, *The Night of the Iguana*. It is no coincidence that these plays enjoyed long, successful New York runs, for critical acclaim and commercial appeal usually coexisted on the Broadway of Williams's time.

But since he first gained international attention with the production of *The Glass Menagerie* in 1945, his plays, even those now considered American classics, have been by turn ignored, scorned, morally condemned, or seriously misunderstood. The successful runs during the 1940s and 1950s were punctuated by productions of plays whose names do not spring to mind readily: *You Touched Me!*, *Stairs to the Roof*, *Camino Real*, *Orpheus Descending*. And while none of his late plays stormed Broadway, he had modest success with plays produced elsewhere. Indeed, reassessment of all the works continues; one imagines that the final analysis will be deferred as long as his writings remain under the critical microscope. The following survey hits the highs and lows of his career as a Broadway playwright, and suggests that the complexity of his critical reputation matches that of his publication history: nothing about Tennessee Williams, it seems, is uncomplicated.

The Theatre Guild's production of *Battle of Angels* at the Wilbur Theater in Boston premiered on December 30, 1940, and prompted excitement of the kind that, though perhaps not a forecast of the young playwright's later success, foreshadowed the kind of controversy that frequently engulfed a Williams production. Called by one reviewer "the maddest night of melodrama," *Battle of Angels* prompted members of Boston's city council to denounce it on moral grounds and call for its censure (*Boston Post*). Closing after two weeks, and prompting the Theatre Guild to apologize in writing to its subscribers for having gambled on the drama, the production offered little evidence of Williams's future success.

Exactly four years later, *The Glass Menagerie* opened in Chicago, after a difficult rehearsal period that called into question the viability of both the script and the lead actress. Initial audience response was lukewarm, the box-office returns meager. But the play caught the attention of two influential Chicago critics, Ashton Stevens and Claudia Cassidy; the latter wrote in her first-night review: "If it is your play, as it is mine, it reaches out tentacles, first tentative, then gripping, and you are caught in its spell" (Cassidy, "Fragile"). In another review, however, she allowed that approval might not be unanimous: "If you like this play, you love it – and maybe it works the other way around, too" (Cassidy, "On the Aisle"). The enthusiastic critical responses convinced the producers to delay the closing, the mayor of Chicago was persuaded to subsidize tickets for city employees, Ashton and Cassidy attended repeat performances and continued to praise the show in their columns, and by the end of January the show was consistently sold out. In March *The Glass Menagerie* moved to Broadway, where it captured the New York Drama Critics' Circle Award for the best play of the 1944–1945 season.

While the production's Broadway critics spent most of their review time praising Laurette Taylor, the craftsmanship and fragile beauty of the play were frequently noted. Not everyone thought the play a masterpiece, however: its episodic structure and lack of discernible plot provoked suspicion among some reviewers. Some called Williams's talent into question when the rumor spread that lead actor Eddie Dowling, who also co-directed and co-produced the play, had made crucial script changes. The play's debut in London three years later was far from an overwhelming success. One reviewer expressed confusion about why it had so captivated the American imagination: "*The Glass Menagerie* has come from America to the Haymarket on a great gale of acclamation, and it is difficult to understand why. Mr. TW may be the outstanding playwright New York declares him to be, but we shall require weightier proof of it than this patchwork bubble of sentimental imagining" ("At the Play").

Proof of Williams's genius, or at least reaffirmation of it, was demanded by American reviewers too, when, after *Menagerie*'s New York success, his collaboration with Donald Windham produced *You Touched Me!* The play, which opened in late September of 1945, was identified by critics as "a slight fall from grace," "a tenuous and fragmentary comedy," and "an odd work of sex and symbolism." Burton Rascoe represented the minority opinion with his wholehearted recommendation of the play, in his view "a work of art, edification and entertainment." The play closed in early January.

Premiering December 3, 1947, *A Streetcar Named Desire* did provide the evidence many critics needed to declare Williams the most talented playwright working in the theatre. Critics such as Joseph Wood Krutch confirmed Williams's craft: "From the moment the curtain goes up until it descends after the last act everything is perfectly in key and completely effective. The extent of Mr. Williams's range is still to be demonstrated." Richard Watts declared Williams "an oncoming playwright of power, imagination and almost desperately morbid turn of mind and emotion" (Watts, "Striking"). Called "the event of the season," "the most creative play of the season," and the "season's high," *Streetcar* was awarded both the Pulitzer Prize and the New York Drama Critics' Circle Award. Throughout the time since its opening, the play has been the most consistently praised drama in the Williams canon.

When *Summer and Smoke* was produced on Broadway in October 1948, Ward Morehouse's statement about the play indicated that Williams's reputation for theatrical highs and lows was already forming. Morehouse declared the play "definitely one of Tennessee Williams's lesser achievements." Morehouse was not alone in stressing the shortcomings of the play; John Mason Brown argued that *Summer and Smoke* "fails most where it needs and means most to succeed. Its bad man may become good and its good girl bad, but the true complexities of their altering natures are not revealed."

During the first few years of the next decade, two Williams plays appeared that departed significantly from the kind of treatments audiences expected of him. *The Rose Tattoo* (1950) and *Camino Real* (1953) represented experiments in form and content that disappointed most critics. From Walter Kerr:

> It is this reviewer's opinion that Tennessee Williams is the best playwright of his generation. It is also the reviewer's opinion that *Camino Real*, which opened at the National last night, is the worst play yet written by the best playwright of his generation. Mr. Williams is hopelessly mired in his new love – symbolism. (Kerr, "*Camino*")

Kerr's assessment, to which Williams responded with a letter of protest, encapsulates a perspective on the playwright that had been forming since *Menagerie*'s success: that he wrote bad plays as well as good ones.

Critics agreed that *Cat on a Hot Tin Roof* was the good one they had been waiting for; Williams's seventh play on Broadway in ten years, it won for him his second Pulitzer Prize and his third New York Drama Critics' Circle Award. Running for 694 performances, it played at the Morosco Theater from March 1955 to November 1956. Williams considered *Cat* his most tightly-constructed drama. Brooks Atkinson put this another way: "one of its great achievements is the honesty and simplicity of the craftsmanship. It seems not to have been written. It is the quintessence of life. It is the basic truth" (Atkinson, "Williams' *Cat*"). But at the same time that most critics were cheering, Eric Bentley criticized the disjunction between play and production, and in direct counterpoint to Atkinson's assertion, argued that Sincerity and Truth in the play are "mere abstractions with capital letters."

With another new play on Broadway a mere four months after *Cat* closed, Williams continued to provide New York reviewers with raw material for their columns. The premiere of *Orpheus Descending* (1957), the revised *Battle of Angels*, opened to mixed notices, faring neither as well as *Cat*, nor as badly as *Battle*. Walter Kerr noted "a serious loss of sustained power" (Kerr, "*Orpheus*"), while Tom Donnelly suggested the play's failure in his review title, "Tennessee Williams Loses Round Two of His Battle." *Orpheus* either pleased or disappointed, called in turn "one of Mr. Williams's pleasantest plays . . . with some sensitive philosophical comments in passing about the loneliness of the human being condemned in his soul to solitary confinement for the whole of his life" (Atkinson, "Rural *Orpheus*") and "a highly unsatisfactory play, saying very little about any recognizable human experience."

Suddenly Last Summer appeared with *Something Unspoken* as part of a double bill called *Garden District* the following year. Williams claimed to have chosen off-Broadway for the production because of the experimental and controversial nature of the plays. Harold Clurman called them "marginal efforts by a leading dramatist" which nevertheless merited attention (Clurman, "Theatre"). Although some critics claimed that *Suddenly Last Summer* was a sordid shocker, Brooks Atkinson praised Williams for using "ordinary words with so much grace, allusiveness, sorcery and power" (Atkinson, "*Suddenly*"). *Garden District* was a box-office success that ran for 216 performances. The next year sent Williams back to Broadway with *Sweet Bird of Youth*, the headlines proclaiming the play's success: "Williams's Best," "Tennessee Williams Does It Again," and "Williams's *Sweet Bird of Youth*: Weird, Sordid and Fascinating."

By the end of the decade, "weird, sordid and fascinating" had become adjectives evoked frequently to describe Williams's dramas. In 1960, Williams defended his plays in the *New York Times Magazine* against charges of sensationalism, asserting that "the theater has made in our time its greatest artistic advance through the unlocking and lighting up and ventilation of the closets, attics, and basements of human behavior and experience" (Williams). Ironically, however, in his next play he departed radically from the horrific themes that had become his trademark, with a "serious comedy," *Period of Adjustment*. John Chapman even believed this effort to be a demonstration that Williams had not "type-cast himself as a narrator of doom, horror, and confusion." John McClain called it, "quite simply, a resounding success."

Williams named the 1960s his "stoned age," and both he and his critics acknowledged later the artistic decline that resulted from his constant and massive consumption of drugs and alcohol during this decade. But as early as 1961, when *The Night of the Iguana* won Williams his fourth New York Drama Critics' Circle Award, earned him the title of "the greatest living playwright anywhere" from *Time* magazine, and for many reviewers offered no indication that he had reached the end of his fifteen-year success spree, detractors suggested Williams's creative declivity. John Simon, for instance, disputed *Iguana*'s coherence: "Williams has done it all before . . . the play is not really a play . . . the play does not have a clear-cut profile: instead of having a meaningful structure, it is allowed to deliquesce and inspissate at random." Robert Coleman "found it difficult to discover the major point" and called it "second-rate Williams." For those critics, then, the descent had begun.

The Milk Train Doesn't Stop Here Anymore opened at the Morosco Theater, New York, on January 16, 1963. Once more the reviews indicated mixed reactions that still managed to convey Williams's sustained power to mesmerize his theatre audiences. "Most ambitious" and "most arresting" are among the superlatives used to describe a play that has generated little interest in the long term. A revised version ran briefly on Broadway one year later but closed after four performances. A time of increased depression and restlessness for Williams following the death of Frank Merlo, the mid-1960s were nonetheless a time of productivity. Two years after the revision of *Milk Train* failed to materialize into a successful Broadway comeback, Williams's double bill *Slapstick Tragedy* (1966) became his third Broadway production of the decade. The critics agreed that Williams was not at the top of his form: "this brilliant talent is sleeping," and "what has happened to Tennessee Williams is the saddest thing that has happened to the current theatre in the last decade" (McClain, "Out").

Two years later, the critics expressed disappointment and more when *The Seven Descents of Myrtle* (alternately titled *Kingdom of Earth*) ran for less than a month at the Ethel Barrymore Theater. Richard Watts tried hard to like the show but ultimately could not sustain his praise: "[the play]contains some of the distinguished dramatist's most probing and compassionate reflections on lost souls of this sad world. Yet there is no denying the fact that I thought its final effect was one of a let-down" (Watts, "Misfits"). This comment is fairly indicative of the reviews Williams's plays received during the sixties. The critics continued to demonstrate their belief in his greatness, and continued to find elements of talent and genius in plays that became known, nonetheless, as lesser works. Even guarded praise proved impossible for reviewers of *In the Bar of a Tokyo Hotel*, which opened off-Broadway on May 11, 1969. Martin Gottfried declared in amazement: "I don't think anyone should be allowed to see it. Much worse than being an awful play by a great writer, it is a terribly naked work that reveals more about its author than he could have possibly intended" (Gottfried, "*Bar*"). The unanimously negative response to *Bar* prompted Richard Watts to defend the New York critics and their assessment of Williams's latest play:

> I firmly believe there is not a responsible critic in New York who doesn't approach his work with a warm feeling of respect and admiration that is close to a kind of personal affection, and a genuine attitude of the deepest distress when we have to express dissatisfaction with it.   (Watts, "Notes")

At the close of the second full decade of nearly constant public exposure, Williams evoked more pity than praise.

A chorus of critical disappointment and distress continued to haunt Williams during the 1970s, beginning when *Small Craft Warnings* opened in its off-Broadway production on April 2, 1972. Martin Gottfried called the play "one more stumble in the tragic collapse of one of the finest playwrights in theatre history" (Gottfried, "*Warnings*"). T. E. Kalem was kinder, claiming that Williams "reminds us of the size and scope of his genius, but displays it diminuendo." His next play to reach Broadway, *Out Cry*, had already been produced elsewhere under both that title and its alternate, *The Two-Character Play*. Closing after only twelve performances, *Out Cry* in its Broadway version evoked more confusion than repulsion: Richard Watts called it an enigma, but claimed it to be "written so expertly that it not only retains an astonishing share of theatrical interest but creates two characters who may be lunatics but are both believable and touching" (Watts, "Enigma"). As had become commonplace, however, at least one critic found nothing redeeming: Rex Reed called the drama "pretentious, static, and all but incomprehensible."

The *Red Devil Battery Sign* (1975) previewed at the Schubert Theater in Boston. It was the second time in Williams's career that Boston proved an inhospitable site for one of his plays, for as with *Battle of Angels*, the negative reception was enough to close *Battery Sign* before it could reach New York. Carolyn Clay called the play "an embarrassing exercise in ethnic hysteria." The play's abrupt closing prompted the reviewer Douglas Watt to ask the question, "Tennessee Williams: Is His Future Behind Him?" Watt allowed that despite the endurance of Williams's early plays, the absence of a major success since 1961 called into question his chances for future dramatic triumphs. Perhaps this assessment relied too heavily on the assumption that success on Broadway was the only success that counted, even though Watt himself acknowledged that alternative theatre centers in New York and elsewhere could accommodate the playwright in evolution towards new forms or new themes. To some extent, Williams had already been forced to seek out other venues for his work, and a number of plays during the late 1970s were staged outside of New York. *This Is (An Entertainment)* (1976) premiered in San Francisco; *Vieux Carré* had a brief New York run, but was much better received in London a year later; *Tiger Tail*, Williams's rewrite of the *Baby Doll* screenplay, was a hit in Atlanta. Clearly, however, Williams continued to hope that the plays opening elsewhere would reach Broadway, and both he and his reviewers continued to measure success by this established pattern. Standing ovations in Atlanta were a long way from Pulitzer Prizes and extended Broadway runs.

A radically revised version of *Summer and Smoke* ran for twenty-four performances at the Morosco Theater in late 1976. Clive Barnes found *The Eccentricities of a Nightingale* so different from the original as to be really another play entirely, superior in his mind to its predecessor. The play was originally written as a rewrite Williams intended to have staged in London in 1951; he arrived too late with the script, for the cast was already rehearsing the *Smoke* version. Other reviewers did not see the virtues of this radical revision first produced twenty-five years later, and felt that the paring down resulted in a less comprehensible, "skeletal," even "incomplete" play.

Those who saw in the long-delayed production of *Eccentricities* a sign of Williams's return to forms and themes of the past were no doubt pleased with their prediction when the following year brought *Vieux Carré* to the New York stage. Martin Gottfried's remembrance of Williams's past is palpable in his review, when he calls the play "a glimmer" and argues that it "attempts the characters, the compassion and the poetry that once enriched Williams's plays and our lives; that gave masterpieces to the world" (Gottfried, "Glimmer"). Other critics were embarrassed by what they perceived to be personal confessions about Williams's own homosexuality in the portrait of the aging Painter, and found no merit in the playwright's return to a naturalistic style and a familiar setting.

A comedy written in the late 1970s and produced off-Broadway in 1979 also found favor with Clive Barnes, for he called *A Lovely Sunday for Creve Coeur* an exceptional excursion in which pathos is "brightly linked with comedy" (Barnes, "Excursion"). Douglas Watt called it "trivial and uneven" (Watt, "*Sunday*"), however, while Richard Eder declared that *Creve Coeur* had "many of the elements of a fine play; but not a central one." The show ran for thirty-six performances, but like other Williams productions of this time, was not received well enough to find a more permanent home.

Williams's last original full-length play to reach Broadway, *Clothes for a Summer Hotel*, opened at the Cort Theater in March, 1980, and closed less than two weeks later. Harold Clurman maintained that the play failed, despite good writing, good direction, and good acting, because Williams's creative practice and his inner self were disconnected, and because the playwright "persists in expression when the impulse to express has become merely a professional obligation" (Clurman, "*Clothes*"). Howard Kissel remarked on the close parallels between Williams and F. Scott Fitzgerald, a central character in the play, and reported having hoped that these similarities might produce something in the "great Williams tradition." Kissel was forced to conclude, however, that the play did not further an understanding of the Fitzgeralds or Williams.

Scarcity of space has permitted discussion of only the major productions of full-length plays or double bills; Williams's *œuvre* and production history are much more extensive than this brief survey would indicate, and the production chronicle continues to evolve. For even as this glance backward seeks to modify the notion of Williams's simple rise and fall, the current generation of producers and reviewers works at re-presenting and reassessing his plays: those celebrated and those reluctantly or glibly condemned by the reviewers of the time. One need not look far to locate a production of *A Streetcar Named Desire* or *The Glass Menagerie*, while late plays *In the Bar of a Tokyo Hotel*, *The Two-Character Play*, and *Clothes for a Summer Hotel* find new audiences and new critics. Williams's reputation will be altered with each revival or reassessment.

BIBLIOGRAPHY

Atkinson, Brooks. "Theatre: Rural *Orpheus*." *New York Times*, March 22, 1957: 28.
"Theatre: *Suddenly Last Summer*." *New York Times*, January 9, 1958: 23.
"Theatre: Tennessee Williams's *Cat*." *New York Times*, March 25, 1955: 18.

"At the Play." *Punch*, August 11, 1948: 132–33.

Barnes, Clive. "Stage: Williams's *Eccentricities*." *New York Times*, November 24, 1976: 23.

"Williams's *Creve Coeur* is an Exceptional Excursion." *New York Post*, January 22, 1979.

Bentley, Eric. "Tennessee Williams and New York Kazan." *What is Theatre?* New York: Atheneum, 1968: 224–31.

Brown, John Mason. "People Versus Characters." *Saturday Review* 31 (30 October 1948): 31–33.

Cassidy, Claudia. "Fragile Drama Holds Theater in Tight Spell." *Chicago Tribune*, December 27, 1944: 11.

"On the Aisle." *Chicago Sunday Tribune*, January 7, 1945. Books Section: 3.

Chapman, John. "Williams's *Period of Adjustment* is an Affectionate Little Comedy." *New York Daily News*, November 11, 1960: 60.

Clay, Carolyn. "Dead Battery: The Streetcar Breaks Down." *Boston Phoenix*, June 24, 1975: 6.

Clurman, Harold. "*Clothes for a Summer Hotel*." *Nation* 230 (April 19, 1980): 477.

"Theatre." *Nation* 186 (January 25, 1968): 86–87.

Coleman, Robert. "Williams at 2nd Best in *Iguana*." *New York Mirror*, December 29, 1961: 28.

Donnelly, Tom. "Tennessee Williams Loses Round Two of His Battle." *New York World-Telegram*, March 22, 1957: 22.

Eder, Richard. "New Drama by Tennessee Williams." *New York Times*, January 22, 1979, section C: 15.

Gibbs, Wolcott. "Well, Descending, Anyway." *New Yorker* 33 (March 30, 1957): 84–86.

Gottfried, Martin. "Theatre: *In the Bar of a Tokyo Hotel*." *Women's Wear Daily*, May 12, 1969.

"Theatre: *Small Craft Warnings*." *Women's Wear Daily*, April 4, 1972.

"Williams's *Carré* a Glimmer." *New York Post*, May 12, 1977.

Kalem, T.E. "The Theater." *Time*, April 17, 1972: 72–73.

Kauffmann, Stanley. "Theater: Tennessee Williams Returns." *New York Times*, February 23, 1966: 42.

Kerr, Walter F. "*Camino Real*." *New York Herald Tribune*, March 20, 1953: 12.

"Orpheus Descending." *New York Herald Tribune*, March 22, 1957: 12.

Kissel, Howard. "Clothes for a Summer Hotel." *Women's Wear Daily*, March 27, 1980.

Krutch, Joseph Wood. "Drama." *Nation* 165 (December 20, 1947): 686–87.

McClain, John. "The Out and the Abstract." *New York Journal-American*, February 23, 1966: 17.

"Tennessee at His Best." *New York Journal-American*, November 11, 1960.

"Miriam Hopkins at Wilbur; *Battle of Angels* is Full of Exciting Episodes." *Boston Post*, December 31, 1940: 8.

Rascoe, Burton. "*You Touched Me!* a First Rate Comedy." *New York World-Telegram*, September 26, 1945: 34.

Reed, Rex. "Tennessee's *Out Cry*: A Colossal Bore." *Sunday News*, March 11, 1973: 5.

Simon, John. "*The Night of the Iguana.*" *Theatre Arts* 46 (March 1962): 57.

Watt, Douglas. "*Lovely Sunday* is trivial and uneven." *New York Daily News,* January 22, 1979: 27.

——— "Tennessee Williams: Is His Future Behind Him?" *Sunday News,* October 19, 1975: 3.

Watts, Richard, Jr. "The Drama of Three Misfits." *New York Post,* March 28, 1968: 67.

——— "Notes on Tennessee Williams." *New York Post,* May 31, 1969.

——— "*Streetcar Named Desire* is Striking Drama." *New York Post* 4 December 1947.

——— "Tennessee Williams's Enigma." *New York Post,* March 2, 1973.

Williams, Tennessee. "Tennessee Williams Presents His POV." *New York Times Magazine,* June 12, 1960: 19, 78.

SELECTED BIBLIOGRAPHY

PRIMARY WORKS

Collection

The Theatre of Tennessee Williams. 8 volumes. New York: New Directions, 1971–1992.

Books

Battle of Angels. New York: New Directions, 1945.
27 Wagons Full of Cotton and Other One-Act Plays. Norfolk, CN: New Directions, 1945; London: Grey Walls, 1947. Contains *27 Wagons Full of Cotton, The Purification, The Lady of Larkspur Lotion, The Last of My Solid Gold Watches, Portrait of a Madonna, Auto-Da-Fé, Lord Byron's Love Letters, The Strangest Kind of Romance, The Long Goodbye, Hello from Bertha, This Property is Condemned, Talk to Me Like the Rain and Let Me Listen . . .,* and *Something Unspoken.*
You Touched Me! with Donald Windham. New York: French, 1947.
A Streetcar Named Desire. New York: New Directions, 1947; London: Lehmann, 1952.
One Arm and Other Stories. New York: New Directions, 1948.
American Blues: Five Short Plays. New York: Dramatists Play Service, 1948. Contains *Moony's Kid Don't Cry, The Dark Room, The Case of the Crushed Petunias, The Long Stay Cut Short, or The Unsatisfactory Supper,* and *Ten Blocks on the Camino Real.*
Summer and Smoke. New York: New Directions, 1948; London: Lehmann, 1952.
The Roman Spring of Mrs. Stone. New York: New Directions, 1950.
The Rose Tattoo. New York: New Directions, 1951; London: Secker & Warburg, 1954.
I Rise in Flame, Cried the Phoenix. New York: New Directions, 1951.
Camino Real. Norfolk, CN: New Directions, 1953; London: Secker & Warburg, 1958.
Hard Candy: A Book of Stories. New York: New Directions, 1954.
Cat on a Hot Tin Roof. New York: New Directions, 1955; London: Secker & Warburg, 1956. Revised edition, New York: New Directions, 1975.

In the Winter of Cities: Poems. Norfolk, CN: New Directions, 1964.

Baby Doll. New York: New Directions, 1956; London: Secker & Warburg, 1957.

Orpheus Descending. London: Secker & Warburg, 1958. *Orpheus Descending, with Battle of Angels.* New York: New Directions, 1958.

Suddenly Last Summer. New York: New Directions, 1958.

Garden District. London: Secker & Warburg, 1959.

Sweet Bird of Youth. New York: New Directions, 1959; London: Secker & Warburg, 1961.

Period of Adjustment. New York: New Directions, 1960; London: Secker & Warburg, 1961.

Three Players of a Summer Game and Other Stories. London: Secker & Warburg, 1960.

The Night of the Iguana. New York: New Directions, 1962; London: Secker & Warburg, 1963.

The Milk Train Doesn't Stop Here Anymore. New York: New Directions, 1964; London: Secker & Warburg, 1964.

Grand. New York: House of Books, 1964.

The Eccentricities of a Nightingale and Summer and Smoke. New York: New Directions, 1964; Toronto: McClelland & Stewart, 1964.

The Knightly Quest: A Novella and Four Short Stories. New York: New Directions, 1967. New York: New Directions, 1967. Revised and enlarged as *The Knightly Quest: A Novella and Twelve Short Stories.* London: Secker & Warburg, 1968.

Kingdom of Earth (The Seven Descents of Myrtle). New York: New Directions, 1968. Revised edition, New York: Dramatists Play Service, 1969.

The Two-Character Play. New York: New Directions, 1969.

Dragon Country: A Book of Plays. New York: New Directions, 1969; Toronto: McClelland & Stewart, 1969. Contains *In the Bar of a Tokyo Hotel, I Rise in Flame, Cried the Phoenix, The Mutilated, I Can't Imagine Tomorrow, Confessional, The Frosted Glass Coffin, The Gnädiges Fräulein,* and *A Perfect Analysis Given by a Parrot.*

In the Bar of a Tokyo Hotel. New York: Dramatists Play Service, 1969.

Small Craft Warnings. New York: New Directions, 1972; London: Secker & Warburg, 1973.

Out Cry. New York: New Directions, 1973.

Eight Mortal Ladies Possessed: A Book of Stories. New York: New Directions, 1974.

Moise and the World of Reason. New York: Simon & Schuster, 1975; London: Allen, 1976.

Memoirs. Garden City, NY: Doubleday, 1975; London: Allen, 1976.

Androgyne, Mon Amour: Poems. New York: New Directions, 1977.

Where I Live: Selected Essays. (Ed.) Christine R. Day and Bob Woods. New York: New Directions, 1978.

Vieux Carré. New York: New Directions, 1979.

A Lovely Sunday for Creve Coeur. New York: New Directions, 1980.

Clothes for a Summer Hotel: A Ghost Play. New York: New Directions, 1983.

Stopped Rocking and Other Screenplays. New York: New Directions, 1984. Contains *Stopped Rocking, All Gaul is Divided, The Loss of a Teardrop Diamond,* and *One Arm.*

The Red Devil Battery Sign. New York: New Directions, 1988.
Something Cloudy, Something Clear. New York: New Directions, 1995.

Collected Letters and Interviews

Conversations with Tennessee Williams. (Ed.) Albert J. Devlin. Jackson: University Press of Mississippi, 1986.
Five O'Clock Angel: Letters of Tennessee Williams to Maria St. Just, 1948–1982. With commentary by Maria St. Just. New York: Alfred A. Knopf, 1990.
Tennessee Williams's Letters to Donald Windham 1940–1965. (Ed.) Donald Windham. New York: Holt, Rinehart & Winston, 1977.

SECONDARY WORKS

Biographies

Choukri, Mohamed. *Tennessee Williams in Tangier.* Translated by Paul Bowles. Santa Barbara: Cadmus, 1979.
Hayman, Ronald. *Tennessee Williams: Everyone Else is an Audience.* New Haven: Yale University Press, 1993.
Leavitt, Richard, (ed.). *The World of Tennessee Williams.* New York: Putnam, 1978; London: Allen, 1978.
Leverich, Lyle. *Tom: The Unknown Tennessee Williams.* New York: Crown, 1995.
Maxwell, Gilbert. *Tennessee Williams and Friends.* Cleveland: World, 1965.
Rasky, Harry. *Tennessee Williams: A Portrait in Laughter and Lamentation.* New York: Dodd, 1986.
Smith, Bruce. *Costly Performances. Tennessee Williams: The Last Stage.* New York: Paragon House, 1990.
Spoto, Donald. *The Kindness of Strangers: The Life of Tennessee Williams.* Boston: Little Brown, 1985. Reprinted, New York: Ballantine, 1986.
Steen, Mike. *A Look at Tennessee Williams.* New York: Hawthorn, 1969.
Van Antwerp, Margaret A., and Sally Johns, (eds.). *Dictionary of Literary Biography, Documentary Series,* volume IV: *Tennessee Williams.* Detroit: Gale, 1984.
Williams, Dakin, and Shepherd Mead. *Tennessee Williams: An Intimate Biography.* Arbor House, 1983.
Williams, Edwina Dakin, as told to Lucy Freeman. *Remember Me to Tom.* New York: Putnam, 1963.
Windham, Donald. *Lost Friendships: A Memoir of Truman Capote, Tennessee Williams, and Others.* New York: Morrow, 1987.

Bibliographies and Checklists

Adler, Thomas P., Judith Hersch Clark, and Lyle Taylor. "Tennessee Williams in the Seventies: A Checklist." *Tennessee Williams Newsletter* 2 (Spring 1980): 24–29.
Arnott, Catherine M. *File On Tennessee Williams.* London and New York: Methuen, 1985.
Carpenter, Charles A. "Studies of Tennessee Williams's Drama: A Selective Inter-

national Bibliography: 1966–1978." *Tennessee Williams Newsletter* 2 (Spring 1980): 11–23.

Chesler, S. Alan. "Tennessee Williams: Reassessment and Assessment." *Tennessee Williams: A Tribute.* Jackson: University Press of Mississippi, 1977: 848–80. "A Streetcar Named Desire: Twenty-Five Years of Criticism." *Notes on Mississippi Writers* 7 (Fall 1974): 44–53.

Cohn, Alan M. "More Tennessee Williams in the Seventies: Additions to the Checklist and the Gunn Bibliography." *Tennessee Williams Review* 3 (Spring/ Fall 1982): 46–50.

Crandell, George. *Tennessee Williams: A Descriptive Bibliography.* Pittsburgh: University of Pittsburgh Press, 1995.

Gunn, Drewey Wayne. *Tennessee Williams: A Bibliography.* Metuchen, NJ: Scarecrow, 1980. Revised 1991.

Habib, Imtiaz H. *Tennessee Williams: A Descriptive Bibliography.* Dhaka, Bangladesh: University Press, 1986.

Hayashi, Tetsumaro, (ed.). *Arthur Miller and Tennessee Williams: Research Opportunities and Dissertation Abstracts.* Jefferson, NC: McFarland, 1983: 61–124.

McCann, John S. *The Critical Reputation of Tennessee Williams: A Reference Guide.* Boston: G. K. Hall, 1983.

McHaney, Pearl Amelia. "Tennessee Williams." *American Dramatists: Contemporary Authors Bibliographic Series.* vol. III (ed.) Matthew C. Roudané. Detroit: Gale, 1989: 385–429.

Presley, Delma Eugene. "Tennessee Williams: Twenty-Five Years of Criticism." *Bulletin of Bibliography* 30 (January/March 1973): 21–29.

Critical Studies: Books

Adler, Thomas P. *'A Streetcar Named Desire': The Moth and the Lantern.* Boston: Twayne Publishers (Twaynes Masterwork Series, no. 47), 1990.

Boxill, Roger. *Tennessee Williams.* London: Macmillan, 1987.

Donahue, Francis. *The Dramatic World of Tennessee Williams.* New York: Ungar, 1964.

Falk, Signi L. *Tennessee Williams.* Boston: Twayne, 1961. Revised 1978.

Fedder, Norman J. *The Influence of D. H. Lawrence on Tennessee Williams.* The Hague: Mouton, 1966.

Griffin, Alice. *Understanding Tennessee Williams.* Columbia: University of South Carolina Press, 1995.

Hirsch, Foster. *A Portrait of the Artist: The Plays of Tennessee Williams.* Port Washington, New York: Kennikat, 1979.

Jackson, Esther Merle. *The Broken World of Tennessee Williams.* Madison: University of Wisconsin Press, 1965.

Kataria, Gulshan Rai. *The Faces Of Eve: A Study of Tennessee Williams's Heroines.* New Delhi: Sterling Publishers Private Limited, 1992.

Londré, Felicia Hardison. *Tennessee Williams.* New York: Ungar, 1979.

Murphy, Brenda. *Tennessee Williams and Elia Kazan: A Collaboration in the Theatre.* Cambridge: Cambridge University Press, 1992.

Nelson, Benjamin. *Tennessee Williams: The Man and His Work.* New York: Oblensky, 1961.

Phillips, Gene D. *The Films of Tennessee Williams*. East Brunswick, NJ: Associated University Presses, 1980.

Presley, Delma E. *The Glass Menagerie: An American Memory*. Boston: G. K. Hall, 1990.

Sahu, Dharanidhar. *Cats On A Hot Tin Roof: A Study of Alienated Characters in the Major Plays of Tennessee Williams*. Delhi: Academic Foundation, 1990.

Shaland, Irene. *Tennessee Williams on the Soviet Stage*. Lanham; London: University Press of America, 1987.

Thompson, Judith J. *Tennessee Williams's Plays: Memory, Myth, and Symbol*. New York: Peter Lang, 1987.

Tischler, Nancy M. *Tennessee Williams: Rebellious Puritan*. New York: Citadel, 1961.

Weales, Gerald. *Tennessee Williams*. Minneapolis: University of Minnesota Press, 1965.

Yacowar, Maurice. *Tennessee Williams and Film*. New York: Ungar, 1977.

Zeineddine, Nada. *Because It Is My Name*. Braunton and Devon, UK: Merlin Press, 1991.

Collections

Bloom, Harold (ed.). *The Glass Menagerie: Modern Critical Interpretations*. New York: Chelsea House, 1988.

A Streetcar Named Desire. Modern Critical Interpretations. New York: Chelsea House, 1988.

Tennessee Williams: Modern Critical Views. New York: Chelsea House, 1987.

Kolin, Philip C. (ed.). *Confronting Tennessee Williams's "A Streetcar Named Desire": Essays in Critical Pluralism*. Westport CN: Greenwood, 1993.

Miller, Jordan Y. (ed.). *Twentieth Century Interpretations of A Streetcar Named Desire: A Collection of Critical Essays*. Englewood Cliffs, NJ: Prentice-Hall, 1971.

Parker, R. B. (ed.). *The Glass Menagerie: A Collection of Critical Essays*. Englewood Cliffs, NJ: Prentice-Hall, 1983.

Stanton, Stephen S. (ed.). *Tennessee Williams: A Collection of Critical Essays*. Englewood Cliffs, NJ: Prentice-Hall, 1977.

Tharpe, Jac (ed.). *Tennessee Williams: 13 Essays*. Jackson: University Press of Mississippi, 1980.

Tennessee Williams: A Tribute. Jackson: University Press of Mississippi, 1977.

Critical Studies: Journals and Newsletters

Tennessee Williams Newsletter. Volumes 1–2 (January 1979–Fall 1980).

Tennessee Williams Review. Volumes 3–4 (Spring 1981–Spring 1983).

Tennessee Williams Literary Journal. Volume 1, no.1 (Spring 1989).

Critical Studies: Book Sections

Adams, Julie. *Versions of Heroism in Modern American Drama: Redefinitions by Miller, Williams, O'Neill and Anderson*. London: Macmillan, 1991.

Adler, Thomas P. *American Drama 1940–1960: A Critical History*. New York: Twayne, 1994.

Bernstein, Cynthia Goldin (ed.). *The Text and Beyond: Essays in Literary Linguistics*. Tuscaloosa: University of Alabama Press, 1994.

Bigsby, C. W. E. *A Critical Introduction to Twentieth-Century American Drama, volume 2: Williams, Miller, Albee*. Cambridge University Press, 1984.

Modern American Drama, 1945–1990. Cambridge; New York: Cambridge University Press, 1992.

Bock, Hedwig and Wertheim, Albert (eds.). *Essays on Contemporary American Drama*. Munich: Hueber, 1981.

Broussard, Louis. *American Drama: Contemporary Allegory from Eugene O'Neill to Tennessee Williams*. Norman: University of Oklahoma Press, 1962.

Cohn, Ruby. *Dialogue in American Drama*. Bloomington: Indiana University Press, 1971.

Cushman, Keith and Dennis Jackson (eds.). *D. H. Lawrence's Literary Inheritors*. New York: St. Martin's Press, 1991.

Debusscher, Gilbert and Henry I. Schvey (eds.). *New Essays on American Drama*. Amsterdam; Atlanta, GA: Rodopi, 1989.

Dickinson, Hugh. *Myth on the Modern Stage*. Urbana: University of Illinois Press, 1969.

Dynes, Wayne R. and Donaldson, Stephen (eds.). *Homosexual Themes in Literary Studies*. New York: Garland, 1992.

French, Warren (ed.). *The Fifties: Fiction, Poetry, Drama*. DeLand, FL: Everett/Edwards, 1970.

Gillen, Francis (ed.). *Forms of the Fantastic: Selected Essays from the Third International Conference on the Fantastic in Literature and Film*. Westport CN: Greenwood, 1986.

Hartigan, Karelisa V. (ed.). *The Many Forms of Drama*. Lanham, MD: University Presses of America, 1985.

Hauptmann, Robert. *The Pathological Vision: Jean Genet, Louis-Ferdinand Celine, and Tennessee Williams*. New York: Peter Lang, 1984.

Heilman, Robert Bechtold. *The Iceman, the Arsonist, and the Troubled Agent: Tragedy and Melodrama on the Modern Stage*. Seattle: University of Washington Press, 1973.

Lilly, Mark (ed.). *Lesbian and Gay Writing: An Anthology of Critical Essays*. Philadelphia: Temple University Press, 1990.

Parker, Dorothy (ed.). *Essays on Modern American Drama: Williams, Miller, Albee, and Shepard*. University of Toronto Press, 1987.

Porter, Thomas E. *Myth and Modern American Drama*. Detroit: Wayne State University Press, 1969.

Redmond, James (ed.). *Drama and Symbolism*. Cambridge University Press, 1982.

Madness in Drama. Cambridge University Press, 1993.

Violence in Drama. Cambridge University Press, 1991.

Robinson, Marc. *The Other American Drama*. Cambridge University Press, 1994.

Savran, David. *Communists, Cowboys, and Queers: The Politics of Masculinity in the Work of Arthur Miller and Tennessee Williams*. Minneapolis: University of Minnesota Press, 1992.

Scanlon, Tom. *Family, Drama, and American Dreams.* Westport, CN: Greenwood, 1978.

Schlueter, June. *Dramatic Closure: Reading the End.* Rutherford: Fairleigh Dickinson University Press, 1995.

Schlueter, June (ed.). *Feminist Rereadings of Modern American Drama.* Rutherford: Fairleigh Dickinson University Press; London and Toronto: Associated University Presses, 1989.

Sievers, W. David. *Freud on Broadway: A History of Psychoanalysis and the American Drama.* New York: Cooper Square, 1955.

Taylor, William E. (ed). *Modern American Drama: Essays in Criticism.* DeLand, FL: Everett/Edwards, 1968.

Mead, Shepherd 246
Member of the Wedding 98
Men, The 220
Meredith, Lee 83
Merlo, Frank 67, 259
Merrick, David 200
Meyerhold, Vsevelod 196
Michelangelo 147
Mielziner, Jo 17, 33, 77, 195, 239, 248
Millay, Edna St. Vincent 16, 149, 150, 157
Miller, Arthur 1, 2, 31, 72, 135, 198, 205,
  206, 207, 216, 231, 233, 236, 253
Miller, Jordan 252
Mills, Clark 15, 151
Moon is Blue, The 228
Moveable Feast, A 241
Murphy, Brenda 7, 9, 62

Nathan, George Jean 193, 194
Negulesco, Jean 212
Nelson, Benjamin 89, 251
New School for Social Research 20
Newman, Paul 221, 227, 229, 231
Nicol, Alexander 109
Now, Voyager 213

Oakes, James 102
"Ode to the West Wind" 154
Odets, Clifford 1, 2, 3, 20
O'Conner, Jacqueline 9, 10
O'Connor, Flannery 103
O'Donnell, Anna Jean 19
Olivier, Laurence 102, 202
On the Waterfront 217
O'Neill, Eugene 1, 3, 14, 48, 167, 201, 205
Oppenheimer, George 83
Orpheus 22
Osborne, John 14
Ovid 24

Pacino, Al 83, 84
Pagan, Nicholas 244
Page, Geraldine 117, 199, 200, 201, 227
Parker, R. B. 252
Palmer, R. Barton 4, 8, 62
Parsons, Estelle
Peyton Place 229
Phillips, Gene D. 250
Pike, James 225
Pinter, Harold 167
Pirandello, Luigi 167
Piscator, Erwin 21
"plastic theatre" 3, 24

Plato 154
Playbill 189, 192, 200
Poe, Edgar Allan 149
Pollock, Jackson 149
Porter, Thomas E. 173, 254
Postlewait, Thomas 48, 329
Powell, Addison 82
Preminger, Otto 228
Presley, Delma E. 248
Production Code Administration 211, 212,
  218, 228
Proust, Marcel 69, 90, 152
Psacharopoulos, Nikos 85

Quintero, José 7, 82, 83, 117, 196, 199, 200,
  201, 202, 219
Quintus, John Allen 181

Rader, Dotson 245
Ramsay, Robert 14, 150
Rapper, Irving 209, 212, 213
Rascoe, Burton 257
Rasky, Harry 17, 245
Rawlins, Lester 82
Reardon, Dennis J. 63
Redford, Robert 221
Redmond, James 254
Reed, Rex 260
Reflections in a Golden Eye 231
Rembrandt, van Rijn 147
Rhodes, Russell 81
Rice, Elmer 2
Rich, Frank 25
Rilke, Rainer Maria 15
Rimbaud, Arthur 2, 114, 152
Robinson, Marc 254
Robson, Mark 229
"Rocking Horse Winner, The" 15
Ross, Marlon B. 118
Rossen, Robert 231
Roudané, Matthew C. 247, 268
Rousseau, Jean-Jacques 151, 160
Rubin, Gayle 5

Sahu, Dharanidhar 249
Salome 177
Sancho Panza 6
Sappho 114
Sartre, Jean Paul 2
Savran, David 5, 10, 236, 237, 238, 253
Schlueter, June 62, 254
Schneider, Alan 202, 236
Schvey, Henry I. 54, 60